Finding Meaning in Dreams

A Quantitative Approach

EMOTIONS, PERSONALITY, AND PSYCHOTHERAPY

Series Editors:

Carroll E. Izard, *University of Delaware, Newark, Delaware*
and
Jerome L. Singer, *Yale University, New Haven, Connecticut*

Recent volumes in the series

THE COGNITIVE FOUNDATIONS OF PERSONALITY TRAITS
Shulamith Kreitler and Hans Kreitler

FINDING MEANING IN DREAMS: A Quantitative Approach
G. William Domhoff

IMAGERY AND VISUAL EXPRESSION IN THERAPY
Vija Bergs Lusebrink

THE PSYCHOBIOLOGY OF EMOTIONS
Jack George Thompson

THE PSYCHOLOGY OF EMOTIONS
Carroll E. Izard

QUANTIFYING CONSCIOUSNESS: An Empirical Approach
Ronald J. Pekala

THE ROLE OF EMOTIONS IN SOCIAL AND PERSONALITY
DEVELOPMENT: History, Theory, and Research
Carol Magai and Susan H. McFadden

SAMPLING INNER EXPERIENCE IN DISTURBED AFFECT
Russell T. Hurlburt

SAMPLING NORMAL AND SCHIZOPHRENIC INNER EXPERIENCE
Russell T. Hurlburt

THE TRANSFORMED SELF: The Psychology of Religious Conversion
Chana Ullman

A Continuation Order Plan is available for this series. A continuation order will bring delivery of each new volume immediately upon publication. Volumes are billed only upon actual shipment. For further information please contact the publisher.

Finding Meaning in Dreams

A Quantitative Approach

G. William Domhoff

University of California
Santa Cruz, California

Plenum Press • *New York and London*

Library of Congress Cataloging-in-Publication Data

On file

ISBN 0-306-45172-7

© 1996 Plenum Press, New York
A Division of Plenum Publishing Corporation
233 Spring Street, New York, N. Y. 10013

10 9 8 7 6 5 4 3 2 1

Printed in the United States of America

To the memory of Calvin S. Hall (1909–1985),
the first American psychologist to study dream content
systematically, whose ideas and research are the basis
for this book

Preface

This book brings together, in one place for the first time, the excellent quantitative studies of dream content based on the detailed empirical coding system developed by Calvin S. Hall and Robert Van de Castle (1966). This volume includes many previously unpublished studies by Hall that contain major new findings, especially on cross-cultural comparisons and consistency in what people dream about over many years. The result is a comprehensive picture of dream content that is far more worldwide and impressive than I realized it would be when I set out to assess the literature. These findings show that the Hall/Van de Castle system has stood the test of time and is poised to take advantage of new developments in computer software for data storage and analysis.

The book contains every method and finding needed by anyone who wishes to carry out quantitative studies of dream content using the Hall/Van de Castle system. It is both an empirical contribution to our understanding of dream meaning and a practical manual on how to do new studies of dream content. Because the book containing the Hall/Van de Castle system has been out of print for many years, I have included the original presentation of the coding rules, complete with examples, to help ensure that future studies are compatible with past ones. In addition, a statistical appendix makes it easy for newcomers to use our simple but revealing indicators and indexes without having to run any statistical tests: everything that is needed can be derived directly from our tables. The book is meant to be user-friendly in the style and manner that it introduces our methods and indicators, and it assumes no knowledge of mathematics or statistics beyond arithmetic and percentages.

The many findings that have accumulated in the 30 years since the Hall/Van de Castle system was first published make it possible to put forward new theoretical ideas about dreams and their relationships to our waking lives. In the final chapter, I argue that findings with the Hall/Van de Castle system can be linked with studies of traumatic dreams and recurrent dreams to suggest there is a "repetition dimension" in dreams that tends to be overlooked because most theorists focus on one dream at a time. I also claim that studies of relaxed waking cognition, such as daydreams and passing thoughts, allow us to theorize about dreams on the basis of new ideas in cognitive psychology. At the most general level, dreams reveal our self-conceptions and our emotional preoccupations, and they tend to be more continuous with our waking thoughts and concerns than we generally realize.

Both the accuracy and readability of this book were improved immeasurably thanks to an extremely careful and thoughtful reading of the first draft by one of the leading experts on dream content, Deirdre Barrett of Harvard University Medical School. I am deeply grateful for her time and effort. I also want to thank David Foulkes, the preeminent laboratory investigator of dreams for the past 30 years, for his very helpful and reassuring substantive comments on the second draft of the manuscript, and Richard L. Zweigenhaft, my longtime co-author on social psychology topics, for his frank and useful editorial suggestions on the second draft. My thanks, also, to my colleague Dane Archer in the Department of Sociology at the University of California, Santa Cruz, for advice on statistical questions, and to Mark Mizruchi of the Department of Sociology at the University of Michigan for his important corrections to my statistical appendix. Further thanks go to my colleague Daniel Guevara of the Department of Philosophy at the University of California, Santa Cruz, for his thoughtful comments on what philosophers say about the meaning of "meaning."

The help of one of my former students, Adam Schneider, was essential to me in the final stages of the manuscript. He mastered the coding system and did creative work on three final analyses that added greatly to the argument. He utilized his outstanding computer skills to improve the accuracy of the tables and to check many previous calculations. He also caught many errors in his careful proofreading of the manuscript.

I also want to thank another of my former students, Veronica Tonay, now a published scholar in her own right, for taking the time to code several dream samples for me; her contributions are noted at several places in the main text. Still another former student, Susan Cermak, did excellent research on typical and recurrent dreams, and helped in proofreading the manuscript, for which I am very grateful. The contributions of many other fine and energetic students too numerous to mention here have aided me in various ways over the years, and I thank them one and all for their insights and critiques.

It would not have been possible to complete this manuscript and provide it in this form without the excellent work and patience of the Word Processing Center at the University of California, Santa Cruz. I especially want to thank Zoë Sodja, Joan Tannheimer, and Cheryl Van De Veer for their help.

Although Calvin Hall died in 1985, I thought very seriously about listing him as a co-author here, because this book includes so much of his thinking and unpublished work. It would not have been possible for me even to contemplate this book if his files had not been in my possession. I have used his findings, concepts, and writings at every juncture, sometimes with only the slightest paraphrase. Thus, readers should be aware that I am claiming little or no originality for my contribution to this book. Except for the final chapter, my role is primarily as an organizer and expositor. Nevertheless, the final responsibility for the opinions, ideas, and conclusions in the text is mine. I therefore have not included my teacher and mentor from my graduate school days as the co-author that he is in all but name. I will, however, use the editorial "we" in the text as a reminder that my writing is based in his work.

G. WILLIAM DOMHOFF

Santa Cruz, California

Contents

Finding Meaning in Dreams

A Quantitative Approach

The Scientific Study
of Dream Content

INTRODUCTION

The purpose of this book is to search for meaning in dreams through the quantitative study of dream content. It will do so in three senses of that elusive term. First, it will demonstrate an internal coherence or regularity in the dreams of specific groups, such as men, children, or members of hunting and gathering societies. Second, it will show there is consistency in what individuals dream about from year to year and even over decades. Third, it will reveal correspondences between dream content and waking life; more specifically, it will show a direct continuity between dream concerns and waking concerns.

The book will attempt to realize its purpose through the version of content analysis created by Calvin S. Hall and Robert L. Van de Castle (1966) on the basis of earlier work by Hall (1947, 1951, 1953a) and his students (e.g., Cook, 1956; Meer, 1955; Paolino, 1964; Polster, 1951; Reis, 1951). The Hall/Van de Castle coding system was constructed gradually through the empirical study of thousands of dream reports collected from college students in the 1940s and 1950s. It is the most comprehensive and detailed system for the study of dream content developed to date. Given the explicit coding rules developed by Hall and Van de Castle, all of which will be presented in this book, their categories can be used by any investigator willing to take the time to learn the system.

The Hall/Van de Castle system may be unique among methods of dream analysis in that it relies *entirely* on the dream reports themselves in order to determine whether there is meaning in dreams. It does not use free associations, amplifications, biographical information, or any other information provided by the dreamer. Nor does it draw upon metaphoric, linguistic, or literary methods of interpretation. The Hall/Van de Castle system makes comparisons of dream reports in three different ways to search for dream meaning. First, it compares new dream reports with normative information on American college students and other population groups. Second, it compares one dream or type of dream within an individual dream series with other dreams in the series. Third, it compares reports of specific types of dreams collected from many people, such as dreams of flying or of appearing partially clad in public, with each other and with the norms for dreams in general.

The quantitative study of dream content begins with the careful formulation of categories to encompass the many different elements appearing in dreams. In the case of the Hall/Van de Castle system, these categories include characters, social interactions, settings, the activities engaged in by the dreamer and other dream characters, and a wide range of objects. There are also coding categories for emotions, temporal references, successes and failures, good fortunes and misfortunes, and many other aspects of dream content. Categories can be expanded or combined to fit the needs of specific research questions, and new categories can be created.

As will be shown, the Hall/Van de Castle system has a number of advantages over other coding systems, and in fact encompasses most other systems. For one thing, it is possible to achieve high intercoder reliability. For another, its categories have been shown to be psychologically relevant in terms of the waking concerns of those who have contributed dream reports. Furthermore, its normative findings on the dream reports of American college students, replicated several times, provide a comparison point for studies of dream content all over the world. It therefore has been used by investigators in many different countries, including India and Japan, for a wide range of projects. This widespread use makes it possible for findings to be cumulative and therefore to serve as a reference point for new studies.

Studies of over 10,000 dream reports using the Hall/Van de Castle system have yielded consistent developmental, gender, and cross-cultural differences as well as a core of findings stable across gender lines and cultural boundaries. Studies of lengthy dream diaries from a diverse array of individuals reveal that there are large individual differences in dream content as well as a high degree of consistency in what a person dreams about over the space of several months or years, or even 40 and 50 years in the cases of the two longest dream series analyzed to date. There are also striking continuities between dream content and waking life, making possible accurate predictions about the concerns and interests of the dreamers.

To link dream content with the waking thoughts and behavior of the dreamer, the Hall/Van de Castle system makes one basic assumption: the frequency with which a dream element appears reveals the concerns and interests of the dreamer. That is, *frequency* is assumed to be an indicator of *intensity* (Hall & Van de Castle, 1966:13–14). The idea that frequency reveals concerns and interests means any statistically significant deviation from the norms in either a high or low direction should relate to psychologically unique aspects of the dreamer's waking thoughts or behavior. The formula for the significance of differences between two independent proportions is used to determine statistically significant deviations from the norms; more important, the magnitude of any statistically significant differences, that is, the "effect size," is determined by Jacob Cohen's (1977: Chap. 6) "h" statistic. For readers unfamiliar with statistics, these methods are explained in an appendix. To make it unnecessary for readers to calculate either of these two statistics, the appendix includes tables from which they can be determined with considerable ease. This statistical appendix is best read in conjunction with the introduction to Chapter 4.

DREAMS AND DREAM REPORTS

Just what is being studied when we say we are analyzing "dream" content? The word "dream" has three possible meanings. It can refer to (1) an experience during sleep; (2) what is remembered upon awakening; or (3) what is reported to others, usually prefaced by "I had this dream" or "Last night I dreamt that..." Put another way, there is an experienced dream, a remembered dream, and a reported dream. Unfortunately, there is no way of knowing what people are dreaming or what they remember until they report their recall of the dreaming experience in words. Thus, only the reported dream has an objective, or public, existence. Of necessity, then, this book will deal only with the reported dream, usually referred to as a "dream report" or "dream narrative." The phrase "dream content" will be used to designate what is found in the dream report (Hall & Nordby, 1972:12; Hall & Van de Castle, 1966:17–18).

Dream reports are a unique type of document. Most of what is spoken or written is meant to influence other people or communicate with them, but dream reports are descriptive accounts based on memories of an experience that happened during sleep. On occasion they might be used to influence a psychotherapist or communicate something to a friend, but for the most part they are "representational," not "instrumental," communications. Moreover, dream reports of the kind used by dream researchers are not generally self-initiated. That is, very few of the people who provide dream reports for our studies would have written down their dreams if they had not been asked to do so, although those who keep dream diaries for their own personal reasons are an important exception. Then too, because dreams are usually experienced as something that just happens to the dreamer, and not as something intended, people do not tend to accept as much responsibility for their dreams as they do for what they say or write during waking life. In all these ways, dream reports differ from other types of oral or written reports (Hall & Van de Castle, 1966:21).

The quantitative study of dream content is not without difficulties. There can be problems of bias in the collection of dream reports; for example, aspects of dream content may be altered or deemphasized on the basis of instructions given to the dreamer. Nor is there any guarantee that some subjects do not make up dream reports or alter details of what they actually remember. However, none of these problems is a serious one. Most of the dream reports utilized in the studies to be discussed in this book were collected from anonymous volunteer subjects with basically the same instructions. As for the fabrication of some dreams in a sample, or the deliberate alteration of certain details, this presents no problem in terms of our general findings because they are based on very large numbers of dream reports.

DREAM SERIES AND DREAM SETS

Dream reports can be grouped in two different ways, as "dream series" or as "dream sets." A "dream series" consists of two or more dream reports from the same person; a "short" dream series contains anywhere from 2 to 74 dream reports, and a "long" dream series contains 75 or more dream reports. The phrase "dream set" is used to describe both (1) dream reports from persons of a certain "type" (e.g., men, women, children, schizophrenics, Americans) or (2) dream reports of a certain "type" collected from a wide range of people (e.g., dreams of being chased, dreams of falling). The same dream reports are sometimes part of both a series and a set. For example, if we took all dream reports of being chased from hundreds of different dream series, we would have a set of chase dreams. For our purposes, the most important example of a dream set drawn from many dream series concerns the normative studies of the dream reports of European-American college men and women reported in detail in Chapter 4. This normative study is based on five dream reports drawn at random from longer series contributed by 100 men and 100 women at Case Western Reserve University and Baldwin-Wallace College in Cleveland, Ohio, between 1947 and 1950 (Hall & Van de Castle, 1966:158).

THE IMPORTANCE OF "BLIND ANALYSIS"

It is our strong belief that content analyses should be done with no knowledge of the dreamer if such studies are to be convincing evidence for

the usefulness of content analysis. Such "blind analyses" are essential because there is always the possibility, even with this objective and quantitative
method, that the analyst is reading into the dream reports what she or he
already knows from free associations or biographical information, rather
than gaining new insights and information from the dream reports themselves.

It is, of course, necessary and inevitable that a dream analyst will have
other information if he or she is treating the dreamer in a clinical setting. But
such clinical analyses, however beneficial therapeutically or useful in gener-
ating testable hypotheses about dream meaning, always will be suspect by
rigorous scientific standards. This is not only because the analyst has other
information available that might be influencing interpretations, but also because such dream analyses are a form of "post hoc" interpretation based on
reasoning from the present to the past. The criticism of "retrospective" analyses as unable to demonstrate the existence of causality is a problem of all
clinical theories.

Unfortunately, it is not possible to answer this type of criticism with
experimental studies in the case of dreams. Experimental studies of the
cognitive process of dreaming have shown that some external (e.g., water
drops, hearing significant names) and internal (e.g., thirst) stimuli can sometimes have a modifying influence on dream content, and heightened emotional or motivational states can change the general vividness or emotionality
of dreams (e.g., Berger, 1963; Bokert, 1967; Hoelscher, Klinger, & Barta, 1981;
Witkin, 1969; Witkin & Lewis, 1967). Beyond a general demonstration of the
psychological lawfulness of the dream process, however, experimental studies
have not been able to tell us very much about the meaning of most dream
content or about the relationship between dream content and either waking
thought or behavior (cf. Antrobus, 1990:4; Cartwright, 1990:179).

Given the limited usefulness of retrospective analyses on the one hand
and experimental studies on the other in the study of dream content, blind
analyses using quantitative methods become the best approach to the scientific study of dream meaning. As we will see, this approach is especially
compelling when dream series are used to make many specific predictions
about a person's conceptions, concerns, and interests. In those cases where
the dreamer is known to the researcher, predictions should be made in
advance about the nature of the dream content, and the dream reports should
be coded by someone who does not know the predictions.

Not all the studies reported in this book are based on blind analyses,
but in many studies the person doing the quantitative content analysis knew
only the gender and/or nationality of the dreamer, or was unaware of the
purpose of the study. Whatever the limitations of previous studies, however,
the future clearly lies with blind analyses of dream content if the study of
dream meaning is to be taken seriously by social scientists.

DREAMING AND DAYDREAMING

Many different questions can be asked about dreaming and dreams, and there is a large literature on each of them. Since the discovery in 1953 of two different types of sleep—active, fast-wave rapid-eye-movement (REM) sleep and quiescent, slow-wave non-REM (NREM) sleep—there have been thousands of psychophysiological studies of sleep and dreams by researchers all over the world (e.g., Aserinsky & Kleitman, 1953; Dement, 1955; Dement & Kleitman, 1957; Hartmann, 1967; see Ellman & Antrobus, 1991, for one major summary). In psychological terms, these researchers are searching for physiological correlates of dreaming. Some of them believe dreaming occurs almost exclusively in REM sleep, and that we therefore know something about the neurophysiology of dreaming (e.g., Hobson, 1988; Hobson & McCarley, 1977; McCarley, 1989), but others dispute this conclusion, claiming that the presence of fully developed dreams shortly after sleep onset and during NREM sleep suggests we still know little about the psychophysiology of the dream process (e.g., Cavallero, Cicogna, Natale, & Occhionero, 1992; Cicogna, 1994; Foulkes, 1962, 1985, 1993a; Vogel, 1978).

There is also an important literature on dreaming as a cognitive process. It builds on the burgeoning research in the area of waking cognition to show that much of what was previously inexplicable about dreaming can be understood in terms of recent findings and concepts developed in the study of waking consciousness and memory. David Foulkes has been the major contributor to this effort; his *Dreaming: A Cognitive-Psychological Analysis* (1985) synthesizes what is known about dreaming from laboratory studies with findings on waking cognition and presents many new hypotheses for future investigation. The studies of John Antrobus (1977, 1990), Harry Hunt (1986, 1989), and Donald Kuiken (1986) also are important in this area. Still others have done ingenious experimental studies in the sleep laboratory, suggesting possible psychological functions for dreams. The major contributor to this area of study has been Harry Fiss (1983, 1986, 1991).

Although the work on dreaming as a cognitive process is fascinating and informative, it will not be discussed in this book because it does not provide detailed answers to questions about dream content and its correspondence to waking thought and behavior. The biology of dreaming does not tell us the psychological meaning of dreams (cf. Fiss, 1979, 1991). The dreaming brain and the dreaming mind are two different issues, one neurophysiological, one psychological. Similarly, the study of dreaming as a cognitive process has made a great contribution by showing that dreams are psychologically meaningful in a general sense, but few of these studies help us to understand the meaning of specific dream reports or the relationship between dream content and waking thought or behavior. Then too, dreams could have no "functions" at all in terms of either evolutionary survival or individual adaptation, but still be psychologically meaningful in terms of internal coherence and correlations with waking thought and behavior (e.g., Antrobus, 1993; Foulkes, 1993a).

There is also an interesting literature on daydreaming, reveries, and extraneous thoughts, based in a variety of techniques, including thought-sampling by means of pagers carried by people going about their everyday lives. Just as our studies show that dream content has continuities with waking life, these studies suggest the dreamlike nature of some waking thought (e.g., Foulkes, 1994; Klinger, 1971, 1990; Singer, 1966, 1975, 1988; Starker, 1978). This literature will figure importantly in our theoretical comments in the final chapter. Relevant findings also will be referred to at a few places in the intervening chapters. To underscore the relationship between dream content and relaxed waking thought, we have adopted Klinger's (1971) phrase "current concerns" because it characterizes the major content of both forms of cognition. Our former phrase, "emotional preoccupations," will be used interchangeably. "Unfinished business" and "unfinished intentions" also express part of this concept, but "current concerns" and "emotional preoccupations" allow for the positive interests sometimes appearing in dreams.

For the most part, though, this book will be focused on the quantitative study of dream content and its relationship to such factors as gender, age, nationality, and individual differences. Its findings stand on their own, whatever theory turns out to be right concerning the neurophysiological correlates of dreaming, or whatever cognitive theory eventually explains the production of the dreams reported to investigators. Similarly, there are enough differences between dreams and daydreams to justify our exclusive focus on dreams until we come to the final chapter.

THE MEANING OF CONTENT ANALYSIS

In the most general sense, "content analysis" is the search for meaningful regularities and patterns in written documents. In principle, it can be done "qualitatively," as when we use our intuition or our general understanding of language, or it can be done "quantitatively." Historically, however, content analysis as the phrase is used by social scientists has meant the attempt to convert verbal, written, or other symbolic materials into numbers so that statistical analysis can be performed. This purpose is accomplished by formulating categories, tabulating frequencies for those categories, and determining percentages, proportions, or ratios. Comparisons are then made with "norms" or control groups.

In practice, there is not a hard and fast line between the qualitative and the quantitative. One can shade into the other. We often begin with an implicit set of categories and develop a rough idea of the frequency of elements fitting into those categories. Next we create more explicit, carefully defined categories, and then we make a more detailed search of the document for exact frequencies. This is, in fact, the process used by Hall (1951) in his early work.

Thus, quantitative content analysis often develops out of impressionistic qualitative analyses as an attempt to minimize personal bias and make possible greater agreement among investigators who are studying the same type of documents, whether newspapers, plays, folktales, political party platforms, or dream reports. One early content analyst said content analysis consists of "methods in which the bias of the analyst is at least minimized, in which the essential operations can be made explicit and the conclusions thereby more easily replicated, and in which the findings can be communicated in meaningful numbers" (Osgood, 1959:34). Cartwright (1953:466) concluded that the "fundamental objective" of content analysis is to convert the "symbolic behavior" of people into "scientific data," by which he meant (1) objectivity and reproducibility, (2) susceptibility to measurement and quantification, (3) significance for either pure or applied theory, and (4) generalizability. To the degree that the study of dream content can meet the standards set forth by Osgood and Cartwright for content analysis in general, it can be called a "scientific" study of meaning in dream reports.

There is nothing arcane, abstract, or theoretically difficult about the idea of content analysis. Nor are its methodological issues hard to grasp. However, doing content analysis is not an easy task. It is difficult to formulate categories having both reliability and validity. It takes time to learn to use a coding system. Great care must be taken to ensure that the material under investigation is categorized, tabulated, and analyzed accurately. Indeed, some of the disagreements in the literature on dream content are due to the fact that some of the studies were not very well done.

No one content coding system works for all kinds of verbal or written materials. Consequently, there has been little or no use of content categories developed for studies of other written material in the study of dream reports. Instead, several different systems have been developed for analyzing one or another aspect of dream content. In the next chapter, we will explain the development of one of these systems, that of Hall and Van de Castle, and present an overview of its coding rules. This system then will be compared with other coding systems to suggest that it is more comprehensive and more objective than most other systems. In short, we believe it is a sound basis for a scientific study of dream meaning.

The Hall/Van de Castle
System of Content Analysis

INTRODUCTION

The first task for a dream content coding system, as for any content analysis, is the formulation of a set of categories encompassing the relevant aspects of dream reports in a reliable and useful way. In an abstract sense, the categories in a system of classification can be either theoretical or empirical. A theoretical category is one derived from a theory of personality and applied to a dream report. For example, a category derived from Jung's theory of archetypes or Freud's theory of the castration complex is a theoretical category. An empirical category, on the other hand, is one developed in a trial-and-error fashion from a reading of numerous dream reports with no theoretical intentions in mind. "Friends," "aggressive interactions," "physical activities," "misfortunes," and "successes" are examples of empirical categories in the Hall/Van de Castle system.

In practice, however, some categories or groups of categories are both theoretical and empirical. In the Hall/Van de Castle system, for example, aggressions are categorized in terms of aggressor and victim, and friendly interactions are classified in terms of who initiated or received the friendly act (befriender and befriended). These are strictly empirical categories. A score combining the percentage of initiated aggressive and friendly encounters might, however, be designated as a measure of assertiveness, a theoretical category (Van de Castle, 1969:189).

In this book, only empirical categories will be utilized because there are more of them and they have proved to be more interesting and useful. Moreover, theoretical categories are far more difficult to develop, not only because the investigator must be steeped in the theory he or she wishes to utilize, but also because even proponents of the theory may disagree about which empirical elements in the dream report are embodiments of the theorist's claims. In other words, both theory interpretation and dream interpretation are difficult enterprises.

The problems with theoretical scales can be seen in the short history of the castration anxiety, castration wish, and penis envy scales Hall and Van de Castle attempted to develop on the basis of psychoanalytic theory. They defined castration anxiety as (1) an injury or threat to the dreamer's body; (2) an actual or threatened injury or loss to any animal or object belonging to the dreamer; (3) the inability of the dreamer to use a gun, piece of machinery, or vehicle; or (4) a male dreamer changing into a woman, acquiring a woman's secondary sexual characteristics, or wearing women's clothes (Hall & Van de Castle, 1966:126–130). Castration wish was operationalized in terms of the same four criteria, except they happen to another person in the dream report. Penis envy was indexed by (1) acquisition of an object with "phallic" characteristics; (2) admiration of a man's physical characteristics or possessions; or (3) a female dreamer turning into a man or acquiring male secondary characteristics (Hall & Van de Castle, 1966:131–133).

In an initial study, Hall and Van de Castle (1965) found in accord with psychoanalytic theory that significantly more males than females displayed castration anxiety, whereas significantly more females expressed castration wish and penis envy. When they tried to replicate the study with a larger sample as part of their normative study, however, they found more penis envy in men's dreams (25 dreams in 500 dreams) than in women's dreams (13 dreams in 500 dreams). The small number of occurrences for both genders is as damning for the usefulness of the categories as the unexpected findings. The differences on the Castration Wish Scale also were reversed in the normative study, with 45 such dreams for males and 39 for females. Only the difference on castration anxiety was replicated.

To make matters worse, the only other use of one of these scales suggested it was measuring power disparities between males and females, not the castration complex. Women living in traditional preindustrial societies with high male dominance scored higher on the alleged penis envy scale than women in more egalitarian traditional societies (Nathan, 1981), not a finding expected from psychoanalytic theory. This study, combined with Hall and Van de Castle's inability to replicate their earlier study, leads to the conclusion that there is no future for these theoretical scales. The only positive note coming out of the effort is the reassurance that the coding system was objective enough to lead to results contrary to the expectations Hall and Van de Castle developed from their original study.

The empirical categories in this book were formulated after reading and studying a large number of dream reports. No class of items appearing fairly frequently was omitted. On the other hand, some classes with low frequencies were included because of their potential psychological significance or to give completion to a larger set of classes of which the small class was one part.

The first step in creating good and useful categories is ensuring that their scope and limits are defined clearly so there can be a high degree of agreement between coders as to what elements in a dream report should and should not be included in a given category. No matter how psychologically significant a category may be potentially, it is useless and has to be discarded if there is no intercoder reliability.

Developing reliable categories, as noted earlier, is not an easy task. It can be accomplished only by painstaking trial and error, and then examples must be developed to aid new investigators in using the system. Even with all this effort, there are *always* gray areas at the boundaries and new elements that do not fit the coding system. Difficult coding decisions and elements that cannot be coded are often frustrating, especially for newcomers and those who do not realize that there is an arbitrary element in any classificatory system. Difficult coding decisions, combined with the considerable amount of time it takes to use the system, are among the reasons why some investigators prefer to use quicker and more subjective global rating systems that assign a single score to a dream report. Such problems cause others to drop quantitative content analysis altogether in favor of qualitative analyses based on traditional dream theories or metaphoric understandings common to all of us.

There are no established rules or guidelines for constructing empirical categories. That is, there are many different ways a set of elements can be organized. Hall and Van de Castle tried to create categories that seemed to fit with everyday conceptions and at the same time would prove to have psychological significance. Whether their judgment was good or bad should be decided by the results obtained using the system, and by comparing their system with those created by other investigators.

Although the system to be presented in this chapter is in a certain sense arbitrary, we believe anyone starting out to devise a set of empirical categories based on reading thousands of dream reports would end up with a very similar system. In fact, we will present evidence to this effect later in the chapter when we compare the Hall/Van de Castle system with coding schemes developed by other investigators. This similarity of coding systems is due to the fact that most dream reports have a setting or series of settings, and one or more characters who think, act, interact, and express emotions. Dreams, in other words, have some resemblance to plays.

In principle, categories can be either "nominal," standing by themselves, or "hierarchical," meaning each category is a point along a general continuum. Hierarchical categories involve ratings, rankings, or the assignment of "weights." They represent different degrees of a phenomenon: more or less, greater or smaller, stronger or weaker. They assume one category is more or less than any other category. A hierarchical scale is called a "rank scale" or "ordinal" scale if the categories are arranged only from highest to lowest, with no implication that they are equal distances from each other. If all categories are equally distant from each other, the scale is called an "equal interval" scale. If a scale has an exact zero point, such as weight does, as well as equal intervals, it is called a "ratio" scale.

There are serious difficulties with hierarchical scales in studying dream reports. For example, when rating scales are based on subjective estimates concerning "vividness," "confusion," or some similar dimension, they are often less reliable because coders have to make difficult comparative judgments. When "weights" are assigned to different elements arranged along a scale, there are often implicit assumptions that are difficult to justify in psychological terms. In one hostility scale, for example, a death is coded a "4," an injury is coded a "2," and discomfort is coded a "1" (Sheppard, 1964). By this reckoning, two injuries or four discomforts have the same "weight" as a death. In one dependency scale, one point is given if partial reliance on another individual is mentioned, but six points are given if there is a specific reference to food or eating (Whitman, Pierce, Maas, & Baldridge, 1961). This assumes that mentioning a sandwich shows six times as much dependency as accepting a helping hand from another (cf. Van de Castle, 1969:193, for an elaboration of this critique).

To avoid these problems, all the scales in the Hall/Van de Castle system are nominal ones. They assign no ranks or weights. Instead, they compare various discrete categories as equals and aggregate discrete categories for overall scores. The eight categories of the Hall/Van de Castle "scale" for aggressions provide an example of this point. Each aggression in a dream report is tabulated into categories ranging from (1) covert feelings of hostility to (2) verbal criticism to (3) rejection or coercion to (4) verbal threat of harm to (5) theft or destruction of a person's possessions to (6) chasing, capturing, or confining to (7) attempts to do physical harm to (8) murder. The frequencies for each category can be compared with norms. Categories one through four, the nonphysical types of aggression, are summed, as are categories five through eight, the physical aggressions. Finally, all categories of aggressions can be totaled for an overall aggression score. There is no information lost in this system, and there are no assumptions made about how much "stronger" or "weightier" one aggression is compared to another.

In closing this introduction to the Hall/Van de Castle system of content analysis, it cannot be stressed enough that empirical content scales such as those about to be presented yield "findings," but not explanations for the findings. That is, it is essential to make a distinction between "findings" and "interpretations." For example, as will be shown in Chapter 4, there are some gender differences in the dream reports of American college students. There is nothing in these findings, however, that tells us whether the differences are cultural, psychosocial, biological, or some complex combination of these

factors. Unlike the situation with good theoretical scales, where correct predictions are in effect "interpreted" by the theory, it is necessary to search
further for interpretations of empirical findings. Sometimes plausible interpretations can be found by looking at results with other empirical categories;
sometimes they can be found in comparisons with other individuals or
groups. We will be making very few interpretations in this book, and none of
the interpretations we do make is tied to any of the classical dream theories
derived from clinical practice. Our approach may be useful to those researchers who want to test hypotheses derived from clinical theories, but this
book is not based on or beholden to any of them.

We now turn to an overview of the coding system so that readers can
gain a general sense of its breadth and depth. The emphasis will be on
definitions, rationales, and highlights because the system can appear overwhelming in its intricacy and detail when it is first encountered. A complete
presentation of the system and how to use it accurately can be found in
Appendix A, where each coding rule is followed by examples of codeable
and noncodeable items. As a further aid to those who want to use the coding
system for their own research, Appendix B presents Hall and Van de Castle's
original coding of every codeable element in 10 dream reports from a young
adult male.

The Hall/Van de Castle system consists of 10 general categories, most of
which are divided into two or more subcategories. The 10 general categories
are as follows:

- Characters
- Social interactions
- Activities
- Striving: Success and failure
- Misfortunes and good fortunes
- Emotions
- Physical surroundings: Settings and objects
- Descriptive elements
- Food and eating
- Elements from the past

We begin our exposition of the system with the characters category.

THE CLASSIFICATION AND SCORING OF CHARACTERS

The characters category consists of people, mythical figures, and animals. These three general types of characters are then broken down in a
number of different ways. First, all three general types can appear as individuals or groups. Thus, "a woman," a "Greek god," or "my favorite kitten" is

one character, but so is "a group of women," "three goddesses," or "a litter of kittens." If characters were not differentiated into individuals and groups, problems would arise about estimating group sizes, and groups consisting of what the dreamer thought to be dozens or hundreds of people could introduce serious distortions into a simple frequency count of individual characters. Still, we can make differentiations from within a group that allow for individuality. If the dreamer reports that he or she was "talking with a group of women, one of whom was my mother," we code for both a group (the women) and the individual character who was singled out (the mother).

For human and mythical characters, there are three additional general categorizations: gender, identity, and age. In the gender category, individual characters can be male, female, or "indefinite," with "indefinite" meaning that gender is not identified in the dream report. Groups of characters can be male, female, indefinite, or of both genders (that is, identified in the dream report as a group containing both men and women).

The identity classification of characters concerns such factors as relationship to the dreamer, occupation, ethnicity, and the prominence or celebrity of characters. For example, characters can have the following relationships to the dreamer: immediate family, other relatives, known characters (friends, acquaintances, classmates), and strangers (unknown to the dreamer).

Both the list of occupational identifications and the list of ethnicities are very large. "Prominent" characters is a category for famous people who are known to the dreamer by general reputation, but not personally (e.g., leading political figures, famous entertainers, and sports stars). Fictional, dramatic, imaginary, and supernatural characters are also included as "prominent" characters because they are familiar to the dreamer by their reputation (e.g., cartoon characters, mythical figures, characters in TV serials). Finally, there is a residual identity coding category called "uncertain" for those characters whose identities cannot be established with certainty from the dream report.

Age is the fourth and final general category after individual/group, gender, and identity. The four age categories are adult, teenager, child (ages 1 to 12, or referred to as a child in the dream report), and baby (under age 1 or referred to as a baby or infant).

There is one major coding issue with regard to the character categories: deciding when to code for the presence of a character. After trying several alternatives, Hall and Van de Castle found they could achieve the highest reliability and make the maximum use of all the information in the dream reports if there is a coding for characters even if they are only mentioned (e.g., "I told him my dad was a good person"), referred to (e.g., "I told him about my sister's new car"), or thought about (e.g., "I wondered how my brother was doing"). Conversely, there are conventions precluding the coding of characters mentioned in a generic sense (e.g., "Anyone can sing," "Dogs are friendly animals") or referred to in order to establish that they were not in the dream (e.g., "It was not my older son, but my younger one"; here the "older son" is not coded).

As Appendix A explains, there is a detailed notational system for describing each character in a dream report. "A man I did not know" is a 1MSA, that is, an individual character (1), a male (M), a stranger (S), and an adult (A). "A little baby girl that I knew" would be a 1FKB, that is, an individual character (1), a female (F), a person known to the dreamer (K), and a baby (B). In other words, a coding is assigned to each human and mythical character for each of the four general categories in the order the categories were introduced previously in this volume.

Each immediate family member has her or his specific coding symbol, but we will leave most of the details for Appendix A. We note here, however, that 1MFA is a "father" and 1FMA a "mother" to show how important sequence is. That is, an M in the second position in the sequence means "male," but an M in the third position means "mother"; an F in the second position means "female," but an F in the third position means "father." Such little details of the coding system are slowly learned as one works with it. Once learned, the efficiency and usefulness of the system become apparent. Animals, incidentally, have one generic coding symbol for all of them, which is "ANI." They are coded only for individual or group. Thus, two spiders, three bears, or a herd of buffalo all would be coded 2ANI, and nothing more.

In all, the entire character system is only slightly more detailed than the summary we have provided here. The complications caused by dead characters, imaginary characters, and characters who change into another character in the dream report are discussed in Appendix A.

THE CLASSIFICATION AND SCORING OF SOCIAL INTERACTIONS

With the cast of characters introduced, attention turns to the unfolding of the play. Lines are spoken and the plot develops. The relative emphasis given to dialogue as contrasted with actions will depend on the author of the dream and the message he or she wishes to express. A character's remarks may serve to insult, flatter, or "proposition" another character, or a character may act by assaulting, supporting, or seducing another character. These social interactions may occur between individual characters, or sometimes groups of characters may be involved.

Three kinds of social interactions are classified in the Hall/Van de Castle system: aggressions, friendliness, and sexuality. Those actions and feelings of characters that are not classified as social interactions are discussed in subsequent sections.

Aggressive Interactions

Aggression has a specific definition in the Hall/Van de Castle system. It is a deliberate or intentional feeling or act on the part of one character meant to harm or annoy another character. Injury or adversity to a character happening by chance or environmental circumstances does not count. Most aggressive acts involve a character who is the *aggressor* and a character who is the *victim*. On occasion, the victim will respond with counteraggression, called *reciprocated aggression*. In cases where there is no clear aggressor or victim, the interaction is coded as a *mutual aggression*. In addition, aggressions can involve the dreamer or merely be *witnessed* by the dreamer (e.g., "I saw two men fighting"). On rare occasions there is *self-directed aggression* (e.g., "I was so angry at myself I bit my finger until it hurt").

As noted earlier in the discussion of nominal and hierarchical scales, there are eight nominal subclasses of aggression. Each class is designated by the letter A followed by a number:

A8: An aggressive act resulting in the death of a character.

A7: An aggressive act involving an attempt to harm a person physically, whether through personal assault or with a weapon.

A6: An aggressive act involving chasing, capturing, confining, or physically coercing another character into performing some act.

A5: An aggressive act involving the theft or destruction of possessions belonging to a character.

A4: An aggressive act in which a serious threat or accusation is made against a character.

A3: An aggressive act in which a character is rejected, exploited, controlled, or verbally coerced through such activities as dismissals, refusals, demands, disobedience, or any other type of negativistic or deceitful behavior.

A2: Aggression displayed through verbal or expressive activities like yelling at, swearing at, scowling at, or criticizing a character.

A1: A covert feeling of hostility or anger without any overt expression of anger.

The categories A5 through A8 can be summed into a "physical aggressions" category. Similarly, categories A1 through A4 can be added up to create a "nonphysical aggressions" category. Finally, the sum total of the aggressions in all eight categories can be treated as a general category of aggressions.

There are many do's and don'ts in the coding of aggression and other social interactions. These specifics are reserved for Appendix A. There is also a set of coding notations that will be saved for the appendix except for a few brief examples. D A2 > 1MFA says that the dreamer (D) swore at or was critical of (A2) his father (1MFA). By the same token, 2MSA A5 > D says a group of males unknown to the dreamer destroyed or stole one of the dreamer's possessions. We use these shorthand summaries of all the aggressions in a dream set or series to answer such questions as the frequency of the dreamer's involvement in aggressions, the frequencies of different types of aggressions, and the frequency of victimization and reciprocation.

When the scoring of a dream report is done on the kind of scorecard shown in Appendix B, which has separate columns for entering aggressive, friendly, and sexual interactions, there is no need to include the A in the scoring of an aggressive interaction. However, if the scoring is being done in the margins of the dream report, which is more feasible in a day when extra copies can be made easily through photocopying, then the interaction should be scored as D A2 > 1MFA so that it can be readily distinguished from the F2s and S2s to be introduced shortly. We now do most of our coding on photocopies of dream reports to improve ease of checking.

Friendliness

The coding system for friendliness closely parallels that for aggressions. First, friendliness is defined as a deliberate purposeful act, only this time involving support, help, kindness, gift giving, or any other type of friendly act toward another character. Second, there is a distinction between involvement and mere *witnessing* of the friendly interaction. Third, there are categories for the initiator (the *befriender*) and the recipient (the *befriended*) of the friendly interaction, as well as for *reciprocated, mutual,* and *self-directed* friendliness. Fourth, there are several subclasses of friendliness that are defined in Appendix A.

The subclasses of friendship usually are brought together as one overall category of friendliness for purposes of analysis. The notational system is similar to that for aggressions. For example, D F4 > 1ANI means the dreamer helped an animal. D F6 = 1MKA means the dreamer and a known male exchanged slaps on the back or maybe an embrace—the friendliness was mutual. 1FMA F6 > 1FTA means the dreamer witnessed her mother hugging her sister. The details of how to code for all the intricacies of friendly interactions are once again left for Appendix A.

Friendly interactions are usually not as frequent as aggressive ones in dream reports, but they are nonetheless a very useful coding category, especially when they are joined with aggressions for various kinds of comparisons.

Sexual Interactions

Sexual interactions involve everything from sexual fantasies about a character to sexual intercourse. As with aggressive and friendly interactions, a distinction is made between *initiators* and *recipients*, and there are categories for *reciprocated* and *mutual* sexual interactions. The dreamer can be involved or a *witness*, and there is a category for *self-directed* sexuality. There are five subclasses of sexual interactions.

The five subclasses of sexual interaction can be added together for one overall "sexual interaction" score, which often is a necessity because there are relatively few sexual interactions in most series or sets of dream reports. Given this tendency to use one overall score, any difficulties in distinguishing among subclasses become a minor matter. The notational system for sexual interactions is the same as for aggressive and friendly interactions. The following is a steamy sexual scene that also shows how we code a sequence of social interactions:

$$D\ S2\ >\ 1FKA$$
$$1FKA\ S4R\ (R\ =\ reciprocates)\ D$$
$$D\ S5\ =\ 1FKA$$

THE CLASSIFICATION AND SCORING OF ACTIVITIES

Activities are defined as anything characters *do* in dreams, such as run, walk, talk, or think. Activities can be done by one character acting alone (e.g., thinking), in conjunction with other characters (e.g., laughing, jogging), or in interactions between characters (e.g., talking). Although most activities are *not* social interactions by the definitions used in this coding system, activities and social interactions are not mutually exclusive. For example, an aggression can also be a physical activity (e.g., hitting) or a verbal activity (e.g., scolding). There are eight subclasses of activities. The activities categories can be reduced to a physical activities category and a nonphysical activities category. One overall activities score can be derived by adding the frequencies for all eight categories.

THE CLASSIFICATION AND SCORING OF STRIVING: SUCCESS AND FAILURE

Some social interactions and activities involve striving to succeed. The character can "try" to think of a solution to a problem, "try" to fix a fence, or "try" to run from a dangerous character. That is, once a character is described as expending energy and showing perseverance in pursuit of a goal, no matter how trivial the goal is, then the character is involved in striving. If the goal is reached, a "success" is coded. If the goal is not reached, a "failure" is coded. Striving can involve an individual or a group, it can be physical or nonphysical, and it can or cannot be part of a social interaction.

Provision is also made in the coding system for including any aftermath or "consequences" of success or failure. For example, a failure might be followed by a helping hand from another character, which is a friendly interaction as a "consequence" of failure. In practice, we find very few consequences of success or failure.

THE CLASSIFICATION AND SCORING OF MISFORTUNES AND GOOD FORTUNES

In the preceding three sections, emphasis has been placed on the various interactions and activities of the characters. They may fight, dance, make love, converse, walk around, look, listen, or struggle to accomplish something. All of these acts involve some deliberate voluntary choice on the part of the character engaging in them. As the result of these acts, characters may be killed, hurt, or defeated, or they may become engaged, popular, or prosperous. These bad and good outcomes are, therefore, the consequences of what the characters have done or attempted to do.

Sometimes bad or good outcomes happen to a character independent of anything he or she may have done. Fate, in a sense, has stepped in and produced certain results over which no character has any control. In the Hall/Van de Castle coding system, these impersonal "fatalistic" events are called "misfortunes" when bad things happen to a character and "good fortunes" when good things happen to a character. A misfortune is any mishap, adversity, danger, or threat happening to characters through no fault of their own and without intent of aggression on the part of some other character. The six subclasses of misfortune range from death, accidents, and illnesses to being lost or late. A good fortune is something positive, like finding money or winning the lottery, that happens "out of the blue," by luck. No one "caused" the happy event, nor is it the result of striving by the character. Because good fortunes are relatively rare in dream reports, no attempt was made to create any subclasses for them.

THE CLASSIFICATION AND SCORING OF EMOTIONS

Emotions are defined as any feeling states explicitly stated in the report as experienced by a dream character. The emphasis has to be on "explicitly stated" because there is a great temptation to infer unexpressed feelings when dreamers describe emotion-arousing events such as falling, being chased, or facing great danger. The only exception to the explicitness rule is if the dreamer describes the kind of autonomic nervous system activity accompanying an emotion in that situation, such as tears upon hearing news of a death (sadness), or sweating and trembling when cornered by a dangerous animal (apprehension).

Developing a coding system for emotions was an extremely difficult task because there are so many different words for the different affective states, and these affective states can shade one into the other. There also was the problem of whether or not to code for varying intensity in emotions. After trying various coding classifications, Hall and Van de Castle learned that they could achieve good intercoder reliability only if they limited the emotional states to five in number and made no attempt to discriminate levels of intensity. There is, however, a separate coding system for all types of intensity that is part of the descriptive elements category. The five categories for the emotions are anger, apprehension, sadness, confusion, and happiness.

It is surprising how seldom emotional states are mentioned in dream reports unless they are asked for explicitly, and even then they are not always present. Moreover, most of the emotions fall into one of the four categories of "negative" emotions (anger, apprehension, sadness, and confusion). Pleasant emotional states are so few that there is little need to distinguish between types of happiness. Thus, the five categories turn out to be quite adequate for the limited role they are called on to play in the quantitative study of dream content.

THE CLASSIFICATION AND SCORING OF PHYSICAL SURROUNDINGS: SETTINGS AND OBJECTS

The characters in a dream report do not act, interact, emote, strive, and meet their fate in a vacuum. The dream report usually contains physical surroundings that are divided into two very general categories in the Hall/Van de Castle system: settings and objects.

Settings

Almost all dream reports include some form of recognizable setting, and people frequently begin their reports by saying something about the setting. Just as there are often several acts and scenes to a play, so, too, is it common for the setting to change during the course of a dream narrative, sometimes quite abruptly.

Establishing the categories for settings was the most difficult aspect of the entire coding system. The initial efforts to classify settings included a rather extensive number of possible settings. It proved impossible, however, to obtain adequate intercoder reliability when such a large number were involved, so Hall and Van de Castle eventually collapsed all settings into two broad groupings—indoor and outdoor settings. Indoor settings are ones in which the dreamer is in a building or in an area attached to or part of the exterior of a building. Outdoor settings are those where the dreamer is described as being out-of-doors or outside a building, even if in a vehicle or a cave. If the setting cannot be determined with certainty, it is coded as ambiguous. Settings also are coded for their familiarity to the dreamer. Five levels of familiarity are described in Appendix A.

Objects

To provide a more detailed picture of the physical environments dreamers create for the enactment of their nightly dramatic productions, attention must also be paid to the various "props" that are on the initial stage or introduced as the play proceeds. These "props" are classified under the heading of objects.

An object is a "thing" having tangibility, palpability, dimensionality, and definite physical boundaries or limits. Intangibles such as air, wind, fog, and sky are excluded by such considerations, as are songs or sounds, which have temporal boundaries but not physical ones. Locations such as cities, streets, rooms, and lakes have physical boundaries and are consequently classified as objects. Persons and animals are not coded as objects because they are handled separately under the classification of characters, but parts of persons and animals are treated as objects.

Because any object we encounter in waking life can be represented in dreams, along with some we would be startled to see with our eyes open, the problem of formulating a system for the classification of objects was a tedious one. The number of possible groupings could be very large if one chose to categorize by reference to size, shape, color, weight, age, composition, ownership, location, function, and other qualities that could readily be suggested. After several arrangements had been tried, Hall and Van de Castle finally settled on a system that includes 12 broad classes, three of which are further subdivided, plus a miscellaneous class. All objects appearing in dreams are therefore classifiable under one of these headings. They are as wide as "nature," "region," and "travel," and as narrow as "food," "body parts," "clothing," and "money." These highly detailed categories are not regularly used in every investigation, but some of them have proven to be helpful in specific instances.

THE CLASSIFICATION AND SCORING
OF DESCRIPTIVE ELEMENTS

In addition to characters, actions, interactions, and emotions in a physical surrounding of settings and objects, dream reports also contain a very wide range of descriptive terms characterizing people and things. Dreamers are in "fast" cars, see "young" men, feel "intense" anger, and perform "gracefully." Dream reports also may refer to a particular time of the day or note that a certain amount of time has passed. They may use negative terms in order to describe what people or things are not (e.g., "not a big car, but a small one"). All of these are called "descriptive elements" in the Hall/Van de Castle coding system, and they are broken into three general categories—the modifier scale, the temporal scale, and the negative scale.

The Modifier Scale

The modifier scale consists of adjectives, adverbs, and phrases used for descriptive elaboration. There are nine subclasses. Each of the nine subclasses ranges along a bipolar dimension, and so can be coded with a plus or minus sign to indicate which pole of the modifier is present in the dream report. "Size," "velocity," and "intensity" are examples of the modifier subclasses.

Temporal Scale

This scale is for (1) specific units of time, such as "a few minutes," "a week," "a long time," or even "the night shift," or (2) references to a particular time for the purpose of dating an event, such as "tomorrow," "early in the morning," "6 p.m.," or "Christmas day." The trick with this scale is not to code age, sequences of events (e.g., after, next), or greetings like "good morning" or "good night."

Negative Scale

This straightforward scale is used to code all negative descriptions. Negative descriptions are of two types. First, there are common negative words like "no," "not," "none," "never," "neither," and "nor." Second, there are a set of negative words formed by the prefixes "un-," "im-," "il-," "ir-," and "non-"; here the rule is that a word is coded on the negative scale if the word "not" could be substituted for the prefix without changing the meaning of the word. For example, "illegal" is "not legal," "inexcusable" is "not excusable," and "improper" is "not proper."

FOOD AND EATING SCALE

The food and eating scale was created because of the possibility that it might reflect the great concern with these issues in industrial urban societies. The scale consists of eating, drinking, the activities leading to eating and drinking, and the surroundings in which these activities occur. The five subclasses can be added together for one overall code.

ELEMENTS FROM THE PAST

It is sometimes claimed that the elderly and the psychologically disturbed tend to live more in the past than other people. Some theorists believe that dreams are often about the past or are "regressive" in nature. The Elements from the Past Scale was created so that these kinds of claims could be addressed in a quantitative way. There are seven straightforward subclasses that encompass such events as being younger, being in locales not recently visited, and seeing someone the dreamer has not visited for over a year.

The Elements from the Past Scale is the final empirical scale in the original Hall/Van de Castle coding system. We now turn to some new developments since the scales were created.

DRAMATIC DREAM REPORTS AND UNREALISTIC DREAM ELEMENTS

Because of common beliefs that dreams are packed with drama and bizarreness, many scales have been developed to study these aspects of dream reports. Some of these scales will be mentioned briefly in a later section of this chapter. Most of them suffer from an attempt to make a global rating of a dream report on a continuum from highly dramatic to mundane or from bizarre to realistic. Such judgments, as we pointed out at the beginning of this chapter, are difficult to make with a high degree of intercoder reliability.

In this section, we present two very different scales to deal with what may be two different dimensions of dreams—their degree of excitement, "jazziness," or "dramatic intensity" on the one hand and their degree of unreality or unusualness on the other.

We believe that the dramatic intensity of a dream report is best indexed by a simple summation of the number of scores entered in the following seven content categories: aggression, friendliness, sex, success, failure, misfortune, and good fortune. For example, a dream report with three aggressions, two friendly interactions, two successes, and two misfortunes would receive a Dramatic Intensity (D.I.) score of nine; a dream report with one occurrence in each of the seven categories would receive a D.I. score of seven; and a dream report with no entries in any of these seven categories would receive a D.I. score of zero. This scale was first used by Hall (1966a: Chap. 3) in a study comparing dreams collected at home with dreams collected in the sleep laboratory. He found that home dream reports tended to be more dramatic than laboratory dream reports. The Dramatic Intensity Scale also was used in a study of dream recall (Trinder & Kramer, 1971).

We also have developed a set of coding categories for unrealistic elements in dreams. These unrealistic elements range from the improbable to the impossible. They include unusual activities and occurrences, distortions, and metamorphoses. We agree with Bonato et al. (1991) that "unrealistic" is a better designation for these kinds of elements than the term "bizarre" now common in the literature. A detailed account of the Unrealistic Elements Scale is presented at the end of Appendix A.

Contrary to what might be expected on the basis of popular stereotypes about dreams, unrealistic elements are relatively rare in the dream reports we have analyzed. For example, Hall and Van de Castle (1966:168) found only 24 metamorphoses in 1,000 dream reports from college men and women. They found that only 4% of the settings in the same dream reports were distorted in any way. When Hall (1966a:40–41) applied the Unrealistic Elements Scale to the same home and laboratory dream reports that he coded for Dramatic Intensity, he found only 10.4% of 815 dreams that had even one unrealistic element. Unlike what he found with the scale for dramatic quality, there were no more unrealistic elements in the home dream reports than in the laboratory dream reports. Several other investigators using very similar scales (Bonato et al., 1991; Dorus, Dorus, & Rechtschaffen, 1971; Snyder, 1970) also have reported very low frequencies of unusual, magical, or impossible elements in dream reports.

The findings with these two scales suggest there may be two different dimensions underlying our popular conception of dreams as wild or otherworldly. It is also likely that there are individual differences in the dramatic or unrealistic quality of people's dreams and in the categories of unreality emphasized from dreamer to dreamer. One dreamer may be high on metamorphoses, for example, another on unusual occurrences. Such findings would be another argument against global ratings of dreams as ranging from highly unusual to mundane. Not only are such ratings usually unreliable, but they might throw away information about individual differences in dream content.

PSYCHOPATHOLOGY AND DREAM CONTENT

The preceding sections of this chapter presented a wide range of empirical coding categories. We believe these categories encompass virtually all elements to be found in dreams, a point we will demonstrate more concretely in a later section of the chapter discussing coding systems developed by others. For many readers, however, the coding system may appear to be lacking in one major component: a scale for inferring psychopathology from dream reports. This omission might seem especially striking because many psychotherapists and dream theorists consider dreams to be a rich source of insights into a person's psychopathology.

Several scales have been constructed to assess "ego strength" or "adjustment" (e.g., Polster, 1951; Sheppard, 1964). They are usually ordinal scales requiring the coder to judge the degree to which settings are realistic, themes are logical in structure, reactions to other dream characters are appropriate, and solutions to problems are reasonable. In some cases, implicit value judgments are built into the scale. In the Polster scale, for example, an aggressive response to aggression is classified as "appropriate" and a nonaggressive response to aggression is "inappropriate" (Hall & Van de Castle, 1966:208). Thus, if a person escapes from an aggressive character, this is supposedly a sign of low ego strength. Given the problems of using rating scales, and especially ones based in value judgments, very little work has been done with ego-strength scales.

We therefore think that a very different approach to the issue of possible psychopathological indicators in dream content should be taken, one based on the empirical categories already presented in this chapter. In our view, it is not productive, at least at this stage of development in dream content studies, to search for something as general as "psychopathology" because dream content may reveal many different kinds of specific problems. For one person, the problem may be the absence of a capacity for friendly interactions; for another, feelings of victimization; and for another, gender confusion or feelings of sexual inadequacy.

We thus believe that several different percentages and indexes derived from our empirical categories hold out the most promise for revealing various kinds of psychopathologies and maladjustments through the study of dream content. As will be seen in later chapters, several of these indicators have been of use in one or more of our studies. However, very little work has been done as yet on this issue. We therefore put forth the following indexes as *hypotheses* to be *tested*. The normative expectations for each of them are presented in Table E.1 in Appendix E.

In addition, we believe a summary profile using some or all of the following indicators will prove useful. This summary profile, to be introduced and explained in Chapter 4, is based on the magnitude of a person's or group's deviation from the norms on each of our indicators.

1. *Friends percent.* First, a lack of friends and acquaintances in dreams, as opposed to an abundance of family members, strangers, and other human character categories, is a potential indicator of adjustment problems, as will be shown later in a case study. This is because people with few friends in their

dreams may be unable to develop relations beyond their family. A "lack of friends" is defined as significantly fewer friends and acquaintances (known characters) as a percentage of all human characters:

$$\text{Friends percent} = \frac{\text{Known characters}}{\text{All human characters}}$$

2. *F/C index.* Second, a lack of friendly interactions with the characters who appear in dream reports, whether friends, strangers, or family members, is considered a potential indicator of psychological problems. A "lack of friendly interactions" is defined as a significantly low score on an index in which friendly interactions are divided by the total number of characters in the dream reports (F/C). The F/C index also can be figured for specific classes of characters, such as males, females, family members, or strangers.

It needs to be emphasized that the friends percent and F/C index are very different measures. The first concerns types of characters; the second concerns types of interactions. That is, a person could report that friend A and friend B were present in the dream, but that he or she did not have any friendly interactions with them. Conversely, a dreamer can have friendly interactions with strangers or parents or any other characters in the dream series, not just with friends.

3. *Aggression/friendliness percent.* A third indicator of possible psychopathology, the "aggression/friendliness percent," is derived by dividing the number of aggressive interactions by the total number of aggressive and friendly interactions. Note that this measure is independent of the number or type of characters appearing in the dream reports. The aggression/friendliness percent can be figured for specific classes of characters, such as friends or strangers, or for specific characters, such as father or mother.

4. *A/C index.* Fourth, it is a possible sign of psychopathology if there is a significantly high rate of aggressive interactions with the characters appearing in the dream reports (A/C). This indicator is parallel to the F/C index. As with the F/C index, it can be figured for specific classes of characters as well as for all characters.

5. *Victimization percent.* Fifth, it is a possible sign of psychopathology when dreamers are disproportionately victims in the aggressive interactions in their dream reports. This percentage is determined by dividing the number of instances where the dreamer is the victim by the number of instances where he or she is either the aggressor or the victim in an aggressive interaction:

$$\text{Victimization percent} = \frac{\text{Victim}}{\text{Aggressor} + \text{Victim}}$$

6. *Unusual aggression/friendliness.* An unusual pattern of aggressive and friendly interactions with males and females may be an indicator of

possible pathology. This indicator entails findings in a 2 × 2 table to be explained in Chapters 4 and 9.

7. *Misfortunes.* A very large percentage of dream reports with misfortunes in them may be a sign of potential maladjustment. Misfortunes, as noted earlier in the chapter, are basically any negative events in the dream report not caused by a dream character.

8. *Low success percent.* A very low success percent in striving attempts, in other words, a very high rate of failure, may be an indicator of psychopathology. The success percent is calculated in the same way as earlier percents presented in this section:

$$\text{Success percent} = \frac{\text{Dreamer-involved successes}}{\text{Dreamer-involved successes} + \text{dreamer-involved failures}}$$

9. *Negative emotions percent.* It may be a potential sign of psychopathology if the "negative emotions percent" is significantly higher than the norm:

$$\text{Negative emotion percent} = \frac{\text{Negative emotions}}{\text{Negative + positive emotions}}$$

10. *Torso/anatomy percent.* Findings in one clinical case presented in Chapter 9 suggest that a preoccupation with certain parts of the body may indicate a psychological disturbance in body image. Specifically, we determine a "torso/anatomy percent" based on dividing the sum of the mentions of the torso, anatomical parts, and sexual organs by the total number of all body parts mentioned.

11. *Bodily misfortunes percent.* It may be a potential sign of psychopathology if there are a disproportionate number of "bodily misfortunes," defined as illnesses, injuries, bodily defects, or mental problems suffered by a dream character. The death of a character through illness, injury, or some unknown cause is also considered a bodily misfortune. The bodily misfortune percent is determined by dividing the number of bodily misfortunes by the total number of misfortunes:

$$\text{Bodily misfortunes percent} = \frac{\text{Bodily misfortunes (M5 + M6)}}{\text{All misfortunes}}$$

We stress again: these potential indications of psychopathology in dream content are based on a very few cases. They must be tested on a wide range of individuals and groups. Moreover, some of the indexes may prove to be more useful than others. Then, too, it might be necessary to make small adjustments in some of the indexes to make them more useful. For example, it is an empirical question as to whether "witnessed" elements are as useful as "dreamer-involved" elements in such indexes as the torso/anatomy percent and the bodily misfortunes percent. Finally, as noted earlier in this section, we think it highly likely that a pattern of scores on several indicators is more likely to be useful in distinguishing types of psychopathology than any single indicator alone. A method of displaying such patterns using the h statistic will be introduced in Chapter 4.

THE ISSUE OF INTERCODER RELIABILITY

Interjudge (intercoder) reliability, as we have stated several times, is a critical issue in constructing and assessing a content analysis system. It is not, however, a straightforward task to decide what constitutes agreement between two coders because there are several ways comparisons can be made. For example, we can compare the total number of codings that two coders make for several samples of dream reports. Although such an approach has its uses, it does not determine whether or not the coders are actually coding the same elements in arriving at what may be very similar totals. Thus, the most meaningful and stringent measure for our purposes is to determine the percentage of times that the coders agree on the number and types of specific elements occurring in each dream (see Hall and Van de Castle, 1966:144–149, for a discussion of the various ways of assessing intercoder reliability). We call this preferred method the "percentage of perfect agreement" approach. It is always based on just those elements coded as present by at least one coder. The numerator contains the number of coding agreements, and the denominator consists of the number of agreements plus the number of disagreements.

It is not, however, enough to ascertain intercoder reliability. It is necessary for the investigator and coders to discuss and resolve any coding differences. The final results should be based on the consensus results of the coders. This approach corrects for the blind spots that particular coders may have, meaning that some coders may overlook one category, for example, while others may confuse or overlook other categories. This procedure not only improves the quality of findings, but increases reliability of coding for future studies.

In the best of all possible worlds, the issue of reliable coding would transcend individual investigators or investigative teams. Dream content researchers would periodically compare their coding of the same dream series or dream set in order to ensure that everyone is using the Hall/Van de Castle system in the same way. Such comparisons would help to increase confidence that different findings from research group to research group are real findings, not artifacts of differences in coding. In this regard, it should not be forgotten that sleep researchers in different laboratories had to work very hard for 2 years to achieve reliability in their scoring of sleep EEG records (see Rechtschaffen & Kales, 1968).

To determine the reliability of their system, Hall and Van de Castle did a new study in which each of them scored from 50 to 100 dream reports for each separate category, then compared their results. They first of all found very high levels of agreement in the overall frequency of elements for each category; their correlation coefficients concerning the total number of elements present, as well as the number of elements within separate categories, were generally above .90. The figures on perfect agreement ranged from about 60% to 90%, depending on the complexity of the scale being coded.

Deciding among the hundreds of possible character combinations in 100 dream reports, Hall and Van de Castle agreed exactly on the number, gender, identity, and age of 76% of the characters. They agreed on the presence of a character 93% of the time, on gender 89% of the time, and on age 92% of the time. In the settings category, where there are 16 different codings if we include "no setting," there was 73% agreement. The percentages were in the 80s for objects, activities, and modifiers.

Generally, the greatest difficulties were in the coding of social interactions. Although Hall and Van de Castle agreed almost perfectly on the total number of social interactions in 50 dream reports, the percentage of perfect agreement ranged from 54% for aggressive interactions to 64% for sexual interactions. It must be remembered, however, that coding a social interaction involves a number of components. For perfect agreement to occur, the coders had to agree that a social interaction was present, then agree as to the coding for the characters involved, and finally agree as to the appropriate subclass of the interaction and whether it was an initiated, reciprocated, mutual, or self-directed interaction. When a more lenient criterion was followed whereby the coders could disagree on a single component, such as the subclass number, then the level of agreement was over 70% for each of the three types of social interactions.

A summary of the findings from Hall and Van de Castle's reliability study can be found in Table 2.1. These findings show that the coding system can be used with great reliability by those willing to take the time to master it. We suggest that the best way to do this is for two or more people to learn it together. This helps to maintain interest in the learning process, provides an incentive to try harder, and makes it easier to pinpoint and overcome blind spots.

To aid in the task of learning to use the system in a reliable fashion, as noted earlier, Appendix B provides Hall and Van de Castle's coding of 10 dreams from a young adult male. His series was selected because it had a large number of difficult coding decisions. Once new investigators have learned the rudiments of the system and tried to apply it to 25 or 30 dream reports that they have available to them, we suggest that they then read through and code the 10 dreams reports in Appendix B and compare their coding to that by Hall and Van de Castle.

Table 2.1. Reliability Findings by Frequency and Method of Perfect Agreement

Category	Number of dreams	Codings by A	Codings by B	Percent one detail wrong	Percent perfect agreement
Characters	100	276	276		
Presence	100				93
Single/group	100				92
Gender	100				89
Identity	100				81
All correct	100				76
Interactions					
Aggressions	50	45	46	72	54
Friendliness	50	38	38	70	61
Sexuality	50	12	12	71	64
Success	50	6	8		56
Failure	50	4	4		100
Misfortune	50	23	18		71
Good fortune	50	5	6		83
Settings[a]	100	139	142		73
Objects[b]	50	298	300		83
Activities[c]	50	245	251		85
Emotions[d]	100	78	70		63
Modifiers[e]	50	97	94		81
Temporal	50	26	25		75
Negative	50	91	87		96
Food/eating	50	9	11		82

[a]There were 16 possible combinations for settings.
[b]There were 24 object classes.
[c]There were 8 activities classes.
[d]There were 5 emotions classes.
[e]There were 9 modifier classes.

OTHER CODING SYSTEMS

As noted in the first chapter, many other coding systems for the content analysis of dreams have been developed over the years, and here we can add that new investigators often develop new scales, ignoring what has been done in the past. Most of the older coding systems have been brought together in Hall and Van de Castle (1966: Chap. 15) and Winget and Kramer (1979). There are drawbacks with these other coding systems, however, as will be shown in this section. Moreover, their categories can be found in the Hall/Van de Castle system or can be duplicated by bringing together two or more categories from the Hall/Van de Castle system. If the arguments and evidence brought together in this section are convincing, thereby leading new dream researchers to use the Hall/Van de Castle system, then the possibility for an accumulation of findings on dream content will be increased.

Weaknesses of Other Coding Systems

The first and biggest problem with most other coding systems is that the categories are not defined clearly enough to make it possible to develop a high level of interrater reliability. Even when good reliability can be achieved among coders in the same laboratory, there often is difficulty in obtaining the same levels of reliability when investigators from outside the original research group try to use it.

These problems concerning reliability are demonstrated with an Imagination Scale developed by Foulkes and Rechtschaffen (1964) to determine the effects of two different films shown just prior to bedtime on the degree of elaboration and reality in subsequent dream reports. This weighted scale is summarized in Table 2.2, which is adapted from Winget and Kramer (1979:118).

In the original reliability study with the scale, the two coders' ratings were quite similar. The Pearson correlation coefficient based on an average score for each subject was .78 for REM dream reports and .86 for NREM reports. To his great credit, however, Foulkes candidly reports that it was difficult to obtain good levels of reliability with new coders when he moved to a new university setting:

> Unfortunately we found the scale difficult to communicate to new judges, the choice of the original dream standards apparently somewhat idiosyncratic to the judges who selected them, and reliability difficult to achieve. In this regard, the reliability achieved by the original set of judges, particularly in view of their extensive training, was not totally satisfactory. (Winget & Kramer, 1979:117)

The second major problem with most other coding systems is one we noted earlier: they are constructed as rating scales, requiring the coders to make difficult and often subtle judgments about more or less imagination, more or less hostility, or more or less ego strength. Moreover, as we also noted earlier, some rating scales are based on questionable assumptions about which elements in a dream deserve greater weight. Rather than refer readers to the earlier examples, we present in Table 2.3 the weighting system for the first two categories of Sheppard's eight-category Ego Scale of Integrative Mechanisms (1963, 1969), as summarized in Winget and Kramer (1979:100–101).

We do not think there is a strong rationale for such an 8–4–2–1 weighting system. Nor is it obvious, even if a weighting system is accepted, why a mutilation is only half as significant as a deformity, for example.

There is a third problem with most other scales. They have been used in only a small number of investigations, usually one or two. Rarely have any other scales except those developed by Hall and Van de Castle been used by anyone except the original investigators. There is thus a proliferation of scales, none of which has been used enough to establish its general validity or usefulness.

Table 2.2.   The Foulkes/Rechtschaffen Imagination Scale

Weight	Elaboration	Violation of "laws of nature"	Unusualness of topic
1	Basically none	None	Not extremely unusual
2	Basically none	None	Extremely unusual
2	Some, within context of one scene	None	Not extremely unusual
3	Some, within context of one scene or several related scenes	None	Somewhat unusual
3	Same as 3, above	Minimal, as changed identity maintained throughout dream *or* vague hints as to unusual causality	Everyday-ish
4	Fair amount: several related scenes or one fairly elaborated sequence	None	Everyday-ish
4	Fair amount, as in 4, above	None	Partly unusual, partly not
4	Little or none	More than minimal, as identity fluctuation/transformation, unusual causality	Partly unusual, partly not
5	Elaborated: several more or less distinct scenes or parts	Some	Partly unusual, partly not
6	Elaborated	Several kinds of unreality or one violation that is prominent in theme	Fairly unusual
7	Highly elaborated	Numerous violations, including perhaps object transformations	Many incongruities

Duplication

Beyond the three serious weaknesses of other coding systems, most of them duplicate the Hall/Van de Castle system or can be constructed in a more objective fashion by combining elements of the Hall/Van de Castle system.

To take the most striking example of overlap, Rychlak (1960; with Brams, 1963) breaks the dream report into five categories very similar to those developed by Hall in 1951 and then incorporated into the Hall and Van de Castle system:

Table 2.3. Ego Scale of Integrative Mechanisms

The dream element or dream theme containing the reference to ego function is the unit to be coded. Each category must be coded at least once, and a class within a category may be coded only once. A complete coding manual with examples and expanded rules is available from Sheppard.

Class weight	Category
	A. *Reality of Setting*: The degree to which the environment in the dream conforms to reality or to the environment in which the dreamer lives.
8	Bizarre, unrealistic, weird, impossible, opposite to the dreamer's waking environment.
4	Possible but not probable, realistic but terrifying, disturbed realistic background such as a storm.
2	Familiar setting altered, some minor problem in the setting, or the dreamer has the feeling that there is something wrong with the place.
1	Realistic, benign, conforming to reality and not threatening. Use this class if no setting is specified.
	B. *Body Image*: The degree to which personae are represented as in good health. The same code is given for threatened, imaged, feared, or negatively presented states of impaired health as for actual impairment.
8	Bizarre, bizarre deformity or illness as in psychosis, suicidal or homicidal.
4	Mutilation, critical injury.
2	Mild illness, something wrong, curable illness.
1	Healthy, no mention of ill health or disturbance for persons in the dream. If the dream contains both healthy and unhealthy characters to various degrees, it is coded accordingly.

1. Location: where the dream is taking place
2. Actors: human and/or other animate actors
3. Action: the story line
4. Mood terms: the emotions expressed
5. Implements: inanimate materials used in the action of the dream

There is also considerable overlap with Brenneis's (1967, 1970, 1975) "34 Dimensions in Ego Styles," summarized in Winget and Kramer (1979:96–97). We present the first 11 questions on this scale to give readers a flavor:

The Ego Modalities

1. The events of the dream took place mainly (a) indoors, (b) outdoors, (c) within an enclosure (such as a stadium), (d) in an uncertain setting.
2. The dream occurred in a setting which seemed (a) well known and

familiar, (b) distinctly unknown, alien, or very different, (c) unspecified.
3. The setting in which the dream occurred was described, for the most part, (a) in a fair amount of detail, (b) in very little or no detail at all.
4. The most important inanimate objects in the dream, if noted at all, were mainly (a) stationary, (b) capable of moving on their own but not in motion (such as a parked car), (c) distinctly in motion.
5. The events of the dream, as they were dreamt, seemed (a) entirely within the dreamer's control, (b) at some point out of his control, (c) completely within his control.
6. The space in which the dream occurred was, by its own nature, (a) very big (such as a large building or a broad street), (b) of ordinary size (such as a typical room).
7. The dream contained (a) no people or one person, (b) two people, (c) three people, (d) more than three people.
8. The dreamer's mother or father appeared in the dream.
9. The people in the dream aside from the dreamer were (a) predominantly male, (b) predominantly female, (c) equally divided, (d) impossible to tell.
10. The people aside from the dreamer were (a) by and large personally well known and familiar, (b) by and large personally unknown, unfamiliar, or unidentifiable, (c) equally divided between familiar and unfamiliar.
11. There were children or animals in the dream.

Systematic evidence for our claim of overlap between the Hall/Van de Castle system and other scales can be found in a study by Hauri (1975) comparing many different coding systems. Hauri began his study by putting together a set of 100 randomly selected REM dream reports—50 from men, 50 from women—collected in 10 different sleep laboratories. Hauri (1975:272) explained his starting point as follows:

> Ten different laboratories involved in REM-dream work were each asked to provide ten dream reports from normal adults (five males, five females). Each of the dream reports had to be collected after at least ten minutes of REM sleep and be at least 100 words long.

Hauri then sent these 100 dream reports to the authors of many different dream scales for coding by the authors or their close associates. After receiving the various codings of the dream reports from the different investigators, Hauri did a factor analysis. He found six basic factors or dimensions in the various scales:

1. Dreamlike quality (vivid fantasy, imagination, distortion)
2. Hostility and anxiety

3. Motivation to self-improvement
4. Sex
5. Activity
6. Compulsivity of reporting

Can these factors be duplicated with the Hall/Van de Castle scales? We think they can for all but the final one, compulsivity of reporting. Factor 1, dreamlike quality, brings together scales for distortion, imagination, vivid fantasy, and primary process. We saw one of these scales already when the reliability of the Foulkes/Rechtschaffen Imagination Scale was discussed. Other of these scales use dimensions like "plausibility," ranging from plausible and realistic in terms of the subject's everyday life to implausible and bizarre. We believe the dimensions of dream content being tapped by these scales can be duplicated by the combination of the two scales presented in the previous section of this chapter: the Dramatic Intensity Scale and the Unrealistic Elements Scale.

Factor 2, hostility and anxiety, picks up hostility, anxiety, unhappiness, and lack of human relationships according to Hauri (1975:272). Most of this factor is contained in the Hall/Van de Castle categories for aggression. The rest of it is picked up by the percentage of negative emotions and the aggression/friendliness percent, presented earlier as possible indicators of psychopathology.

Factor 3, motivation to self-improvement, involves three categories from the Hall/Van de Castle system: the initiation of friendliness, the initiation of aggression, and successful striving. In the Hall/Van de Castle system, a person who befriends dream characters more often than he or she is befriended by them, who is an aggressor more often than a victim, and who has more successes than failures would score high on this factor. Factor 4, sex, essentially overlaps the detailed Hall/Van de Castle coding categories for sexuality. Factor 5, activities, overlaps the detailed Hall/Van de Castle coding categories for activities.

Factor 6, labeled "compulsivity of reporting" by Hauri, contains only a category for the number of words in the dream report and a coding scale for "anality" developed by Sheppard (1964). There does not seem to be any obvious relationship between this scale and the number of words in dream reports. Nor is there any Hall/Van de Castle scale that duplicates this factor. In any case, it does not seem to us to be a very coherent or useful scale, and it never has been used by anyone but its author.

"Masochism" and Dream Content

Support for our claim that scales developed by others can be encompassed within the Hall/Van de Castle system can be found in a study by

Clark, Trinder, Kramer, Roth, and Day (1972). The study compares the findings from a "masochism" scale with the findings from three Hall/Van de Castle scales focused on the same dream elements as the alleged "masochism" scale. The scale makes questionable assumptions about what dream elements show a love of suffering and sexual submission, and it never has been validated for the theoretical claims in its label. The "masochism" scale was developed by investigators to test their hypothesis that depressives had a greater number of masochistic dreams than nondepressives (Beck & Hurvich, 1959; Beck & Ward, 1961). It is one of the few scales ever used by other than the original investigators (e.g., Cartwright, 1992; Kramer et al., 1965, 1966, 1969). The scale can be summarized as follows:

1. Negative representation of the self: the dreamer is portrayed in a negative way. He or she has unpleasant attributes not present in reality or exaggerated in the dream. He or she is deficient or defective in some way.
2. The dreamer suffers physical discomfort or injury.
3. Thwarting: the dreamer does something or tries to do something but the outcome is unsatisfactory.
4. The dreamer suffers a disappointment, loss, or lack.
5. The dreamer suffers a physical attack.
6. The dreamer suffers a nonphysical attack, such as ridicule, blame, or scolding.
7. The dreamer is left out, rejected, or displaced by another person.
8. The dreamer is lost.
9. The dreamer receives punishment from a legal agency or an authority figure.
10. The dreamer fails in a specific activity.

(For more detailed statements of this scale, see Hall and Van de Castle, 1966:205–208, or Winget and Kramer, 1979:85–86.)

After comparing the categories in the "masochism" scale with the Hall/Van de Castle system, Clark et al. (1972) concluded that all of the alleged "masochism" categories were encompassed by just three categories in the Hall/Van de Castle system: victimization, failure, and misfortune. They then coded 21 morning-collected dream reports from manic-depressive patients and 91 laboratory-collected dream reports from depressive patients using both the "masochism" scale and the three Hall/Van de Castle scales. The percentage of agreements between the two systems was 81% for the manic-depressives' dream reports and 91% for the depressives' dream reports. When the investigators compared the points of disagreement between the two coding systems, they found that in 11 of the 12 instances the Hall/Van de Castle system coded a "masochistic" element while the other scale did not. Thus, the Hall/Van de Castle system is more comprehensive than the original scale. The authors conclude, "The results of the present study indicate the feasibility and the potential advantages of deriving new dream content scales from existing reliable and valid coding systems rather than increasing the already large collection of independent scales" (Clark et al., 1972:118).

Additional evidence for the similarity of the "masochism" scale to a combination of Hall/Van de Castle scale" can be found in a gender difference in "masochism" reported by Cartwright (1992:82). Analyzing dream reports from men and women going through divorce, Cartwright found that all the women in the study, whether depressed or not, had higher scores on the "masochism" scale than did the men. This theoretically anomalous finding may be explained within the Hall/Van de Castle system with findings on college men and women to be presented in Chapter 4: college women are slightly more likely to be victims of aggression than are college men (67% versus 60%) and to have a lower success percent (42% versus 51%). Moreover, they have a higher bodily misfortunes percent (35% versus 29%). Thus, the alleged difference in men and women on "masochism" probably is accounted for by victimizations, failures, and bodily misfortunes.

CONCLUSION

In this chapter, we have presented an overview of the Hall/Van de Castle system and shown that it is empirical, objective, and comprehensive. Furthermore, we have demonstrated that it can be coded with good reliability on a very stringent measure, the percentage of perfect agreement. Throughout the remainder of this book, we will show that the Hall/Van de Castle system has been learned and used by investigators all over the world solely on the basis of the coding instructions and examples presented in Appendixes A and B. We stress again that everything a person needs in order to learn and utilize this system is included in this book.

This chapter also has shown that the Hall/Van de Castle system encompasses most, if not all, other coding systems. It has argued that the Hall/Van de Castle system is more useful than the others because (1) its coding categories are more explicit; (2) it does not make unwarranted ranking or weighting assumptions; and (3) it can be used to create a set of psychopathology indicators.

But does the system have "validity"? Does it give us results that make sense in terms of what we already know about gender, age, and cultural differences, and does it give us new hypotheses about dream meaning or a dreamer's personality that turn out on further investigation to be accurate? Before we can answer these questions, it is necessary in the next chapter to address the quality of our data. No matter how reliable the coding system may be, we will not be able to obtain useful findings if the quality of the data is poor.

3

The Quality of the Data

INTRODUCTION

There are serious obstacles to systematic studies of dream content. First, as noted in the first chapter, it is not possible to introduce stimuli that regularly produce predictable variability in dream content, so an experimental approach is not very useful. Second, not all subjects are willing or able to report dreams, raising questions about the representativeness of those subjects who do report dreams. Third, even high dream recallers do not report dreams every morning at home or every time they are awakened in a laboratory setting, raising questions about the representativeness of the dreams recalled by subjects. Fourth, variability in how dreams are collected may affect the content of the reports. Finally, there are no independent checks on the accuracy of the reports provided by subjects; elements of the dream could be omitted or changed, or the entire "dream" could be a made-up story. Given these problems, it is not surprising that many psychologists raise questions about the quality of the data used in studies of dream content.

The purpose of this chapter is to argue on the basis of several different types of evidence that the quality of our data is very good despite the difficulties and uncertainties involved in obtaining them. It can be shown that the subjects who provide dreams are a surprisingly representative sample of the general population in terms of their personality structures and cognitive styles, and that the dream reports they provide are very likely a fairly representative sample of their overall dream life. The dream reports we analyze are based on a standardized form, and there are reasons for believing the reports are honest.

INDIVIDUAL DIFFERENCES IN DREAM RECALL

The representativeness of the subjects in studies of dream content can be approached through the large number of studies attempting to find personality, cognitive, and other differences between those who are frequent dream recallers and those who are less frequent recallers (see Cohen, 1979, and Goodenough, 1991, for complete overviews of this literature). Most of these studies are correlational in nature. Recall frequency is determined by either brief questionnaires or daily diaries, which have been found to correlate highly with each other (Cohen, 1979:159–160).

First, and most important for our purposes, the great preponderance of studies conclude that the personality dimensions traditionally studied by psychologists play little or no role in determining who is and is not a frequent recaller in everyday life (e.g., Berrien, 1933; Cohen, 1970, 1973, 1979; Domhoff & Gerson, 1967; Farley, Schmuller, & Fischbach, 1971; Redfering & Keller, 1974; Robbins & Tanck, 1971; Stickel, 1956; Tonay, 1993; Trinder & Kramer, 1971). Cohen (1979:161) speaks for most investigators in this field when he says, "Correlations between dream recall frequency and specific personality measures have been weak, trivial, or inconsistent," as does Kramer (1982:89) when he concludes that "for the general population personality traits are not a significant factor in determining dream recall." The one possible exception to this conclusion is the finding in one study that people with "thin" personal boundaries, as measured by a new paper-and-pencil test, tend to be better recallers than those with "thick" boundaries. However, the thinness or thickness of personal boundaries did not correlate with traditional personality measures (Hartmann, Elkin, & Garg, 1991). Thus, if the "meaning" of dream content inheres in good part in its relationship to "personality" broadly defined, then for our purposes we have a representative sample of subjects for studying this relationship.

Second, cognitive variables have an influence on differences in everyday dream recall, but the influence is not much larger than personality variables (Cohen, 1971, 1979; Cory, Ormiston, Simmel, & Dainoff, 1975; Fitch & Armitage, 1989; Hiscock & Cohen, 1973; Martinetti, 1983). Third, physiological factors unrelated to personality and cognitive variables seem to have a part in making some people less able to recall their dreams. This possibility was first raised in sleep laboratory studies of recall that found gradual arousals substantially decreased recall from REM periods (Goodenough, Lewis, Shapiro, Jaret, & Sleser, 1965). This led to a study showing that some low recallers had high waking thresholds and were difficult to arouse in the sleep lab (Zimmerman, 1970).

None of these factors, however, seems as important in adults as interest, motivation, or a belief that dreams are meaningful or important (e.g., Cohen & Wolfe, 1973; Strauch, 1969; Tonay, 1993). Emphasis on these more mundane and changeable factors is given added support by the fact that there is very little variation in recall by subjects who are studied in the sleep laboratory. Interest and motivation are the factors, of course, likely to lead a person to volunteer to take part in a dream content study, so it is important to note that an interest in dreams does not correlate with personality variables.

Recall frequencies also vary with mood and stress, which suggests, along with the findings on interest level, that dream recall is largely independent of personality and cognitive variables. For example, in one study people instructed to keep dream diaries reported more dreams when they were in a bad mood, especially if they tended to be low recallers (Cohen, 1974). Moreover, there may be gender differences in the effects of such variables. Armitage (1992), in a diary study of 15 male and 15 female young adults over the space of 1 month, found that women recalled more dreams when they were under high stress and males recalled more dreams when they were under low stress.

When we add up all these studies, we conclude that we do not have any one or two strong predictors of frequency of dream recall. We agree with Goodenough (1991:157) when he says, "People apparently may be nonreporters for a variety of distinctly different reasons." It thus follows that a representative sample of people are able to contribute to studies of dream content, meaning there will be the usual individual differences on personality and cognitive factors in any large-scale study of dream content.

This does not mean, however, that all the samples used in dream content studies are equally good. The same issues making for a representative or unrepresentative sample in other types of psychological studies remain relevant. For our purposes, the most important of these issues is sample size. A handful of dreams from each of a few subjects does not constitute a study with replicable or generalizable results. As will be seen, our studies are usually based on dozens of subjects contributing hundreds of dream reports, and in a few cases we have thousands of dream narratives from thousands of subjects, or several hundred dreams from a single subject. Studies with inadequate samples should not be given the same weight as ours in making generalizations about meaning in dream content.

In any case, the representativeness of the subjects in normative dream content studies should not be a concern. They are typical people with a wide range of individual differences.

THE REPRESENTATIVENESS OF RECALLED DREAMS

It seems likely that every person is having at least four to six dreams per night. It is estimated that less than 5% to 10% of all dreams are remembered. This is a very small sample, and thus is a sample that may be biased. Even the highest of recallers, two or three dreams every day, are remembering only from one-third to one-half of their dreams.

For some purposes, it is not relevant if the few dreams we recall are representative or not in their content. Harold Sampson (1969:222) argues that, for cross-cultural and personality studies, the important point is whether the dreams lead to useful and reliable conclusions about group differences or a given subject's personality. Rather than comparing samples of dreams, such as those recalled at home with those collected in the sleep laboratory, Sampson suggests comparing the conclusions about dream meaning and the relationship of dream content to personality derived from studies of the two types of samples. Although we agree with Sampson up to a point, the fact remains that no one has compared conclusions drawn from the two different types of report samples. Moreover, it is possible to present an argument based on systematic evidence that the dreams we recall are a fairly representative sample of our total dream life, making it unnecessary to compare conclusions drawn from home and laboratory dream samples. We say "fairly representative" because there is evidence of a tendency to remember the most dramatic dreams, but even here there are other factors leading to recall of many prosaic dreams.

We begin our analysis of the representativeness of dream reports by focusing on sleep laboratory studies because they make it possible to sample throughout the night from both REM and NREM stages of sleep. Furthermore, there is anywhere from 70% to 90% recall from REM periods, making it easy to collect a large number of reports fairly quickly. Most dream content studies in the laboratory have focused on REM periods, but this is no problem for our purposes because research has shown there is little or no difference between REM and NREM reports. For example, using data collected by Foulkes and Rechtschaffen (1964), Hall found in an unpublished study with the Hall/Van de Castle coding system that many NREM reports from late in the sleep period scored as high on the dramatic intensity index as REM reports. Antrobus (1983) and Foulkes and Schmidt (1983) found few or no differences when they controlled for report length.

The first relevant sleep laboratory finding is that there are no differences on the Hall/Van de Castle coding scales between early and late REM periods except for some minor exceptions due to the shortness of the first REM period of the night (Domhoff & Kamiya, 1964b; Hall, 1966a; Strauch & Meier, 1996). Thus, if there is a tendency for people to recall only their last dream of the night, as studies we will present in a moment do suggest, then this tendency does not introduce a bias into our sample of dream content. In fact, the greater the importance of "recency" in everyday dream recall, the more we are assured of a representative sample.

The second relevant finding from sleep laboratory studies is that there are only slight differences between the home and laboratory dream reports in four different studies using the Hall/Van de Castle coding system (Bose, 1983; Domhoff & Kamiya, 1964a; Hall, 1966a; Strauch & Meier, 1996). Then, too, there were no differences in a comparison of 51 home reports with 51 laboratory reports from nine female subjects (Domhoff, 1962), but 51 reports per condition is a very small sample. The primary difference in two of the studies was a greater dramatic intensity in the home reports; in particular, there were more aggressive and sexual acts. Hall (1966a) and Domhoff (1969) originally argued that inhibitory effects in the laboratory setting were probably as much of a factor in explaining these differences as selective recall for more dramatic dreams at home, but subsequent research by Foulkes (1979; with Weisz, 1970) has shown the differences can be accounted for by selective recall of everyday dreams.

But what factors seem to be involved in which dreams are recalled at home, and how important is selection for dramatic intensity? In our view, the most interesting evidence on this issue comes from laboratory studies comparing what subjects report from REM awakenings with what they remember in the morning. In the first of these studies, Meier, Ruef, Ziegler, and Hall (1968) studied the night and morning recall of an adult male subject who was awakened at the end of every REM period for 45 nights. The subject recalled 138 dreams when awakened, 88 of which he still remembered in the morning.[1] When the dreams recalled in the morning were compared with those not recalled, it was found that dreams late in the sleep period were recalled more frequently (83% for the last 105 minutes versus 63%, 55%, and 52% for the three preceding 105-minute periods). The intensity of the dream, as judged independently by the dreamer and his Jungian analyst, also predicted recall, with high-intensity dreams being recalled in the morning more frequently than low-intensity dreams (83% versus 56%). Longer dreams were recalled better than shorter dreams (87% versus 48%). The number of awakenings per night also had an effect, with more awakenings decreasing morning recall, but that variable will not be considered further here because it has less relevance outside the laboratory.

The interactions among the three main variables influencing morning recall were then analyzed. It was found that recency can compensate for low intensity and shortness of reports, and length can compensate for low intensity. If these results can be generalized outside the laboratory, they suggest that recency and length are giving us many dreams not unusually high in dramatic intensity.

---

[1]Before serving as a subject in the laboratory, this middle-aged man kept a dream diary for about 1½ years (560 nights), during which time he recorded 105 dreams, or about one every five or six nights. Prior to keeping the dream journal as part of a Jungian analysis, he remembered only a few dreams in his entire life. The subject held an executive position in a large pharmaceutical company at the time of the study.

Three similar studies using a larger number of subjects also found that recency and length were major factors in the morning recall of reports from REM awakenings in the sleep laboratory (Baekeland & Lasky, 1968; Strauch, 1969; Trinder & Kramer, 1971). Two of the three (Strauch, 1969; Trinder & Kramer, 1971) also agreed that dramatic intensity correlated with recall of REM reports in the morning.

Domhoff's (1969) naturalistic study of the factors involved in everyday recall over a 2-week period suggests that recency and mundane memory cues figure in a large portion of our total recall. Six male and six female students at California State University, Los Angeles, were recruited from the student employment office to record their dreams and the events surrounding recall as soon as the dreams were recalled. The subjects were not selected in terms of interest in dreams or frequency of recall, but all said they recalled dreams at least occasionally.

In a counterbalanced design, subjects wrote their dream reports one week and telephoned them to an answering machine the other. After recording the dream, subjects were instructed to answer a series of questions concerning the correlates of the dream recall. The questions concerned the time, location, mood, thoughts, activities, and number of companions at the time of recall. Subjects were also asked to give their opinion as to why they recalled the dream, and to search for links between the dream and any specific events that may have led to the recall.

The 12 subjects made 30 telephone reports and 27 written reports. There were no differences in content or recall factors between the two types of reports. There were wide individual differences in frequency of reporting. Two subjects reported no dreams at all, one coming by regularly with great apologies, the other uncommunicative. Two others reported only one dream each. Two subjects provided two and three telephone reports, respectively, before dropping out. Six subjects accounted for 23 of the 30 telephone reports and all 27 written reports.

The overwhelming majority of reports (72%) were made immediately on awakening. Thirty-seven of those awakening reports came in the morning, and four came right after afternoon naps. Contrary to what we expected, only two reports (4%) came from night awakenings, and both of those were from the same subject. The rest of the recall came from late morning (6%), afternoon (12%), or evening (6%). Nonmorning recall seemed to be related to one or both of two factors, neither of which concerns dramatic intensity. First, minimal external cues seem to suddenly bring back dreams in which the external cue triggering the dream memory may play only a small part. Second, nonmorning dream recall seems to occur when the dream memories are in some way linked to thoughts and associations the person is having in a relaxed, sometimes daydreamy mood; often, as might be expected, he or she is alone.

Here are some examples of each type. A male subject, talking one evening with his girlfriend about the movie they were about to see, suddenly remembered a dream from the night before in which he had been talking to Peter Sellers. The whole dream was then available to him in considerable detail, including the fact that he had told Peter Sellers he was engaged to a friend of Sellers. Another male subject, telling a friend about his car, suddenly remembered a dream in which the paint was peeling off the car. In this case, the recall was very fragmentary, consisting of two short images. A female subject, about to sit down in chemistry class, spotted a friend and suddenly recalled in detail a dream about a person's supposed failure in the chemistry laboratory. Another time, this same subject was watching a television ad about skiing that brought back a skiing dream.

Examples of internally triggered recall are as follows: A female subject was sitting alone studying when her mind wandered to a recent date and the movie they had seen. Suddenly, she remembered a dream about a monster trying to get her (without, we might add, suggesting any connection with the male escort). A female subject daydreaming about getting married vividly recalled a complicated dream in which she was a housewife.

A female subject from whom we have not drawn any previous examples presented a case where internal and external cues combined to produce an afternoon recall. Her report, phoned in immediately, began as follows:

> My code letters are GG. It's 1:15 Sunday afternoon and I was doing my homework. I've been sitting in the sunshine, but the sun is moving and so it's getting to be half sun and half shade in my chair, and I started getting cold, and when I got cold I started thinking about the trip I'm going on in 2 weeks with the Photo Club, and while I was thinking about the trip, then I happened to remember the dream I had last night....

Perhaps the factors of external cue, relaxed state of mind, and being alone are best summarized in the following early-evening recollection, the only dream reported by this male subject:

> I'd come home and I was relaxing and sitting around. I lit a cigarette and all of a sudden I remembered that this is what I'd dreamed about [he dreamed he burned his fingers lighting a cigarette, then it burned down and burned his fingers again]. I wasn't thinking about anything in particular at the time. I was kind of relaxed and sitting alone.... I was relaxed, I think, for the first time today.

Some of these recall data are anecdotal in nature, but they are worthwhile for the point they make: recency, length, and intensity are not the only factors involved in everyday dream recall. Simple everyday external cues and internal associations also may be important (cf. Foulkes, 1985:81–87, for a discussion of "retrieval cues" in explaining dream recall).

Putting together the various findings from different studies of factors that relate to dream recall, we can say there is good reason to believe the dreams recalled by our subjects are a fairly representative sample of their dream lives *on the elements we quantify*. True, there is a strong tendency to remember dreams occurring just before we awaken, but that is no challenge to the representativeness of our data because of the laboratory evidence that there are no systematic differences in dream content throughout the night. True, too, there is a tendency to remember longer dreams, but that is an aid in terms of representative dream content because many long dreams have low-intensity content. True, also, there is a tendency to remember more intense or dramatic dreams, but that tendency is counterbalanced to some extent by the fact that external stimuli and drifting thoughts can trigger what seem to be very mundane, not intense, dream reports.

The argument that we obtain a large number of relatively mundane dream reports from everyday dream recall will be strengthened by the normative findings in the next chapter. Only about 10% of dream reports from college students contain any sexual content, for example. Misfortunes occur in one of every three dreams. Most important, perhaps, only 44% of female reports and 47% of male reports contain any aggression. If we look at dream reports from a psychological standpoint, we might argue that the amount and intensity of aggression in dream reports is high, but in terms of an argument that only dramatic or intense dreams are recalled, the important point is how many dreams do not contain dramatic or aggressive content.

THE STANDARDIZATION OF DREAM REPORTS

As with any personal information, the nature and quality of dream reports can be shaped by experimenter effects and the demand characteristics of the experiment. For example, Kremsdorf, Palladino, and Polenz (1978) found in a study of five male and five female subjects that opposite-sex interviewers received dream reports with less sexual content and more conflict elements than did same-sex interviewers. Stern, Saayman, and Touyz (1983), in a study using both home and laboratory dream reports from 12 college students, varied the instructions on the report forms, requesting subjects to pay special attention to either the outdoor/nature settings or the urban settings in their dreams. They found statistically significant differences in the relative frequencies with which the two types of settings were reported.

To deal with these kinds of problems, the dream reports utilized in most of our studies have been collected in written form with complete anonymity for the subjects through the use of a code number or a self-chosen code name. The completed forms are placed in a large envelope or box with a minimum of interaction with the person in charge (usually an instructor in a classroom). Sometimes the dream reports are mailed to the investigator. As will be seen in the next chapter, we have found no differences in dream content in studies conducted by men or women. The instructions on our form, reported in

Appendix C, are similar to those used in most dream content studies. Some studies by other investigators have used our form exactly.

We said in the previous paragraph that "most" of our studies have used this form. This qualification was necessary for five reasons:

1. Many of the young children's dream reports in our studies were told to teachers or parents.
2. Some of our dream reports from psychiatric patients were told to psychotherapists.
3. Most of our long dream series were written down by their authors for their own purposes and without knowledge of our work on dreams.
4. Some of the reports used in our studies were tape-recorded in sleep laboratories and then transcribed.
5. Most of the dreams in our cross-cultural studies of preliterate societies were written down by ethnographers.

The fact that young children are telling their dreams to adults in an interpersonal situation may well affect the nature of their reports, but there is little other choice until children are old enough to write full reports. There are relatively few such reports in our studies, and the differences in the content of children's reports presented in Chapter 5 are likely due to developmental factors discovered by Foulkes (1982) in a 5-year longitudinal study.

With psychiatric patients, there may well be a selective factor in which of their dreams they tell their therapists. This point was demonstrated empirically by Whitman, Kramer, and Baldridge (1963), who found that the dreams two subjects reported after REM awakenings in the sleep laboratory were not always the same ones they told their therapists the next day.

Tape-recorded reports in laboratory studies are usually longer than written reports. They often contain more characters and more descriptive details. These factors sometimes need to be corrected for in comparing tape-recorded reports to written reports. In terms of the percentages and indexes we use in our analyses, the greater length of tape-recorded reports is not a problem.

Dream content analysts are not unmindful of the many possible methodological issues involved in the collection of adequate dream reports (Urbina, 1981). These problems are minimal, however, if we collect reports in an anonymous and written fashion with written instructions of the kind we and other investigators commonly utilize.

THE HONESTY OF DREAM REPORTS

Some investigators may be concerned with whether dream reports are invented by subjects. Those concerns are addressed by studies comparing "real" and "made-up" reports on content dimensions or asking judges to try to distinguish the two types of narratives. Brenneis (1967:86) and Carswell and Webb (1985), the latter using 180 dream reports and 278 artificial reports, found content differences, but Cavarello and Natale (1988–1989), using 24 dream reports and 12 artificial reports, did not. With regard to judges, Darbes (1952) found that a group of people who had little or no experience with dream reports were able to make the distinction, but Carswell and Webb (1985) and Cavarello and Natale (1988–1989) found that judges couldn't tell the two types of report apart.

Although we realize it is possible that some subjects invent or purposely alter details in the dream reports they give to investigators, we believe this problem is rare as long as subjects are anonymous and participation is voluntary. Most people do not feel enough personal "responsibility" for the content of their dreams to have any motivation to censor them (Foulkes, 1979:249). We believe further that the large number of subjects and dream reports in our studies make the impact of any invented reports extremely minor.

Some indication of the frequency of invented reports and the crucial importance of voluntary participation is demonstrated in a normative study of women's dreams by Veronica Tonay (1990–1991) discussed in the next chapter. After collecting dream reports on a voluntary basis from some of the students in a large psychology class, Tonay administered a postcollection informational questionnaire to all students in the class. It included two questions concerning artificial reports. Four of her 104 subjects (3.8%) said they made up one or more of the five dream reports they turned in. Forty-three percent of all students in the class, which means both participants and nonparticipants in Tonay's study, said they probably would have made up dream reports if participation in the study had been required. Tonay's findings give us confidence in the quality of our data, but they also warn us it would be a serious mistake to require the reporting of dreams.

CONCLUSION

In all, then, we think there is every reason to believe that our findings are based on representative subjects, a representative sample of their dream life, and honest dream reports. The consistency of the findings reported in later chapters, including correlations with cultural patterns and personal concerns, will be further evidence for this point.

Studies of dream content from REM awakenings in the laboratory assure us that any differences from everyday home-recall reports are matters of degree, not of kind. There are no types of dreams or dream experiences that were unknown before laboratory studies of dream content began in the latter half of the 1950s. Some differences in dramatic intensity may need to be corrected for, however, in comparing laboratory and home samples. In particular, laboratory studies using the norms to be presented in the next chapter should not make too much out of lower frequencies on the dramatic intensity scale categories presented in the previous chapter. This is particularly the case with sexual and aggressive elements.

To say that the quality of our data is generally good does not mean all studies of dream content are good. There are large variations in the quality of such studies. The problems of uneven quality are then compounded by the fact that some authors of summary papers and popular books take every study at face value, turning poor studies into conventional wisdom and giving the false impression that there is more disagreement and confusion in the literature than there really is. Then too, theorists with axes to grind are often uncritical of the quality of studies that reach conclusions favorable to their viewpoints.

Dream content studies can be of poor quality for a number of reasons. Sometimes the number of subjects or reports in a study is very small, making any conclusions dubious at best. Sometimes studies are based on brief dream reports that are clearly hasty or half-hearted productions. Sometimes the dream narratives have been collected by asking for only a memorable dream, making comparisons with everyday dream reports collected over the space of days or weeks a highly questionable enterprise. Sometimes the studies lack adequate comparison groups. Some studies draw conclusions without a knowledge of previous research that should be taken into consideration. Others misinterpret previous findings or use inappropriate statistical tests. Still others do not make clear that the findings are based on questionnaire surveys asking for the subject's opinion on his or her dream content; conclusions from such studies cannot be compared directly with quantitative studies of dream content. For all these reasons, it is an unpleasant but necessary task to point out the weaknesses and misinterpretations in some of the studies cited in later chapters.

If our criticisms of inadequate studies are correct, then we will have strengthened our case for the quality of the data used in good quantitative studies of dream content. In other words, the problem with the research literature on dream content is not the quality of the data, but the varying quality of studies based on that data, along with the uncritical acceptance of poor studies by partisans and popularizers.

We are now ready to consider the most systematic findings we have using the Hall/Van de Castle coding system.

Normative Findings on American College Students

INTRODUCTION

The findings presented in this chapter are based on studies of American college students over a 45-year period. Although such findings may seem limited because most students come from a narrow age range and a small portion of the socioeconomic ladder, this is in fact the greatest strength of the findings because they are not attenuated by other variables. They provide an anchor point for investigations of the relationship of dream content to such factors as age, ethnicity, race, class, nationality, and individual differences.

Moreover, college students are an ideal group to study if the primary goal is to understand the meaning of dreams because they are introspective, articulate, and often interested in understanding their own dreams. They are at an open and inquiring age, and many are willing to cooperate wholeheartedly in dream studies. Although many dream theorists believe that we will learn more about dream meaning from studying the dream reports of children, psychiatric patients, and preliterate people living in small traditional societies, in our experience the most useful findings on dream content come from studying the dream reports of college students or the dream diaries of highly motivated postcollege adults.

Hall and Van de Castle (1966: Chap. 14) carried out their first study using the new coding system on 500 dream reports from 100 European-American female students and a similar number of reports from 100 European-American male students, all of whom were between 18 and 25. Five reports from each student were randomly selected from dream series containing between 12 and 18 dreams. Dream reports that had fewer than 50 words or more than 300 words were eliminated before the selections were made. The findings from this study provide the "norms" for the Hall/Van de Castle system for home dream reports for college students.

There are two issues of critical importance in analyzing findings of the type presented in this chapter. First, dream reports from different groups or individuals may differ in length; because longer dream reports might be expected to have more of everything in them, some kind of correction must be made for this possibility. In Hall and Van de Castle's normative sample, for example, women's dream reports were on the average 8% longer than those from men. Therefore, the tables presented in this chapter generally show higher frequencies of dream elements for women than for men. In our experience, this is a fairly typical gender difference. However, a reversal of the pattern on dream report length in a study by Kramer, Kinney, and Scharf (1983), criticized at the end of this chapter, has led to a great amount of confusion in the literature on gender differences in dream content. The second problem in analyzing findings with the Hall/Van de Castle coding system is that the frequencies of social interactions are affected by the frequencies with which various types of characters appear as well as by dream length. For example, because there are more male than female characters in the dream reports of men, there is a greater possibility for social interactions with male characters.

We use several different strategies to deal with these two related problems. Sometimes, as in the case of the normative study to be presented in this chapter, we do not use dream reports under 50 words in length. In one or two instances we have divided the frequency of an element by the number of words or lines in a report. We do not, however, think these approaches are the best possible solution, a conclusion based in part on a finding by Trinder, Kramer, Riechers, Fishbein, and Roth (1970) that the relationship between dream report length and frequency of elements is not a linear one for all content categories.

Instead, we apply a variety of solutions to the length and frequency problems that allow us to bypass any correction for the length of the dream report. Basically, we create various ratios, rates, and proportions that are called "indexes" and "percentages" in the terminology of this book. For example, when subclasses of such general categories as settings, characters, activities, or objects are being compared in different samples, the effect of report length can be eliminated by converting each frequency of a subclass into a percentage of the total frequency of the category. Thus, we determine what percentage of the total human characters in a sample are male or female, what percentage of the combined friendly and aggressive interactions are aggressive ones, what percentage of the total number of aggressions are physical ones, and what percentage of the total number of activities are physical ones (cf. Hall, 1969a:153–154).

Similarly, the comparison of social interactions between the dreamer and other characters can be standardized by creating an index controlling for the different number of characters in different samples. For example, we simply divide the number of aggressive interactions by the number of characters, creating an "aggressive-interactions-per-character" rate, which we call the "A/C index." Such indexes can be created for any character subclass to learn if a dreamer has a higher A/C index with men or women, children or adults, relatives or strangers. In short, our "unit of analysis" for aggressive interactions, and all other social interactions, is characters (cf. Hall, 1969a:154).

We do not propose to present all of our specific percentages and indexes at this point. Instead, they will be introduced at the appropriate place in the discussion of various findings, where the context will make them more immediately understandable. The important conclusion for now is one we stated at the beginning of this discussion of percentages and indexes: all of these strategies eliminate the necessity to correct for dream length, so we do not have to talk in terms of "mean frequencies" per dream report or per dream-report sample. Whether this approach is the better course to take can be determined only by seeing if the results it provides make psychological sense and inspire new investigators to do further studies using it. This approach is, however, based on long experience.

The issue of how to deal with inevitable differences in report lengths and variations in raw frequencies also brings us to the question of what form our statistical analyses should take. As we explain in more detail in Appendix D, we have chosen statistics that are based in percentages and percentage differences for a variety of reasons. The most important of those reasons is that these statistics allow us to analyze the particular kind of data we had to create in order to correct for dream length and differential frequencies for some kinds of elements.

Rather than discussing statistics in the main text of this book, we ask readers interested in the rationale for our statistical approach to turn to Appendix D before reading the rest of this chapter. Here we will say only that the main test of statistical significance we use is called the "significance of differences between two independent proportions" and that it yields the same results as better-known alternatives such as correlation and chi-square with our particular kind of data. Beyond that, we need only add that statistical significance is a minor issue for us, in good part because our large sample sizes ensure that even small differences are found to be statistically significant. The main issue for us, therefore, is the magnitude or size of differences, which we measure with Cohen's (1977) h statistic, explained in Appendix D.

We now turn to a presentation of the results of Hall and Van de Castle's normative study of European-American college men and women. We first discuss the findings of this study and then present the results of subsequent investigations of American college students by several different investigators. The chapter includes three recent innovations with the potential to make dream content studies easier and more interesting. First, we will show that it takes only 100 to 125 dream reports from the normative sample of 500 dreams to obtain roughly the same findings. Second, we will argue that one "Most Recent Dream" from 100 to 125 students makes it possible to replicate the normative findings. Taken together, these two points mean that comparisons of subgroups with each other and with our norms can be done much more efficiently than in the past and with confidence in any differences discovered. Third, we will present the h-profile as an effective method to display the ways in which a subgroup or individual differs from our norms, making it easy to see possible patterns in the findings.

To avoid inundating readers with dozens of frequencies and percentages in this chapter, we present only some of Hall and Van de Castle's major findings for each content category. The complete findings are displayed in highly detailed tables in Appendix E, which makes it easy for readers to use them for research purposes. To make this appendix even more useful, the normative expectations for all our major categories are shown in Table E.1.

THE HALL/VAN DE CASTLE NORMATIVE STUDY

Characters

There are several main findings in the realm of characters. We will use these findings to introduce readers to how we use percentages to correct for dream length. We also will show how we use comparative findings to begin to make sense out of our data, but the full implications of most of our findings will become apparent only in the context of the findings presented in later chapters. We begin with simple findings, as displayed in Table 4.1.

Table 4.1. Frequencies and Percentages
of Selected Subclasses of Dream Characters

	Men		Women	
	f	%	f	%
Total characters	1,180		1,423	
Average number per dream	2.4		2.8	
Total animal characters	71	6	60	4
Total human characters	1,108	94	1,363	96
Total male characters	587	67	507	48
Total female characters	286	33	547	52
Total familiar characters	501	45	796	58
Total unfamiliar characters	607	55	567	42

As the table reveals, there are two to three characters aside from the dreamer in the average dream report. The exact figures are 2.4 for males and 2.8 for females, but we need to recall that women's dream reports are 8% longer than those of men; this finding does not correct for the difference in length. We also need to remember that groups of any size count as only one character. The mean number of characters per dream is not a finding we use often. It is merely a rough benchmark, as is the fact that less than 5% of dream reports are without any characters aside from the dreamer.

We next see in Table 4.1 that most of the characters in the dream reports of these college students are other human beings. This is a useful finding when we use it as part of an equation we call the "animal percent." According to our norms, 6% of the characters in the dream reports of men are animals; the figure is 4% for women dreamers. These findings have no particular relevance in and of themselves, but they start to take on meaning when they are compared with findings for children (where the animal percent is much higher), or dreamers in small hunting and gathering societies (where it is also much higher), or dreamers in Japan (where it is below 1%).

The "finding" on the percentage of animal characters allows us to return to the issue of how we deal with differences in dream length. Here we have used the "total characters" as our unit of analysis. In future studies, whatever the length of the average dream report, and whatever the total number of characters in the dream reports, we can speak of the person's or group's "animal percent" in a directly comparative way because it is always a function of "total animals" divided by "total characters."

We next note in Table 4.1 that there is a gender difference in how often men and women include male and female characters in their dreams: men dream twice as often about other men as they do about women (67% versus 33%), and women dream equally about both sexes (48% men, 52% women). If we put the numbers in the kind of 2×2 table discussed in Appendix D, and then perform our statistical operations, we find that this difference of 19 percentage points has an h value of .39 (defined as a medium effect size in Appendix D) and is statistically significant well beyond the .01 level of significance (see Table 4.2). As Table 4.2 also shows, however, the confidence interval for this finding ranges from .30 to .48.

Table 4.2. Gender Differences in Male and Female Characters

	Male dreamers	Female dreamers
Male characters	587 (67%)	507 (48%)
Female characters	266 (33%)	547 (52%)

$h = .39$; $p = > .000$; 95% confidence interval = .30 to .48

We call this finding the "ubiquitous" gender difference in dreams (Hall, 1984; Hall & Domhoff, 1963a), and we label it the "male/female percent." Men have a male/female percent of 67/33, and women have a male/female percent of 48/52. This difference is not found in every study, but it is found in most of them. It is a totally unexpected outcome of the coding system. This discovery has its counterpart in published short stories written by male and female authors (Hall & Domhoff, 1963a) and in stories made up by preschool children (as reported in the next chapter). There is no obvious or certain "interpretation" of this finding, but it is the type of finding that may lead eventually to a theory of dream meaning, as will be shown in subsequent chapters.

In Table 4.1, we also see there is a gender difference in the percentage of "familiar" and "unfamiliar" characters, which basically means people we know, such as extended family and friends, or do not know. This information can be used to create a "familiarity percent," determined by dividing the number of familiar characters by the total number of familiar and unfamiliar characters. A comparison of male and female dreamers on familiarity percent is presented in Table 4.3; this same comparison is also used in Appendix D in explaining a 2 × 2 table. Once again, the magnitude of the difference is in the medium range, the level of significance is well beyond the .01 level, and the confidence interval for the effect size is fairly wide.

If we ask ourselves why there is a gender difference on familiarity percent, we may be given a start toward the answer in the findings on unfamiliar males and females presented in the more detailed table in Appendix E on characters (Table E.2). There we learn that men dream more often of unfamiliar males than do women (28% versus 15%), but men and women dream equally about familiar males (25% versus 23%). Conversely, women dream more often of familiar females (29% versus 16% for the males), but males and females dream about equally of unfamiliar females (10% for males and 11% for females). In short, these comparisons tell us that "unfamiliar males" in male dreams and "familiar females" in female dreams create the difference on the familiarity percent.

We do not want to give the impression from the findings presented so far that our primary interest in the norms is in the gender differences. For our

**Table 4.3.   Gender Differences
in Familiarity Percent**

	Male dreamers	Female dreamers
Familiar characters	501 (45%)	796 (58%)
Unfamiliar characters	607 (55%)	567 (42%)

h = .26; p = > .000; 95% confidence interval = .18 to .36

purposes, gender differences are most important as a starting point for the study of individual differences. For example, if we were to study a male dream series that had an animal percent of 18 instead of the usual 6, a male percent of 90 instead of the usual 67, and a familiarity percent of 25 instead of 45, we might start to suspect we were studying a fairly unusual person. In an individual study, the only importance of the gender differences is that we know we must use different norms for uncovering individual differences in males and females.

We now turn to the highlights of our findings on the various types (subclasses) of human characters categorized in the Hall/Van de Castle system. Both genders dream most frequently about known characters. Women are a little more likely to dream about family members and known characters, and men are a little more likely to dream about strangers, but we already knew most of this from the findings on familiar and unfamiliar characters. The complete findings on types of human characters can be found in Table E.3.

Although Table E.3 is not used as frequently as Table E.2, it is the basis for our normative expectations on one of our possible psychopathology indicators, the "friends percent." Recall from the discussion in Chapter 2 that for this indicator we divide the number of known characters by the total number of human characters. The normative percentage is 37 for women and 31 for men.

The findings on characters are useful in and of themselves, but they become of even greater interest in indexes involving aggressive, friendly, and sexual interactions. Thus, we often begin an investigation of a dream series or dream set with an analysis of the characters.

Social Interactions

Social interactions are usually the most revealing aspects of a dream series or dream set. The first consistent finding is that aggressions outnumber friendly interactions for both genders. Sexual interactions are a very distant third, contrary to many popular stereotypes of dream content. Forty-seven percent of men's dreams and 44% of women's contain at least one aggressive interaction. For friendliness the percentages are 38 for men and 42 for women, and for sexuality the percentages are 12 and 4.

Because aggression is the most frequent social interaction, we begin with a number of findings on aggressions. We first note that men have more aggressive interactions in their dreams than women, a point we will come back to in more detail when we discuss the ways in which we correct for differences in dream length and number of characters in analyzing aggressions and friendliness. In terms of our eight subclasses of aggression, men tend to have more physical aggressions and women far more interactions in the "rejection" category. The net result is that there is a gender difference in the physical aggression percent, calculated by dividing the number of physical aggressions by the total number of aggressions. Males have a physical aggression percent of 50, whereas for females the percentage is 34 (h = .33). Note that the relationship being expressed here, between physical and nonphysical aggression, is entirely independent of dream report length, number of dream characters, or number of aggressions. It is a comparison we often make, and it is one of our hypothesized indicators of possible psychopathology. The detailed findings for the types of aggressions in dream reports can be found in Table E.4.

With regard to the interaction dimension of aggressions, summarized in Table E.5, there are two main findings. First, dreamers are involved in about 80% of the aggressions in their dreams. Percentages that are much higher or lower are of potential interest to us, especially when they are compared with the percentages for involvement in other social interactions. Second, we find that dreamers are more often victims than they are aggressors, as best shown in the victimization percent, which is independent of dream length, number of characters, or number or type of aggressions. If we use only the categories for aggressor and victim in Table E.5, ignoring witnessed, reciprocated, mutual, and self aggressions, we can figure the normative victimization percent for men and women as follows:

Males

$$\text{Victimization percent} = \frac{\text{Victim (153)}}{\text{Aggressor (100)} + \text{(153)}} = 60\%$$

Females

$$\text{Victimization percent} = \frac{155}{76 + 155} = 67\%$$

If the victimization percent is above 50, the dreamer is a victim. If it is below 50, the dreamer is an aggressor. This percentage can be determined for every major class of character with whom the dreamer interacts. From this we can learn that the dreamer may be an aggressor in relation to some people and a victim in relation to others. For example, both men and women are likely to be victims of animals and male strangers, a point we will demonstrate after we look at the main findings on friendliness.

Friendliness

Women have more friendliness in their dreams than do men if we look at the raw frequencies alone. The subclass for "helping and protecting" has the highest frequency for both genders, followed by friendly remarks and compliments, which we call "verbal friendliness." Findings on the frequencies and distribution of friendly interactions by seven subclasses are presented in Table E.6.

There are three main findings in terms of the interactions within which acts of friendliness occur. First, dreamers are involved in almost all of the friendly interactions in their dream reports. Second, there is little or no mutual, reciprocal, or self friendliness. Third, we expect the typical college dreamer, whether male or female, to initiate friendly interactions about as often as they are received. This figure, the befriender percent, is 50% for males and 47% for females. The befriender percent does not include "reciprocal" and "mutual" friendly interactions. When looked at in conjunction with the victimization percent, it gives us some idea of the dreamer's assertiveness in her or his dreams. The complete results on friendly interactions are presented in Table E.7.

Aggression and Friendliness

The findings on aggressive and friendly interactions take on even more interest when they are compared with each other. We do this in two different ways that correct for the fact that there tend to be more characters in female dream reports. The first way is to divide the total number of dreamer-involved aggressions by the total number of dreamer-involved aggressions plus friendliness. This yields the "aggression/friendliness percent" mentioned in Chapter 2 as a possible indicator of psychopathology in dreams. A percentage over 50 indicates a greater amount of aggression; a percentage less than 50 indicates a preponderance of friendliness. The aggression/friendliness percent is over 50 for both men and women; for men the figure is 59, and for women it is 51. Men have more aggressive interactions with males and more friendly interactions with females, whereas women have about equal amounts of aggression and friendliness with both male and female characters. Women are very friendly with familiar males but have a preponderance of aggressive interactions with unfamiliar males. If we define "enemies" as characters with whom the aggression/friendliness percent is over 60, then male strangers and animals are "enemies" in the dreams of both men and women. These and other findings are displayed in Table E.8.

Our other strategy for comparing aggressions and friendliness while controlling for the number of characters is to divide the number of aggressions or the number of friendly interactions by the total number of characters or the total number of characters in a given subclass. For example, if we divide the total number of aggressions (402) in male dream reports in our normative sample by the total number of characters (1,180), we have an A/C index of 34. If we do the same for female dreamers, 337/1,423, the A/C index is 24. Thus, male dreamers are found to be even more aggressive in their dream reports than raw frequencies suggest if we control for characters. If we compute the same figures for friendliness, the male F/C index is 21, and the female index is 22. These indexes are also useful when they are computed for specific classes of characters, especially males and females.

As we noted briefly in Chapter 2 when talking about possible indicators of psychopathology, we have found it useful to look at people's patterns of friendliness and aggression with males and females by means of a 2 × 2 table that we call the "A/F square." This table, which appears as part of Table E.1, shows that men are more aggressive with other men and more friendly with women in their dream reports, whereas women have both more aggression and more friendliness with male characters than they do with female characters. We think that atypical A/F squares might be of great use in studying individuals and groups. There have been a few revealing studies with males that will be presented in Chapter 8 but none with females. We are hopeful that the great potential in using this 2 × 2 table in studying women of varying personality and sexual orientations will be tested in the next few years.

To reinforce our point about animals as dangerous characters in dreams, Table 4.4 presents the A/C and F/C indexes with animals for both men and women.

Sexual Interactions

After the several interesting and useful findings on aggressions and friendliness, the few findings on sexual interactions will come as a letdown. The two meager findings emerging from Table E.9 are (1) men report more sexual dreams than women and (2) female dreamers have more sexual interactions with familiar characters, whereas male dreamers have more with unfamiliar characters. Not only are the findings meager, but they may reflect the greater likelihood of sexual activity on the part of college males in the past. We think that our norms for sexuality in dreams should be used with caution, especially with women, and that not too much should be made out of them. We also note that sexual interactions in dreams are far more likely to be fraught with negative emotions than popular stereotypes suggest (Jerasitis, 1992).

Table 4.4. Relations with Animals in Dream Reports

	Men	Women
A/C with animals	38	33
F/C with animals	8	10

Activities

The main findings on activities can be summarized very briefly. The details can be found in Table E.10. First, activities are frequent in dream reports, averaging 4.7 per dream report for males and 4.9 for females. Second, physical activity, movement, and talking account for 74% of men's activities in dreams and 71% of women's. Finally, we think it may be useful in future studies to divide the number of dreamer-involved physical activities by the total number of dreamer-involved activities to derive a "physical activities percent." The normative expectation for men is 61% and for women 56%. We use the activities categories primarily for normative comparisons with other societies, not for individual studies unless we notice some unusual frequencies.

Successes and Failures

Successes and failures are not very frequent in the dream reports of either males or females. Most successes and failures occurred to the dreamer. There was rarely a "consequence" of a success or failure in the normative study. We use these findings to determine if the dreamer has an unusually large percentage of dreams with successes or failures in them. We also use these findings to derive our "success percent," which is the number of dreamer-involved successes divided by the number of dreamer-involved successes and failures; this percentage is 51 for men and 42 for women. The details for the findings on successes and failures can be found in Table E.11.

Misfortunes and Good Fortunes

Misfortunes occur in 36% of men's dream reports and 33% of women's. Good fortunes happen in only 6% of dream reports for both men and women. Misfortunes are followed by good fortune, success, or friendliness about 10% of the time for men and 6% of the time for women. In the normative sample, good fortunes were never followed by any "consequences," positive or negative. Misfortunes are of use to us in two ways. First, we always check the percentage of dream reports in a series or set with at least one misfortune. Second, we use the "bodily misfortunes percent" as a possible psychopathology indicator, as explained in Chapter 2. This figure is 29% for men and 35% for women. The specific findings on misfortunes and good fortunes can be found in Tables E.12 and E.13.

Emotions

As mentioned in Chapter 2, it is surprising how few emotions are included in dream reports. Women express more emotions than men, but the distribution of types of emotions is about the same. Negative emotions account for 80% of all emotions reported. This figure is our normative expectation when using the negative emotions percent as a possible indicator of psychopathology. The figure is 79% for men and 82% for women if only emotions expressed by the dreamer are included. The main findings on emotions are presented in Table E.14.

Settings

Few dreams lack a setting. There were virtually identical numbers of settings in both samples, 644 in the 500 male dream reports, 654 in the 500 female reports. Our quantitative findings on the nature of settings are generally prosaic, however, perhaps because the categories had to be so few and so general to achieve adequate intercoder reliability.

In our experience, the most useful of the findings on settings concern the dimensions of indoor/outdoor, familiar/unfamiliar, and distorted/normal, although there are usually very few distorted settings. To make the findings on indoor/outdoor more clear, we ignore findings on "ambiguous" and "no setting" codings, where there are small numbers and no gender differences. We then can say that when a setting can be coded indoor or outdoor, women are indoors 61% of the time and men 48% of the time. This finding is presented in Table 4.5.

If we look only at settings that can be clearly coded as familiar or unfamiliar, there is once again a gender difference. Although familiar settings predominate for both men and women, women are more likely to be in familiar settings than men. This finding is presented in Table 4.6. The details on all the findings on settings are presented in Table E.15.

Objects

There are many objects in dreams. The typical dream report has between 2 and 9 objects, with a mean of 4.8 for men and 5.3 for women. Only 20 male dream narratives and 11 female dream narratives in the normative sample

**Table 4.5.   Frequency and Percentage
of Indoor and Outdoor Settings
in Men and Women's Dream Reports**

	Men	Women
Indoor settings	284 (48%)	362 (61%)
Outdoor settings	302 (52%)	229 (39%)

$h = .26; p > .000; 95\%$ confidence interval $= .15$ to $.37$

Table 4.6. Frequency and Percentage
of Familiar and Unfamiliar Settings
in Men's and Women's Dream Reports

	Men	Women
Familiar settings	197 (62%)	241 (79%)
Unfamiliar settings	123 (38%)	65 (21%)

h = .38; $p = > .000$; 95% confidence interval = .22 to .54

had no objects in them. These categories are of greatest use in the study of individual dream series in which there is an unusually high percentage of some rare category. Two gender differences in the objects category have been of use in later replication studies: although the frequencies are small, men are three times as likely to dream about implements, such as tools and weapons, and women are more likely to dream about clothing.

Table E.16 presents the large number of specific findings on objects in dream reports. This table provides the basis for determining the "torso/anatomy percent" presented in Chapter 2 as a possible indicator of disturbances in bodily image. As noted there, the torso/anatomy percent is determined by dividing the sum of torso, anatomy, and sexual organ references by the frequency of all body parts. The normative torso/anatomy percent is 31 for men and 20 for women.

Remaining Categories

The findings for modifiers, negatives, temporal references, and food and eating are presented in Tables E.17 through E.20. These categories have not been used as frequently as the categories presented earlier. The findings are worthy of only the briefest mention here. The frequencies are not large in most instances, with the exception of "size" (large/small) and "intensity" on the modifiers scale. There are no major gender differences, although women tend to use more negatives in their reports than men. We have created no percentages or indexes using any of these findings. These findings await further exploration and creative development.

There are no norms for the Elements from the Past or Unrealistic Elements scales.

THE h-PROFILE

It is often difficult to comprehend a large number of numerical comparisons. A graphic display of results makes the task easier and more interesting.

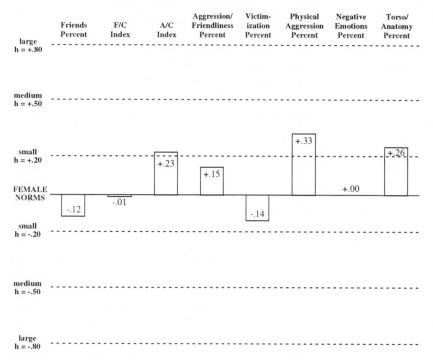

Figure 4.1. h-Profile of males compared to female norms. The h-profile is explained in Appendix D.

It also allows us to detect patterns more quickly if we are making comparisons among many groups or individuals. We therefore use our effect sizes to create what we call the "h-profile," defined as a display of the differences between one group and another (or our norms) for any combination of our percentages and indexes we may choose to compare. In Figure 4.1 we present the h-profile for male dreamers as it compares with our female norms on several major indexes. As can be seen, it immediately shows the most salient differences, those related to aggression. It gives a sense of pattern.

HOW LARGE SHOULD SAMPLES OF DREAM REPORTS BE?

As noted at the outset of the chapter, the norms for the Hall/Van de Castle coding system are based on 500 dream reports from 100 females and a similar number of reports from the same number of males. But were that many dream reports necessary to obtain a representative sample of the dream life of these college students? More exact, how large a subsample is necessary to approximate the overall findings with the full sample? We think the answer to this question is very important because it gives us a good idea of how large samples of dream reports should be in order to be confident that we have an accurate (representative) portrait of a group's dream life. To answer our question, Adam Schneider compared randomized subsamples of 25, 50, 75, 100, 125, and 250 dream reports coded by Hall and Van de Castle for the original normative study. Schneider used dream reports from the male sample, the only one we could find in Hall's files. The findings for each sample size were compared in terms of their average departure in percentage points or index points from the norms.

The important finding that emerges from the many comparisons computed by Schneider is that it takes 100 to 125 dream reports to approximate the norms. At one extreme, sets of 25 have widely fluctuating departures from the norms and are almost certainly not useful. At the other extreme, 250 dream narratives replicate the norms almost exactly; this finding could be of great use to those who might wish to generate new norms for people in other countries. With sets of 50, the findings on most of our measures have settled down considerably compared to sets of 25, but the average departure from the norms for most indicators was usually over 10 percentage points. By comparison, the average departures from the norms were generally cut in half with 15 samples of 100 dream reports each, and were small enough to make samples of that size useful on most of our measures. For example, the average departure from the male/female percent of 67/33 was ±4.4 percentage points, which means that the male/female percent was between 62.6/37.4 and 71.4/28.6 in most sets of 100 reports.

The main findings from Schneider's analyses are displayed in Table 4.7, which shows that some measures have reasonable stability at 50 or 75 dream reports, such as the A/C and F/C indexes, but that 100 narratives are needed to bring the average departure from the norms to under 10 percentage points for most measures. The information on the stability of specific measures can be used in two ways. First, it can tell researchers what sample size is needed if they are interested in focusing on only a few measures for one theoretical reason or another. Conversely, if researchers find themselves with samples of only 50 or 75 dream reports that cannot be augmented, this table tells them what indicators they can use with some degree of confidence.

The findings presented in this section can be used as one factor in judging the usefulness of past studies of the dream life of a group. These findings also could be used to set the minimal sample size for publishable quantitative studies of dream content using the Hall/Van de Castle system. We recognize that statistical tests might be able to detect large differences

Table 4.7. Average Departures from the Male Norms
with Numerous Random Samples of Varying Sizes[a]

	Norm	Sets of 250	Sets of 125	Sets of 100	Sets of 75	Sets of 50	Sets of 25
Characters							
Animal percent	6	± 0.9	± 1.3	± 1.7	± 1.9	± 4.4	± 7.6
Male/female percent	67/33	± 1.6	± 4.3	± 4.4	± 6.0	± 8.4	± 13.6
Familiarity percent	45	± 0.3	± 3.4	± 5.3	± 4.4	± 8.4	± 13.4
Friends percent	31	± 0.9	± 3.1	± 5.7	± 6.2	± 11.7	± 16.1
Social interactions							
A/C Index	34	± 1.8	± 4.8	± 4.4	± 5.7	± 6.5	± 13.6
F/C Index	21	± 0.4	± 2.1	± 2.7	± 3.2	± 5.0	± 11.7
Aggression/friendliness percent	59	± 1.3	± 4.6	± 5.0	± 6.2	± 8.8	± 18.8
Victimization percent	60	± 1.3	± 7.1	± 7.0	± 8.2	± 14.9	± 29.2
Befriender Percent	50	± 2.0	± 8.8	± 10.1	± 11.8	± 18.0	± 30.3
Physical Aggression Percent	50	± 1.2	± 4.5	± 7.2	± 8.1	± 15.4	± 25.6
Settings							
Indoor setting percent	49	± 1.2	± 3.2	± 5.2	± 5.0	± 8.7	± 13.4
Familiar setting percent	62	± 1.3	± 6.5	± 5.5	± 9.6	± 13.1	± 24.6
Other categories							
Dreamer-involved success percent	51	± 5.1	± 10.9	± 10.5	± 13.5	± 26.3	± 48.1
Bodily misfortunes percent	29	± 0.8	± 2.3	± 4.4	± 8.6	± 12.1	± 25.9
Torso/anatomy percent	31	± 0.8	± 7.2	± 11.1	± 9.2	± 17.3	± 28.6
Negative emotions percent	80	± 2.6	± 6.2	± 7.5	± 9.1	± 13.4	± 20.3
Percentage reports with at least one:							
Aggression	47	± 1.9	± 5.7	± 7.4	± 7.6	± 11.3	± 17.3
Friendliness	38	± 1.0	± 4.0	± 4.7	± 8.0	± 10.7	± 18.0
Sexuality	12	± 2.2	± 3.7	± 4.0	± 5.1	± 7.3	± 14.7
Misfortune	36	± 0.4	± 2.8	± 4.6	± 6.2	± 8.7	± 17.3
Success	15	± 1.1	± 3.2	± 5.4	± 5.6	± 10.0	± 15.3
Failure	15	± 1.9	± 4.1	± 5.2	± 6.2	± 8.7	± 15.3

[a]Three sets of random numbers were utilized, making it possible to draw 20 sets of 25, 10 sets of 50, 6 sets of 75, 5 sets of 100, 4 sets of 125, and 3 sets of 250 three different times from the full set of 500 dream reports, thereby creating a total of 60 sets of 25 reports, 30 sets of 50 reports, 18 sets of 75, 15 sets of 100, 12 sets of 125, and 6 sets of 250. The phrase "average departure from the norms" is used to avoid any confusion that might arise from the use of the statistical terms "deviation" and "range." The numbers in the table are an average of all the departures from the norms for a given set of samples. The use of the plus and minus signs indicates that the departure is on the average that many percentage or index points above or below the normative figure in the lefthand column of the table. For example, the ± 1.7 for the animal percent for sets of 100 dream reports means that the departures fell on the average between 4.3% and 7.7% (the normative figure is 6%). Similarly, the figure ± 4.4 for the A/C index for sets of 100 dream reports means that the departures fell on the average between 29.6 and 38.4 (the normative figure is 34).

between two or more groups with sample sizes smaller than 100. The focus of future research using this coding system should, however, be on what we believe is a more useful kind of comparison, namely, one with the Hall/Van de Castle norms. Sample sizes of at least 100 are needed to approach this goal.

MOST RECENT DREAMS: A NEW METHODOLOGY

Some potential dream content analysts may worry that they will not be able to obtain enough dream reports to do good studies, but we have found there is a simple and excellent way to create very large representative samples. Because the Hall/Van de Castle norms can be approximated with 100 to 125 everyday dreams from 100 to 125 people, it follows that 100 to 125 Most Recent Dreams should provide an adequate sample. We have tested this hypothesis and found support for it with 100 Most Recent Dreams from women students at the University of California, Santa Cruz, in 1992 and 1993. We simply ask students to write down the most recent dream they can remember, whether it was "last night, last week, or last month." To reinforce this emphasis on recency, we first ask people to write down the date and the time of day they recalled the dream. This information also can be used to screen out dreams not recalled within the past few days, thus making even more certain that the dream reports in the sample are recent ones. The instructions we use are reprinted in Appendix C.

The importance of emphasizing Most Recent Dreams in such studies cannot be overestimated because of the tendency for people to report a recurrent dream or nightmare, or an especially unusual dream if they are asked in a general way to report a dream. This is what happened, for example, when Stanley Krippner asked a television audience to send him a dream: 33% of the dream reports he received were described as recurring ones, and many respondents reported that they experienced the dream years earlier, sometimes in childhood (Rubenstein & Krippner, 1991:41). It is not surprising that the findings differed from the Hall/Van de Castle norms.

Studies based on Most Recent Dreams hold out the possibility of expanding dream content studies to a wide range of subgroups within the college population from skydivers to racial minorities to gays and lesbians. They also hold the potential for cross-national studies in which Most Recent Dreams are collected on the same date in many different universities around the world. Moreover, large samples of Most Recent Dreams can be analyzed very quickly by focusing on the question of what percentage of the reports have at least one aggression, friendliness, sexuality, misfortune, success, or failure. This approach allows investigators to bypass coding the dream narratives for characters and avoids detailed classification of social interactions.

Given the solid rationale for studies of Most Recent Dreams using 100 or more subjects in each group, the day of studies using small samples of two to five dreams from a handful of subjects should be over. If it is not possible to obtain lengthy dream series from individuals, then it is far better to work with one recent dream from each of many subjects, as our research demonstrates. It is also easier to obtain one Most Recent Dream from students in a classroom, dorm, or dining hall than it is to obtain dream diaries with five dreams in them from more than a handful of subjects.

REPLICATIONS AND FOLLOW-UPS

We turn now to several follow-up studies that can be seen in part as attempts to replicate the findings presented so far in this chapter. They are more than replications, however, for some of them sought to determine if historical changes, all-female settings, or racial and ethnic differences might influence the findings.

The Richmond Study

Dream reports collected from predominantly European-American students at the University of Richmond in 1979 for a study of emotions in dream reports (Stairs & Blick, 1979) provided an unplanned opportunity to see what, if anything, had changed in the dreams of college students over a 30-year period (Hall, Domhoff, Blick, & Weisner, 1982). This Richmond sample, as we came to call it, consisted of three, four, or five reports by each of 53 males and 69 females for a total of 263 male reports and 340 female reports. The reports were collected with instructions very similar to those Hall used in his earlier work. Case Western Reserve University and the University of Richmond, although in different parts of the country, are both private, urban coeducational universities whose students come from the middle and upper-middle socioeconomic strata. The dream reports were collected in psychology classes at both universities.

Because of time constraints on the investigators, only selected categories from the Hall/Van de Castle system were utilized. The categories were selected on the basis of three criteria. First, they were used in several studies subsequent to the normative study. Second, they were categories with large frequencies. Third, some of them showed gender differences and others did not.

The findings of this study can be presented in two ways. First, the Richmond males and females can be compared with the Hall/Van de Castle norms for males and females. The results of the comparison show that there are few differences and that the differences are relatively small in magnitude even when they are statistically significant. Specifically, Richmond males and females report a higher percentage of familiar characters than the norms.

Richmond males have a lower percentage of total friendliness, friendliness with males, and friendliness with unfamiliar characters. Richmond females have a lower percentage of total friendliness. Richmond males have a lower percentage of dreams with at least one sexual encounter and with references to clothing. Richmond females also have a lower percentage of references to clothing. In all, of 40 comparisons, only 9 are statistically significant, 6 for males, 3 for females.

The second way to compare the findings is to see if the gender similarities and differences for the norms are the same as they are for the Richmond study. Rather remarkably, there was not a single change. Where there were gender differences in the norms, there were gender differences in the Richmond study. Where there were no gender differences in 1950, there were no gender differences in 1980.

Hall et al. were careful to note that they did not know why there were so few differences between the two sets of dream reports. They mentioned three "possible" answers: that "human nature" has not changed, that 30 years is too short a time for the effects of social changes to manifest themselves in dream reports, and that any changes in American society in the past 30 years have not been very significant (Hall et al., 1982:193). They then wrote that "we cannot say which, if any, of these answers is the correct one..."

Despite this caution, some dream researchers have misinterpreted their conclusions. For example, after reporting the findings accurately, Cartwright and Lamberg (1992:82) imply that the authors attribute the lack of differences to the alleged fact that "human nature has not changed." Because few readers of Cartwright and Lamberg's popular book are likely to read the original report, this mischaracterization of the "interpretation" of the findings can be described not only as inaccurate, but as unfortunate. Statements like Cartwright and Lamberg's obscure the fact that extremely important findings were reported. Such statements also steer feminist social scientists away from quantitative content analysis.

The Salem College Study

Salem College is a small, private, all-women college in Winston-Salem, North Carolina. It is very similar to Case Western Reserve and the University of Richmond in that its students are mostly European-Americans who come from middle and upper-middle social strata. In 1987, Linda Dudley and one of her students (Dudley & Fungaroli, 1987) collected dreams from 12 female students enrolled in a special upper-division topics course in psychology to see if the dream reports of students at a women's college differed from those of women in the normative sample. With a sample of 141 dream reports, they found there were both striking similarities and some interesting differences. The consistencies were found for character and settings. The male/

female percent for Salem women was 46/54 as compared with 48/52 in the norms. The familiarity percent was 65 at Salem compared with 58 for the norms. The percentage of indoor settings was 60 at Salem compared with 61 for the norms.

There were some interesting differences in the patterns of social interactions. Whereas women in the Hall/Van de Castle normative study had more aggressive acts with males than with females (22% with males and 14% with females in the norms), the women at Salem College had the same percentage of aggressions with male and female characters (14% and 15%) because of less aggressive interactions with males. In keeping with this finding for aggressions, it was found the Salem women had a greater percentage of friendly interactions with women than the normative group (21% and 15%) even though their level of friendly interactions with male characters remained higher than with female characters (27% for Salem, 24% for the norms). Taken together, these findings lead to the cautious "interpretation" that the all-women environment led to less aggression with men and more friendliness with women. These findings are clearly worth testing in other social situations.

In spring 1990, Dudley did a follow-up study with 33 women in an introductory psychology class (Dudley & Swank, 1990). The women's average age was 18.5. The findings were very similar to those in her first study. The women continued to have a higher percentage of friendliness with women than did women in the normative group. The decline in aggression with male characters was not as great, however, perhaps because they had not been at Salem College as long. The findings for the two Salem studies are compared with the norms in Table 4.8.

By using their unique situation to collect dream reports, Dudley and her students have made an important contribution to the quantitative study of dream content. Their findings have strengthened our confidence in the normative findings and given us new hypotheses to explore about why dream reports may vary in their percentages of friendly or aggressive interactions with male and female dream characters.

The Berkeley Study

The first study of the dream reports of women at a major public university was made by Tonay (1990–1991). Moreover, that university was the best-known campus in the state of California, the University of California at Berkeley. Tonay's study included many safeguards to improve the quality of her data. It also included an ethnicity component. It did not include men because not enough of them turned in dream reports.

The subjects were 100 of 220 women attending an upper-division psychology class on the Berkeley campus. They participated voluntarily and

Table 4.8.   Comparison of Norm Women
with 1987 and 1990 Salem Women across Content Categories

Content variable	Hall/Van de Castle norms	1987 Salem	1990 Salem
Characters			
Percent male	48	46	49
Percent female	52	54	51
Percent familiar	58	65	65
Interactions			
Aggression with males	22	14	19
Aggression with females	14	15	14
Friendliness with males	24	27	27
Friendliness with females	15	21	21
Percent dreams with sex	4	Not studied	8
Settings			
Indoor	61	60	61
Outdoor	39	40	39

Adapted from Dudley, L., & Swank, M. (1990). A comparison of the dreams of college women in 1950 and 1990. *ASD Newsletter* 7(5), 3.

received no compensation. Students were invited to submit five consecutive dreams on basically the same forms originally used by Hall, and they were assured of anonymity. After 3 weeks, 109 dream booklets had been collected. Five subjects said they recalled no dreams during the time period, leaving 104 subjects. Four other subjects later admitted on the poststudy questionnaire (discussed in Chapter 3) that they had made up dreams, leaving 100 subjects and 500 dream reports. The typical subject was 21 years old, single, middle class, and a social science major with a 3.22 average. Most of the subjects were European-American or Asian-American. The volunteer subjects did not differ on any of these variables from the students in the class who did not participate.

The dream reports were put into a common pile and randomized before they were coded by two female undergraduate assistants trained by Tonay. Dreams were randomized again after the coding for each category. A third person compared the coding by the two raters. The rare disagreements were resolved by agreement between the two raters. The findings for 24 comparisons in the categories for characters, settings, friendliness, and sexuality did not reveal a single significant difference from the norms. For emotions and aggressions, there were three differences, all of which may be plausibly interpreted as showing more assertiveness and outgoingness on the part of these women. First, there were more emotions in their dream reports. Second, they were more likely to be victims of women characters than in the past. Third, they were more likely to be aggressors than in the past, meaning in the terms adopted for this book that their victimization percent had declined.

Tonay counted aggressions reciprocated by the dreamer as instances of being an aggressor, however, so her findings are not strictly comparable to the norms on this issue. Including reciprocal aggressions in our equation for the victimization percent drops it from 67 to 60 for women and from 60 to 52 for men.

Tonay's study included a comparison of Asian-American and non-Asian-American women. As Table 4.9 shows, there were very few differences between the two samples. The Asian-American women were more likely to be in unfamiliar settings. They were less likely to act as the aggressors in their dreams and were more often the victims of male characters than were non-Asian-Americans. Citing studies of the deferential way in which Asian-American women are often socialized (Chow, 1984; Fong, 1973; Hsu, 1971), Tonay (1990–1991:93–94) hypothesized that the differences on the aggression scores were consonant with subcultural differences.

Table 4.9. Subcultural Comparison: Dream Content of Asian-Americans and Non-Asian-Americans at Berkeley

Category	Percentages	
	Asian-Americans	Non-Asian-Americans
Characters		
Animals	1	4
Humans	97	95
Males	30	35
Females	40	33
Familiar	51	56
Unfamiliar	49	43
Setting		
Indoor	49	41
Outdoor	32	32
Familiar	25	28
Unfamiliar	29*	4
Friendliness		
Dreamer-involved	80	80
D as befriender	38	39
D as befriended	54	42
Emotions		
D-experienced	90	81
Aggression		
Dreamer-involved	79	84
D as aggressor	27*	49
D as victim of males	50*	36
D as victim of females	35	35

*$p < .05$, two-tailed.
Note: Various percentages do not sum to 100 (e.g., indoor/outdoor, familiar/unfamiliar, befriender/befriended) because findings for some categories are not included in the table. N = 32 for Asian-Americans.

The few interesting differences aside, the findings of these first three replication studies are consistent with previous findings. Dream reports collected at Case Western Reserve (1950), the University of Richmond (1979), the University of California, Berkeley (1986), and Salem College (1987 and 1990) all provide essentially the same results. This is an impressive record of replications. Thus, the norms for the Hall/Van de Castle system are reliable for the study of home dream reports from European-American and Asian-American college students.

Crane Community College: An African-American Sample

In spring 1967, Stephen Gornik, an instructor in psychology at Crane Community College in Chicago, offered to collect dream reports for Hall in his psychology class. All of the students were African-Americans. Students were asked, but not required, to turn in their dreams on the standard report form. Gornik received 101 reports from 12 males and 233 reports from 25 females. The students ranged in age from 18 to 29; most were in their early 20s. Unlike our earlier samples, many of these students still lived at home, which may be a factor in some of the differences Hall found. Gornik characterized these students to Hall in the following words:

> The student population represents what I would call a rising Negro middle class. While they come from poverty areas, they are strongly motivated to achieve and improve themselves, but in a direction that is not clearly delineated for them. (Personal letter to Calvin S. Hall, August 16, 1967)

Hall analyzed the dream reports for all the Hall/Van de Castle categories except settings, activities, and descriptive elements. The findings for males and females were compared with the Hall/Van de Castle norms and then with each other. There were a great many similarities with the norms, but there were some interesting differences as well. We begin with a brief summary of the similarities.

There were no differences between the two groups on objects, emotions, misfortunes and good fortunes, success and failure, number of sex dreams, or number of food and eating dreams. There were no differences between African-American males and European-American males on overall aggression or on any of our measures relating to friendliness. Where, then, do any differences lie?

First, African-American males differed from European-American males in five areas—three in character categories, two on aggression measures:

1. The male/female percent for African-American males was much lower (53/47% versus 67/33%, significant at the .001 level, h = .29). This means there were more female characters in their dream reports.
2. There were more familiar characters (66% versus 45%, significant at the .001 level, h = .43).

3. There were more family members and relatives in the dream reports of African-American males (30% versus 12%, significant at the .001 level, h = .45), which is the main reason why there were more familiar characters in their dream reports.
4. African-American males had less aggressive interactions with female characters than did European-Americans (A/C index = 8 versus 17, significant at the .05 level, h = .30).
5. African-American males had slightly more physical aggressions with all classes of characters than did European-American males (59% versus 50%, significant at the .001 level, h = .18).

Before we comment on these differences, let us look at the several differences between the African-American and European-American females:

1. Like African-American males, the African-American females differed from their European-American counterparts in having more family members in their dream reports (29% versus 19%, significant at the .001 level, h = .24).
2. Like African-American males, the African-American females differed from their European-American counterparts in having a higher proportion of physical aggression (47% versus 34%, significant at the .01 level, h = .27).

What is most striking between the two sets of women, however, is that the African-American females were both more friendly and more aggressive in their dream reports:

1. More total friendliness (F/C index = 31 versus 22, .001 level, h = .21).
2. More friendliness with male characters (F/C = 38 versus 24, .001 level, h = .30).
3. More friendliness with female characters (F/C = 23 versus 15, .001 level, h = .21).
4. More total aggression (A/C = 39 versus 24, .0001 level, h = .33).
5. More aggression with male characters (A/C = 29 versus 22, .05 level, h = .16).
6. More aggression with female characters (A/C = 22 versus 14, .01 level, h = .21).

Taken as a whole, what do these differences between European-Americans and African-Americans seem to indicate? At this point in our presentation of the full range of findings with the Hall/Van de Castle system, we are not prepared to make a case for a relationship between dream content and either personality or culture. Nor do we have enough information on the people in this sample to make a very strong argument even if we were ready to do so. Then too, the higher percentages for family members may be due to living at home instead of in a dorm or separate apartment.

Still, we hazard two hypotheses, which we will immediately "test" when we compare gender differences within the African-American sample. First, unlike the European-American sample, women and the family seem to be as salient in the dreaming minds of the men as they are in the minds of the women. Second, there is less of a gender difference in social interactions in the African-American sample. Let us now see how these suggestions fit with gender findings within the African-American sample.

For most of our categories, the gender differences within the African-American sample are similar to those in the Hall/Van de Castle norms. This finding is in effect contained within the long list of "no differences" between the two groups of males and two groups of females with which we began a recounting of our findings several paragraphs ago. However, some of the differences we then reported between the two groups of males and females also imply gender differences within the African-American sample. These differences are potentially quite interesting.

First, the usual gender difference in the male/female percent disappears, showing an equal saliency of male and female characters in both genders. This point is made in Table 4.10, comparing male and female dreamers in both samples.

Second, the gender difference on the familiarity percent is reversed. For European-Americans, women have the higher familiarity percent; for the African-Americans in this sample, men have the higher familiarity percent. This reversal is entirely due to the difference between the two samples of males, as can be seen in Table 4.11.

Finally, the gender difference in the A/C index is reversed. For European-Americans, the males have a higher A/C index. For African-Americans in this sample, women have the higher A/C index. This reversal is due to the difference between the two samples of females, as can be seen in Table 4.12.

As we just noted, we are not in a position to draw conclusions from these findings, but interesting and suggestive patterns are implied. There seem to be subcultural differences between the two groups, and the findings on gender differences suggest that gender relations may be very different in the two groups. It is also noteworthy that African-American women in this

Table 4.10.   Male/Female
Percent for African-American
and European-American
College Students

	Men	Women
African-Americans	53/47	54/46
European-Americans	67/33	48/52

Table 4.11. Familiarity Percent for African-American and European-American College Students

	Men	Women
African-Americans	66	56
European-Americans	45	58

sample are both more friendly and more aggressive with each other in their dreams than European-American women are with each other.

The foregoing paragraph is very far from an analysis. We would need behavioral information of the kind we present in Chapter 8 before we could begin a serious analysis. We also would want to replicate the findings in other African-American samples. The findings would be even more powerful if they could be replicated in other tight-knit communities, or in other groups where male/female power relations are thought to be more equal, whatever the race or ethnicity of these groups.

Mexican-Americans at Two Different Universities

The Hall/Van de Castle system was used in one study relating to Mexican-American college students (Kane, Mellen, Patton, & Samano, 1993). The study compared Mexican-American and Anglo-American women from four colleges and universities in San Antonio with each other and with Mexican women from four universities in Mexico City. The students were given dream diaries in which they were asked to record the first five dreams they recalled in a 3-week period. Many hundreds of dream reports were collected. A random sample of 30 women was drawn from each group of between 40 and 50 women, and one dream was drawn randomly from the series provided by each of the 30 women. The dream reports were compared

Table 4.12. A/C Indexes for African-American and European-American Men and Women

	Men	Women
African-Americans	31	39
European-Americans	34	24

for number of characters, emotions, aggressions, friendly interactions, sexual interactions, achievement strivings, and misfortunes and good fortunes. There were no statistically significant differences between the Mexican-American and Anglo-American women in any category. There were two significant differences between Anglo-Americans and Mexicans: there were more emotions and more misfortunes and good fortunes in the dream reports of the Mexicans. There is, unfortunately, one serious drawback with this study. There are only 30 dream reports in each sample. The rest of the dream reports need to be analyzed, or else new studies need to be done, before we can be confident of the reported findings.

Although there are no studies using the Hall/Van de Castle system that included Mexican-American male students, Brenneis (1976) and Brenneis and Roll (1975) compared the dream reports of Mexican-American and Anglo-American male and female students at the University of New Mexico using the scale of "34 ego dimensions" developed by Brenneis and discussed in Chapter 2. Their results are not strictly comparable with other findings in this chapter, but there is enough overlap in some of the scales to make several of their findings of interest.

For this study there were 42 Chicano males, 65 Chicana females, 61 Anglo males, and 74 Anglo females. All were volunteers. The average age for all four groups was between 20 and 21. The Chicano volunteers were accepted if Spanish was spoken in their homes and if they identified themselves as Chicanos. There was a total of 1,123 dream reports, 203 from male Chicanos, 309 from Chicanas, 283 from male Anglos, and 328 from female Anglos (Brenneis, 1976:281).

If we look first at the findings for the Mexican-Americans, we see there are a number of gender differences that are by now familiar to us. There are more characters in women's dreams, and a greater percentage of them are known to the dreamer. There is a higher percentage of male characters in the men's dream reports. Male dreamers more often have "contentious" or "negative" interactions; there is more aggression, sexuality, and depiction of physical injury in their dream reports. Women are more likely to be in enclosed and familiar settings, men to be in larger and more open settings (Brenneis, 1976:283–284; Brenneis & Roll, 1975:179).

The main cultural difference between the Mexican-Americans and Anglo-Americans was a greater exaggeration of the gender differences in Mexican-Americans (Brenneis, 1976:287). In addition, more familiar settings appear in the dream reports of Mexican-Americans, and there was a tendency—which did not reach statistical significance—for there to be more characters (Brenneis, 1976:284). Brenneis (1976:287) also claims that "death themes" appear more frequently in the dream reports of Mexican-Americans. He does so on the basis of earlier studies by Roll and Brenneis (1975) and Roll, Hinton, and Glazer (1974). In the first of these two studies, there is no analysis of

dream content, nor even any dream reports, but only the results of a questionnaire in which subjects were asked "Have You Ever Dreamed Of ..." for 48
topics.

Perhaps because the weaknesses of questionnaire studies of "dream
content" were recognized, a second study was done in which five dream
reports were analyzed from 40 male and 40 female Mexican-American college students and 40 male and 40 female Anglo college students at the
University of New Mexico. The study claims there is the same difference in
"death themes," but the evidence for this claim is doubtful at best. In this
study, the problem lies in the coding categories, which include (1) "clear and
obvious" death themes and (2) allegedly "symbolic" death themes (Roll &
Brenneis, 1975:380). The "obvious" death themes were (1) seeing dead people
appear as though alive; (2) seeing a relative or friend dead; (3) seeing yourself
as dead; (4) being hanged by the neck; (5) being buried alive; (6) seeing
mortuaries or graveyards; and (7) being in heaven or hell after death. The
allegedly "symbolic" death themes are (1) losing a limb; (2) being unable to
breathe; (3) seeing lunatics or insane people; (4) having teeth fall out or be
pulled out; (5) being tied and unable to move; (6) seeing a creature that is part
animal and part human; and (7) seeing a body change grotesquely (Roll &
Brenneis, 1975:380). No evidence is presented that any of these elements
relates to death, but this symbolic scale is the key to the whole study, as we
shall now show.

The alleged cultural differences achieved statistical significance for
women only. However, "if the realistic and symbolic content areas were
treated separately, they do not achieve statistical significance" (Roll & Brenneis, 1975:381). In other words, the claim stands or falls, to the degree it can
stand when males do not show the difference, on the validity of the allegedly
"symbolic" death themes. Roll and Brenneis provide no frequency counts by
categories, so it is impossible to know where the two samples of women
students may differ. To satisfy empirical curiosity, it would be interesting to
know how often these students dream of seeing mortuaries, being hanged by
the neck, being in heaven or hell, losing a limb or teeth, or seeing insane
people. Our guess, based on our studies, is that it would not be very often.

Further support for the relative lack of differences between Mexican-
American and Anglo-American dreamers can be found in a study using the
Hall/Van de Castle scales to study aggressions and misfortunes in the dream
reports of 140 Mexican-American and Anglo-American teenage delinquents
and nondelinquents in Tucson, Arizona (Leman, 1967). Subjects were matched
for age, intelligence, and socioeconomic level. There were no ethnic differences on either scale.

Overall, the dream reports of Mexican-Americans seem very similar to
those of Anglo-Americans. There may be some cultural differences, but the
similarities and the common gender differences seem to be greater.

Gender Changes or Flawed Methods?

Milton Kramer and his colleagues at the University of Cincinnati have applied the Hall/Van de Castle coding system to dream reports collected in the laboratory. Most of their work is innovative and useful. One of their studies concerned the norms for the character categories (Reichers, Kramer, & Trinder, 1970), where they reported a great similarity between the distribution of characters in their sample of 418 laboratory reports and the Hall/Van de Castle norms.

Another study concerned gender differences in laboratory dream reports (Kramer et al., 1983). It was based on 11 males and 11 females, ages 20–25, who were students at the University of Cincinnati. Subjects were awakened at the end of each of the first four REM periods and asked to report what was going through their minds. In all, 1,190 reports were collected from 1,659 awakenings, for a recall rate of 72%.

The authors found there were no gender differences in the percentage of reports containing at least one aggression or at least one misfortune suffered by the dreamer. Aggressions appeared in 12% of the dream reports of both men and women. Women had misfortune to themselves in 12% of their reports, men in 9%. The authors conclude that well-known gender differences on aggression have thus disappeared, but their conclusion is mistaken.

According to the Hall/Van de Castle norms, 47% of male dream reports have at least one aggression as compared to 44% of female dreams. Thus, there never was a difference between males and females on aggression if the focus is on the percentage of reports with at least one aggression. What the findings by Kramer et al. (1983) show is a smaller percentage of aggression reports for both sexes, which is in keeping with the differences between laboratory and home reports discussed in the previous chapter. The same analysis pertains to misfortunes, as can be seen in Table 4.13.

Kramer et al. (1983) also coded the dream reports using Hall/Van de Castle scales for characters (10 subscales), activities (9 subscales), and modifiers (21 subscales). They found that male dreams had more male characters and more strangers, which is consistent with the Hall/Van de Castle norms. Males tended to mention large sizes more, also in keeping with the norms.

Table 4.13. Percentage of Dreams with at Least One Misfortune

	Men	Women
Hall/Van de Castle norms	36	33
Kramer et al. (1983)	9	12

However, Kramer et al. also found that men were higher on five subscales where there had been no gender difference previously, but the reasons are methodological, as we shall soon show. Most of these differences are on minor elements, tending to occur infrequently in the Hall/Van de Castle norms. We report the Hall/ Van de Castle findings on these elements in Table 4.14, then show what Kramer et al. did.

Using raw frequencies for each element, Kramer et al. (1983) turned the Hall/Van de Castle findings into male/female ratios. They then compared these ratios to their ratios in Table 4.15.

Using the same procedure, Kramer et al. (1983) found women to be higher on two other minor subscales in the modifier category that previously had shown no gender difference (Table 4.16).

The findings of Kramer et al. (1983:1) do not support their claim that the "sexual revolution of the past two decades has indeed had some psychological impact in altering some of the traditional differences" between the sexes. The different findings are in fact an artifact of their flawed methodology.

The first problem with these findings is that the authors used *raw frequencies* for male and female dreamers in the Hall/Van de Castle norms to create their M/F ratios. Such a procedure does not correct for report length or different numbers of characters, activities, and modifiers in male and female reports. In the Hall/Van de Castle norms, the women's dreams were 8% longer and contained more characters (1,423 versus 1,180), more activities (2,470 versus 2,362), and more modifiers (1,458 versus 1,110). Thus, ratios based on raw frequencies will be higher than a comparison based on indexes that control for differences in length of reports and raw frequencies. Ratios based on raw frequencies may create "differences" where there are none when the proper corrections are not made for differing report lengths and frequencies. For example, the percentage of single characters for female dreamers (72%) is not much higher than for male dreamers (69%) even though there are more single characters in women's dream reports. The

**Table 4.14. Hall/Van de Castle
Percentages on Selected Categories**

	Men	Women
Single characters	68.7	71.9
Auditory activity	1.6	1.4
Achromatic (color minus)	3.9	4.6
Mention of old age (age plus)	4.0	4.2
Mention of density (density plus)	1.6	1.5
Linearity plus (straightness)	0.4	0.4

Table 4.15.   Comparison of M/F
Ratios of Significant Variables

	Cincinnati	Norms
Single characters	1.44	0.79
Male characters	2.70	1.17
Strangers	5.25	1.08
Auditory activity	2.45	1.04
Color minus	1.86	0.64
Size plus	2.57	1.04
Age plus	2.33	0.75
Density plus	4.88	0.82
Linearity plus	3.55	0.69

Cincinnati study turned this small difference into an M/F ratio of .79 by using raw frequencies.

With this information as a context, we can now see the second reason for the differences from the norms in the study by Kramer et al. (1983): the men's dream reports turn out to be longer than the women's for a change (116 words versus 92). Thus, there is likely to be "more" of everything.

There is a third problem. It is not a good statistical practice to use ratios with very low frequencies. Just a few cases can change ratios dramatically. Let us use the mention of straight lines ("straight plus") as an example. The M/F ratio for Cincinnati is 3.55, and it is only .57 for Hall/Van de Castle; however, in the Hall/Van de Castle norms we are talking about a frequency of four out of 1,110 modifiers in male dreams and a frequency of seven out of 1,458 modifiers in female dream reports. That is, the .57 M/F ratio is based on dividing seven into four. Moreover, if we use percentages, as we should, there is no gender difference—"straightness" is used as a modifier 4% by males and 4% by females in the Hall/Van de Castle norms.

We have focused on the findings and claims of Kramer et al. (1983) for two reasons. First, it is always a good idea to check for methodological differences when new findings contradict established findings, rather than immediately to assume the differences are real and then begin theoretical

Table 4.16.   The Normative and Cincinnati
Findings on Two Modifier Scales

Scale	Cincinnati M/F	Normative M/F
Thinking activity	.05	.67
Intensity plus	.16	.75

speculations. There often are real changes, but all explanations in terms of sampling and statistical procedures should be thoroughly examined before the findings are assumed to be different. In this particular case, the samples are different (men's reports are longer) and percentages are not used. It is essential to follow all the rules of the system to make future findings compatible and cumulative.

The second reason we have discussed these findings at length is that they have been used to question the current accuracy of the Hall/Van de Castle norms (e.g., Lortie-Lussier, Schwab, & De Koninck, 1985:1012; Lortie-Lussier, Simond, Rinfret, & De Koninck, 1992:81,93; Rinfret et al., 1991:180; Rubenstein, 1990:139). There is thus a danger that those new to dream research will believe that the Hall/ Van de Castle findings are "outdated." But they are not, as the replication studies from the 1980s cited earlier in this chapter have demonstrated, and as a revised analysis of the Cincinnati findings also indicates.

CONCLUSION

The numerous findings presented in this chapter give us strong reason to believe that we know what American college students dream about. The findings are robust over 45 years and across different regions of the country. They come from both male and female investigators. In short, these findings with the Hall/Van de Castle system are the most reliable, systematic, and potentially useful quantitative findings on dream content ever developed. They deserve to be taken seriously as a starting point for further research investigating the possible relationships of age, class, race, ethnicity, and nationality to dream content. Studies concerning these variables now can be done with confidence with one Most Recent Dream from each of 100 to 125 subjects.

These findings also give us our first reason to believe that there is meaning in dreams because they show a coherence or regularity in the relatively small but consistent differences in what women and men dream about. In that regard, the findings on dream reports are similar to what is found in many other psychological studies comparing women and men. The reasons for these small differences are many and varied, but they are not our concern here. What is important for our purposes is the regularity of the findings in several different samples from various time periods and regions of the country.

Age Differences
in Dream Reports

INTRODUCTION

Age is a defining issue in the waking lives of all Americans. It is now time to see if this is also the case in their dreaming lives. Reversing the usual order for discussions of age, we will start with adults and end with children. The chapter begins by comparing college-age findings with those for postcollege groups. It next turns to teenagers (defined as ages 13–17) and then to children (defined as ages 2 to 12). The longest section of the chapter concerns a detailed comparison of conflicting findings on the dream reports of young children. This discussion shows how important the adoption of a common coding system could be in avoiding misunderstandings, but it also shows that with children there are likely to be larger differences between dreams collected in the home and laboratory than we think is the case with adults.

YOUNG ADULTS VERSUS OLDER ADULTS

Using an earlier version of the Hall/Van de Castle coding system that varies only slightly from its final form, we did studies in the early 1960s of characters, aggressions, and friendly acts in dream reports of young and older adults. These studies allow us to make comparisons between college students, all of whom were between 18 and 25, and older adults who ranged in age from 30 to 80 (Hall & Domhoff, 1963a, 1963b, 1964). The older adult sample was developed by taking one dream from dream series provided by 281 males and 281 females. These dream series were given to Hall by a wide variety of people.

The main age-related findings in these studies are brought together in Table 5.1. There is stability in the male/female percent, but a decline in friendly interactions and aggressions.

Harold Zepelin (1980–1981, 1981) did a very good and thorough study of age differences in 58 males ages 27 to 64 using both laboratory and home dream reports. He used both his own scales and some of the Hall/Van de Castle scales. There were very few age differences. As in the Hall and Domhoff (1963b) study, there was a slight age-related decline in aggression. There also was a decline in "distortion" on a scale designed by Zepelin. Family-related content was most prominent from ages 35 to 55, which makes sense in terms of the focus on child rearing for most adults in those years. However, Zepelin stresses how few changes there were in the several dozen comparisons he made, and notes that the correlations were low even where there were changes.

As one part of an in-home mental health survey conducted in Cincinnati with a representative sample of 300 men and women age 21 or over, the interviewers asked the subjects to relate their most recent dream (Kramer, Winget, & Whitman, 1971; Winget, Kramer, & Whitman, 1972). Sixty-four men (53% of the male sample) and 118 women (65% of the female sample) provided a total of 182 dream reports. The dream reports were compared for gender and age differences on the major Hall/Van de Castle scales. Four age classifications were used: 21 to 34, 35 to 49, 50 to 64, and 65 and over.

Most of the usual gender differences were found. The women's reports contained more characters, friendly interactions, emotions, indoor settings, and mentions of family, while the men's dream reports had more aggression and successful striving (Winget et al., 1972:203). The only age difference was a lower amount of aggression for those in the 35 to 49 age category as compared to those who were younger or older. There is one reason for caution

Table 5.1.   Age Differences in Selected Content
Categories for Young versus Old Adults[a]

	Males	Females
Male/female percent	66/34 (68/32)	52/48 (55/45)
F/C index overall	13 (21)	4 (14)
A/C index overall	22 (34)	7 (24)
A/C index with male characters	18 (27)	3 (17)
A/C index with female characters	5 (14)	3 (13)

[a]Young adult findings in parentheses.
$h = .21$ between younger men and over-30 men on F/C overall
$h = .34$ between younger women and over-30 women on F/C overall
$h = .49$ between younger women and over-30 women on A/C overall
Note: Findings in parentheses do not conform to current norms because they are based on an earlier version of the coding system.

with these findings. The mean length of the dream reports was only 21 words, with a range of 2 to 68 words. They were thus far shorter than the reports Hall and Van de Castle used to establish their norms; their dream reports averaged about 125 words, with a range of 50 to 300 words. After noting the differences in the length of reports, Kramer et al. (1971:89) concluded that "the striking feature that emerges is how similar the dream content of the two samples turns out to be."

Brenneis (1975) compared 148 dream reports from 38 college women ages 18 to 26 (mean age: 20.5) with 185 reports from 43 women ages 40 to 86 (mean age: 56.8). The dreams of the older women were obtained from friends of the author and friends of friends (a "snowball" sample). The dream reports of the younger women were obtained through college classes. All but one of the older women had attended college. All but one was or had been married; eight were widows. Brenneis compared the two sets of dream reports on his ego dimension scale briefly described in Chapter 2; however, most of his comparisons are subjective and interpretative. For our purposes here, his main finding was that there was less aggression in the older women's reports, with levels of robust and energetic activities remaining high. There was no decline in sexual elements (Brenneis, 1975:433).

A study of how college-age and elderly women (59 to 87 years) rated the emotionality of their dream reports supports the idea that there is a decline in aggressive/hostile dream content in older adults (Howe & Blick, 1984). Both sets of women kept dream diaries for 6 weeks and rated each dream on a 10-item emotional checklist developed for dream studies by Stairs and Blick (1979). The authors found that anger–rage and fear–terror were checked significantly less often in relation to the dream reports of the elderly; enjoyment–joy accounted for a significantly higher proportion of emotions related to the dream reports of the elderly.

The findings with American subjects are supported in a study of 47 French-Canadian women who ranged in age from 25 to 56, each of whom contributed two dream reports to the study (Lortie-Lussier, 1995). Seventeen of the women were from 25 to 35, 20 from 36 to 45, and 10 from 46 to 56. The dream reports were scored on the Hall/Van de Castle scales for characters, settings, activities, emotions, and aggressive and friendly interactions, and then sorted into the three age groups. There was a slight decline in the total number of emotions, and there were more pleasant outcomes in the oldest group; otherwise, there were no age differences. Although we cannot be confident of these findings with only 20 to 40 dream reports in each age group, they point in the same direction as the studies of older Americans.

Ideally, these cross-sectional findings should be checked against longi-tudinal studies to make sure the few differences are not due to cohort effects. However, systematic longitudinal studies of dream content over a period of years or decades are not likely to be undertaken. A few multiyear dream series are discussed in Chapter 7 on consistencies in long dream series. To anticipate, the findings from those dream series support the cross-sectional findings in showing little or no change over the span of decades. Unfortunately, these few series are not helpful on the issue of changes in aggressive content because they come from mild-mannered people who started their dream journals in their mid-20s or early 40s with very low levels of aggression that remained constant thereafter.

TEENAGERS (13 TO 17)

There is very little information on the dream reports of teenagers, and some of what we have is disappointing because it is not understandable in terms of the Hall/Van de Castle norms. Moreover, some of the trends, such as on aggressive interactions, are contradictory. There are also some reassuring consistencies, such as on characters, settings, and objects, but we need better studies before we can be confident about extending the norms to teenagers. Because it is not easy to obtain dream reports on a regular basis from teenagers over the space of several weeks, studies relying on the Most Recent Dream approach outlined in the previous chapter may be the best way to conduct future studies of this age group.

Hall and Domhoff (1963b, 1964) analyzed one dream report from each of 138 male and 138 female teenagers, ages 13 to 18, as part of their larger study of aggressions and friendliness in different age groups. For our purposes here, we will compare those findings with their study of one dream report from each of 200 males and 200 females ages 18 to 27 rather than the Hall/Van de Castle norms because of small changes in the coding system made when the norms were created. The point for now is only to see how closely the teenagers approximate the young adults.

As Table 5.2 shows, there are some differences. The teenage males express more friendliness than the young adult males (F/C index). Conse-

Table 5.2.   Differences between Teenagers and Young Adults in Selected Content Categories[a]

	Males	Females
F/C index	21 (11)	13 (12)
A/C index	29 (31)	22 (16)
Aggression/friendliness percent	59 (74)	63 (57)
Victimization percent	73 (55)	76 (63)
Physical aggression percent	47 (61)	48 (36)

[a]Young adult findings in parentheses.

quently, the teenage males have a lower aggression/friendliness percent. They are also more likely than young adult males to be victims of aggression, but a smaller percentage of the aggression in their dream reports is physical. For women, the differences are in aggressions. As young teenagers they have a higher A/C code, a higher rate of victimization, and a higher percentage of physical aggression. Consequently, the aggression/friendliness percent for teenagers is slightly higher than it is for young adult women.

A rigorous dissertation compared dream reports from high school and college students in Ames, Iowa, using the Hall/Van de Castle coding categories (Howard, 1978). Unfortunately, it did not use the Hall/Van de Castle methods of analyzing the data, so the results are not comparable with the Hall/Van de Castle norms.[1] The author compared dream reports from 44 students, ages 15 to 16 (17 males, 27 females), at Ames High School with those from 54 students, ages 20 to 22 (22 male, 32 female), in upper-division psychology courses at Iowa State University. All subjects recorded their dreams at home for 1 week in a booklet consisting of six lined pages. The difficulty in obtaining the high school reports is seen in the fact that only 32 of the 63 original high school volunteers returned any dreams; the figure was 13 out of 23 for the second volunteer group. One student returned only one report of nine words and had to be dropped. By contrast, 54 of the 56 college volunteers returned the dream booklet (Howard, 1978:54). There were 381 usable reports in all.

There is no information on how these dream reports were distributed by age and gender. Howard (1978:36, 56) does, however, report that the small number of high school males in the sample was compounded by the fact that they produced the fewest dream reports and used the fewest words to describe their dreams (76 words per dream report versus 117 for college males; by comparison, high school girls wrote an average of 105 words, college females 120 words; Howard, 1978:56). The high school boys were the least clear in their descriptions, and they had the lowest scores for many content categories. In short, they do not sound like eager participants, and comparison of them with the other three groups must be made with caution.

All dream reports were randomized, then rated independently by two judges on the following variables: dream length, setting, characters, aggression, friendliness, sexual content, references to the body, food, clothing, weapons, emotions, references to the past, negative affect, unusual elements, and negative words (Howard, 1978:34). Reports of fewer than 15 or more than

---

[1]There is also a dissertation on aggression in the dream reports of high school students in Detroit that has major methodological weaknesses, so it will not be included here (Buckley, 1970). For example, it did not correct for report length by dividing aggression frequencies by number of characters, and some of the N's involved are extremely small. None of its claims can be taken seriously except for the difficulties in obtaining dream reports from teenagers.

175 words were excluded. Eight of 389 reports were eliminated because they contained fewer than 15 words. None was eliminated for being too long (Howard, 1978:54).

Howard made her analysis so that she would have one score for each subject for each coding category. This controlled for dream series of different lengths. Here is how she did it:

> To obtain one score per subject on each variable, an average score per dream or mode was established first, then an average or mode of all the dreams produced by the subject was determined. This procedure established the number of subjects rather than the number of dreams as the basis for analysis. (Howard, 1978:51)

Howard used chi-square, Pearson r, and analysis of variance to analyze her findings. She found very few age differences. The two age groups were similar on settings, objects, characters, friendly and aggressive interactions, and unusual elements. The high school students were higher on the descriptive and evaluative scales, meaning they used more modifiers such as size, speed, and intensity to describe people, objects, and events. College students had more male figures in their dream reports. They also expressed more negative emotions and used more negative words (Howard, 1978:63, 96, 102, 106, 111, 138).

On the other hand, there were several gender differences. College males expressed more aggression than females. High school and college males had more outdoor settings, whereas high school and college females had more indoor settings and more indoor and outdoor settings in the same dream report (Howard, 1978:61, 90). High school and college females scored higher than males in female characters, friends, friendly interactions, and references to food (Howard, 1978:71, 78, 93, 138).

If we assume Iowa State University students are similar to those at the universities discussed in the previous chapter, an assumption supported by the gender differences reported by Howard, then we can conclude tentatively that the Hall/Van de Castle norms might be of use for teenagers as young as age 15. However, we need further studies before we can be confident of that conclusion. Specifically, given our own findings with young teenagers, and the fact that Howard did not control for gender differences in report length or number of characters, we are uncertain about her findings on aggressive and friendly interactions. We are not confident about our own findings, but we are not confident about hers either.

Foulkes (1982) conducted a laboratory study of teenagers' dream reports as the final part of a longitudinal study of dreaming and dream reports in children from ages 3 to 15. It will be reported on in the next section on children's dream reports. It did not use the Hall/Van de Castle system, but some of its results are roughly comparable.

CHILDREN'S DREAM REPORTS

As part of their developmental study of characters, aggressions, and friendliness, Hall and Domhoff (1963a, 1963b, 1964) analyzed 217 dream reports from 119 boys ages 2 to 12 and 274 reports from 133 girls in the same age group. Hall later increased the sample size to 600 reports in an unpublished study. Findings from both analyses will be reported in this section.

College students, parents, and teachers in home, nursery school, and school settings collected these dream reports for Hall. There were usually only one or two dream reports from any one child. Most of the dream reports came from children over the age of 6. It is likely, as we will see, that this sample is biased toward memorable or frightening dream reports, so the findings need to be treated with more caution than the teenage findings, at least for some categories. Moreover, the children's reports are shorter than those of teenagers or young adults.

An analysis of the characters in the children's reports showed a gender difference on male/female percent—69/31 for the boys, 50/50 for the girls. Because we have so few dream reports from children under age 5, we also determined the male/female percent in the narratives that a sample of children ages 3 to 6 produced when they were asked to tell a story (Pitcher & Prelinger, 1963). The results are very similar to what we found in dream reports, as shown in Table 5.3. The biggest difference between child and adult dreams on the character scales is the much larger number of animals in children's dream reports, which manifests itself as a higher animal percent. This high animal percent also appears in young children's stories, as shown in Table 5.3. Table 5.4 presents the animal percent findings in a separate unpublished study by Hall. They are not as high as in children's stories. The animal percent declines with age. In a later, even more detailed study, Van de Castle (1983) reported similar findings using dream reports he collected with the aid of teachers as well as dream reports in Hall's collection.

Table 5.3. **Male Percent and Animal Percent in Children's Stories**

Age	Number of stories		Mean characters		Male/female percent		Animal percent	
	M	F	M	F	M	F	M	F
2.5–2.11	30	30	1.90	2.23	71/29	27/73	40	48
3.0–3.5	23	27	2.74	2.63	75/25	40/60	40	38
3.6–3.11	37	33	2.65	3.06	70/30	40/60	49	46
4.0–4.5	23	36	2.74	3.50	72/28	48/52	46	52
4.6–4.11	37	24	3.16	3.21	82/18	62/38	38	43
5.0–5.5	17	19	3.65	4.70	85/15	53/47	47	39
5.6–5.11	13	11	3.85	4.73	56/44	44/56	42	52

Table 5.4.   Animal Percent
in the Dream Reports of Children Ages 2 to 12

	Number of dreams		Mean characters		Animal percent	
Age	M	F	M	F	M	F
2–6	106	100	1.72	2.07	32	24
7–12	196	200	1.90	2.13	14	14

A higher animal percent in children's dream reports also was found in the first laboratory study of children's dream reports. Foulkes, Pivik, Steadman, Spears, and Symonds (1967) collected dream reports from 32 boys ages 6 to 12 who slept two nights in the laboratory and compared them to laboratory reports from young adults. Animals accounted for 16% of the characters in the boys' narratives; no animals were found in the reports of the young adult males.

Turning now to social interactions, Hall and Domhoff (1963b) found there is more aggression in children's dream reports than in adults' reports in terms of the A/C index. Much of this larger amount of aggression is with animals, and the child is usually the victim of an attack by the animal. After animals, males are the most frequently involved character in the aggressions in children's dream reports. The rate of aggressions that girls have with male characters declines into adulthood, but there is no difference between boys and college males in this respect. In terms of the victimization percent, children are more likely to be victims of aggression than are adults. In keeping with these findings on higher rates of aggression, children in this study also have more dreams with at least one misfortune than do adults. The F/C index shows there is almost as much friendliness in children's dream reports as in those of adults. For boys, the rate of friendliness with other males increases with age. For girls, the rate of friendliness with both genders stays the same as they grow older.

To summarize, the key differences between the children's sample and adult dream reports are as follows:

1. Children have a higher animal percent.
2. Children have a higher A/C score.
3. Children have a higher victimization percent.
4. Children have a higher percentage of dreams with at least one misfortune in them.

As stated at the outset of this section, these findings on children may be biased by a very selective sample. It is therefore necessary to see how they compare with findings from an extensive developmental study of dreaming in the sleep laboratory.

The Foulkes Study

One of the best studies of dreams and dreaming ever conducted in the sleep laboratory, and by far the most comprehensive study of dreaming in children, was carried out over a 5-year period at the University of Wyoming by David Foulkes (1982). The basic study involved two groups of children who slept in the laboratory every other year for nine nonconsecutive nights over a 5-year period. Subjects were awakened three times per night. The children in the first group were between 3 and 4 years of age when the study started. The children in the second group were between 9 and 10. Thus, Foulkes has information on the dream reports of children ages 3 to 15. Foulkes also gave the children a wide range of cognitive and personality tests, observed them at a summer play school, interviewed their parents, and had them write down their home-recalled dreams at one point in the study. The study began with 30 children in the two groups; six boys ages 11 to 12 were added at the start of the third year, and seven girls ages 7 to 8 were added at the start of the fifth year. In all, 46 children were studied—26 for all 5 years, 34 for at least 3 years, and 43 for at least 1 complete year. Foulkes made 2,711 awakenings over the 5-year period.

Perhaps the most surprising finding of the study was the low amount of recall from REM periods in the 3- to 5-year-olds, and the static, bland, and underdeveloped content of the few reports that were obtained. Only 27% of the REM awakenings yielded any recall that could reasonably be called a dream. The reports became more "dreamlike" (characters, themes, action) in the 5- to 7-year-olds, and increased in frequency in the 7- to 9-year-olds, but it was not until the children were 11 to 13 years old that their dreams began to resemble those of adult laboratory subjects in frequency, length, and overall structure (Foulkes, 1982:217).

Using a cross-sectional design, Foulkes later replicated his most important findings at the Georgia Mental Health Institute with 80 children, 10 boys and 10 girls each at ages 5, 6, 7, and 8. He and his co-authors summarized their findings as follows:

> Dreams were reported relatively seldom (median report rate of 20%); until age 7, their imagery was reported as more static than dynamic; until age 8, a passive-observer role for their self character was most common; until age 8, dream activity evidenced very simple forms of narrative structure; waking visuospatial, but not verbal, skills predicted dream-report rates, with Wechsler Block Design the single best such predictor. (Foulkes, Hollifield, Sullivan, Bradley, & Terry, 1990:447)

We now need to compare Foulkes's findings with those from the Hall collection, especially because children's dream reports do not seem to be as full of aggression and misfortune as the Hall and Domhoff findings would lead us to expect. It is difficult to make a detailed comparison, however, because Foulkes utilized his own coding system, and it does not correspond completely with the Hall/Van de Castle system. We therefore have to piece together a comparison with great care.

First, we do know that the gender difference in male/female percent is present in Foulkes's dream reports because Hall coded them on this dimension (Hall, 1984:1115). Because the reports of the younger children were short and contained few characters, Hall combined the data for ages 3 to 9. The percentage of male characters in 209 male dream reports was 70/30 as compared to 51/49 in 146 female reports. In the longer and more numerous narratives of the 9- to 15-year-olds, there was no systematic variation from year to year in the male/female percent, so Hall combined them into one group. The 510 male dream reports in this group showed an even higher male percent (76/24), whereas the 496 female reports had an even lower male percent (43/57).

Second, we know that animals appeared in a very high percentage of the young children's reports in the Foulkes study, and this percentage declined with age, as it did in the study by Van de Castle (1983). Foulkes (1982:48) reports that animals were the "major" characters in the dream reports of children ages 3 to 5. They appeared in 45% of girls' dream narratives and 33% of boys' reports. Animals appear in 38% of REM reports for 5- to 7-year-olds, most of whom by then are having narrativelike dreams with social interaction and physical movement (Foulkes, 1982:80). At this age, boys are dreaming more often of animals than are girls. In the years 7 to 9, a decline in dreams with animal figures in them begins (Foulkes, 1982:113, 115, 234).

Third, there was at least some aggression in the dream reports in the Foulkes study. Between the ages of 5 and 7, one dream in four for both boys and girls "contained a hostile (attack) initiation by one character to another" (Foulkes, 1982:9–90). At this age, all but one of these hostile attacks were initiated by some character other than the dreamer, and the dreamer was rarely the victim. The same low level of aggression was found at ages 7 to 9, although the dreamer now initiated some of the acts—in 9% of the girls' dream reports and 4% of the boys' reports (Foulkes, 1982:120).

Within this context of low overall levels of hostility, there were nonetheless gender differences. At ages 5 to 7, girls had far more reports with nonhostile social interactions (56% versus 21%), and at ages 11 to 13 the "prosocial initiations" were higher in girls than in boys (Foulkes, 1982:89, 189–190). Conversely, boys 11 to 13 had more "antisocial acts or misfortunes" (Foulkes, 1982:189–190). The increased gender difference at ages 11 to 13 was due to a decline in aggressions in the dream reports of the girls (Foulkes, 1982:193).

At ages 13 to 15, the dream reports of Foulkes's subjects became more like the Hall/Van de Castle norms. First, there was less prosocial behavior and there were more ascriptions of anger to other dream characters (Foulkes, 1982:229). For girls there was an increased amount of victimization (Foulkes, 1982:231). There was a general decline in dreaming about family members, especially for males, and the tendency for girls to be in home or residential settings became statistically significant (Foulkes, 1982:230, 235, 247).

Overall, the findings on the male/female percent and the animal percent, and the gender differences on family members, aggressions, and settings, are similar to what was found by Hall and by Hall and Domhoff. However, there is less aggression, misfortune, and negativity in the Foulkes data. Between the ages of 11 and 13, for example, "prosocial initiations" outweighed "antisocial" ones by a ratio of two to one, and even in the less prosocial reports of 13- to 15-year-olds, there were more prosocial motives than antisocial ones (Foulkes, 1982:189, 231). By contrast, in the Hall and Domhoff (1963b, 1964) findings, there was more aggression than friendliness, although it should be noted that the F/C index was higher for teenage males than for either younger boys or male college students. Part of this difference between the two sets of findings may be due to differences in the coding systems, but it probably means Hall and Domhoff had selective samples of dream reports for children and teenagers.

To bring some new findings to bear on these differences, we asked Tonay to apply several Hall/Van de Castle coding categories to the dream reports Foulkes et al. (1990) collected in their cross-sectional replication study. Tonay coded the reports without knowledge of the gender or age of the dreamer. Table 5.5 shows the findings for settings. Both boys and girls tend to be outdoors or in no setting at age 5, but by age 7 the girls tend to be indoors and the boys to be outdoors. This finding would come as no surprise to either Hall or Foulkes. The number of dreams at each age level is relatively small, so we do not want to make any statistical claims.

Table 5.6 presents the main findings for characters. Consistent with the adult norms, there are more characters in the girls' dream reports. The usual

Table 5.5. Percentage of Indoor, Outdoor,
No Setting, and Familiar Settings

Age	Number of dreams		Indoors		Outdoors		No setting		Familiar	
	M	F	M	F	M	F	M	F	M	F
5	24	17	30	16	47	53	24	26	35	37
6	31	10	44	42	22	42	33	16	37	58
7	16	35	33	50	61	43	6	10	44	43
8	25	25	42	59	52	35	10	6	26	68

Table 5.6. Findings with Characters

Age	Number of dreams M	F	Mean number of characters M	F	Male/female percent M	F	Familiarity percent M	F	Animal percent M	F
5	24	17	1.00	1.82	58/42	41/59	44	85	17	29
6	31	10	1.45	2.10	71/29	44/56	77	51	9	0
7	16	35	1.88	1.83	71/29	53/47	48	57	23	6
8	25	25	3.32	3.64	75/25	56/44	55	71	12	9

findings on the male/female percent appear from age 5, and the findings on the familiarity percent appear at age 7. The animal percents are not greatly different from those in Table 5.4.

The findings on social interactions, misfortunes, and negative emotions are in basic agreement with Foulkes's earlier findings. Furthermore, Tonay found no failures, very few misfortunes, and few negative emotions. There is more friendliness in the girls' reports, but relatively little aggression in the boys' reports. Several of these findings are presented in Table 5.7. The number of aggressive and friendly interactions is too small to make statistical claims.

When all the comparisons of the Hall and Foulkes data on children and young teenagers are taken into consideration, it is clear that Foulkes is right when he says our findings on aggression and misfortune in the dream life of children between the ages of 2 and 12 are based on a selective sample. At the same time, several of the adult gender differences appear in Foulkes's University of Wyoming and Georgia Mental Health Institute data by age 7 or 8, and other previously reported adult gender differences appear by the ages 13 to 15. We also note that he found the same developmental trends on the decline of animal percent, the increase in male strangers, and the victimization percent.

Table 5.7. Aggression and Friendliness

Age	Number of aggressions M	F	A/C index M	F	Number of friendliness M	F	F/C index M	F
5	1	1	4	3	0	4	0	13
6	1	0	2	0	0	2	0	10
7	3	2	10	3	0	2	0	3
8	9	9	11	10	4	12	5	13

Thus, not all the differences are due to the nature of the samples. Some of them are due to differences in the coding systems. The Hall/Van de Castle coding system obtains somewhat different results because it has different coding rules for friendliness and because it corrects for the larger number of characters in girls' and women's dream reports.

Findings similar to those in the Foulkes data are being produced in an ongoing longitudinal study in Switzerland of 12 boys and 12 girls between the ages of 9 and 15 (Strauch, 1995). For example, only a small percentage of their dream reports (12% to 24% when they were between ages 9 and 12) contained either a friendly or an aggressive interaction. Nonetheless, dream reports with at least one aggression outnumbered those with at least one friendly interaction for both boys and girls by age 12, and the victimization percent began to approach that of young adults by the same age in the relatively few dream reports with aggressions. Laboratory dream reports will be collected from the subjects when they are ages 15 to 16, and the final report from the study will include a comparison with their home-recalled dreams over the same 6-year age span. The overall study promises to add significantly to our understanding of how dream content develops in the teenage years.

There are not likely to be many more large-scale studies of children's dreams in the laboratory because laboratory studies are expensive and time consuming. The next feasible step in trying to resolve any remaining differences between the earlier studies therefore might be to see if the Most Recent Dream approach could be extended to younger children, perhaps with teachers reading them the instructions and asking them to write out their dream reports anonymously for the investigator while they are sitting at their desks. The younger the children, the more likely they might be to respond in terms of a memorable, recurrent, or frightening dream. However, large samples revealing consistent findings at ages 9 to 12 would be a useful addition to our understanding, especially if they could be coupled with Most Recent Dream studies of teenagers, where the method is definitely feasible.

Some indication of what might be possible is seen in a pilot study of Most Recent Dreams from 64 male and 80 female seventh graders, ages 12 to 13, in two middle schools in California (McNicholas & Avila-White, 1995). In keeping with adult differences, the reports from the girls were longer. Parallel to other findings mentioned earlier in the chapter, the animal percent was 13 for boys and 2 for girls, and the male/female percents were very close to the adult norms. The percentage of dreams with at least one aggression was 47 for the boys, which is exactly what it is for young adult males, and the figure for girls was 37, which is not far from the young adult female norm of 43. The percentage of dreams with at least one friendly interaction was 56 for the girls, not too far above the young adult female norm of 42. The only atypical finding was the low percentage of boys' dreams with at least one friendly interaction, 17, as compared with the normative figure of 38. These findings need to be replicated with larger sample sizes in a variety of settings, but they are an encouraging starting point.

CONCLUSION

We conclude that age is not a major factor in shaping dream content once Americans have reached young adulthood. One exception is the possible decline of aggressive acts in the dream reports of people over age 30. Thus, in studying individual dream series or dream sets from people over age 30, we should not be surprised by aggression scores lower than the norms. Instead, perhaps we should pay closer attention to aggression scores only slightly above the norms. In all, however, the important point is that norms based on college students are useful in studying postcollege adults.

Still, the norms have to be used with a certain amount of common sense. For example, it should not come as a surprise if parents dream of their children, thus increasing the percentage of youthful characters over the young adult norms. Such findings are not criticisms of the norms, but are evidence of their usefulness in developing our understanding of the relationship between waking preoccupations and dream content.

With regard to people under the age of 15 or 16, we have little confidence in our norms in the categories of social interactions and misfortunes. We believe that Foulkes (1982) has demonstrated dramatic developmental changes in dream content between the ages of 3 and 15, and that the dream life of children has less aggression and misfortune than Hall's sample led us to believe. Foulkes's findings support some of the gender differences and developmental trends in the Hall data, but they also support Foulkes's claims that the Hall sample is selective for dramatic intensity. Hall (1953c) and Hall and Domhoff (1963b) are guilty of exaggeration.

We conclude that children are important subjects for studying the cognitive development of dreaming as a psychological process, but not good subjects for studies of meaning in dream content. Foulkes's finding of poor recall with young children, as well as the difficulties of obtaining permission to use children as subjects and then gaining their cooperation, convinces us that the primary focus of content analysts should be on those people whose dreaming capabilities are fully developed and who are interested in participating in dream content studies. Still, it would be useful to know if the Most Recent Dream methodology could yield consistent findings with older children and teenagers.

We thus repeat what we think is the most important conclusion of this chapter: the findings on the dream reports of adult subjects show that our college student norms can serve as a basis for studies of dream meaning with unique adult groups or individual dream series. Before we turn to examples of such studies, however, we need to see what we learn by comparing our norms with findings from a wide range of nations and small preliterate cultures.

Cross-Cultural Studies
of Dream Content

INTRODUCTION

In this chapter, we present findings on dream content from a wide range of other nations and cultures. Some of these cultures are very similar to the United States in level of education or degree of urbanization and industrialization. Others are preliterate in nature, including some of the smallest and least structured societies in the world. Whatever the size of the society or its material base, however, the chapter shows there are both similarities and understandable differences in the findings when compared with our norms. The chapter begins with findings from such modern nation-states as the Netherlands, Argentina, India, and Japan, and then turns to findings on dreams collected by cultural anthropologists in past decades from small-scale societies.

Before we present the findings, it is essential to stress that there are great difficulties in doing cross-cultural research on dream content. These difficulties multiply as the differences between American society and the group under study increase (cf. D'Andrade, 1961; Dentan, 1983, 1986, 1988; Eggan, 1961; Kracke, 1979, 1987; Tedlock, 1981, 1987, 1991). For example, there are issues of access, trust, and rapport. There are problems of common understanding in many cases. Even when these obstacles are overcome, there can be problems obtaining a representative sample of dreamers. Informants, once established, may be eager to report dreams that are part of the cultural lore rather than their own dreams, or they may be reluctant to report certain dream contents to outsiders.

With a clear understanding of the obstacles to cross-cultural studies in mind and the likely uneven quality of the data, we turn to the substance of the findings.

LARGE-SCALE NATIONS

The Netherlands

Three Dutch investigators (Waterman, de Jong, & Magdelijns, 1988) have provided us with what is in effect a replication of aspects of the Hall/Van de Castle norms for the Netherlands. The study was designed to see if what they call "sex role orientation," that is, the mixture of "masculine" and "feminine" attributes in a person, was more important than gender itself in predicting dream content. They found that gender differences were more important than sex role orientation, and their findings were similar to those of the Hall/Van de Castle norms.

The subjects were students in a college psychology class in Amsterdam, 34 women and 32 men, ages 19 to 31. Each contributed five dreams for a total of 330 dream reports. The reports were coded for aggressions and friendliness. The results were analyzed using some of the percentages and indexes presented in Chapter 2 of this book. The formula for the significance of differences between proportions was utilized. The results of this significance test were checked with three separate log linear analyses ($2 \times 2 \times 2$ design) using the raw data.

As with the Hall/Van de Castle norms, there was more aggression than friendliness in both male and female dream reports, and the aggression/friendliness percents were higher for the male dreamers. A comparison of Dutch and American dreamers on aggression/friendliness percents is presented in Table 6.1.

The American and Dutch dreamers also were similar in their degree of victimization, with women in both cultures having a higher victimization percent than men. Here the one difference for sex role orientation occurred: the most "feminine" women were more often victims than the most "masculine" women.

Table 6.1.   Aggression/
Friendliness Percents

	Male	Female
Dutch	62	52
American	59	51

Table 6.2.   Physcial
Aggression Percent[a]

	Male	Female
Dutch	32	14
American	50	34

[a]h = .37 for males; h = .48 for females.

Finally, there was a far lower physical aggression percent for both males and females in the Netherlands, as can be seen in Table 6.2. This finding provides our first cross-cultural difference. If the finding on physical aggression percent were to be repeated in other Dutch samples, then the fact that the United States is by far the most violent industrialized nation in the world, and the Netherlands one of the least violent, would become of great interest. Furthermore, we would begin to wonder if the national violence rankings that can be derived from the highly detailed homicide and violent crime statistics compiled and analyzed by Dane Archer and Rosemary Gartner (1984) might correlate with the physical aggression percent in dream reports.

Switzerland

Inge Strauch of the University of Zurich, one of the pioneers of the new laboratory dream research in the 1960s, and her collaborator, Barbara Meier, studied 500 REM dream reports collected in their sleep laboratory over the years (Meier & Strauch, 1990; Strauch & Meier, 1992, 1996). The 500 dream narratives came from 44 subjects who spent a total of 161 nights in the sleep laboratory, each contributing between 2 and 19 reports. The 26 women subjects contributed 331 (66%) of the reports, and the 18 male subjects contributed 169 (34%). The women's dream reports were longer and more detailed than those of the men (Strauch, personal communication, July 1, 1993). The subjects ranged in age from 19 to 35 years.

The dream reports were coded for settings, characters, and social interactions with the Hall/Van de Castle scales. They also were classified for realism, references to everyday life, and references to leisure activities with Strauch and Meier's own rating system. We will focus here on the findings with the Hall/Van de Castle categories, although it can be said in passing that Strauch and Meier rated most dream reports as creative elaborations of realistic situations dealing with leisure, household, and other aspects of everyday life.

As can be seen in Table 6.3, there were very few differences between the Swiss laboratory dream reports and the American norms in the categories of

Table 6.3.   A Comparison of Swiss and American
Dreamers on Selected Categories of Settings and Characters

	Women		Men	
	Swiss	Americans	Swiss	Americans
Average settings	1.5	1.3	1.3	1.3
Indoor setting percent	59	61	58	48
Average characters	3.2	2.8	2.3	2.4
Male/female percent	55	48	63	67
Percent known	35	37	30	31
Percent strangers	24	17	25	23
Animal percent	5	4	4	6

settings and objects. The Swiss women are similar to the American women except for a higher percentage of male characters and strangers, and the Swiss men were similar to the American men except for a higher percentage of indoor settings.

The differences between the Swiss and American samples are greater in the categories of aggression and friendliness, as seen in Table 6.4. This table shows that a smaller percentage of the Swiss dream reports contain at least one aggression, with an especially dramatic difference between the males (23% Swiss versus 47% American). However, this difference has to be interpreted with caution because of the fact, reported in Chapter 3, that laboratory dream reports in the United States also show less aggression (Domhoff & Kamiya, 1964a; Hall, 1966a). Thus, the more interesting finding may be the lower physical aggression percent for Swiss men and women, with the largest difference once again between the males (29% Swiss versus 50% American, h = .43). It is also noteworthy that the figure for Swiss males is close to the 32% for Dutch males (shown in Table 6.2).

There are also differences in the types of friendliness expressed by Swiss

Table 6.4.   A Comparison of Swiss and American
Dreamers on Aggression and Friendliness

	Women		Men	
	Swiss	Americans	Swiss	Americans
Percent dreams with aggressions	33	44	23	47
Percent dreams with friendliness	41	42	31	38
Physical aggression percent	23	34	29	50
Inviting and verbal friendliness	48	34	57	28

and American dreamers, a finding made even more interesting by the fact the differences in the percentage of dream reports with at least one friendly interaction are relatively small for men and nonexistent for women. Swiss dream reports are more likely to contain friendly interactions of a verbal nature, such as invitations, compliments, or greetings. Conversely, the friend-liness in American dream reports is more likely to involve gift giving, efforts at help or support, and physical displays of friendliness.

In all, there are both reassuring similarities and intriguing differences in the detailed and careful work of Strauch and Meier. The fact that the Swiss sample is from the laboratory and the American norms from everyday recall injects a note of caution about some of the findings on social interactions, but the Swiss picture on physical aggression percent is also consistent with findings on Dutch dreamers reported in the previous section.

Canada

In a series of investigations, Monique Lortie-Lussier and her colleagues and students at the University of Ottawa in Canada have studied French-Canadian and British-Canadian citizens to see if and how social roles influ-ence dream content. One primary focus has been on the dream reports of married, college-educated mothers who are exclusively homemakers as com-pared to those of married, college-educated mothers who are employed outside the home. Female college students and college-educated, employed fathers also have been studied (e.g., Lortie-Lussier, Schwab, & De Koninck, 1985; Lortie-Lussier, Simond, Rinfret, & De Koninck, 1992; Rinfret, Lortie-Lussier, & De Koninck, 1991).

There are many similarities between the findings of these investigators and the Hall/Van de Castle norms. For example, findings on various Hall/ Van de Castle scales for 15 college-educated French-Canadian housewives (Lortie-Lussier et al., 1985:1016) and 18 single, French-Canadian undergradu-ates ages 18 to 22 (Rinfret et al., 1991:187) are compared with the American female norms in Table 6.5.

For the issues of concern to Lortie-Lussier and her co-authors, the varia-tions among their samples are more important. In the first study, however, Lortie-Lussier et al., (1985:1015) found only one statistically significant differ-ence between homemakers and wage-earning women out of 10 comparisons. This comparison showed more negative emotions in the dream reports of the wage earners. The investigators then turned to a statistical technique called discriminant analysis to see if patterns of differences could be detected in their data. This analysis revealed a four-variable pattern that was created by slightly more residential settings and overt hostility in the homemakers' reports, and slightly more indoor settings and negative emotions in the wage earners' reports. In the study by Rinfret et al. (1991:184–186), the working

Table 6.5.   A Comparison of French-Canadian and American
Women on Selected Content Categories

	French-Canadian homemakers	French-Canadian students	American female norms
Male/female percent	46/54	51/49	48/52
Familiarity percent	63	55	58
A/C index	30	51	24
Physical aggression percent	27	31	34
F/C with male characters	8[a]	43	24
F/C with female characters	16	8	15

[a]Recall that the F/C index was 4 for women over 30 in Table 5.1.

mothers ages 27 to 39 dreamed more often of the work environment, their husbands, their children, and unpleasant emotions than did college-age women students. Another paper from this group (Lortie-Lussier et al., 1992) claims "convergence" between the dream content of employed fathers and employed mothers as compared to women homemakers, suggesting that work roles can be as influential as gender roles.

We believe that these findings show there are considerable cross-national similarities. Nevertheless, the paper by Lortie-Lussier et al. (1985) is often joined with the mistaken interpretations by Kramer et al. (1983), discussed at the end of Chapter 4, to criticize the Hall/Van de Castle norms. For example, Garfield (1988:26) uses the findings by Lortie-Lussier et al. (1985) with discriminant analysis to refute her own false claim that Hall and Van de Castle "were the first to say that a woman's place was in the home" in her dreams. Aside from the technical point that no one finding can be isolated from the pattern in a discriminant analysis without losing its significance, and that there were no differences in the mean number of indoor settings in a direct comparison of the two samples, Garfield's comment ignores the fact that the working women, not the homemakers, had more indoor settings. She also overlooks the fact that the Hall/Van de Castle system codes only for "indoors" and "outdoors," and "familiar" and "unfamiliar." It says nothing about "the home," and Hall and Van de Castle never made the assertion that Garfield unfairly attributes to them. Similarly, Moffitt (1990) says that the findings by Lortie-Lussier et al. (1985) refute the "biological" underpinnings of quantitative content analysis. He thereby ignores the fact that content analysis is a methodology, while at the same time blurring the distinction between "findings" and "interpretations." Rubenstein (1990:139), in addition to accepting uncritically the mistaken interpretations by Kramer et al. (1983), wrongly claims that Lortie-Lussier et al. (1985) found "few indoor settings" for the working mothers, which is exactly the opposite of what they actually report: homemakers had more residential settings, and working mothers had more indoor settings.

The false claims by Garfield, Moffitt, and Rubenstein, based on a misunderstanding and misuse of very small differences that could be detected only through an analysis of general patterns, have been a source of major confusion in the literature on dream content. Contrary to their conclusion, the similarities between the two French-Canadian samples, and between the American norms and the overall French-Canadian findings, are far greater than the differences.

Three Latin American Countries

The focus of this section is on dream reports from children, teenagers, and young adults in Argentina, Mexico, and Peru. The dream reports were collected in urban schools in the early 1960s and translated for Hall by college students in these countries whom he hired expressly to gather dream reports on forms he provided. The verbal and written instructions to the students were to write down a recent dream. Each student wrote down one dream. In effect, this was the first use of the Most Recent Dream methodology.

The sample for Argentina consisted of 239 males, ages 12 to 17, and 149 females, ages 18 to 21. The Peruvian sample came from 276 males, ages 12 to 19, and 192 females, ages 13 to 20. There were 178 Mexican males, ages 16 to 24, and 54 Mexican females, ages 18 to 21. The findings with these groups were compared with each other and with those for American teenagers. These findings have not been previously published.

Overall, the similarities outweighed the differences. For example, the familiarity percent was above 55 for both males and females in all four countries, but there were always more familiar characters in women's dreams, as can be seen in Table 6.6.

There were similar findings for other content categories. Aggression was more common in male dream reports than in female dream reports in all four national groups, but there was always more aggression than friendliness irrespective of gender. Male dreamers in each of the four countries had more aggressive interactions with other males than female dreamers did, but both genders had more aggressions with male characters than with female ones.

Table 6.6. Familiarity Percents

	Peru	Mexico	Argentina	United States
Males	57	56	56	56
Females	67	77	70	68

There was, however, one striking difference in these comparisons. Peruvians and Mexicans differed from Argentinians and Americans on the male/female percent. Contrary to the usual European-American pattern, male Peruvians and Mexicans dreamed equally about male and female characters, whereas Peruvian and Mexican women tended to dream more about male characters than about female characters (Table 6.7).

Urbina and Grey (1975) also found a low male/female percent for men in Peru. They used dream reports collected in Lima from 48 male and 48 female college students, 18 to 20 years of age. Each student turned in eight dream reports over a period of 2 weeks to 3 months. Urbina and Grey argue that the difference in their findings from our earlier American findings is due to the fact that they computed the percentage of male characters for each dreamer, and then obtained the mean of these percentages. They believe this method is superior. In fact, they are mistaken. For group comparisons, it does not make any difference whether the percentage for a group of dream reports or the mean percentage is used. Hall (1984:1110) demonstrated this point empirically with findings for 20 dream reports from each of 20 males and 20 females. The percentages for the 400 male and 400 female dream reports were 68 and 48, respectively. The mean percentages for 20 males and 20 females were 67 and 48, respectively. Contrary to Urbina and Grey, then, we have to conclude that the Peruvian college students may be a rather unique group of dreamers.

The possibility that the male/female percent may be higher for Mexican women is supported by an unpublished study Hall did on 152 dream reports from an adult woman in Mexico City; her figure of 55/45 is below the 61/39 finding for his youthful Mexican sample, but higher than the normative figure of 48/52.

Thus, the findings for Peru and Mexico may indicate a genuine cultural difference on male/female percent. The Argentinian findings reinforce this conjecture because Argentine culture, with its large number of German and Italian immigrants and its minimal number of indigenous peoples in Buenos

Table 6.7.   Male/Female
Percent[a]

	Males	Females
Peru	51/49	55/45
Mexico	50/50	61/39
Argentina	70/30	50/50
United States	67/33	48/52

[a]h = .33 between American and Peruvian males; h = .26 between American and Mexican females.

Aires, where the dreams were collected, is very different from that of most other Spanish-speaking countries in Latin America.

Latin cultures are thought to be more "macho" than North European cultures. This may lead to the speculation that the male/female percent should be higher for males, not lower. But even if we assume that Latin cultures are more "macho," are they necessarily more "patriarchal"? Is there a strong "matriarchal" element in Latin cultures? Whatever the answers to those questions might be, we would not want to build a theory on the basis of the small number of findings we have for Latin American countries. Although the findings seem fairly solid, it would be essential to study more dream reports up and down the age scale in Peru or Mexico before serious inferences could be drawn. The Most Recent Dream approach makes such studies feasible.

India

There have been three studies of dream reports collected from college students in India, one at Allahabad University in Northern India (Grey & Kalsched, 1971), the other two at Andhra University in Southern India (Bose, 1983; Prasad, 1982). All three make use of the Hall/Van de Castle coding system, and all three report findings similar to those for the United States. There are also findings that may be culturally specific.

The dream reports for the Grey and Kalsched study were collected from 45 female and 51 male college students in 1962–1963 when Grey was a Fulbright Senior Lecturer at Allahabad. An adaptation of the Hall/Van de Castle instructions was used on the report forms. The students contributed a range of 4 to 25 reports for a total of 941 dream narratives. They also filled out a "Traditionalism Index" to see how closely they were tied to orthodox Hindu culture.

The reports were later utilized to test Hall and Domhoff's (1963a) claim of a "ubiquitous" gender difference in dream content on the male/female percent. Grey and Kalsched (1971:344) report very similar findings in Table 6.8.

Table 6.8.   Male/Female
Percent in India and
the United States[a]

	Males	Females
India	71/29	46/54
United States	64/36	52/48

[a]h = .15 for males; h = .12 for females.

In making this comparison, Grey and Kalsched (1971) use the findings from the older article by Hall and Domhoff (1963a) instead of from the norms, even though they were using the finalized Hall/Van de Castle (1966) system in coding the Indian dream reports. If they had stayed consistent, the findings would have been even more similar, as shown in Table 6.9.

The authors agree that their finding "seems to confirm" Hall and Domhoff's (1963a) earlier finding with American, Australian aboriginal, and Hopi dreamers (Grey & Kalsched, 1971:344). However, they stress the fact that Indian males dream even more of males and Indian females even less. They think the difference of seven percentage points for males and six for females is significant statistically and theoretically. They "reject" the alleged "assertion of universality" because they predicted that the greater gender segregation in India would lead to the larger differences they found.

Grey and Kalsched go on to report some very interesting findings. First, they confirm that there are individual differences in male percent for both male and female dreamers. Second, students who score high on the "Traditionalism Index," meaning they are devout Hindus and live in highly gender-segregated milieus, have a lower percentage of opposite-sex characters in their dream reports than students making a transition to more secular identities (r = .37 for males, .51 for females). The finding may not be as solid as it sounds because some of the male percents are based on only four or five dream reports and may therefore be unreliable, but it is suggestive in the context of other findings in this chapter.

The second Indian study is based on 1,000 dreams collected in the years 1968–1970, with exactly 10 reports from each of 50 males and 50 females (Prasad, 1982). The study was undertaken as a complete normative comparison with the Hall/Van de Castle norms. The Hall/Van de Castle instructions were followed in collecting the dream reports, and every Hall/Van de Castle coding category was used in analyzing the dream reports. The subjects are described as "graduate" and "postgraduate" students at Andhra University in Southern India. They ranged in age from 18 to 25. The author recruited volunteers by going to different classrooms and explaining the nature of the

Table 6.9. Male/Female
Percent in India and
the United States Using
the Hall/Van de Castle Norms[a]

	Males	Females
India	71/29	46/54
United States	67/33	48/52

[a]h = .09 for males; h = .04 for females.

study. He returned to the classrooms each morning to collect dream reports until each subject turned in 10 reports. Over 300 students volunteered to be involved, but many subjects dropped out or were not able to remember 10 dreams.

The data were analyzed for differences with the American male and female norms using the z score. No analyses are reported for possible gender differences between Indian males and females. The author reports there were a few significant differences between Indian and American males and females in virtually every general category, but the lack of differences on most comparisons is even more striking to us. Unfortunately, it is not easy to gain a full sense of the findings because no percentages are presented. Table 6.10, on settings, is typical. The table shows that Indian males and females are more likely to be in familiar settings than American males or females. Americans, on the other hand, are more likely to be in indoor settings. But we know nothing of the magnitude of the differences. Nor do we know if Indian males and females differ in the same way American males and females differ in their percentages of indoor and familiar settings. Indians (male and female) dream more of familiar characters, and Americans dream more of unfamiliar characters. Indians dream more of family members and relatives, whereas Americans dream more of strangers. In Prasad's (1982) tables, there appear to be no differences between the two countries in the male/female percent in either men or women's dream reports. We cannot be sure, however, because there are no numbers. Here we see again why it would be helpful to have a conventional format for presenting the results of quantitative dream content studies.

Despite the problems of comparing Prasad's findings with the American norms, it seems likely that he has found a cluster of cultural differences where Indian males and females alike differ in the same way from their American counterparts. Indians are more likely to be in familiar settings, interacting with family members and other relatives. They are more likely to witness aggression than to be involved in it (but there is apparently the same frequency of aggression in their dreams). They are more likely to dream of food and nature. They express more happiness in their dream reports. If these are the main differences, however, as his tables imply, then Prasad also has

Table 6.10. Prasad's Table
on Settings

Setting	Indian	American
Male dreamer	Familiar	Indoor
Female dreamer	Familiar	Indoor

shown there are great similarities between the dream reports of Indian and American college students.

A second study at Andhra University by V. S. Bose (1983) was designed to compare home reports with laboratory reports collected at different times with different awakening strategies. The larger purpose of this sophisticated investigation was to see if the memory processes by which dream reports are revised could be determined. These larger issues need not concern us here. For our purposes, it is sufficient to compare the findings on home dream reports with the American norms. No overall tables are presented because this was not a normative study, so the findings on home dream reports must be taken from comparisons Bose made between home reports and the various types of laboratory reports. The study is based on 175 dream reports from 44 male college students between the ages of 19 and 26 who kept a dream diary at home for 5 days and slept in the laboratory for 11 nights. All of the Hall/ Van de Castle coding categories were utilized. The available comparisons are shown in Table 6.11. As can be seen, the differences between the Bose findings for India and the Hall/Van de Castle findings for the United States are minimal.

In a later analysis using the 175 home-recalled dream reports from the original study, Bose and Pramilia (1993) made a detailed comparison of their findings with the American norms for all Hall/Van de Castle content categories. Their findings are very similar to those of Prasad's (1982) sample from a decade earlier, providing a historical continuity for Indian college students reminiscent of the University of Richmond, Salem College, and University of California, Berkeley, replications of the original Hall/Van de Castle findings from 30 years before. There were more familiar settings and more familiar characters than in the American studies. The percentage of male characters was slightly higher than the American norms by five percentage points, but the results were not statistically significant at the .05 level of confidence. The

Table 6.11.   Indian and American Comparisons

	Indian males	American males
Average number of characters	2.5	2.4
Human percent	93	94
Animal percent	6	6
Mean number of settings	1.44	1.29
Outdoors percent	40	47
Percent of all objects that are architectural	28	27
Percent of all objects that are body parts	11	10
Percent of all objects that are nature	9	9
Mean number of modifiers/dream	1.77	2.22
Percent of dreams that are sexual	4	12

only differences on social interactions were a greater number of dreamer-involved sexual interactions on the part of the American males; there also was a tendency that did not quite reach statistical significance at the .05 level for Indian college males to witness the aggressions in their dreams more often than did the American males. There were no differences in successes and failures, misfortunes and good fortunes, or emotions.

Indian dreamers showed some differences in the categories of objects, activities, and descriptive elements. For example, they were more likely to dream of food and drink, clothes, and communications. They were more likely to engage in verbal activities and experience location changes, and less likely to have movement. They also had more temporal elements and less mentions of intensity.

Bose and Pramilia (1993:6) conclude that there are few differences in the more "dynamic" aspects of the dream reports of the two samples, by which they mean social interactions, activities, and striving, whereas there are some differences in settings, characters, and types of objects. They further argue that the differences are "integrated, consistent, and meaningfully related" in terms of differences between the two cultures (Bose & Pramilia, 1993:7).

If we look at the preponderance of evidence from the three studies in India, we have to conclude that the dream reports of college students at the Indian universities are very similar to those of American college students. This does not deny that there are some interesting cross-national differences, nor does it ignore Grey and Kalsched's (1971) finding of a correlation between Hindu traditionalism and a lower percentage of opposite-sex dream characters. However, it does suggest, in conjunction with previous findings in this chapter, that there are some powerful cross-national variables operating as well. For some purposes the similarities may be useful; for others the differences may be of interest.

Japan

There is a major study of dream reports in Japan by Tadashige Yamanaka, Yusuke Morita, and Junji Matsumoto (1982). It is, in effect, a replication of home and laboratory comparisons in the United States. The main difference is that the "home" reports were collected in an apartment by watching the eye movements of the sleeping subjects and awakening them during what appeared to be REM periods. Given the intensity of this procedure, perhaps it is not surprising that the high rate of home recall (76%) approached that for the laboratory (86%). Nor is it surprising that under these circumstances there were even fewer differences between "home" and laboratory reports.

The subjects in the nonlaboratory portion of the study were 6 male and 12 female students, 19 to 21 years of age, at the University of Tokushima in the city of Tokushima. There were 11 males and 10 females of the same age range and university affiliation in the laboratory portion of the study. A questionnaire based on the Hall/Van de Castle coding system was used to question subjects about dream contents at each awakening. Subjects in the "home" study were awakened until at least 10 dreams were reported; 220 dream reports were collected under this condition. Each subject in the laboratory portion of the study spent one night in the sleep laboratory; 77 dream reports were collected (Yamanaka et al., 1982:34–35, 38). Once it was determined that the two samples had few differences, they were merged for purposes of comparison with the Hall/Van de Castle findings.

The researchers coded the dream reports for all Hall/Van de Castle categories except settings and friendliness. We begin with the similarities to the Hall/Van de Castle norms and then turn to the interesting differences. Yamanaka et al. (1982) did a detailed analysis of objects and activities in the 104 male and 193 female dream narratives. The similarities with the findings for American college students are almost uncanny; comparisons of the Japanese and American results are presented in Tables 6.12 and 6.13. There are more mentions of food and drink in Japanese reports, and more physical movement like running and playing in American reports, but even these differences are not large. The great similarities in objects and activities mean any differences in characters or social interactions will be all the more interesting.

Table 6.12. Frequencies and Percentages of Objects in Dream Reports from Japanese and American College Students (percents in parentheses)

	Japan			Norms		
	Males	Females	Total	Males	Females	Total
Architecture	56 (26.8)	116 (26.5)	172 (26.6)	655 (27.1)	843 (31.7)	1,498 (29.5)
Houshold articles	27 (12.9)	60 (13.7)	87 (13.4)	197 (8.2)	278 (10.4)	475 (9.3)
Food, drink	11 (5.3)	32 (7.3)	43*(6.6)	44 (1.8)	55 (2.1)	99*(1.9)
Travel	12 (5.7)	29 (6.6)	41 (6.3)	271 (11.2)	223 (8.4)	494 (9.7)
Street	25 (12.0)	32 (7.3)	57 (8.8)	163 (6.7)	118 (4.4)	281 (5.5)
Nature	7 (3.3)	19 (4.3)	26 (4.0)	221 (9.1)	199 (7.5)	420 (8.3)
Regions	16 (7.7)	26 (5.9)	42 (6.5)	135 (5.6)	126 (4.7)	261 (5.1)
Body part	13 (6.2)	35 (8.0)	48 (7.4)	246 (10.2)	314 (11.8)	560 (11.0)
Clothes	13 (6.2)	39 (8.9)	52 (8.0)	139 (5.7)	271 (10.2)	410 (8.1)
Communication	17 (8.1)	24 (5.5)	41 (6.3)	95 (3.9)	112 (4.2)	207 (4.1)
Money	4 (1.9)	7 (1.6)	11 (1.7)	36 (1.5)	19 (0.7)	55 (1.1)
Miscellaneous	8 (3.8)	19 (4.3)	27 (4.2)	220 (9.1)	101 (3.8)	321 (6.3)
Total	209 (100)	438 (100)	647 (100)	2,422 (100)	2,659 (100)	5,081 (100)

*$p < 0.05$ (χ^2-test)

Table 6.13. Frequencies and Percentages of Activities in Dream Reports from Japanese and American College Students (percents in parentheses)

Activities	Japan			Norms		
	Males	Females	Total	Males	Females	Total
Verbal	128 (24.8)	207 (23.4)	335 (23.9)	511 (21.6)	646 (26.2)	1,157 (23.9)
Physical	108 (20.9)	209 (23.7)	317 (22.6)	627 (26.5)	482 (19.5)	1,109 (23.0)
Movement	82 (15.9)	79 (8.9)	161^b(11.5)	586 (24.8)	621 (25.1)	1,207^b(25.0)
Location change	59 (11.4)	119 (13.5)	178 (12.7)	194 (8.2)	182 (7.4)	376 (7.8)
Visual	54 (10.4)	83 (9.4)	137 (9.8)	280 (11.8)	307 (12.4)	587 (12.1)
Auditory	29 (5.6)	49 (5.5)	78 (5.6)	38 (1.6)	36 (1.4)	74 (1.5)
Expressive	19^a(3.7)	80^a(9.1)	99 (7.1)	51 (2.2)	83 (3.4)	134 (2.8)
Cognitive	38 (7.4)	57 (6.5)	95 (6.8)	75 (3.2)	113 (4.6)	188 (3.9)
Total	517 (100)	883 (100)	1,400 (100)	2,362 (100)	2,470 (100)	4,832 (100)

$^a p < 0.05$ (χ^2-test).
$^b p < 0.01$ (χ^2-test).

There are more characters in Japanese reports, but women have more characters in their reports than men, as in the United States. It is possible that the number of characters is slightly inflated because of the intensive method of immediate awakening by which the nonlaboratory dream reports were collected. However, if we take it for a real difference, which makes sense in terms of other findings on characters to be presented in a moment, then we can conjecture that the Japanese live in a more socially dense—"peopled"— environment than do Americans.

Even fewer of the characters in Japanese dream reports are animals than in American reports. The percentage is less than 1 for both men and women, whereas it is 6 and 4 for American men and women, respectively. The Japanese dreamers live in an intensely "human" world, which fits with the fact that there are very few pets in large urban areas. Far more of the characters in Japanese reports are familiar to the dreamer, which is another way of saying that there are fewer "strangers" in Japanese dreams. Here it is interesting to note that Japanese men have the highest proportion of familiar characters and American men the lowest. Both male and female Japanese dreamers live in an intensely familiar world (Table 6.14).

The "ubiquitous" gender difference on the male/female percent disappears for Japanese dream reports because the women have a pattern that is the mirror image of the men's pattern (Table 6.15). Thus, Japanese dreamers live in an intensely gender-segregated world. We have found no other society, as will be seen in the remainder of this chapter, where women have such a low male/female percent.

The analysis of aggressions was limited to the percentage of dreams in

Table 6.14.   Familiarity
Percent in Japan
and the United States

	Men	Women
Japan	74	67
United States	45	58

which an aggression occurred. The percentage of the aggression dreams in which the dreamer was the victim or aggressor also was determined. Both males and females have a very low percentage of dreams with aggressions in them—only 14% for males and 26% for females. The men are aggressors in 9 of their 15 aggression dreams (60%); the women are victims in 35 of their 51 aggression dreams (68%). On both measures, the males are more atypical than females in terms of our American norms.

The number of sexual dreams is also very low. The men reported 3 in 104 dream reports (3% versus 12% in American males) and the women 1 in 193 reports (0.5% versus 4% in American females). Here we have to be careful, however. We do not know enough about Japanese culture to be certain that subjects would feel comfortable telling sexual dreams in the "home" condition to the experimenter (always of the same sex as the dreamer). As for the laboratory, we know sexual reports there are rare in both the United States (Domhoff & Kamiya, 1964a; Hall, 1966a; Snyder, 1970) and India (Bose, 1983).

It would be fascinating to know if the unreported patterns of aggressive and friendly interactions in these dream reports relate to the atypical findings presented on characters and aggressions. For now, however, we have more than enough data to be certain that there are great similarities in Japanese and American dream reports (objects and activities) as well as intriguing differences (characters, aggressions) worthy of further study to help us understand the relationship between dreams and culture.

Table 6.15.   Male/Female
Percent in Japan
and the United States

	Men	Women
Japan	68/32	29/71
United States	67/33	48/52

[a]h = .39 between Japanese and American women.

Stepping back for a moment, perhaps the numerous similarities in the cross-national findings presented so far in this chapter are not as surprising as they may seem at first. Most of the subjects are college students. Many of them speak English as a first or second language. All are from urban areas in industrialized, class-stratified societies. They probably have more in common than we may realize if we focus only on "culture."

The differences may, however, reflect differences in cultural patterns. There may be higher levels of aggression in American dream reports. There seem to be more familiar characters in the reports of Indian and Japanese college students. The low male/female percent in Japanese females especially catches our interest. Does this relate to the extremely strong male dominance in Japan? If so, what do we make of the national cultures at the other extreme on male/female percent, Mexico and Peru? A large sample of Most Recent Dreams collected in those and other nations in the same time period might be a way to answer these questions.

Perhaps further light can be shed on these issues in comparisons with preindustrial peoples who live in small bands, tribes, and villages, and often hunt and fish for much of their livelihood. Several such comparisons will be made in the remainder of the chapter.

SMALL-SCALE SOCIETIES

Hall's Yir Yoront and Hopi Study

We begin this section with a consideration of dream reports from the Yir Yoront of Australia and the Hopi of the American Southwest because they provide two of the best dream collections available on small-scale societies. In an unpublished study, Hall (1964) compared the dream reports from these two cultures with each other and with findings on American college students.

The dreams from the Yir Yoront, one of many distinctive aboriginal societies in Australia, were collected in the 1930s as part of field work by Lauriston Sharp (1934, 1939, 1952), who was intimately knowledgeable about this culture. The Yir Yoront put no special emphasis on dreams and made no use of them in ceremonies. Nor were dreams anything but a peripheral part of Sharp's work (e.g., Sharp, 1969). According to David Schneider (1969:15), who was responsible for giving the dream collection to Hall and later publishing it, Sharp collected them "primarily to bring up new ethnographic material, and to establish and maintain rapport. Dreams were a neutral subject that could be exploited without offending anyone; no one seemed to care enough about them to get upset."

The Hopi dream reports were collected by Dorothy Eggan (1949, 1952,

1961, 1966), who had a strong interest in dreams as part of her focus on the relationship between culture and personality. She had a detailed knowledge of Hopi culture.

The Yir Yoront collection consists of 140 dream reports from 43 men and 10 reports from 8 women. One man contributed 14, another 11, and the rest from 1 to 5 each. The Hopi collection came from four men who contributed 24, 18, 10, and 6 dream reports for a total of 58, and three women who contributed 60, 18, and 18 dream reports for a total of 124. There is every reason to believe these are good reports because of the anthropologists' familiarity with the cultures and their close relations with their informants.[1]

Schneider (1969) did his own quantitative analysis of the Yir Yoront dreams. He found sexual content in 19 of the 140 male dreams, mostly with younger women as sexual partners, and only one with the person's wife as the sexual partner. Reports of sexual activity with women in prohibited kinship categories more often included interruptions and unsatisfactory outcomes (Schneider, 1969:22–23). Thirty-nine male dreams contained 73 acts of human aggression. The dreamer witnessed 18 of these aggressions, initiated 14 of them, and was a victim of 41 of them (Schneider, 1969:26–27). In our terms, the victimization percent was very high. Almost all of the aggression (68 of the 73 instances) was directed against adult males.

Eggan (1949, 1952) did not do group or quantitative analyses of the dream reports she collected. Instead, she focused on themes in an individual's dream series and showed how these themes related to the person's personality and cultural beliefs.

Hall's unpublished study comparing Yir Yoront and Hopi dream reports to those from American college students tested the hypothesis that the *similarities* in content categories for the three different groups would be greater than *differences* to a statistically significant degree. He then compared American, Hopi, and Yir Yoront males to American and Hopi females. The Yir Yoront females were not included because there were only 10 dream reports from them.

Hall used direction of difference between categories rather than magnitude of difference to test his hypothesis. That is, he determined whether the difference between content category A and content category B for each group was systematically positive or negative. To take a specific example, he deter-

---

[1]Tedlock (1991:162), in an article suggesting content studies are outmoded in anthropology and should be replaced by studies of how dreams are understood and used in different cultures, claims cross-cultural content studies by people such as Hall (1951, 1953c) are based on dream reports collected in an inadequate fashion. Hall used only American data in the publications Tedlock cites, however, and never made more than a few passing comments in print on cross-cultural findings. Hall's cross-cultural findings never have been published until now. It is not clear from Tedlock's paper why she made these gratuitous and inaccurate comments about Hall's work.

mined the male percent and compared it to a female percent, as in Table 6.16. In this example, four of the five difference codes are in the same direction. Hall used this method for this cross-cultural study because he believed that the magnitude of scores in each content category could be affected by many factors not present in within-culture studies. These include possible sampling problems, the age and gender of the anthropologist, and the type of relationship between the anthropologist and the dream reporters.

This approach allows for a rigorous statistical test of the hypothesis using a theoretical distribution of difference scores obtained from the expansion of the binomial theorem. Because five groups of dream reports are being compared, there are five differences in direction for each pair of content categories. If all five comparisons are positive, the difference score is +5. If four of the five are positive, the difference score is +4; if three are positive, +3; if two are positive, +2; if one is positive, +1; and if none is positive, 0. For purposes of statistical analysis, however, the +2 is changed to −3 so it can be grouped with +3, and the +1 is changed to −4 and the zero to −5 so they can be grouped with +4 and +5. There are then three types of scores: +5, −5; +4, −4; +3, −3. To test the hypothesis of greater similarity than difference, it was assumed that the empirical distribution of difference scores would differ significantly from the theoretical distribution. Specifically, there should be a preponderance of +5's and −5's if the hypothesis is correct.

Hall developed eight tables containing comparisons involving various proportions using the coding categories for characters, aggressions, friendliness, misfortunes, and good fortunes. There are many more similarities among the three groups (and between males and females) than there are differences. These similarities manifest themselves despite the fact that there are such uncontrolled variables as age, number of dream reports per informant, and conditions under which the dream reports were collected. Hall concluded on the basis of his tests of statistical significance that the hypothesis was supported.

Perhaps these findings can be made more concrete by focusing on the few differences among the three societies. Most of the differences occur in the Yir Yoronts. Yir Yoront males dream more about animals, have a higher

Table 6.16.   Male and Female Percents for Yir Yoronts, Hopis, and Americans

	American males	Yir Yoront males	Hopi males	American females	Hopi females
Category one (M/M + F)	61	73	81	54	48
Category two (F/M + F)	39	27	19	46	52
Direction of difference, one minus two	+	+	+	+	−

proportion of aggression with animals and a very high percentage of physical aggressions, and a higher frequency of friendly encounters with humans, particularly with familiar female characters. Much of the friendliness with others consists of the dreamers sharing meat from the animals they have killed.

These findings suggest a correspondence between the dream life and waking life of Yir Yoront males. They hunt and kill animals far more than do Hopi or Americans, who grow their food. They do a great deal of individual squabbling among themselves, and they share their kills with relatives and friends. This correspondence between dream life and waking life is similar to what we found in the cross-nation comparisons, only on different dream elements. Both types of differences are evidence that there is meaning in dreams.

The only differentiating feature of Hopi male dream reports is a larger number of aggressive encounters with females, for which we have no ready cultural explanation. There are no major deviations for Hopi females or American males and females from the overall findings.

The findings of this rigorous study with three good dream collections are impressive evidence that the Hall/Van de Castle coding system is applicable to dream reports from anywhere in the world and may pick up cultural differences as well. The biggest drawback to the investigation is the limited number of cultural groups employed. The groups come from different parts of the world and have radically different ways of life, but the fact remains that there are only three of them.

Hall's Larger Cross-Cultural Study

To expand the scope of the previous investigation, Hall did a second unpublished study using dream reports from a wider range of societies. Most of the dream collections were provided to him by Schneider, who gathered them from a variety of anthropological sources.

Schneider (1969) did his own analysis using dream reports from the following societies: Tinguian, Hopi, Yir Yoront, Alor, Ifaluk, Baiga, Navaho, Kwakiutl, Truk, Buku, Hopi-American, and Kiwai. He wrote (1969:55) that his study "seems to support the contention that (1) there are certain regularities in the manifest content of groups of dreams regardless of the society and culture of the dreamer, and (2) there are certain differences between groups of dreams that seem to be a function of the culture of the dreamers." For example, in all groups the dreamer is more often the victim than the aggressor in aggressive interactions, but there are cultural differences within that general context (Schneider, 1969:56). Schneider's method and findings are supportive of the Hall study of Yir Yoront, Hopi, and American dreamers.

Hall supplemented the Schneider collection with dream reports obtained from other sources. He then made dozens of comparisons on characters, aggressions, friendliness, and misfortunes. Again, he found there were more similarities than differences across groups for any given content category, but a few groups show differences.

One of the most consistent similarities concerned the male/female percent. There was no male group where the male percent was below 59 and no female group where it was below 48. There was one small female set of dream reports where the male/female percent was an unusually high 66. All of Hall's findings on this issue in small-scale societies, including the Hopi and Yir Yoront, are brought together in Table 6.17.

Hall's main findings for the five small-scale groups where he had both male and female dream reports are brought together in Table 6.18. There is some variability from culture to culture, but for us the similarities are striking. There are always more single than plural characters, more humans than animals, and more familiar than unfamiliar characters. The A/C index is higher than the F/C index with one exception (the Hopi). Dreamers everywhere are more often victims of aggression with two exceptions, one of which is not shown in the table (Yir Yoront), and there is usually more physical than nonphysical aggression.

Two findings concerning the animal percent are noteworthy. First, it ranges from a high of 34 and 31 for Biaga and Yir Yoront males, not shown in Table 6.18, to 6 for Hopi females. Second, it is always higher for small-scale societies than it is for large-scale ones, although Hopi females (6%) come close to our female norms (4%). Because these small-scale societies are in

Table 6.17. Cross-Cultural Findings on Male/Female Percent

	Males			Females			
Subjects	n	Number of dreams	Male/female (percent)	n	Number of dreams	Male/female (percent)	p
United States	281	281	66/34	281	281	52/48	< .001
Ifaluk	23	51	80/20	17	19	53/47	< .001
Tinguian	11	27	61/39	49	95	66/34	ns^a
Alor	4	68	68/32	5	61	58/42	< 0.05
Skolt	17	132	73/27	6	44	48/52	< .001
Hopi	16	171	63/37	19	157	51/49	< 0.01
Northwest Australia	27	59	80/20				
Baiga	32	73	59/41				
Kuatiutl	42	56	72/28				
Navaho	37	63	71/29				
Yir Yoront	42	140	76/24				

[a]Not significant.

Table 6.18.   Cross-Cultural Findings with Five Small-Scale Societies

		(Male findings in parentheses)			
	Ifaluk	Tinguian	Alor	Skolt	Hopi
Number of subjects	17 (23)	49 (11)	5 (4)	6 (17)	19 (16)
Number of dream reports	19 (51)	95 (27)	61 (68)	44 (132)	157 (171)
Percent single characters	59 (59)	69 (59)	68 (66)	60 (59)	61 (53)
Animal percent	27 (14)	10 (09)	13 (12)	22 (20)	06 (17)
Familiarity percent	62 (54)	70 (55)	88 (81)	77 (61)	66 (64)
Overall A/C index	52 (33)	32 (41)	25 (37)	37 (32)	25 (29)
A/C index with animals	62 (32)	44 (50)	26 (24)	53 (36)	16 (26)
Victimization percent	85 (75)	50 (54)	62 (61)	72 (60)	54 (61)
Physical aggression percent	40 (60)	46 (55)	61 (53)	68 (70)	39 (40)
Overall F/C index	7 (16)	25 (27)	20 (18)	13 (12)	34 (40)
Befriender percent	50 (37)	27 (33)	53 (58)	87 (29)	49 (44)
Percent sexual reports	0 (06)	12 (07)	0 (04)	0 (08)	1 (01)

greater proximity to animals and nature than the urbanized populations from large-scale societies for whom we have dream reports, we think this difference in animal percent is a cultural difference revealing a relationship between dreams and waking life.

Unfortunately, it is difficult to do much more with these findings because we do not have enough information to explain the deviant cases. The deviations may be due to cultural differences, but it is risky to make such inferences when the sample sizes are small and so little is known about the representativeness of the samples and the methods of collection. Moreover, we do not know enough about the cultures in many cases. In short, these findings take us as far as we can go without much more information on the dreamers and the cultures. We need to turn elsewhere for further enlightenment on small-scale groups.

The Mehinaku

There are a few investigations of small-scale societies that allow us to see if dream reports and culture are closely linked in them. In particular, Thomas Gregor's (1977, 1986) detailed ethnographic studies of the minuscule Mehinaku Indian village of about 80 to 85 people in the Amazon rain forests of central Brazil afford us a singularly in-depth look at the dream reports of preindustrial men and women known personally to the dream collector. Moreover, Mehinaku life in the Xingu National Park preserve where they hunt, fish, and grow a few staples was essentially traditional when Gregor was there: "The presence of an Indian post and a small air force base [several hours from the village] has had a psychological impact that is visible in Mehinaku dream life, but the villagers thus far remain protected from wage labor, contact with missionaries, squatters, and others who would exploit them or alter their lives" (Gregor, 1981a:354).

Gregor found in the course of his general research that the Mehinaku like to remember their dreams and often tell them to their families. They believe, like many preliterate cultures all over the world, that dreams occur when the soul "leaves its home in the iris of the eye to wander about through a nocturnal world peopled by spirits, monsters, and the souls of other sleeping villagers" (Gregor, 1981a:354; see Gregor, 1981b, for a full statement of Mehinaku dream theory). They also believe that dreams can be a clue to the future. Thus, Gregor found it very easy to collect dream reports from them.

Gregor received at least a few narratives from 18 men and 18 women, most of the adult population of the village. The men reported 276 dreams and the women 109, with 25% of the 385 reports coming from two young fathers (ages 22 and 23) who were chosen for intensive study. Their dream content is sufficiently like that of other males in the sample that including them changes overall percentages by less than 5%. Gregor coded the dream reports for physical aggressions and sexuality with categories fairly similar to those in the Hall/Van de Castle system. He also coded the dream reports for the degree of activity or passivity, as determined by whether the dreamer initiated actions (active) or only observed or reacted to the actions of other dream characters (passive).

Gregor found there is more physical aggression in Mehinaku than in American dream reports, especially with animals, but the gender differences are the same in that men report more physical aggressions than women. Mehinaku are more likely than Americans to be victims of aggression. As with our American norms, Mehinaku women are more likely than Mehinaku men to be victims. Men and animals are the most frequent attackers in Mehinaku dream reports, but spirits and monsters sometimes attack as well (Gregor, 1981a:384–385). Sexual elements appear in 13% of the men's reports and 12% of the women's. The male percentage is virtually identical with the Hall/Van de Castle norms, but the female percentage is three times higher. In men's sexual dreams there is sometimes a fear of assault by jealous male rivals or angry women lovers. Women's dream reports often show a fear of rape and other violent encounters with sexually aggressive men (Gregor, 1981a:388). Sixty-one percent of the men's dream reports were judged as active and 39% as passive. By contrast, 42% of women's dream reports were judged as active and 58% as passive.

Gregor believes his overall findings make sense in terms of Mehinaku culture. There is threat from a wide range of animals and insects, and there is conflict and competition among the men. Most men and women have several lovers as well as a spouse, and women do fear sexual pressures and attacks from men (Gregor, 1986). Moreover, "the relative passivity of women's dreams corresponds to women's position in daily life" (Gregor, 1981a:387). The society is highly patriarchal, and men dominate in the home as well as in the religious and public aspects of village life. At the same time, Gregor notes the similarities with the Hall/Van de Castle findings and emphasizes that the gender differences are of the same nature. He suggests that "with additional cross-cultural data it may be possible to show that the dream experience is less variant than other aspects of culture" (Gregor, 1981a:389).

Gregor's study is an outstanding addition to our knowledge of dream content because of his excellent rapport with his subjects and intimate knowledge of their culture. It is impressive independent verification of the generalizability of the Hall cross-cultural findings to other dream collections from small-scale societies.

The Zapotecs of Mexico

The Zapotecs are a rural Indian people in Southern Mexico whose lifestyle was still very traditional when anthropologists Carl and Nancy O'Nell (1977) collected dream reports from them in the 1960s. Most were engaged in subsistence farming; some were artisans and traders. The extended family and the village were the primary frames of reference. O'Nell and O'Nell collected five dreams from each of 66 males and 66 females for a total of 660 dream reports. The subjects ranged in age from 5 to 97 years. O'Nell and O'Nell used the two samples to make comparisons with Hall and Domhoff's (1963b) study of aggressions in dream reports. They found both similarities and differences.

There were three main similarities between American and Zapotec dreamers:

1. Males have more aggression in their dreams than females (A/C index).
2. In both cultures, people are more likely to be victims than aggressors in aggressive interactions.
3. Both male and female dreamers have more of their aggressive interactions with male characters than with female characters.

There were three main differences:

1. Zapotec dreamers, male and female, had a higher physical aggression percent than did their American counterparts.
2. Zapotec dreamers had more dreamer-involved aggressions than the American dreamers.
3. There was little or no tendency for the A/C index to decline with age for the Zapotecs.

O'Nell and O'Nell do not speculate on the reasons for the cultural differences. We note, however, that the Zapotec's higher levels of physical aggressions are similar to what Gregor (1981a) found for the Mehinaku Indian village in Brazil.

The Gusii, Kipsigis, and Logoli of East Africa

In 1967, while members of the Child Research Unit at the University of Nairobi in Kenya, the American researchers Robert and Ruth Munroe (1977) did a day of testing and interviewing in English in both a male and female secondary boarding school. Among other measures, they requested a recent dream from the students.

The students came from three male-dominant societies of East Africa: the Gusii, the Kipsigis, and the Logoli. Munroe and Munroe (1977:150) emphasized that "the social-structural importance of males, which is based on patrilineal descent and patrilocal residence, is vastly greater than that of females." They therefore predicted there would be a predominance of males in all dream reports they collected.

The Munroes collected 325 dream reports, 182 from males and 143 from females. The breakdown by societal groups is not provided. They coded the dream reports by classifying each report as to whether there was a "preponderance" of male or female characters. Independent judges had a 95% level of agreement on a sample of 40 reports. The frequency of male-character reports among the Gusii was 82% for males and 61% for females. The corresponding figures for the Kipsigis were 82% and 44%, and for the Logoli, 83% and 56% (Munroe & Munroe, 1977:150). The differences were statistically significant using chi-square. Although this is not an ideal type of analysis because of its failure to use total characters as the unit of analysis, it does seem to show the ubiquitous gender difference for three more small societies.

The dream reports were then used in a later investigation to make explicit comparisons with some of the gender differences reported in the Hall/Van de Castle norms. The results were similar to the American findings on four of five comparisons.

1. The young men dreamed more frequently of outdoor settings, the young women of indoor settings.
2. Male dream reports more frequently mentioned implements.
3. Female dream reports more frequently mentioned clothing.
4. Female dream reports contained more mentions of emotions.

The results were statistically significant at the level of .05 or lower using a chi-square test. In addition, within-society trends were "in the same direction as the overall findings except that Logoli men mentioned clothing in a slightly higher proportion of their dreams than did Logoli women" (Munroe et al., 1985:406).

There were, however, differences in aggressions. The East African women students had more dreams with physical aggressions than did American college females, and equaled the East African men students in this regard. The East African women also differed from the Hall/Van de Castle norms in having more nonphysical aggression in their dream reports than the young men.

The reasons for the differences from the Hall/Van de Castle norms on aggressions were explored in a later investigation using 187 male dream reports and 149 female reports, for a total of 336 dream narratives. This investigation concluded that "the relatively high frequency of aggression in women's dreams seems due in part to preoccupation with being victimized" (Munroe et al., 1989:728). The detailed investigation of aggression is also noteworthy for a further difference with the American norms that was discovered. Whereas an animal character initiated the aggression suffered by the dreamer in 9% of American dream reports, it did so in 44% of the East African reports. There was no gender difference. This finding is similar to that of Gregor (1981a) on animals as aggressors in Mehinaku dream reports.

Munroe and Munroe (1992) also studied friendliness in the same collection of dream reports. They found that female dream reports contained more friendly interactions than those of males and approximately equal amounts of friendliness with male and female characters. The male dreamers had more friendly interactions with male characters than with female ones, which is the opposite of the American norms. The Munroes suggest that this male pattern "may reflect the strong male bias in social organizations and groupings" (1992:402).

The four analyses of dream reports from East African students do not have the depth of a study such as Gregor's, based as they are on one day of dream collecting, and the subjects are clearly acculturating if they speak English and attend schools. Nevertheless, these analyses add range to the findings reported earlier in this chapter.

Gusii Women of Kenya

As part of a study of childhood in Gusii communities in southwestern Kenya in the 1970s by Robert and Sarah LeVine, Sarah LeVine collected 88 dream reports from 22 women. Those reports have been analyzed by both LeVine (1982) and Linda Kilner (1988). Kilner used Hall/Van de Castle coding categories. We will combine findings from the two studies.

The women ranged in age from 18 to 45. All were married, and all but one had from 1 to 11 children; 6 of the 22 were married to polygamists. None of the women over age 28 ever attended school; all but one of the younger women attended elementary school, and two attended high school. All the women had agricultural as well as domestic duties.

Dreams are private matters for Gusii. They are not due to spirits or external forces. They are not told to healers. Although the women were open to reporting their dreams to LeVine, they were not interested in discussing their meaning with her (LeVine, 1982:66–68). The dream reports were very brief, averaging only three sentences in length. The longest is nine lines. Three women provided 10 or more dreams apiece.

LeVine looked at settings, characters, aggressions, misfortunes, labor and childbirth, material objects, and the supernatural. We will concentrate on her findings on characters, aggressions, and misfortunes because they have the most overlap with our categories. Kilner used Hall/Van de Castle categories to code for friendliness, sexual interactions, misfortunes, good fortunes, success, and failure. Kilner compared her findings to the Hall/Van de Castle norms and to her own sample of 75 dream reports from an unstated number of adult American professional women who were friends and friends of friends.

LeVine found that the women dreamed most frequently about their children (19), their parents (9), and their husbands (8). They dreamed about the women they grew up with, such as mothers, sisters, and aunts, but rarely the female in-laws with whom they had daily contact. Conversely, they dreamed more often of males from their marital home—husband, his brother, and his male cousins—than of their own father and brothers (LeVine, 1982:69). Only rarely did they dream of unfamiliar characters.

Sixty-six of the 88 reports (75%) contained job loss, accident, illness, the threat of violence, actual violence, murder, or death; that is, they were full of aggressions and misfortunes. In only two reports was the dreamer the aggressor (LeVine, 1982:70). This finding of high victimization replicates the third of the Munroe and Munroe analyses for this group discussed in the previous section.

The Gusii women had fewer dream reports with at least one friendliness (33%) than the Hall/Van de Castle norms (42%). They were more likely to be befriended than to initiate friendly interactions when compared to American women. There was sexual activity in 2 of 88 dream reports (2%) compared to 4% of the normative sample. Gusii women dreamed less often of success or failure, meaning there was very little striving in their dream reports. When they did dream of success, it was more likely to be achieved by some other dream character. Gusii women dreamed twice as often about misfortunes as the Hall/Van de Castle norms (Kilner, 1988:82–83).

Overall, the dream reports of the Gusii women are dominated by a sense of fear, submissiveness, and misfortune. Both LeVine (1982:75) and Kilner (1988:20) argue that the contents of the dream reports reflect the dire life circumstances of women in Gusii culture. As we stated in discussing the

Munroe and Munroe studies, the society is highly patriarchal. Women are not respected until they have succeeded as mothers. They leave home to marry a man from an enemy clan:

> The man pays bridewealth to her father. She is believed to be devoid of good judgment and incapable of undertaking responsibility of any sort other than child care and manual labor. She wins acceptance through compliance with elders, industry in agricultural tasks for her mother-in-law, and most especially through bearing children. The Gusii look upon their children as economic benefits. As a woman's children grow, especially if the children are male and already circumcised, so does the influence and acceptance of the mother. (Kilner, 1988:80)

The interpretations by LeVine and Kilner are very plausible. To make them more convincing, it would be good to have dream reports from comparable adult Gusii males to be sure the differences from American women are not cultural ones shared with males (e.g., low striving, high misfortunes). It also would be good to have a larger sample of women and dream reports. Nonetheless, the findings of these two studies are provocative in terms of the possible continuities between dream content and cultural patterns.[1]

A Missed Opportunity

Julia Levine (1991) did an exceptional job of gathering cross-cultural data that could have led to an excellent comparison of children's dreams in the United States, rural Ireland, an Israeli kibbutz, and a Bedouin tribal group in Israel. Unfortunately, she has missed this opportunity by using an idiosyncratic and subjective rating system for such dimensions as "reality of dream," "self-representation," and "humanness of participants." She did not compare her results with more numerous American findings.

Moreover, she takes a totally uncritical attitude toward poorly done studies of the alleged role of culture in shaping dream content (e.g., Grey & Kalsched, 1971; Roll & Brenneis, 1975; Roll, Hinton, & Glazer, 1974). She goes so far as to claim that questionnaire responses by Japanese and American students on whether they think they have had such common dreams as falling, being chased, or losing teeth (Griffith, Miyago, & Tago, 1958) show the role of "value systems" in shaping dream content; she thereby overlooks the fact that thinking/remembering you once had a dream about something or another is not a study of dream content (Levine, 1991:473).

---

[1]Although its findings are in the expected direction, the brief report by Robbins and Kilbride (1971) on one or two dreams from each of 50 male and 44 female Bantu primary and secondary school students in Uganda is not substantial enough to be discussed here. The authors asked the students to "describe the one dream you remember the most," which is likely to generate atypical reports. Furthermore, the results are not statistically significant. Hall later obtained these reports and scored them for male/female percent. The percentage of male characters in 53 male reports was 82; the percentage in 43 female reports was 43 (Hall, 1984:1111). Both figures are typical of what we have found elsewhere.

Levine collected three to five dream reports from each of 26 children from a seminomadic Bedouin settlement in Israel, 24 Israeli children on a large rural kibbutz, and 27 Irish children from a small fishing village in southwestern Ireland. All the children were between 8.5 and 11 years of age. They were enlisted voluntarily from the third, fourth, and fifth grades of their local elementary school. Levine does not say how many dream reports she collected, but the average was 5 per Bedouin and Irish child, and 3.5 per Israeli child. The children were asked to write down their dreams in the morning, and the dreams were then told each morning for 7 days to Levine and, where necessary, an accompanying translator. The dream reports were tape recorded and later transcribed.

Levine employed three students to code the dream reports on the scales she developed. She trained them to what she describes as a high rate of intercoder reliability on 17 reports, then had each of the three rate one-third of the reports. For the most part, the scales she developed, except for the one on the "reality" of the dream, duplicate the usual content categories found in our system. There are human and nonhuman characters, familiar and unfamiliar characters, activities, and positive and negative emotions. Within her rating system on conflictual dreams, reflecting the usual problems of rating systems, the witnessing of an aggression receives as low a score as being the victim of one. Thus, in one of the sample dream narratives provided by Levine (1991:477), where the dreamer saw his or her father shoot a wolf, the dreamer would receive a low score on "self-representation."

Nonetheless, Levine's findings mostly fit with what we have reported already in this chapter. First, there were twice as many "conflictual" as opposed to "nonconflictual" dream reports in all three cultures (Levine, 1991:479), which seems to parallel the predominance of aggression and misfortune over friendliness and good fortune in most of our samples. Second, dreamers were more "passive and uninvolved" in conflictual dreams, and the "hedonic tone" was more negative in these dreams; here she may be replicating the well-known findings on victimization in aggressive dreams in most societies.

Levine then turns to cross-cultural differences in conflictual dream reports because she has detected few differences in the one-third of the sample that are nonconflictual. In general, the Bedouin children differed from the Irish and kibbutz children, which fits with our findings in this chapter on differences between citizens of nations and members of small tribal groups. For example, there were more "nonhuman characters" (presumably animals for the most part) and familiar characters in the Bedouin children's reports (Levine, 1991:483). She is describing very typical findings in the dream content literature (e.g., Gregor, 1981a; O'Nell & O'Nell, 1977; Van de Castle, 1983), none of which she cites.

Levine (1991:485) starts her discussion section with the claim that she has "replicated" previous research, meaning Grey and Kalsched (1971) and Roll and his associates, in demonstrating "the relevance of culture in the analysis of manifest dream reports." She then makes several plausible glosses of her findings in terms of cultural differences among the three groups, but in the conclusions section she rightly says that "this study lacks data regarding the waking life of the subjects that could substantiate the relationship of culture to the systematic differences found in dream reports" (Levine, 1991:488). In all, then, this is another lost opportunity in terms of developing cumulative findings in the study of dream content.

CONCLUSIONS

We have six general conclusions:

1. There is nothing in the dream reports collected in other societies that cannot be encompassed within the Hall/Van de Castle coding system. Mundane though it may seem, this is probably the most gratifying conclusion from this cross-cultural work. The fact that independent investigators in Europe, India, and Japan found the system useful is part of our evidence for this conclusion.

2. Several of our percentages and indexes provide similar results in most of the cross-cultural samples of dream reports studied to date. There is more aggression than friendliness, for example, and more misfortune than good fortune. Dreamers everywhere are more often victims than aggressors in their dreams.

3. There are several cross-cultural gender differences. Men dream more often of other males, whereas women tend to dream equally about males and females. There usually are more familiar characters in women's dreams. Men usually have more physical aggressions in their dreams, and women are more often victims of aggression.

4. Despite the numerous commonalities of dream reports across societies on many of our coding categories, there is enough variability that the American norms must be used with extreme caution beyond Anglophone Canada and Western Europe. Despite our comments earlier about the fundamental commonalities in all large industrialized societies, there are too many differences with French Canada, Latin America, India, and Japan to use the norms in studying individuals from those countries. Instead, new norms should be created for those countries. In terms of aggression scores, there may be important differences with Europe and Anglophone Canada as well.

5. The variations in dream content from culture to culture seem to relate to unique cultural patterns in the few cases where we have enough information to hazard an opinion. The variations in animal percent support that conclusion, as do the findings on such distinctive and carefully studied groups as the Yir Yoront and Mehinaku. In other words, the differences found

among cultures are a further reason to believe that there is meaning in dreams because these differences "make sense" in terms of what is known about the cultures.

6. Finally, we reluctantly conclude that the problems of doing good studies of dream reports from small-scale societies are so great that the understanding of dream meaning is unlikely to be advanced much further by such studies. The studies presented in the last section of this chapter have taken us about as far as we can go in this area. The assembled studies have shown us cross-cultural similarities and differences, giving us confidence in our coding system and reinforcing the claim that there is meaning in dreams. However, the hopes of finding highly revealing and distinctive dream content once held by those who studied culture and personality have not been realized. Moreover, there are too many difficulties standing in the way of convincing studies with small-scale societies, except in rare cases like Gregor's study of the Mehinaku. Those difficulties include dealing with mutual suspicions and power differentials, establishing rapport, cutting through stereotyped responses based on cultural beliefs, and understanding linguistic and cultural subtleties. Dream research in small-scale societies is probably best left to those who want to study people's folk beliefs and practices relating to dreams.

If the goal is to understand the meaning of dreams, as it is in our case, then it is probably better to study adults who share the same language and culture as the researcher, although the Most Recent Dream methodology may be a promising approach to cross-national studies. Either way, within nations or cross-national, the future of dream content research lies primarily in studies of citizens in large-scale industrialized societies. We turn to such citizens in the remainder of this book, reassured by cross-cultural studies that we have a powerful and universalistic coding system.

Consistency and Change
in Long Dream Series

INTRODUCTION

The previous chapters have established the potential of our coding system in terms of its reliability and its ability to yield findings compatible with common understandings of age, gender, and cultural differences. We are not surprised by the ways children's dream reports differ from those of adults, or men's from women's, nor by the cultural differences in some content categories. In a certain sense we are not enlightened by these findings, for they tell us nothing new about children, gender differences, or cross-cultural psychology. Such findings give us confidence, however, that our coding system is picking up psychologically relevant findings and therefore may lead to new and interesting findings in future studies.

Previous chapters also have given us a normative context for studying the dream reports of specific individuals or groups of individuals. Because we know what is typical and atypical in the dreams of college students in general, we are in a position to understand the possible significance of unusual findings on individual college students or other population groups.

In this chapter, we provide another strong foundation for studying the dream reports of specific individuals by focusing on consistencies and changes in 75 or more dreams written down over months or years, which we call a long dream series. These dream series range in length from 187 to many hundreds of dream reports. The major finding emerging from the analysis is considerable consistency of dream content in categories with large frequencies. However, there are sometimes changes in some content categories in each series that make sense in terms of the person's altered life circumstances.

Although the primary focus of the chapter is on consistency, some of the findings are compared with the Hall/Van de Castle norms in order to show the usefulness of group norms in understanding an individual dream series. We introduce two baselines for studying the dream reports of an individual—comparing the series with the norms and comparing one subset of dreams within the series to another subset.

The several dream series analyzed in this chapter came to Hall from a variety of sources, but mostly from people who heard about his research and wrote to ask if their dream series (or "diary" or "journal" or "log," as they usually called it) could be of any use. Those who volunteered to send their series were asked to put a pseudonym on it and to type the dream reports if possible. Most people sent typed reports.

Far more people keep dream journals than may be realized. Such dream diarists come from all walks of life and keep journals for diverse reasons. Many people write down dreams as part of a more general personal diary. Some write down dreams as a possible source of short stories or paintings. Fewer than might be expected write them down for introspective psychological use, although the patients of Jungian analysts are an untapped treasure trove of long dream series. One house painter who sent Hall hundreds of dream reports originally wrote them down as part of his system for betting on horse racing. Whatever their original motivations, most dream diarists develop a routine that keeps them writing, and most say they rarely study their dream reports. Instead, the reports become a kind of record that they value for its detail and continuity and that they intend to reread in the future.

There are three kinds of consistency in the results presented in this chapter—absolute, relative, and developmental. *Absolute constancy* means the frequency or percentage of an element remains the same year after year. There will always be slight variations, of course, but they are not large, and there is no trend in them. *Relative consistency* means that the incidence of one element always exceeds the incidence of another element even though they both may increase or decrease in frequency; we give examples of relative consistency among as many as four elements, but most of our measures of relative consistency concern two elements. Finally, there is *developmental regularity*, a consistent increase or decrease from one period of time to the next. The ways in which we measure each kind of consistency will be explained when we discuss the first dream series.

Relative consistency is the most frequent kind of consistency in dream series. Absolute constancy occurs slightly less often. Developmental regularities are much less common than the first two. This order of magnitude has held for each series analyzed to date.

We begin the chapter with a discussion of our longest and most carefully studied series. We present our methods and findings in detail with the hope that they can serve as a useful model for future studies, for such studies are very much needed. (Readers who are unlikely to do research on long dream series may want to skim many of the tables or ignore them entirely.) We then turn to briefer treatments of two other series quantified for three or more coding categories. Next we present findings on a long series that is unique because it was recorded over the space of a few months. Then we present findings on the consistency of the male/female percent in series from eight men and three women. We conclude with the results of a study of consistency in the laboratory (Kramer & Roth, 1979a).

Most of the analyses in this chapter were completed by Hall in the early 1960s before the Hall/Van de Castle coding system was finalized. Because there were few major changes from the earlier coding system except on the coding of friendliness and settings, the differences have very little impact, but they do mean that we cannot compare the findings to the norms on some content categories. In any case, the primary focus for now is on the phenomenon of consistency. In Chapter 8, we use the norms with dream series analyzed more recently.

THE JASON SERIES

Data and Method

We begin with the long dream series on which we have done the most extensive analyses. Jason kept a record of his dreams from age 37 until the time of his death in his early 70s. Most of our analyses, however, concern the 600 dream reports he recorded between the ages of 37 and 53. Jason was a middle-class white professional. He was married and a parent when he started his dream journal. In his later years, he left his wife, retired, and moved far from where he spent his work years.

Jason made it a point to write down every dream he remembered, except during a period of 4 years, when he recorded only 15 dreams. He used no special techniques to recall dreams, nor did he make any particular effort to recall them. He was not a frequent recaller. He wrote down dreams exactly as he remembered them. Table 7.1 shows the number of dreams he wrote down in each year of the 17-year span under analysis.

Jason kept his dreams for his own curiosity, but he had a detached attitude toward them. He recorded them as soon as he remembered them and then put them in a file. Every several months he would type them up and read through them.

The consistency scores on Jason's dream reports are presented in sets of 100 because the first important finding from this and other series is that it takes about 75 to 100 dream reports to establish stability from set to set on most content categories. For some categories, such as major character categories, there can be stability in subsets of 25 dream narratives, but for other

Table 7.1.   Jason's Dreams
by Year and Age

Year	Number of dreams	Jason's age
1	70	37
2	103	38
3	88	39
4	51	40
5	32	41
6	23	42
7	18	43
8	11	44
9	4	45
10	1	46
11	2	47
12	8	48
13	13	49
14	18	50
15	26	51
16	62	52
17	70	53
Dream total	600	

categories it takes more, especially for low-frequency categories. When we measure consistency, then, we refer to hundreds of dreams and time spans of months or years. What people dream about usually varies from day to day and week to week. That variation, combined with the fact that most recalled dreams are soon forgotten, contributes to the conception of dreams as an aimless concoction of jumble and jive.[1]

We now need to explain the ways in which the three types of consistency were quantified in this and other long dream series. First, to measure absolute constancy, Hall adopted a simple statistic based on the average of the deviations of the sets from the overall average for all the dream reports together. He called this statistic V for "variation." Table 7.2 shows how it works, using the male/female percent from Jason's dream reports.

The deviations of the six samples from the overall average are .02, 0, −.04, .02, .01, and −.01, respectively. The sum of these deviations, disregarding plus and minus signs, is .10. Dividing this figure by 6 yields an average deviation of .017 (.10/6 = .017). We then figure an average deviation by dividing by the smaller of the two percentages in the male/female percent.

---

[1]Urbina and Grey (1975:360) determined "odd–even reliabilities" on the male/female percent in series only eight dreams in length, and found relatively low reliabilities, but their sample size was far too small to reject the idea of consistency, as we show in this chapter.

Table 7.2. Jason's Male/Female Percent over 600 Dream Reports

Set number	I	II	III	IV	V	VI	Overall
	1–100	101–200	201–300	301–400	401–500	501–600	1–600
Male/female percent	63/37	61/39	57/43	63/37	62/38	60/40	61/39

(We always use the smaller of the two percents in any calculation of V because it gives the most conservative estimate. V is far from being a sophisticated statistic because it becomes smaller as the percentage becomes higher. It is only a rough estimate.) To return to the example we are presenting here, the average deviation of .017 is then divided by the overall average for the 600 dream reports on female percent (39) to obtain V ($V = .017/.39 = .04$).

Now comes the arbitrary part. What is "excellent" or "good" or "poor" consistency? Hall defined them as follows:

1. If the average deviation (V) is one tenth (10) or less of the percentage for the total population of dream reports, the consistency is said to be excellent.
2. If V is between one tenth and two tenths (11 to 20) of the percentage for the total population of dream reports, the consistency is said to be good.
3. If V is between two tenths and three tenths (21 to 30) of the percentage for the total population of dream reports, the consistency is said to be fair.
4. Anything beyond 30 is considered poor consistency.

Since V is .04 for Jason's male/female percent in Table 7.2, the absolute constancy for this category is considered excellent.

With regard to relative consistency, defined as the stability with which codes for one category are consistently higher or lower than codes for another category, we use two measures. When we compare two categories over a series of samples, we use an expansion of the binomial theorem. When there is a large enough number of categories, we use the rank order correlation (rho). Table 7.3, from Jason's dream series, demonstrates how the binomial theorem is used in determining the statistical significance of relative (also called row) consistency. As the table shows, known adult males are more frequent than unfamiliar males in four of the six sets of dream reports. To determine the statistical significance of this finding, we have to expand the binomial theorem $(\frac{1}{2})^6$ to find the probability of obtaining a succession of six codes each of which is higher or lower than the other succession of six codes. The resulting probability is $\frac{1}{64}$ or .016. Six out of six is statistically significant

Table 7.3.   Relative Consistency
of Known to Unfamiliar Characters

Set number	I	II	III	IV	V	VI	Overall
Known adult males	30	32	25	22	19	27	26
Unfamiliar adult males	17	15	24	25	25	21	21

at the .016 level. Five out of six is significant at the .094 level (%64), but four out of six could happen by chance 11 in 64 times—not very good odds that the difference is a nonchance one. In this case, we would reject the idea of relative consistency. Therefore, we use five or six differences in the same direction as our evidence for relative consistency in this study using six sets.

Developmental consistency can be seen in Table 7.4, which shows Jason's A/C index with members of his family. The table shows an increasing rate of aggressive encounters between the dreamer and members of his immediate family as he grows older. When we use the binomial theorem, the criterion of developmental consistency is five successive increments or decrements over the six samples of dream reports. In this case, then, there is developmental consistency for aggression with family members.

We are now ready for the overall findings. We will limit our discussion to characters and social interactions, but there is impressive consistency for our other categories as well.

Characters

Table 7.5 shows the total number of characters in Jason's dream reports and the breakdown of those characters into 10 classes. In this table, absolute constancy, as measured by V, is extremely high for single humans and plural humans. It is low for animals, as it is likely to be with any content category appearing infrequently, given the statistical procedure being utilized. If the three categories (rows 1–3) are ranked, there is perfect relative consistency throughout the six sets of dream reports; the class of single humans is always highest, plural humans second, and animals lowest.

Table 7.4.   Jason's A/C Index
with Family Members

Set number	I	II	III	IV	V	VI
Family members	17	19	21	25	33	68

Table 7.5. Frequencies and Percentages of Characters
in Jason's Dreams Classified into Various Categories

Set numbers	I	II	III	IV	V	VI	Overall	V
Total characters	274	258	205	189	292	254	1,472	
1. Single humans	63	65	62	55	59	57	60	8
2. Plural humans	20	21	20	20	20	21	20	2
3. Animals	2	1	6	8	6	6	5	44
4. Immediate family	21	24	26	19	17	13	20	18
5. Relatives	1	1	0	0	0	1	3	17
6. Known characters	44	41	34	34	31	38	38	11
7. Prominent characters	4	1	1	3	5	5	3	50
8. Strangers	30	33	39	44	47	43	39	14
9. Male percent	63	61	57	63	62	60	61	4
10. Female percent	37	39	43	37	38	40	39	4

Turning to rows 4–8 of Table 7.5, we see no examples of excellent
absolute constancy. The only important relative consistency is that family
characters are always lower than either known or unfamiliar characters. As
we already know, because we used it previously as an example, there is no
relative consistency between known and unfamiliar male characters. The
number of relatives and prominent persons in Jason's dream reports is too
small to be of use in a study of relative consistency.

The percentage of male and female characters, as shown in rows 9 and
10, is an example of both absolute constancy and relative consistency, but this
finding comes as no surprise at this point in the book.

Seven character categories account for 87% of all the single characters
appearing in Jason's dream reports. These seven categories are listed in Table
7.6 with their respective percentages for the six sets of dreams. The absolute
constancy is excellent in the case of adult known females, good for adult
known males and adult male strangers, and fair for person X, indefinite
strangers, and adult female strangers. It is poor for person Y, who appears
least often.

To summarize the findings on characters, a high degree of consistency as
measured by V or by rank order of the categories (relative consistency)
prevails among the various categories of characters in Jason's dream reports.
There do not seem to be any systematic developmental regularities with respect to the characters appearing in Jason's dream reports over the 17-year span.

Aggressions

There are enough aggressions in Jason's dream reports to give us a very
fair overall assessment of consistency. Before presenting findings on consis-

Table 7.6.   The Seven Character Categories
with the Highest Frequencies in Jason's Dreams

	Dreams							
	1–100	101–200	201–300	301–400	401–500	501–600	1–600	V
	Percentages of single characters							
Adult known males	30	32	25	22	19	27	26	15
Adult male strangers	17	15	24	25	25	21	21	17
X (an individual)	11	13	17	08	12	07	12	23
Adult known females	09	07	08	09	10	10	09	09
Indefinite strangers	05	08	07	11	10	06	07	29
Adult female strangers	04	08	06	05	06	11	07	29
Y (an individual)	06	05	08	08	02	03	05	40

tency, however, we should note that Jason has an extremely small amount of aggression in his dream reports. His overall A/C score is only 15 (198/1,472), whereas the typical male dreamer has an A/C score of 34 (h = .45). We might want to allow for the fact that Jason was in his middle 30s to early 50s when he was writing down these dream narratives, but he is indeed a very mild-mannered person, and he reports he always has been. Here we see the usefulness of our norms in studying individuals.

The data for aggressive encounters are brought together in Table 7.7. The first comparison aggregates all the aggressions in the dream reports. The next four comparisons are for aggressive interactions between Jason and single humans, plural humans, and animals, and for aggressions he witnessed. These four categories constitute the sum total of all aggressions in Jason's dream reports.

The absolute row constancies (V) are good for the sum total of all aggressions and for Jason's aggressive encounters with single characters, and they are fair for witnessed aggressions. There are simply not enough aggressions involving plural characters and animals to draw any conclusions regarding consistency. The one developmental trend is the increasing proportion of aggressive encounters between Jason and single characters. In the last 100 dream reports, he is involved in almost twice as many aggressions with them than he is in the first 100 dream reports.

In the rest of the rows in Table 7.7, the A/C scores are computed for single characters only, since most of Jason's aggressions occur with single characters. First, we present the data for Jason's aggressive interactions with characters classified by their relationship to him (rows 6–9). We omit from consideration relatives and prominent people because there is only one aggression involving a relative and there are three involving a prominent

Table 7.7.   Aggressive Encounters in Jason's Dreams (A/C Scores)

	Number of aggressions	I	II	III	IV	V	VI	Overall	
		1–100	101–200	201–300	301–400	401–500	501–600	1–600	V
		29	27	32	38	41	41	198	
1. All characters	198	13	12	18	18	17	16	15	15
2. Single characters	132	11	14	14	14	16	20	15	15
3. Plural characters	15	02	04	07	13	03	04	05	56
4. Animals	17	67	00	50	25	06	14	25	81
5. Witnessed aggressions	34	02	01	03	03	04	04	03	28
6. Family	49	17	19	21	25	33	68	27	45
7. Known characters	33	11	10	12	14	08	07	10	20
8. Strangers	46	08	14	12	09	16	18	13	25
9. Males	62	10	12	11	12	15	17	13	17
10. Females	74	15	20	23	22	22	30	24	17
11. X (an individual)	39	26	27	23	63	47	80	38	50
12. Adult males	30	14	20	13	12	17	23	16	22
13. Adult known males	20	08	09	09	17	03	08	09	30
14. Adult known females	11	13	17	20	11	18	07	14	29
15. Victimization percent		16	26	44	15	43	39	33	17
16. Physcial aggression percent		00	09	22	13	32	09	15	10

person (there are only 3 relatives and 27 prominent persons in Jason's 600 dream reports). The data show clear-cut developmental regularity for aggression with family members. The consistency by rows for known persons and for strangers is just fair. There is no consistency in the relative ranks for known persons and strangers. The absolute constancy of Jason's aggressive encounters with males and females (rows 9 and 10) is good. Unlike most males, he has more aggressive interactions with females than with males. His relative consistency on this issue is perfect.

The relative consistency of rows 11–14 is only fair, mainly because his low A/C scores with adult males and known adult females are so similar, but individual X (row 11) always has the highest A/C score. Although the changes for aggressions with individual X do not meet our criterion for developmental regularity, it is obvious that there is a much higher rate of aggressive interactions between Jason and individual X in the last 300 dream reports than in the first 300.

The findings for victimization percent are presented in row 15, and the findings for physical aggression percentage are found in row 16. The absolute constancy on the victimization percent is good, and it is excellent on the physical aggression percent. Perhaps more interesting to readers becoming familiar with the norms is the fact that Jason is very atypical in the frequency with which he is the aggressor and in the small number of physical aggressions.

In short, the findings on aggressions not only show consistencies of various types for large-frequency categories, but they give us an image of Jason as well. He is not very aggressive, and not at all physically aggressive, but what aggression he has manifests itself through hostile interactions that he initiates with female characters.

Friendly and Sexual Interactions

As noted in the introduction to the chapter, this analysis was completed before the final Hall/Van de Castle system was settled on. One of the major changes from the former system was the decision to separate out friendly and sexual interactions. Thus, the analyses in this section are not comparable with the norms. Taking out sexuality would entail a major reanalysis that would not change the consistency findings, but it would deflate scores. In a later part of this section on Jason's dream series, we will comment on the frequency of his sexual dream reports based on a greater span of years.

Table 7.8 brings together findings for Jason's friendly and sexual encounters with 14 classes of characters. In rows 1–5, the greatest number of these encounters is with single characters. The absolute constancy of rows 1 and 2 is good. The other categories have very low frequencies. There are no developmental trends in rows 1–5. The remaining rows (6–16) are based on an

Table 7.8. Friendly Encounters in Jason's Dreams (A/F Scores)

	Number of friendly encounters	Dreams							V
		1–100	101–200	201–300	301–400	401–500	501–600	1–600	
		58	51	36	47	50	48	290	
1. All characters	290	25	23	20	30	20	19	22	15
2. Single characters	249	29	27	24	39	24	29	28	13
3. Plural characters	13	04	06	07	05	03	02	04	38
4. Animals	13	17	00	17	13	22	29	19	37
5. Witnessed encounters	15	03	01	00	01	01	01	01	50
6. Family	31	28	17	51	25	20	16	17	39
7. Known characters	137	33	42	51	63	32	37	41	22
8. Strangers	69	21	14	18	28	18	23	20	18
9. Males	180	35	37	39	47	31	35	37	10
10. Females	63	22	15	10	27	19	28	20	27
11. Adult known males	106	41	48	53	74	33	36	46	23
12. Adult male stangers	41	14	20	20	31	24	26	22	20
13. Adult known females	22	13	08	40	44	32	43	29	46
14. Y (an individual)	11	27	44	00	37	25	00	24	59
15. Befriender percent	00	83	85	75	89	72	53	76	40

analysis of interactions with single characters. The stability of the scores is good for strangers, fair for known persons, and poor for family members. The scores for known persons are higher than those for family members and strangers in every set of 100 dream reports.

Friendly encounters with males are invariably higher than those with females (rows 9 and 10), in contrast to Jason's greater rate of aggressions with females. Jason, in fact, manifests a very atypical pattern of friendly and aggressive interactions with male and female characters. The stability of the scores as measured by V is excellent for males and fair for females. There are no developmental regularities.

The rates of friendliness for the four classes of characters with whom Jason interacts in a friendly way most frequently appear in rows 11–14. The first two rows (11 and 12) are fairly stable, and the scores for adult known males outrank all other scores with a single exception. There is a suggestion of increasing friendliness with adult known females.

Friendly and sexual encounters are next divided into those in which the dreamer is the befriender and those in which he is befriended. Jason is fairly consistently the one who initiates the friendly or sexual encounter, as row 15 in Table 7.8 indicates, although the V is high because of one set of dream reports where the befriender percent deviates greatly from what is typical.

Overall, the quantitative tables on Jason's dream reports show that there is an impressive amount of consistency over the 17-year period. Many of the V's are excellent, especially on general categories with high frequencies, such as males, females, and aggressions. Four of the poor (i.e., high) V's turn out to show an excellent degree of developmental regularity. Many of the remaining poor V's are high because of the low frequencies involved. Absolute constancy, then, is in the big picture, not in the details. The relative consistencies are impressive for several major categories.

A 30-Year Comparison

After a 15-year hiatus in receiving dream reports because we were doing other work, Jason gave us dream reports when he was 70 at our request. When we compared 100 of those dream reports with 100 from when he was 40, there were very few changes.

Throughout the first 21 years that Jason kept track of his dreams, he had a large number of sexual dreams. At age 70, sexuality still remained an important element in Jason's dreams. He had a sexuality to characters index (S/C) of 15 (82/560) as a younger man, and it was about the same 30 years later. The norm for male college students on this index is 6, so Jason's S/C score is 2.5 times higher than one would expect. Jason's higher rate of sexual encounters may mean there is an increase in sexual dreams for postcollege men, but it is more likely the case that Jason had an unusual number of them.

There were three acts of physical aggression in the age-40 set and two in the age-70 set. The two in the second set were relatively mild, and Jason said they caused him no discomfort: a large insect attacked him, and a boy threw a stone at him.

We compared the two sets for Elements from the Past. Approximately 1 in 10 dream reports can be coded on this scale in both sets. When it is taken into account that Jason had 30 more years of past life to dream about when he was 70, this result is all the more interesting. We will see further evidence for this "present-mindedness" of dreams with the next two subjects. We also see a similar phenomenon in a large cross-sectional questionnaire study of day-dreams and other spontaneous thought intrusions in 1,275 men and women ages 17 to 92 (Giambra, 1977). The older subjects were no more likely to daydream about the past than the younger ones, and neither young nor old thought much about the distant past.

The fact that Jason seldom dreams of the past also fits with the generalization emerging from study of the characters in his dream reports. He dreams about the people who are in his life at the time. The only overlaps of the two sets are his wife, his offspring, his father, a male friend he still saw, and his favorite college professor from 50 years earlier. Even when he was 40, all the known persons in his dream reports were current friends and associates except for his closest friend in high school, whom he had not seen in 20 years.

Given Jason's advanced age, we now looked for increased mentions of injury, illness, or death (misfortunes). There were four dreams of death and none of illness in the first set, and one of death and five of illness in the second set. In only one of these dreams, in the second set, was he the victim—an injury to his arm.

Jason died a few years after the second and final study. His contribution to our research was extraordinary. His dream series first raised the possibility that there may be consistency in what people dream about.

DOROTHEA

Our dream series covering the longest span of years began in 1912 and ended in 1965, four days before the dreamer's death at the age of 78. During this 53-year period, Dorothea wrote down 904 dreams. However, she did not start writing down every dream she remembered until 1959, well after she retired. There are only 54 dream reports from ages 25 to 40 and 85 from ages 41 to 55. We therefore have to show caution about the early years when she wrote down only dreams that interested her, but in all it is a magnificent and useful series.

Dorothea was born in 1887 in Shanghai, China, where her parents were

Presbyterian missionaries. She was the second of eight children. The family returned to the United States when Dorothea was 13. She taught school for many years after graduating from college. In 1925, she earned her doctorate in psychology and for the next 18 years taught in a normal school that later became part of a university. After her retirement at age 56, she remained active as a psychological researcher, publishing over a dozen articles in psychological journals. She never married.

Dorothea lived in a retirement home for women in a tropical climate for the last few years of her life. She was mentally alert and active until the very end of her life. Dorothea was a participating member of many local organizations and belonged to a swimming club until she was 76. She was proud that she had an IQ score of 147 on the Wechsler when she was 74.

Although Dorothea was a psychologist, she had no professional or intellectual interest in dreams. She was an experimental psychologist with no use for Freud or other psychodynamic theorists. She wrote down her dreams for her own interest and did not contact Hall about her dream series until she was in her early 70s.

Hall studied 600 of the first 649 dream reports Dorothea sent him, dividing them into sets of 100. The first set covered her early adult and middle years. The last 100 in the study were written when she was 75. The findings for Dorothea's series are consistent with those for Jason's, so we will not repeat the lengthy list of tables. The percentages of single characters, plural characters, and animals in her dream reports showed only minor fluctuations over the 50-year period. Nor were there any inconsistencies or high V's for the percentages of family members, friends and acquaintances, and strangers. However, there was a considerable change in her male/female percent in her later years—a developmental regularity. Her male/female percent was 53 in the first 100 dream reports, but only 39 in the 100 dreams from her 75th year. As the number of males in her life declined, so too did the number in her dream reports.

Dorothea dreamed about her parents and siblings with the same frequency throughout the 50 years, although her father died when she was very young and her mother died when Dorothea was 61. The number of aggressions, which was very low, did not change significantly over the years; nor was there a significant change in the number of misfortunes.

There were only eight dream reports with sexual activity. Some of these dream reports were very explicit, so it does not seem likely she censored others from a dream journal she never showed to anyone until she was in her early 70s. At age 71, for example, she wrote down the following dream report:

> As I stepped from the shower a man came in and said he wanted me. I said, "I'm all wet." He replied, "That's all right," and led me to the bedroom. I lay down on my back. Then he was on top of me. I felt his muscles moving and it felt like there was a rod up my vagina. I wondered if it was his penis inside.

Dorothea's comment that she "wondered if it was his penis inside" may reflect a genuine question. She wrote to Hall that she had never engaged in sexual intercourse.

In addition to the decline in her male/female percent, there were two other developmental regularities in Dorothea's dream reports. First, she dreamed more about traveling when she was a young woman, which is consistent with the fact that she did much traveling then and virtually none at all in her final 5 or 6 years. Second, she was higher on the misfortune of being ill in her earlier years, which corresponded with the fact that she was more troubled by illness when she was younger.

Madorah Smith and Hall (1964) did a separate study of the first 649 of Dorothea's dream reports to see if there was any tendency for her to dream more often of the past as she grew older. Using the Elements from the Past Scale, they found no difference between 188 dream reports before age 66 and 461 reports after that age (23% versus 29%). This finding is similar to what was reported for Jason's series in the previous section.

If Dorothea dreamed very little of aggression, sexuality, or the past, what then did she dream about? We will save part of the answer for a theoretical discussion of "themes" in long dream series in Chapter 9, but the basic answer is that she dreamed most frequently about food and eating. Dorothea is eating, preparing to eat, preparing a meal, buying or seeing food, watching someone eat, or mentioning she is hungry in 128 of the 600 dream reports Hall used in the consistency study (21%), and in 85 of the 304 reports she sent later (28%), In many of these instances, she is at the family dinner table with her mother and some of her siblings. Her proportion of food and eating dreams is three times higher than our female norms.

Coincidentally, the last dream Dorothea mailed to Hall, 4 days before her death of old age, was an eating dream with her mother and some of her siblings in it. If we did not know how regularly she dreamed about being in this setting and, incidentally, not receiving her fair share of the food, we might infer that this final dream report was about an alleged forlorn existence in her retirement home or an omen of her impending death:

> Mother had dished out too liberally to the younger children so asked E [a brother of Dorothea] to give her some of his. I still had nothing. Then we saw a potato on the floor by the door and it was divided with me.

It seems likely that this dream related to one of Dorothea's lifelong concerns, reminding us once again why norms or long dream series are essential for systematic studies of dream meaning.

Dorothea was a very consistent dreamer for 50 years. As we said at the outset of this section, it would have been even better if we had more dream reports from her early adulthood, but the findings are still impressive. They become even more convincing after we consider the next long dream series.

MARIE

Marie is one of the best coincidences that ever happened to quantitative content analysis. Between 1923 and 1932, when she was young and single, she recorded nearly 100 of her dreams. Most of them were written in 1923 or between 1926 and 1929. In 1933, she married and took a full-time job, and stopped writing down her dreams. Thirty-four years after her last dream entry, in 1966, Marie was a widow living in a small town in central California several thousand miles from where she was born and raised. She started to write down her dreams again. Then she read Hall's *The Meaning of Dreams* (1953c) and wrote to ask if her dream reports would be of interest to him.

When Hall quantified the dream reports, the major frequencies were virtually the same in both sets despite the gap of over three decades. This finding adds to what we already know from Jason and Dorothea because Marie's first early set of dream reports is concentrated in her early 20s. Moreover, Marie's series is important because the continuity in content cannot be due to any "practice effect" from writing down her dreams continuously for the whole span of years. Thus, her series answers what was likely to be the major criticism psychologists would raise concerning our consistency findings.

Despite the quantitative similarities in the type of characters in the two sets of dream reports, the actual cast of characters changed almost completely except for members of her family of origin. Like Jason, Marie dreamed about people with whom she was in contact at the time, even if it was only by correspondence. Aside from her family of origin, the only other person she dreamed about in 1966–1967 who was not in contact with her was her deceased husband. (She didn't know him when she first wrote down her dreams, so he does not appear in that set.)

For all the similarities in the two sets of reports, there were some changes as well. The percentage of unfamiliar characters is higher in the 1960s than in the 1920s, for example. Although Marie's rate of aggressive interactions is low in both sets, she dreamed more often of being a victim of aggression, especially from males, when she was in her 20s, whereas in her 60s she was more often the aggressor. Finally, she had markedly fewer sex dreams in her 60s. She reports she had been sexually active in the 1920s, but because of an operation in the early 1960s, along with the death of her husband, she no longer had sexual relations with anyone.

Marie was a wonderful person with a wide circle of friends and a great interest in working creatively with small hand tools. Her fascination with artistic objects came through in her dream reports, as when she was inspecting a rectangular piece of lucite exactly $2'' \times 1'' \times \frac{1}{2}''$, or describing a beautiful Oriental rug, $8' \times 10'$, in magnificent shades of red.

Marie's contribution to our growing realization that there may be consistency in dreams was very great. She is one of the reasons why we think the understanding of dream content will be advanced through the dream reports of normal adult citizens.

THE ENGINE MAN

The studies by Hall reported so far in this chapter establish consistency in dream reports over a period of years. However, there are not enough dreams in any of the series to tell us if consistency is possible over a few months. A remarkable dream series obtained from a used book dealer by Alan Hobson (1988) provided an opportunity to study consistency in a shorter time period.

The person Hobson calls the "Engine Man" (because of his apparent fascination with train locomotives in his dreams) wrote down 234 dreams in the 3 months between July 14 and October 14 in 1939, strictly for his own curiosity. He was 46 years old at the time. When he died nearly 20 years later, the dream journal was inherited by one of his relatives, who later sold it to the book dealer.

Hobson (1988) utilized these dreams to demonstrate the bizarreness and unreality of dreams in terms of their form, scene changes, and unlikely juxta-positions. Whatever the formal bizarreness of the dreams, they are extremely consistent in their content, as shown in an analysis by Adam Schneider of the 187 reports with 50 or more words. Table 7.9 presents these findings for several selected categories by comparing the overall findings with two sub-sets of 93 and four subsets of 46. The stability of the findings is not good with four subsets, but it is impressive with two subsets except for two or three categories.

To refine the analysis even further, Schneider then compared the findings for the Engine Man's first 25, first 50, first 75, and first 100 dream reports to the overall findings with the 187 reports, and with the findings on average departures from the norms that were presented in Table 4.7. This analysis showed that for the set with 75 dream narratives, the Engine Man was within five percentage or index points of his overall score on 14 of 18 comparisons. By way of contrast, with 50 dream reports, he was more than 5 points away from his overall score on 11 of the 18 comparisons. In terms of the comparisons with the average departures from the norms presented in Table 4.7, the Engine Man showed greater stability in all 18 categories at 25 dream reports, in 17 of 18 at 50, in 14 of 18 at 75, and in 13 of 18 at 100. This result suggests that findings with an individual are likely to reach stability at smaller samples sizes than for a group. This is a finding that makes sense, of course, if we assume that an individual is more consistent than a group of 25, 50, or 75 individuals, but we obviously need further studies to be sure.

Table 7.9.   The Engine Man

	Total (187)	Two sets (93/set)		Four subsets (46 dreams/set)			
Characters							
Male/female percent	70	70	70	65	76	66	74
Familiar characters percent	38	38	37	42	34	41	34
Animal percent	11	14	9	15	13	8	9
Group percent	22	25	19	21	29	14	23
Characters per dream	3.08	3.08	3.02	3.11	3.11	2.59	3.52
Emotions							
Negative emotions percent	79	84	72	89	77	70	73
Dreamer-involved emotions percent	68	68	68	83	46	80	60
Emotions per dream	0.30	0.33	0.27	0.39	0.28	0.22	0.33
Settings							
Indoor settings percent	43	45	41	53	37	40	42
Familiar settings percent	73	76	70	75	76	68	71
Aggression							
Dreamer-involved aggression percent	59	51	66	57	45	67	65
Victimization percent	65	62	68	58	67	60	72
Physcial aggression percent	45	42	45	33	50	38	49
Aggressions per dream	0.55	0.46	0.62	0.46	0.48	0.46	0.80
A/C index	18	15	21	15	15	18	23
Friendliness							
Dreamer-involved friendliness percent	70	68	72	71	65	70	73
Befriender percent	52	44	57	50	40	38	68
Friendliness per dream	0.49	0.43	0.54	0.37	0.50	0.43	0.65
F/C index	16	14	18	12	16	17	19

The Engine Man was not only a consistent dreamer, but also a very unusual one, as revealed in his h-profile in Figure 7.1. He was below the norms in most aggression categories, particularly in terms of his involvement in aggressions. He also was strikingly below the norms in his involvement in friendliness. In other words, the Engine Man was primarily a witness or an observer in his dreams. Sexual interactions were completely absent from his dreams. He was above the norms only on animal percent and familiar settings.

The Engine Man's h-profile anticipates findings we will present in the next chapter because it reveals a great continuity with his waking life, as presented in a four-page obituary in the proceedings of a scientific society. The Engine Man was a naturalist who did very detailed taxonomic studies; these activities are consistent with his high animal percent and his stance

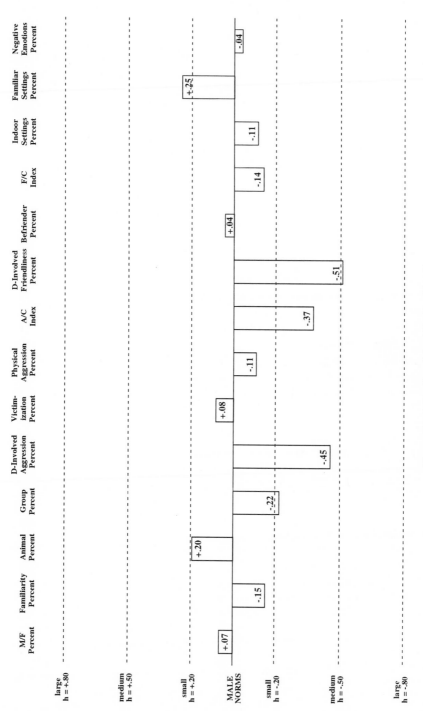

Figure 7.1. h-Profile of the "Engine Man."

as an observer in his dreams, and he was mild-mannered and unaggressive. He was a lifelong bachelor. We have no hesitancy in concluding that there is coherence, consistency, and continuity in the dream life of the Engine Man. In fact, the findings with his dream journal suggest that consistency might be found in dream life over the space of several weeks for some people if enough dream reports are obtained.

CONSISTENCY OF THE MALE/FEMALE PERCENT

As one small part of his study of the male/female percent in several dozen samples of male and female dream reports from all over the world, Hall (1984:1114) compared the male/female percent in early and later parts of 11 long dream series. Eight of the series were from men, and three were from women. As can be seen in Table 7.10, there is great consistency for periods ranging from a few months to many years. There is also consistency for Jason between samples that are 32 years apart. The only change is for Dorothea. Her male/female percent changed from 53/47 in 1912–1933 to 39/61 in 1960–1962, when she lived in a women's retirement home.

We report these results on the male/female percent because this is the largest sample we have relating to the issue of consistency. Male/female percent, because it has been of use in so many of our investigations, is a telltale indicator, but we recognize that more studies using more coding catego-

Table 7.10.   Consistency Over Years for Individual Dreamers
in Male/Female Percent

| Individuals | Period 1 | | | Period 2 | | |
	Time interval	Number of dreams	Male/female percent	Time interval	Number of dreams	Male/female percent
Karl	4/68–6/68	76	69/31	7/68–9/68	73	70/30
Tony	1968	50	73/27	1969	50	64/36
Ted	1966–1968	100	72/28	1979–1980	100	66/34
Dick	3/63–4/63	74	61/39	5/63–6/63	74	67/33
Chris	6/68–9/68	50	68/32	9/68–12/68	50	60/40
Raymond	1950	91	61/39	1952	91	62/38
Jasper	1959	100	68/32	1963	100	67/33
Jason	1947	100	63/57	1979	122	67/33
Lucille	1967	99	42/58	1968	86	43/57
Marie	1966	79	51/49	1967	79	48/52
Dorothea	1912–1933	100	53/47	1960–1962	100	39/61*

*$p < .01$

ries need to be done. We hope such studies will be completed and published by a variety of researchers in the next few years. Establishing consistency in a wide range of dream series would be of considerable theoretical import.

A LABORATORY STUDY OF CONSISTENCY

Kramer and Roth (1979a) have provided further support for the idea of consistency in dream content through an interesting laboratory study in which dream reports were collected from the first four REM periods for 20 consecutive nights from 14 college males. The 820 dream reports they obtained were analyzed for characters, activities, and descriptive elements using the Hall/Van de Castle system. A score for each of these content categories for each night was determined for each subject by adding the findings for all four dream reports of the night. The scores of all subjects for a given night then were used to create a mean score for each night of the study.

Kramer and Roth used the nightly mean score to make a large number of comparisons for pairs of nights and for the first and second weeks of the study. Their most general measure was the mean night-to-night correlations for each of the three categories. They were .45 for total characters, .51 for total activities, and .51 for descriptions (Kramer & Roth, 1979a:322). After reporting that they found a correlation of .44 in their earlier study of the stability of sleep stages from night to night, they conclude that "the stability of dream content across nights is clearly comparable to that of sleep physiology" (Kramer & Roth, 1979a:323). Their conclusion is an impressive commentary on the consistency of dream content. Sleep stages are generally thought of as very regular and stable, just as dreams are thought of as irregular and unpredictable, but it turns out that the two different phenomena are similar in their consistency if dream reports are studied with quantitative content analysis.

CONCLUSION

The rather amazing consistency with which people dream about certain types of characters, social interactions, objects, and activities is a strong argument for the idea that dreams have "meaning" in the sense of psychological coherence and significance. If dreams were only random reactions to internal physiological processes, or entirely at the mercy of too much salsa or a bad day at the office, it is unlikely that their contents would be so consistent over months or years or decades for this set of women and men.

The consistency in long dream series seems to be relatively free of major changes in life circumstances if the findings on Jason, Dorothea, and Marie are any indication. They changed their geographical areas of residence and their family situations, and they retired from their jobs, but they continued to have similar percentages and index scores for most dream content categories. At the same time, a few changes did occur. These changes are important because they help to refute any claim that the consistencies in our findings are a mere "practice effect" created by the process of writing down the dreams. The fact that the changes make sense in terms of changing circumstances in the dreamers' lives also strengthens our belief that our findings are psychologically meaningful.

In general, then, these findings add to our growing body of evidence that dream reports can tell us something meaningful about a person's life. They provide a starting point for future studies of long dream series from people who can give us more psychological information than is available on the people who provided the series used in this chapter. Indeed, we think the future of dream content studies lies primarily in the study of long dream series. If this chapter helps to legitimate such studies in the eyes of more social scientists, it will have gone a long way toward realizing one of the major goals of this book.

The findings in this chapter show that 75 to 100 dream reports are needed to establish reliable (repeatable) quantitative findings on a person's dream life. If we code sets of 25 dreams from a long dream series, we find more variation than if we code 50 or 75 or 100. This finding on reliability within sets from a long dream series is another approach to the issues addressed in Chapter 3 concerning the representativeness of a person's limited number of recalled dreams. In effect, these new findings from long dream series allow us to say that 75 to 100 dream reports are likely to give us a representative sample of a person's total dream life. This is a good starting point for future "personality sketches" based on dream reports. These findings on the number of dream reports needed to ensure reliability in a dream series are the basis for the definition of a "long" dream series provided in Chapter 1. A "long" dream series is defined as one containing 75 or more dream reports because it likely provides a representative sample of a person's total dream life.

Both a reliable coding system (one with high intercoder agreement) and repeatable findings are essential for the scientific study of dream content. However, the biggest challenges in terms of finding "meaning" in dreams are to link their content to waking thought and behavior and to learn something new and important about dreamers that could not be learned through interviews and psychological testing. We turn to those challenges in Chapter 8.

8

The Continuity between Dreams and Waking Life in Individuals and Groups

INTRODUCTION

In this chapter, we show that there is meaning in dreams by exploring the relationship between our dream content categories and waking thought and behavior. This is what people usually have in mind when they ask if dreams have meaning. They want to know if dreams reveal anything about a person's psychological makeup, especially anything not previously known or understood. As should be clear by now, we do think dreams have meaning in this sense of the term. Dreams reveal people's conceptions, concerns, and interests. It is important to understand people's conceptions because they are one basis for their actions in the world. It is important to understand people's preoccupations because they determine where people will expend most of their energies (Hall, 1947, 1953a).

The findings in this chapter demonstrate a continuity between dreams and waking life: the concerns people express in their dreams are the concerns they have in waking life. What they dream about is also what they think about or do when they are awake. We call this claim the "continuity hypothesis." Just as the "consistency hypothesis" characterizes our major findings on people's dream lives over the space of time, so too the "continuity" hypothesis summarizes what we have learned about the relationship between the dreaming and waking minds. Taken together, the consistency and continuity hypotheses are our major evidence for the overall "meaning" of dreams in the sense of (1) regularity and (2) correspondence with other psychological variables.

Although the continuity hypothesis is straightforward and simple, the actual nature of the continuity is somewhat complicated. The continuity usually is with both thought and behavior, but sometimes it is only with waking thought. For example, people who have highly aggressive dreams are not always aggressive people in waking life, but they admit to many aggressive thoughts and fantasies during the day. Similarly, people who have frequent sex dreams are not always sexually active in reality, but they entertain the same thoughts in waking life and sometimes practice frequent masturbation to the accompaniment of their sexual fantasies. These two examples are not happenstance ones. It is our hypothesis, based on a limited number of cases, that sexual and aggressive preoccupations in dreams are the ones most frequently manifested only in waking thought. Our best case example of this point is presented later in the chapter.

Most of our evidence for the continuity hypothesis comes from "testimony" by the dreamer or people who know the dreamer. Sometimes this testimony is augmented by what might be considered more "objective" or "physical" evidence, as when a child molester is jailed for his behavior or mental patients are hospitalized. Most of our evidence comes from testimony, however, and for some of our most satisfying analyses we have relied exclusively on the testimony of the dreamers.

On a few questions, however, the testimony of the dreamer, or at least the initial testimony, has not supported our inferences. What are we to make of such instances? If the person has corroborated our inferences, say, 36 out of 40 times, on what basis do we make rejections of contrary testimony? As we all know, testimony is not always accurate, but that does not resolve our problem. We do not deal with this issue until the conclusion of the chapter, but we want to alert readers to it before it arises.

The search for relationships between dream content and waking behavior has been sidetracked by a repeated—and unexpected—finding: there is little or no relationship between dream content and standard projective techniques such as the Thematic Apperception Test (TAT; see Hall, 1956, for a review of most of these studies). For example, Mary Osterberg (1951) coded dream series and TAT stories obtained from 10 males and 10 females for frequency, intensity, and object of aggression using precursors of the Hall/Van de Castle scales. There was no relationship between dream reports and stories for any of these categories. Gordon's (1953) comparison of dream reports and TAT stories found that dream reports contained more aggression, tension, fear, passivity, and inadequacy. Similar negative findings with the TAT are reported by Ben-Horin (1967), Leman (1967), and Zepelin (1980–1981, 1981). The results with the Rorschach are not any better (e.g., Bolgar, 1954; Eagle, 1964).

Nor is there much evidence for a strong correlation between dream content and objective tests such as the Minnesota Multiphasic Personality Inventory (MMPI), the California Psychological Inventory (CPI), and the Edwards Personal Preference Schedule (e.g., Winget & Kramer, 1979, for a review of such studies through the early 1970s). We will focus primarily on those few studies reporting some positive results, all of which support the continuity hypothesis.

In a summer school session, Rychlak and Brams (1963) collected two or more dreams from 15 males and 15 females ranging in age from 19 to 52. They scored the dreams on four thematic dimensions and several of the content categories in their scoring system, which overlaps greatly with the Hall/Van de Castle system, as shown briefly in Chapter 2. They then compared their findings with many dimensions of the MMPI and the Edwards Personal Preference Schedule for the same subjects. The scores on the dream dimensions and the personality tests were dichotomized at the median, which created a series of 2 × 2 tables that were tested for statistical significance with chi-square. Results at the .01, .05, and .10 levels of significance were reported. Given the number of comparisons they made, several significance differences would be expected by chance alone. No measure of effect size is reported.

There were very few significant relationships between their dream content categories and the tests. The findings on the thematic scoring were, however, generally supportive of continuity between dream content and personality dimensions. For example, people with positive interactions as a main theme of their dreams tended to show more social confidence and social control on the personality tests, and people who were high on "reward" themes involving striving and recognition tended to score higher on scales showing concern with social status. Themes of tension (anxiety, frustration, and hostility) were more often present for those who scored higher on hostility and psychopathology scales. Those who had the most unpleasant dream reports tended to score higher on MMPI scales for dominance and aggression (Rychlak & Brams, 1963:229–231). It is difficult, however, to make very much out of this study because of the small number of subjects and dream reports, the subjectivity of thematic scoring, the large number of statistical tests that were run, and the lack of information on effect sizes.

Foulkes and Rechtschaffen (1964), as one part of a larger study of the effects of different films on the laboratory dream reports of 13 male and 11 female subjects, studied the correlations between 22 MMPI scales and the subjects' own ratings of their dreams for such dimensions as emotionality, unpleasantness, violence, dramatic quality, and degree of distortion. Again, several significant differences could be expected by chance in such a large matrix. Perhaps the most interesting finding for our purposes, and one consistent with those of Rychlak and Brams (1963), was a positive correlation between various hostility scales derived from the MMPI and unpleasantness in dream content (Foulkes & Rechtschaffen, 1964:994). In a later study of dream reports from 14 boys ages 13 to 15 who each spent two nights in the sleep lab, Foulkes et al. (1969) found that the degree of active participation in the dream action correlated positively with dominance on the CPI. They also found a positive correlation between CPI aggression scores and physical aggression in dream reports. Again, these findings are compatible with our continuity hypothesis.

Further tentative support for the continuity hypothesis comes from the findings on two nights of laboratory dream reports from 24 subjects divided into high and low expressors of impulses in waking life, as determined by an MMPI subscale. Those who were high on impulse expression in waking life also tended to express more sexuality and hostility in dream reports (Ben-Horin, 1967). Van de Castle (1968; with Holloway, 1970) reports positive correlations between some Hall/Van de Castle categories and the MMPI profiles of several types of psychiatric patients, but the studies do not involve large numbers of subjects and no details are given. On the other hand, Fletcher (1970), in a study of 529 dream reports, found no relationship between measures of aggression in dream content and various MMPI scales.

The overall findings from these studies hold out some possibility for the use of objective tests in studies of dream content. The results have to be treated with caution, however, because of the relatively small sample sizes and the lack of replication studies. We found no published studies in the *Psychological Abstracts* between 1973 and 1992 that linked specific categories of dream content to dimensions of objective personality tests. This shows how little potential investigators see in such studies after reviewing the literature.

The negative findings with projective techniques and the tentative findings in the few studies with objective personality tests leave personality researchers with no established ways to link dreams with waking life. This is yet another reason why there is so little study of dream content in scientific psychology. If there is going to be any advance in finding connections between dream content and waking life, new directions will have to be taken. That is why we have relied on testimony in our own efforts. It is also why we think analysts of dream content may have to create their own objective tests, based on their findings *within* dream reports, to find the linkages to waking life. The old research strategy started with the existing tests and tried to determine if their dimensions had any connections to dreams. This strategy in effect tested the assumption that the various dimensions of waking personality are reflected in dream content and found little evidence for it.

Similar conclusions can be drawn from a study comparing themes in daydreams to several personality measures (Gold & Reilly, 1985/86). Thirty male and 32 female college students took an objective personality test, listed their most important current concerns, and then kept a diary of their daydreams. No correlations were found between any of the personality dimensions and daydream themes, but a little over half of the daydreams related to the students' five most important current concerns, which is clear evidence for the continuity hypothesis.

Because of the meager findings with personality tests for both dream content and daydream themes, we have adopted a new working assumption: dream content may not be about "personality" in the usual sense of the term. Instead, dream content may provide us with different information about people than most personality tests do. Because dream content reveals conceptions and concerns, that should be our starting point in developing or selecting objective tests for the study of the correspondence between dream content and waking behavior.

Each of the individual case studies in this chapter is a blind analysis in the sense that we did not have any knowledge or expectations about the dreamer. We did have some general impressions of our two most famous subjects, to be introduced shortly, but we had no idea of what inferences might arise from a quantitative content analysis of their dream reports. The individual cases in this chapter are the best we have out of an only slightly larger pool of possibilities. They are the ones on which the most quantitative work has been done and the most information is available. We regret, for example, that we could not report more about the lives of Jason, Dorothea, and Marie (Chapter 7), because their long dream series and consistent patterns would have made them excellent subjects for this chapter.

This chapter consists of eight case studies and a discussion of general findings with various kinds of clinical patients. Although there are some promising leads in the group studies of patient populations, for now we put our greatest stock in the individual cases. They are the most fruitful direction for new research in the next several years.

The following section compares the dream reports of the two most famous dream theorists of the 20th century. Their dream series are not as long as we would like them to be, and we do not have detailed information on all aspects of their personal lives, but we can think of no greater opportunity to test the power of our approach than through the dreams of Sigmund Freud and Carl Jung. To find patterns in the dreams of Freud and Jung that no one has noticed before would be a strong recommendation for quantitative content analysis.

THE DREAMS OF FREUD AND JUNG

The material for this section consists of 28 dreams reported by Freud in two of his books, *The Interpretation of Dreams* (1900) and *On Dreams* (1901), and 31 dreams reported by Jung in his autobiographical *Memories, Dreams, Reflec-*

tions (1963). The two series present us with a handicap because they are so short, although we have found that as few as 20 dream reports may on occasion reveal significant aspects of a dreamer's personality (Hall, 1947).

Moreover, some differential biases may have operated in the selection of the dreams that the two men reported. For example, Freud may have selected dreams favorable to *his* theory, and Jung may have selected dreams favorable to *his* theory. It is evident that the reasons for relating their dreams in the first place were quite different. Freud used his dream reports to illustrate various aspects of his dream theory; Jung's purpose was the more personal one of illuminating the nature of his inner life and development. This difference in purpose is evidenced by the books in which they appeared. Freud's dreams are published in scientific treatises; Jung's dreams are reported in his autobiography. There is also the possibility that these dreams are highly memorable or vivid ones not typical for either dreamer, although our findings cast doubt on this concern.

In spite of the problems of brevity and possible selection biases, we expected our method to reveal differences between the two dream series congruent with the lives of the two theorists. Each dream was typed on a 5 × 8 card. Freud's 28 dreams and Jung's 31 dreams were shuffled together before Hall coded them. Freud and Jung were then compared with each other and American male dreamers.

Characters

Freud and Jung are like each other and the norms in most of the basic character categories, as can be seen in Table 8.1. None of the differences is statistically significant. There are, however, some differences that relate to what we know about the two men. Freud has more characters in his dream reports than Jung does, 85 versus 70, although Jung reports more and longer dreams. The number of lines per character is 3.4 for Freud and 6.5 for Jung. This "density coefficient" for people in dream reports is much higher for Freud than it is for Jung. Jung's dream narratives are filled with descriptions of scenery, architecture, and objects rather than with people. This difference

Table 8.1.   Characters

	Freud	Jung	Norms
Percent male/female	72/28	71/29	67/33
Percent single characters	73	70	70
Percent adults	91	93	97
Percent familiar	53	57	45

appears to be compatible with what is known about the two men. Freud was a highly sociable person. He had many close friends and disciples with whom he interacted on a very personal basis. Jung was more solitary and kept would-be disciples at a distance. He spent much time in scholarly pursuits, poring over old manuscripts, and he was a lover of nature. Jung said of himself, "Today as then [meaning in childhood] I am a solitary" (1963:41–42; cf. 32, 356).

The difference in sociability between the two men is congruent with other evidence from their dreams. Jung's interest in nature is compatible with the fact that he had a higher animal percent than Freud. He writes in *Memories, Dreams, Reflections* that "I loved all warm-blooded animals.... Animals were dear and faithful, unchanging and trustworthy. People I now distrusted more than ever" (1963:67). More mystical, fictional, and historical figures turn up in Jung's dreams than in Freud's. This suggests Jung lived more in a world of the past whereas Freud lived more in a world of the present. Indeed, Jung wrote that for years he felt more closely attuned to the past, especially to the Middle Ages and the 18th century, than to the present (1963:34–35, 87).

Jung dreams more about members of his family, whereas Freud dreams more about friends and acquaintances. This implies that Jung's sociability expressed itself within his immediate family, and Freud's social life was centered more outside of the family. There is evidence in Ernest Jones's (1953–1955–1957) three-volume biography of Freud that he expended an enormous amount of time and energy in keeping up a large network of friendships and in trying to maintain cohesion within the psychoanalytic movement.

Objects

We turn next to the findings on objects because they have some connections with the inferences we made about Freud's and Jung's interests based on the character analysis. There are many more objects in Jung's dream reports than in Freud's, 297 versus 196, which suggests again that Jung was more object oriented and Freud was more person oriented. Further support is provided for this statement by the kinds of objects each dreamed about. Jung dreamed more about houses, buildings, and architectural details, especially windows, doors, and walls, and more about nature and landscape than either Freud or the norm group. Freud, on the other hand, dreamed much more about parts of the body, particularly those located in the head, than either Jung or the norm group.

Jung's dreams contain no references to money, whereas Freud's incidence of dreams of money is the same as the norm group. Both men are low in the implements category, especially references to weapons and recreational equipment, which is not surprising considering that both of them were intellectuals and scholars.

Aggression and Friendliness

The findings so far have been interesting, but hardly earthshaking. They take on more significance from this point on. Freud and Jung have some very revealing differences between each other and the norms in their patterns of aggression and friendliness. However, these differences do not manifest themselves in our most general indicators, the A/C and F/C indexes. There are 16 aggressive and 16 friendly interactions in Freud's dream series; Jung's has 14 aggressions and 11 friendly interactions. Their A/C and F/C codes are much the same, and they are in close accord with our findings for American males between the ages of 30 and 80 (Hall & Domhoff, 1963b, 1964). Nor do they differ from each other or the norms on their degree of involvement in aggressive and friendly interactions, or in the percentage of time they are victims of aggression.

With regard to the role of befriender and befriended, however, the two men are poles apart. In every instance where Jung is involved in a friendly interaction, he initiates the friendliness. Freud, on the other hand, more often plays the role of being the recipient of friendliness (8 out of 11 times). The norms fall midway between the figures for Freud and for Jung. This finding suggests that Freud would expect people to come to him and that he would be sensitive to rejection if they didn't. We do not have a great deal of behavioral evidence on this point, but we do know that Freud was deeply hurt because Jung did not make an effort to visit him when Freud made a trip to Switzerland in 1912, shortly before their close friendship of 6 years dissolved (Jones, 1955:144).

By far the most striking and informative finding in comparing the two series concerns the large differences in the patterns of Freud's and Jung's aggressive and friendly interactions with male and female characters. As we have said perviously, the typical male has more aggressive interactions with males than with females, and more friendly interactions with females than with males. Jung's aggressive and friendly encounters with males and females are fairly typical. He has an aggressive interaction with about one in every four male characters in his dreams and no aggressive encounters with females. Jung has about an equal number of friendly encounters with males and females, which deviates slightly from the norms and makes Jung more friendly with everyone. In Freud's dreams, the typical pattern is reversed. He has an aggressive encounter with one out of every four *female* characters and almost no aggressive interactions with males. On the other hand, he has many more friendly interactions with males than with females. His pattern is similar to what we reported for Jason's long dream series in Chapter 7.

There is evidence that the waking preferences of the two men are compatible with these findings. Jung (1963:48–55, 73, 93–96) felt much closer to his mother than to his father, and the evidence for his conflicts with his father

is abundant in the early chapters of his autobiography. Jung is known to have
had many affairs with women (Wehr, 1985). He did not spend much time in
male social groups. On the other hand, many people have concluded after
reading Freud that he was hostile toward women (a summary of the evidence
can be found in Chodorow, 1978: Chap. 9). Jones (1955:421) says Freud found
women "enigmatic." He also writes that Freud was "quite peculiarly monog-
amous" and that "the more passionate side of married life subsided with him
earlier than it does with many men" (Jones, 1955:386, 421). Jones says, "It
might perhaps be fair to describe his view of the female sex as having as their
main function to be ministering angels to the needs and comforts of men"
(1955:421).

With regard to Freud's feelings for men, we know he had an intense
relationship with his fellow physician Wilhelm Fliess in the 1890s. Freud
spoke of overcoming his homosexuality and said that alternations of love and
hate affected his relationships with men (Jones, 1955:420). Freud wrote to his
friend and colleague Max Eitingon that "the affection of a group of coura-
geous young men is the most precious gift that psychoanalysis has bestowed
upon me" (Jones, 1955:419).

We will return to these findings when we comment on the ending of
Freud and Jung's friendship.

Success and Failure

The experience of success and failure in their dreams also distinguishes
Freud and Jung. Most males, as shown in Chapter 4, have an equal amount of
success and failure in their dreams. This is true of Jung, but Freud has much
more success than failure. In fact, he fails only once and succeeds six times.
This suggests that Freud was more strongly motivated to succeed than Jung
was. Jones's (1955:415) judgment that fame meant very little to Freud does not
correspond with the obvious fact that Freud aspired to greatness. Jung, on the
other hand, although he may have had the same aspiration, did not do many
of those things that would help him to achieve fame. Unlike Freud, he did not
found an international organization with its own journals and publishing
house; he did not establish a chain of institutes throughout the world to
promote his ideas; and he did not encourage disciples. Jung preferred his
stone tower to the bustle of the scientific marketplace. He did not seek
worldly success, although he did not refuse it when it knocked on his door.

Good Fortune and Misfortune

Good fortune in dreams, as we know, is a rare quantity; misfortune is
commonplace. Freud and Jung, true to this cross-cultural pattern, have more
misfortune than good fortune in their dreams. In fact, Freud has no good

fortune at all, whereas Jung has more good fortune than is to be expected. Freud's large amount of success relative to failure, coupled with a lack of good fortune, suggests that he pictured himself as succeeding through his own efforts and not as a result of luck. Jung was more likely to view the world, at least in his dreams, as a cornucopia showering benefits on a person. Jung's autobiography suggests that he was more fatalistic than Freud. He was inclined to let things happen to him, to let his life be lived rather than to live it. He wrote (1963:358) that almost everything in his life "developed naturally and by destiny." Jung (1963:356–357) believed that his life was ruled by forces over which he had no control and that he did not completely understand, although he spent much of his adult life trying to understand them. Freud was more rationalistic. He believed that people could master the world by exercising reason.

Summary and Speculations

The several differences between the dream series of Freud and Jung are congruent with their behavior in waking life. Freud was a striving person who liked the company of other men and held to a theory that has a negative view of women in general. Jung, on the other hand, was more solitary, more interested in nature, and more involved in passionate relationships with women.

The dream evidence may shed light on the breakup of their close friendship. Freud sought intense relationships with other men. He wanted to bring men together into a successful psychoanalytic movement. Given Jung's more solitary orientation, his preference for nature and architecture, and his enjoyment of the company of women companions, it is not difficult to imagine that he would be put off by what he may have seen as Freud's adhesiveness. Moreover, Jung did not share Freud's driving ambition.

Although Freud and Jung came to have strong theoretical differences, such differences do not necessarily mean the end of friendship, or of at least a cordial relationship. By contrast, two other Swiss intellectuals who were attracted to psychoanalysis remained warm friends with Freud even when they developed intellectual differences. One, Oscar Pfister, was a Protestant minister, an unlikely friend for a secular member of the Jewish community (Meng and Freud, 1963, recount Pfister's friendship with Freud). The other, Ludwig Binswanger, who broke with Freud to introduce existentialism and phenomenology into psychiatry, corresponded with Freud for the rest of Freud's life. Binswanger subtitled his book on their relationship *Reminiscences of a Friendship* (1957).

We are not saying theoretical differences are unimportant. We also recognize that Freud was deeply disappointed by Jung's theoretical disagreements because he thought of Jung as the "son" he had "anointed" to take over the helm of the psychoanalytic movement (Jung, 1963:361). Jung also was a far stronger personality than Pfister or Binswanger. Nevertheless, the patterns we have found in the dreams of Freud and Jung are of more than theoretical interest. These patterns seem to relate well to their waking concerns, and that is why we have speculated on their possible usefulness in understanding the relationship between the two men.

This first case analysis shows that quantitative content analysis can extract "meaning" from dream reports. The fact that there were relatively few dream reports and a lack of deep information on the two men makes the case less conclusive than it might be, but perhaps more impressive for the same reasons.

THE DREAM LIFE AND LITERATURE OF FRANZ KAFKA

Franz Kafka (1883–1924), one of the greatest writers of the 20th century, wrote down 37 of his dreams in diaries and letters between 1910 and 1923. Hall and Richard Lind (1970) did a quantitative content analysis of those dreams and then made predictions about his concerns and interests before reading other material in the diaries or any of the biographies and reminiscences on Kafka. The dream reports can be found in Appendix B of Hall and Lind (1970:97–124).

It is not known why Kafka wrote down the dreams in his diaries. He rarely commented on them and never attempted any interpretations. It is known, however, that he was critical of psychology in general and psychoanalysis in particular. In the case of the six dreams he included in letters to Milena Jesenska, a woman with whom he was in love for many years, it seems clear he was using the dreams as a means of communicating his mixed feelings about their relationship.

Despite the fact that there are only 37 dream reports, the quantitative content analysis yields a good portrait of Kafka's personality because there is so much consistency from category to category. This case is also interesting because it shows how useful mundane categories such as "activities" and "objects" can be.

Characters

There were 135 characters in Kafka's 37 dream reports. This is a mean of 3.6 charcters per dream report, which is significantly higher than the mean of 2.4 characters for the normative group. This finding suggests a first inference about Kafka: perhaps he is more preoccupied with people than the typical person. The characters were divided into three usual categories: individuals, groups, and animals. There were no differences from the norms. Ninety-five of the 135 characters in Kafka's dream reports could be identified as individual males and groups of males or individual females and groups of females. Of these 95 characters, 63 were male and 32 female, yielding a male/female percent that is identical with the male norms. The 132 human characters were divided into those who were familiar to Kafka (family, relatives, friends, famous people) and those who were unfamiliar (strangers). Again, the findings were very similar to the norms.

Aggression and Friendliness

Kafka's aggressive and friendly interactions are fairly typical, but there are also some individual differences. At least one aggression occurred in 15 of Kafka's 37 dream reports. This percentage of 41 is not significantly different from the percentage of 47 for the normative sample. When the 24 separate acts of aggression are divided by the number of characters, however, the resulting A/C score of 18 is significantly different from the normative proportion of 34 at less than the .001 level of confidence (h = .37). The physical aggression percent is 38 for Kafka and 50 for the normative group, but that difference is not statistically significant. Kafka is less likely to be involved in the aggressions in his dream reports than the normative group (62 versus 80, h = .40).

When Kafka did take part in an aggression, however, he was far more likely to be the aggressor than the victim, which is opposite of the normative group. His A/C index with males is significantly lower than the norms, but with females it is similar to the normative group. Generally, there is less aggression in Kafka's dream reports because of an unusually low number of aggressive encounters with other males. There is also a strong tendency to witness aggression rather than participate in it.

There are 24 friendly interactions in Kafka's dreams, a number that is exactly equal to the number of aggressive interactions. Although aggressive interactions slightly outnumber friendly interactions in the normative sample, Kafka's aggression/friendliness percent is not significantly different. Similarly, when friendly interactions are divided by the number of characters, the F/C score of 18 is not significantly different from the finding of 21 for the normative group. Nor were there any differences in witnessed versus involved friendliness or in dreamer as befriender versus dreamer as befriended. His distribution of friendly interactions with males and females yielded no statistically significant differences.

When we look at Kafka's patterns of friendliness and aggression with males and females, which was so revealing in the case of Freud, another type of interesting pattern emerges. Unlike the typical male, he has equal amounts of friendliness and aggression with both genders due to less aggression with males and less friendliness with females (see Table 8.2).

Table 8.2.   Aggressions and Friendliness
(A/F²)

	(Male norms in parentheses) A/C index	F/C index
Male characters	11 (28)*	16 (17)
Female characters	13 (17)	19 (29)*

*statistically significant at the .01 level
h = .44 on aggressions with male characters
h = .24 on friendliness with female characters

Activities and Objects

The activities in Kafka's dream reports are similar to the norms in all categories. The objects categories in Kafka's dream reports are comparable to the norms except in one category: body parts. Kafka is three times more likely than the average American male dreamer to mention one or another part of the body, which is an h of .52 when the two percentages are compared. We will return to this interesting finding on body parts after summarizing the findings for other coding categories.

Other Coding Categories

Kafka is typical in most other coding categories. There are no differences on misfortunes, good fortunes, food and eating elements, or emotions. Successes and failures occur with about equal frequency. The only difference in any of these categories is that Kafka witnessed others having success more often than the norms (.44 for Kafka, .11 for the normative group, a difference significant at the .01 level of confidence (h = .78). This witnessing of successes fits with his pattern for witnessing aggression.

A Portrait of Kafka

What kind of picture of Kafka emerges from this analysis? First, he is unusually concerned with people. Second, he is not as aggressive as other males. Third, he seems unusually preoccupied with his body. Finally, his lower level of friendliness with female characters suggests that his feelings toward women are more mixed than is typical for most men.

This portrait of Kafka accords well with what emerges from biographies. He was a quiet, passive person who preferred watching to doing. He worked as a clerk in a quasi-governmental insurance association and never moved out of his parents' home. Kafka never finished writing his three novels. He studied people intently, and his favorite activities were reading, attending the theater, sightseeing, and walking (Hall & Lind, 1970:46–48). He was not involved in any active sports or hobbies. Kafka had deep concern about his body and the bodies of others; he was repelled by bodily imperfections in others. Although he was handsome and 6 feet tall, he thought of himself as skinny and compared himself unfavorably with his more muscular father. There are constant negative comments about his body in his diaries. He was interested in the nudist movement and in natural health practices (Hall & Lind, 1970:39–43).

Kafka had several close relationships with women as a young adult, but they were characterized by hesitation and indecision. He never married. He was engaged to one woman, but the engagement was broken. They became engaged again, and again decided not to marry. He had two other similar relations before developing a satisfying association with a woman toward the end of his life, when he was dying of tuberculosis (Hall & Lind, 1970:51, 75–76).

Hall and Lind also applied the Hall/Van de Castle coding system to Kafka's three novels (*Amerika*, *The Trial*, and *The Castle*). They found few or no connections to his dream reports. They said it was "plainly evident that the interactions between the heroes and other characters in the three novels are much more complex than Kafka's social interactions in his dreams" (Hall & Lind, 1970:67). Kafka's understanding of the human condition was not limited to his own personal preoccupations. His interest in observing others served him well.

We conclude that there is a connection between Kafka's dreams and his waking life, but not between his dreams and his literature. More generally, we suspect that the alleged close connection between dreams and artistic productions is a cultural myth. The "dreams" referred to in such claims are more likely daydreams, reveries, or hallucinations in most instances.

THE DREAMS OF A CHILD MOLESTER

Between September 15, 1963, and February 8, 1967, a convicted child molester, whom we will call Norman, wrote down 1,368 dream reports. He initiated the project for private reasons. He was in a mental institution 80% of the time that he was keeping his dream diary, often writing dreams on paper bags or laundry lists (Bell & Hall, 1971:v, 3). Norman was 34 years of age when he undertook this project and 38 when he ended it.

Alan Bell, a clinical psychologist doing an internship at the hospital where Norman was held, interviewed Norman approximately 20 times between October 1966 and April 1967. During these interviews he learned of Norman's ongoing dream record. Bell later wrote to Hall asking him if he would be interested in analyzing Norman's dream series. Hall undertook the task without knowing anything except the age and sex of the dreamer.

Although Hall knew nothing about Norman when he began the analysis, it did not take long to figure out that he probably was a child molester because of frequent mentions of looking at little girls' genitals or having sexual thoughts when in the presence of children. Hall had previously analyzed the dream series of a 50-year-old transvestite who cross-dressed in his dreams as well as the dream series of male homosexuals, so he knew that the continuity hypothesis had been supported for sexual behavior in at least some cases.

It also was clear from the dream reports that Norman lived at home with his mother and sister when he was not institutionalized, had never married, enjoyed reading and swimming, and worked as a helper in printing shops. Although such information is evidence for the continuity hypothesis, it is not the kind of information sought by those who study dream content. In this particular case, the interesting question became a search for why Norman developed into a child molester.

Once the dream reports were coded, Hall wrote a character sketch of the dreamer. Bell then compared this sketch with his clinical information, test scores, and reports furnished by five different institutions where Norman had been held for 7 years between the ages of 20 and 34 for child molestation (Bell & Hall, 1971:6–9).

Characters

There are many unusual features in the character patterns in Norman's dream reports. His mother appears four times more often than would be expected from the norms. His sister, who is 3 years younger, appears 10 times more often than expected. There is not a single appearance of his father in the 1,368 dream narratives. Given these family patterns, it is not surprising that his male/female percent is extremely low at 50/50 versus 67/33 for the norms (h = .35). Beyond his female family members, Norman dreams primarily of unknown males and unknown females. In particular, there is an extremely low incidence of female friends and acquaintances. As for the males who are known to him, they are usually his fellow inmates, not friends of long standing. There is also a large incidence of minors (characters under age 18) in Norman's dream reports. His friends percent (known characters divided by all human characters) is only 9. This figure is far below our normative figure of 31 for males (h = .57). Combined with the very low male/female percent, it suggests that Norman is an atypical dreamer in terms of characters.

Aggression and Friendliness

There is nothing unusual in Norman's pattern of aggression and friendliness except for the important point that he is a little less aggressive than other males (Table 8.3). Norman is also well below the norms on his physical

Table 8.3.   Aggression and Friendliness
(A/F Square)

| | (Male norms in parentheses) | |
	A/C index	F/C index
Male characters	22 (28)	20 (17)
Female characters	12 (17)	27 (29)

h = .14 on aggressions with male characters

aggression percent (27 versus 50, h = .48). He shows a certain passivity in that he is more likely to be the victim of an aggression and the recipient of a friendly act (the befriended). He has many friendly and few aggressive interactions with minors. If there is a redeeming quality in Norman's dream reports, it is in the fact that he is not a very aggressive person.

Sexual Activity

The typical male dreamer has 12 "sex dreams" per 100 dream reports. Norman has 13 per 100, which is not a statistically significant difference. What distinguishes Norman from most other males is the variety of characters with whom he is erotically involved. Whereas heterosexual adult males have erotic encounters almost exclusively with peer females, Norman is involved in or witnesses sexuality in his dreams with males and females, and adults and minors, as can be seen in Table 8.4.

Moreover, Norman is unusual in the range of sexual acts in which he engages in his dreams. He is both active and passive in his sexual encounters, and he engages in oral, anal, and genital sexual acts. Norman has sexual fantasies more frequently and sexual intercourse less frequently in his dream reports than the male norms, as shown in Table 8.5.

Preoccupation with the Body

The frequency of Norman's references to body parts in his dream reports does not differ from the norms, but the parts of the body he dreams about are different from those the typical male dreams about. In the normative group, references to the head and extremities exceed references to the torso, anatomy, and sexual organs. That is, the "torso/anatomy percent," mentioned in Chapter 2 as a possible indicator of psychopathology, is expected to be 31, but in Norman's case it is 54 (h = .47). This finding fits with his sexual and gender preoccupations.

Table 8.4. Incidence of Sexual Interactions
with Various Classes of Characters

Adult sister	12
Unfamiliar adult females	59
Female adolescent	9
Female child	29
Known adult male	9
Unfamiliar adult male	16
Male adolescent	8
Male child	10
Child (sex not given)	3
Baby (sex not given)	1
Animal	2
Witnessed interactions (Norman is not involved)	18
Grand total	176
Total in which Norman is involved	158
All female categories combined	109
All male categories combined	43
All adult categories combined	96
All minors combined	60

From Bell, A., & Hall, C. S. (1971). *The personality of a child molester: An analysis of dreams.* Chicago: Aldine.

Hall's Portrait of Norman

Hall thought the most extraordinary feature of Norman's personality was his pervasive emotional immaturity. He is dependent on his mother and sister. He has no friends. He prefers to be around children. His sexual desires are unfocused, perverse, and mostly in the realm of fantasy. He suffers from gender confusion. Hall believed that the absence of the father from the dream series might be the key to Norman's problems. He speculated that the father either was absent or had used Norman sexually (Bell & Hall, 1971:84). The evidence further suggested that Norman was ambivalent toward female genitals, and he had a strong feminine identification. The emphasis on fantasy in his sexual activities in dreams suggested that Norman was a compul-

Table 8.5.   Frequencies and Percentages of Various Kinds of Sexual Activities

Sexual interactions	Number	Norman percent	Norms percent
The dreamer has or attempts to have sexual intercourse with another character	27	15	27
The dreamer has foreplay activity, handling the sex organs, with a character	27	15	18
The dreamer kisses or fondles a character	13	7	11
The dreamer makes sexual overtures (verbal and expressive) to a character	28	16	30
The dreamer has sexual thoughts or fantasies about a character	81	46	14

h = .72 on sexual thoughts or fantasies
From Bell, A., & Hall, C. S. (1971). *The personality of a child molester: An analysis of dreams*. Chicago: Aldine.

sive masturbator. The frequent urination and defecation in the dream reports, something we have not mentioned until now, suggested that Norman might still be a chronic bedwetter even as an adult.

Norman's Life History

Norman reported that he was a victim of childhood sexual abuse. This turns out to be a fairly frequent pattern for child molesters. Beginning at around age 4, Norman was forced to perform fellatio on his father for 3 or 4 years. Norman said he enjoyed the experience at the time, but came to have severe guilt feelings about it later on. This testimony confirms Hall's main conjecture: Norman's problems involved his relationship with his father (Bell & Hall, 1971:21). When asked about the most positive influences on his life, Norman named his mother, his sister, his aunt, and a male college professor who had helped him recently; three of the four are women. When asked about the most negative influences on his life, he named four males.

Norman was a frail, unimposing, stooped-over person who lacked energy or aggression in waking life. He seemed to be making an enormous effort at self-control. Norman thought of himself as primarily heterosexual, but he had never had sex with a woman. He said his masturbation fantasies were exclusively heterosexual, unlike his sexual fantasies in dreams. He had had sex with other males and at least once with an animal (Bell & Hall, 1971:25). Norman's main sexual outlet, however, was the same compulsive voyeurism present in his dream reports. He wrote that for "as far back as I can recall, I have had a morbid yet fascinating curiosity about the female genitals" (Bell & Hall, 1971:26). This is what led to his child molestation, which consisted primarily of voyeurism for several years, but included exposing himself at least once and fondling children several times. As time went on, he knew he was becoming more aggressive with the children, and it worried him (Bell & Hall, 1971:28).

Clinical observations and tests supported Hall's view of Norman as an immature and dependent person. They also supported the idea of gender confusion and showed that his sexual life was primarily at the level of fantasy (Bell & Hall, 1971:88–90). There were some disagreements, however, between Hall's predictions and the clinical/test findings. Norman was not a bedwetter, and he successfully resisted masturbation for weeks at a time. He thought masturbation was wrong and often felt depressed afterward (Bell & Hall, 1971:25, 94). Norman was able to resist his preoccupation with his body; he was very interested in spirituality. As Bell and Hall (1971:96) put it, "An analysis of the dream content reveals very little about his defensive maneuvers." For us, this is a very important conclusion.

Norman was released from the hospital in late spring 1966, and he was never hospitalized between that year and 1970, when the book on him went to press. He earned an A.A. degree at a local community college and he spent much of his time reading in his bedroom at home or in the school library. There is even a happy ending to the story as of 1992. Norman continued to stay out of institutions. In the mid-1970s, he married a woman slightly older than he is. In 1992, he was in his mid-60s and living in a sunbelt state with his wife. According to Bell, Norman in his old age is a kind and gentle person (Alan Bell, personal communication, July 22, 1992).

Norman's long and unusual dream series is a graphic demonstration of the continuity between dreams and waking life. It also demonstrates the strengths and weaknesses of using dream content in personality research. Norman's dreams reveal his basic conceptions, concerns, interests, and preoccupations in dramatic fashion, but not all of his behaviors. It seems to us an important lesson that defenses may not be revealed by dreams. We are reinforced in our view that dreams have unique and useful things to tell us, but also in our view that we may not be able to find everything we want to know about personality in dreams. It is no wonder that the attempt to correlate dream content with standard personality tests has not been very successful.

THE DREAMS OF A NEUROTIC PATIENT

In November 1967, clinical psychologist C. Scott Moss sent Hall 58 dream reports from a 28-year-old married man who was in psychotherapy with Moss. Moss (1970: Chap. 3) has provided an account of how the patient analyzed four of these dream narratives while under hypnosis. Knowing only that the dreamer was a male and in therapy, Hall did a quantitative content analysis of the dreams. Hall then rated the patient on 42 brief statements concerning his interests, preoccupations, and attitudes. These ratings were then compared with independent ratings by Moss on the same 42 items. The first unusual feature of this man's dreams is similar to what was found for Norman in the previous section: a low number of friends and acquaintances. The characters in his dreams are either family members or strangers. We are therefore reinforced in our hypothesis that the friends percent may be a useful indicator in predicting psychopathology.

The dreamer is high in aggression with all classes of characters, including females, and low in friendliness with all classes of characters, again including females. He therefore has an atypical A/F square in several ways, but low friendliness with females may be significant in distinguishing males with mental health problems, as will be seen later in the chapter in a study of hospitalized male psychiatric patients. Table 8.6 presents these results.

The problems shown in Table 8.6 are also reflected in his aggression/ friendliness percent (all aggressions divided by aggressions plus friendliness): he is 81, whereas the norms are 62 (h = .43). There are, however, three pieces of better news in the areas of aggression and friendliness:

1. He is not high on the physical aggression percent; thus, he is an angry man, but probably not a physically violent one.
2. His victimization percent is low, which means there is an assertive component to his anger.
3. He has a normal rate of befriending others in the few instances of friendly interactions.

The dreamer has his share of misfortunes, but he is not above the norms on misfortune percent; this is a positive sign for him. The dreamer fails in 9 of 15 strivings, which is slightly above the norms, but with an N too small for statistical significance (60% versus 50%). Here the counterbalancing feature is that he is striving so often. Finally, this man's negative emotions percent is 97, as opposed to the normative percentage of 80 (h = .58). There is only one instance of happiness in 58 dream reports.

Table 8.6. Aggression and Friendliness (A/F Square)[a]

	A/C index	F/C index
Male characters	37 (28)	7 (17)
Female characters	25 (17)	11 (29)

[a]Male norms in parentheses.
h = .19 on aggressions with males
h = .46 on friendliness with females

Hall interpreted these numbers to mean that the patient sees himself as an aggressive, angry person in a hostile and unfriendly world. He sees himself as ineffectual, and he is anxious and unhappy. His strengths are that he is not a victim of aggression and not merely a recipient of friendliness. He fails, but at least he tries. Here we would add one other finding not yet mentioned: he is high on active activities in his dream reports.

To put these and other quantitative findings into a form that could be compared with Moss's clinical observations, Hall then developed 42 brief statements and rated the dreamer as high, medium, or low on each of them. He then asked Moss to make the same ratings. Hall and Moss agreed exactly in 28 of their 42 ratings. They disagreed by one step in nine cases, and they disagreed completely in five instances. The odds of this level of agreement occurring by chance are less than 1 in 1,000 (.0007). From Hall's point of view, the most important items were the five where they disagreed completely. He thus wrote as follows to Moss for further information:

> In his dreams, he had many references to games and sports so I gave him a high score. You said his interest in this area was low. I said he had a low interest in travel because there were few travel references in his dreams, and you said his interest was high. You said his relations with his mother were good, and I said they were poor. Actually, he only mentions his mother once in the 58 dreams, and that is in connection with her apartment. He said, "My brother and I were trapped in my mother's apartment with a dozen women and were preparing to fight off an Indian attack." I figured that anyone who had such poor relations with women, including his wife, must also have poor relations with his mother. Could you enlighten me on this point?
>
> I said he was low on expressions of sorrow because he felt this emotion only once in his dreams. You said he was high. Finally, you said he was a very passive person and I said he wasn't. I judged lack of passivity (or high activity) on the basis of his activities in his dreams which were often strenuous and physical. Is this a case of compensation? In general, I don't feel that dreams are compensatory. An active person has active dreams, a passive person has passive dreams.

Moss replied on each of the issues Hall raised. His replies will be discussed in the following paragraphs. They show that Hall actually was right on three issues—interest in sports, lack of interest in travel, and high level of activity. Hall *may* have been wrong on the emotion of sorrow. Hall very likely *was* wrong on the man's attitude toward his mother for reasons we will discuss shortly. With this overview in mind, we turn to Moss's replies. They are important because they show that theory-based clinical "interpretations" are one thing and personal concerns are another on several issues.

Interest in Sports

Moss agrees that the man was interested in sports, but Moss did not interpret this as an "interest" because the patient was an "abysmal participant" and because he "alluded to sports or 'games of chance' as a means of reflecting how he felt about therapy or his dealings with people."

Travel

Moss agreed that the patient "had no real interest in travel per se." Moss said he rated the patient's interest in travel as high because "he did make periodic references to returning to California where he had been before he was married and used this as an escape mechanism from reality."

Passive

Moss conceded he was on "tenuous ground" in saying the patient was very passive. He agreed the patient was an active person. Moss thought of him as passive in a therapeutic sense, as the following paragraph explains:

> Finally, I did say that he was a very passive person, but here I feel I am on more tenuous ground. The patient was an active (acting out) person all his life, but he came into therapy because his coping mechanisms had failed. He was caught up in a series of self-defeating, hostile, acting out behavior and he reacted to it with an attitude of despair. I thought of him as being "passive" in the sense that he was analyzing this behavior, attempting to work toward something more advantageous. In this sense, he had despaired of trying to work through his problems using his old methods. But it is correct that he was an active person, having active dreams which for the most part reflected the reality of his life, and so I believe that we could agree that he was a high activity person.

Sorrow

Hall inferred that the patient was low on sorrow because it appeared only once in the 58 dream reports. Moss said the depth of the patient's sorrow showed up only in his reactions to the dreams, by which Moss means "guilt and remorse." Here we may see the difficulties of agreeing on what a word means in the realm of emotions. Moss writes:

> The patient's dreams almost inevitably were filled with hostile reactions, but in his interpretation and subsequent evaluation of the dreams, he was often filled with guilt and remorse, particularly in areas involving his wife. The patient throughout most of therapy developed psychosomatic symptoms which I again relate to his conflict and sorrow.

Mother

Hall made his comments on the patient's conception of his mother based on only one dream, a dream in which the patient and his brother were trapped in their mother's apartment. There is no interaction with the mother in the dream, nor any indication of her presence, but only a mention of her. Hall in effect overgeneralizes when he says, "I figured that anyone who had such poor relations with women, including his wife, must also have poor relations with his mother." Moss's reply is very convincing on this point:

> In regard to his attitude toward his mother, the patient's attitude toward both men and women left much to be desired, certainly the attitude towards his wife was fraught with hostility and ambivalence. However, the patient held a rather positive attitude toward the mother throughout therapy as far as I could determine. Early in his life, he held a somewhat fictive goal of rescuing his mother from the tyranny of his father, and throughout therapy he always spoke of the mother in protective, understanding terms.

The Patient's Case History

Moss provides some useful information on the patient's motivations and symptoms in the chapter on the hypnotic interpretation of his dreams. He came to therapy because of marital tension, general nervousness, and physical symptoms such as stomachaches. The patient, who worked as an inventory clerk, had an IQ of 121. Moss says the patient seemed psychologically naive and "exhibited minimal insight into the basis of his difficulties and a proneness to attribute them exclusively to an organic etiology" (1970:33). However, the patient "appeared genuinely motivated and was able to interact effectively despite his anxiety" (Moss, 1970:33). The patient improved considerably in the course of 48 sessions. A follow-up inquiry 10 months after therapy ended found that he was "reasonably satisfied with his marital and work situations and he had not felt the need for additional psychiatric assistance in the interim" (Moss, 1970:56).

The patient had been hospitalized 11 years earlier when he made a "suicidal gesture" while in the military overseas (Moss, 1970:32). He became depressed and received a medical discharge. In an autobiographical sketch he wrote shortly thereafter, he said his family upset him because of constant bickering. He said nothing he did ever pleased them. He characterized his general attitude toward people in a way that fits exactly with Hall's inferences: "I try to stay away from them, they make me sick" (Moss, 1970:32).

Moss characterizes the patient's father as a "strict disciplinarian" who was self-aggrandizing, impatient, and intolerant, and his mother as "meek, hardworking, and long-suffering" (Moss, 1970:38–39). The patient had a younger brother who was more physically robust. The brother had violent quarrels with the father and bullied the patient. The hypnotic dream sessions suggested that the patient was deeply angry with his father, brother, and wife, which fits with the dream findings on aggression. In the course of the treatment, he came to a better understanding of his relationship to his wife and "recalled with remorse the occasions when his wife had tried to communicate with him" (Moss, 1970:38). He came to realize that she couldn't express her feelings any better than he could.

In all, Moss's account of the patient's tensions and insecurities accord extremely well with Hall's quantitative findings and ratings. As with Freud, Jung, Kafka, and the child molester, there is considerable continuity between dreams and waking life. Beyond the general confirmation of the continuity hypothesis, three important points emerge from this collaboration between a quantitative content analyst and a psychotherapist.

First, Hall's incorrect inference on the patient's attitude toward his mother shows that no inferences should be made from one character class to another. Specifically, hostility toward a general category, such as women, should not be presumed to include specific significant others who are included in that category unless there is hostility toward them as well. Conversely, it would be risky to assume from hostile interactions with a mother or sister that the dreamer would have hostile interactions with all women in waking life.

Second, quantitative content analysts have to make very clear what kind of information they want from the psychotherapists after the analysis is completed. Psychotherapists will have a natural inclination to utilize their theories and to provide their interpretations if questions are not very focused, as is evidenced by Moss's reaction to questions about the dreamer's passivity and interest in sports and travel.

Third, extreme deviations from the norms on our key indicators of possible psychopathology were very accurate in this instance, and we will see further support for them in some of the studies of patient groups later in the chapter.

SAM AND TONY

The next two cases concern males who were neither famous nor in psychotherapy. They each separately happened to pick up Hall's *The Meaning of Dreams* (1953c) and then wrote him to offer their dream series for study. They are included here because everything Hall knew about them was learned through their responses to questions he formulated based on a study of each dream series. This gives us an opportunity to show that we do not have to rely on published biographical sources or the judgments of psychotherapists for our information on waking life, as we did in the previous four cases. These examples show that there are simple and objective ways to gain useful information from the dreamers themselves. By this point, there is no need to present the usual quantitative findings from the dream series. We will concentrate on the predictions that were made and confirmed.

Sam was 20 years old when he offered his series of 50 dream reports. From the quality of his letter and his willingness to answer a series of objective questions, Hall decided that he would be a useful subject even though there was nothing very unusual about his dream reports. Based on both high and low frequencies, Hall asked him to respond to what were in effect either/or or yes/no questions. The dreamer, of course, did not know the findings from the analysis of the dream series. The responses are grouped by coding categories.

Settings

Unlike the male norms, there were many more indoor than outdoor settings. Hall therefore inferred that the dreamer preferred indoor activities to outdoor ones. The dreamer was asked whether he preferred one type over the other. He replied he was almost entirely interested in indoor activities.

Objects

There were five atypical frequencies in the objects categories. Sam rarely dreamed about tools, household articles, nature, or clothes. It was inferred he would have little or no interest in craft activities, household chores, nature, or clothes. Sam replied he had no interest in any of them. On the other hand, money appeared more often than expected in the dream reports. Sam said he was very interested in money.

Characters

Because many members of Sam's family appeared in his dream reports, Hall predicted that Sam would say he felt very close to his family. It was also predicted that Sam did not have many close friends because relatively few friends were mentioned in the dream narratives. Both predictions were confirmed.

Social Interactions

Sam had more aggressive interactions with males than with females. He was not above the norms, but he was asked if he thought that males were more hostile than females. He said he believed that males were more hostile. Sam was a victim more often than he was an aggressor in his dream reports. He said that in waking life he thought he was more apt to be the victim of an attack than an initiator. There was more aggression than friendliness in his dream reports, although not unusually so, but he was asked whether people were usually friendly and helpful. He replied that he did not think people were usually friendly and helpful, which fits with his aggression/friendliness percent.

One prediction was not confirmed. Hall thought Sam would be interested in guns and other weapons in waking life because there was an above-average reference to them in the dream reports. He replied that he "hated" guns and weapons and had nothing to do with them. In this instance, it would have been useful to be able to probe further or find other sources of information. Overall, however, the findings from Sam's 50 dream reports allowed Hall to develop a fairly complete and very accurate portrait of the dreamer.

Tony, a schoolteacher in his middle 30s, kept a record of his dreams for a year. His preoccupations, interests, and behavior patterns are reflected extremely well in his dream reports. It is obvious that he is a schoolteacher because frequently he is teaching school in his dreams. He also is worried about growing old, for he dreams of his hair turning gray or falling out, and of physical incapacities and aging. Tony's dream reports show that he is very conscious of time and money and that he has an interest in doing household repairs. He acknowledged these interests. There are few attempts at success and no failures, and Tony reports that he is not ambitious and has no fear of failure. There are few aggressive interactions in his dream reports, and Tony says he is not an aggressive person.

Tony is atypical in his dream interactions in that he has more friendliness with males than with females, which corresponds with his waking feelings. Tony has sexual relations with both males and females in his dream reports, and many of these sexual contacts are with adolescents. He has dreams where he is rejected by women in favor of other men, and where he feels inadequate in sexual relations with women. When combined with the fact that there were slightly more sexual interactions with males than with females, the negative interactions with women suggest that he prefers male sexual partners.

Tony reports the following sexual history. His first sexual experience was with a boy when he was 16. His first heterosexual relation occurred a few years later when he was in the military. Then there were some casual affairs with young women and a 4-year affair with an adolescent boy. At the time he was corresponding with Hall, he was seriously involved with a woman and thought his homosexual feelings were waning. In short, there is great continuity between Tony's sexual patterns in dreams and in waking life.

In summary of this section, Sam and Tony's dream series are fairly typical in showing continuity with both waking thought and behavior. But not all cases are so straightforward, as our following discussion of Karl documents.

KARL: A DIFFICULT CASE

Karl was in his early 30s when he began keeping a record of his dreams. He provided Hall with a little over 1,000 dream reports in a 3-year period. We include the findings from his dream series because they illustrate what appears to be a lack of continuity between dreams and waking life. The large number of dream reports also makes this a useful case because they allowed Hall to focus on dream reports that repeat key content preoccupations.

Karl's parents were divorced when he was age 13. He continued to live in the family home with his mother and two brothers. Karl was a talented football player in high school and played 1 year in college on an athletic scholarship. He married when he was in his early 20s. He and his wife separated toward the end of the 3-year period when he was keeping his dream journal, and they later divorced. They had two children. Karl worked as an engineer and enjoyed running and weightlifting. He was 6'2" tall and weighed over 200 pounds. We will concentrate on three areas where there seemed to be discontinuity between Karl's dream reports and waking life:

1. His interest in football.
2. Violent aggression.
3. The frequency of sexual activity.

Karl had 65 dream reports that included athletic activity. Most of the time he was playing football again. Hall made the simple prediction that the dreamer was very interested in football. At that point, of course, Hall knew nothing about Karl's high school football successes and his college football scholarship. Karl wrote back that, yes, he used to be interested in football, but had taken no interest in the game since he quit it after his first year in college. He said he never watched games after that either.

This was a major disagreement on a simple issue, but it turned out that Karl never really gave up his interest in *playing* football, which is what he continued to do in his dreams. Later he wrote with some embarrassment that several years after he was out of college, just 5 years before he started the dream journal, he tried out for a professional football team but was not successful. He also now wrote that even at that point he would like to work out with a professional team if he had the opportunity. "Who knows," he wrote, "maybe I'm kidding myself about not liking football. Perhaps I do, but I don't want to admit it. I don't really know, but there's some sort of hang-up rooted in it."

If Karl had responded only on a yes–no objective test, Hall's inference would have been scored as incorrect. The lesson is that we should not always take an immediate "no" for an answer, but then the question becomes how to probe further without risking the possibility of suggesting or forcing the desired reply. Here the usefulness of information from others becomes apparent, but that often raises issues of confidentiality and privacy unless clear understandings have been reached with subjects.

Karl had an above-average number of violent and sadistic dream reports. In one dream, for example, he killed his father with a shot from a high-caliber rifle. In another, he saw unknown men starving and tormenting a woman they have chained to a chair. When Hall made the prediction that Karl became involved in fights occasionally and harbored angry feelings, he received a denial. Karl reported that he never engaged in fights. Moreover, he regarded himself as being a friendly, warmhearted, peaceful person.

There are two things going on here. First, Karl was actually not all that friendly to some people. Second, the inference perhaps was too general. It should have been focused on those people with whom Karl had aggressive interactions in his dream reports. Karl readily acknowledged anger toward his mother, father, and wife. His letters to Hall were full of outright hatred for his father and resentment toward his mother and wife. He quit football in his freshman year at the university partially to settle a score with his father, who derived pleasure from his son's successes on the gridiron. Karl wrote as follows about this episode:

> The sorry bastard was all set to soak up the old glory at my expense. No sooner was he all situated [his father became active in the quarterback club and was elected president of the alumni association] than I slipped out of the situation that May. It really left him high and dry, really frosted his ass. It was great, a real pleasure.

Although Karl agreed with his dream reports that he disliked his father and resented his mother and wife, it did not follow for him—and perhaps did not follow in reality—that he was an angry, violent person. This case may demonstrate the opposite type of mistake to the one made with Moss's patient. Hall used the patient's hostile interactions with various women to infer that he disliked his mother, and Hall was probably wrong. With Karl he used hostility toward mother, father, and wife to infer aggressive interactions with a wider range of people, and again perhaps was wrong. In other words, we have findings that support those theorists who argue that at least some aspects of "personality" are situation specific; only here we would call what we have seen "person-specific." In any case, the danger is one of overgeneralization from specific dream content.

Finally, Karl had many passionate sex dreams that were described in vivid and uninhibited detail. Over the 3-year period he had sexual relations in his dream reports with 38 different female characters, many of them repeatedly. Most of the dreams were about women he knew and to whom he felt attracted in waking life. He also had sexual relations with two male characters. Hall therefore inferred that Karl had an active sexual life that may have included some occasional homosexuality.

Hall was wrong again, but this time the problem was not a disagreement with Karl. We include this failed prediction because it shows clearly that sometimes the continuity is with waking thought and fantasy, not with behavior. In actuality, Karl had a miserable, constricted sexual history, adding up to frustrated fantasies and frequent masturbation. Karl did not have sexual intercourse until he was married because he considered premarital intercourse "immoral and unintelligent." From the beginning of his marriage, he did not find sexual satisfaction with his wife and became resentful toward her. He claimed she never "warmly initiated intercourse" and did not like foreplay. He thought this "coldness," as he put it, was the reason he was sometimes impotent when they did have intercourse. Karl did not have extramarital affairs, and he had only one sexual encounter with a woman in the first year or so after he and his wife separated. He never engaged in a homosexual act. Here, then, is a person whose sexual behavior was not predicted from the sexual activity in his dream reports. The continuity is with his waking sexual fantasies. His one sexual behavior was masturbation, once or twice each day.

Most of the lessons we learn from Karl's case are too obvious to summarize. There was far more continuity than seemed apparent at first, but it was masked by his blind spots, or by poor questions. Most of all, though, the findings on aggression and sexuality show that the continuity can be with waking thought only.

This finding on sexuality and aggression with Karl was not unique among the several similar blind analyses that Hall carried out by correspondence with individuals who sent him dream series. Occasionally there would be a lack of behavioral continuity for more mundane content categories, such as a woman who dreamed frequently of foreign travel, but only daydreamed about it in waking life. For the most part, however, such behavioral discontinuities as there were occurred in the areas of aggression and sexuality. In future studies, one major task should be to determine if there are elements in dream reports that will allow us to predict whether the continuity between dream content and wakefulness will be only in the area of thought and fantasy.

PERSON ONE

Person One is a male college student who wrote down 30 of his dreams the summer after he graduated from high school, then another 30 during a 6-week period in his junior year in college, and another 50 a year after his graduation. His series makes possible a consideration of both consistency and continuity. It has two atypical features that make it interesting. Adam Schneider coded it for us.

As Table 8.7 shows, there is a large amount of consistency in what Person One dreams about between the ages of 17 and 22, even though there are only 30 dream reports in each of the first two samples. This consistency is especially striking on his male/female and physical aggression percents and his F/C and A/C indexes, although the A/C index is much lower in one year

Table 8.7.   Consistency in Dream Samples
from 1990, 1993, and 1995 for Person One

	1990	1993	1995
Characters			
Animal percent	4	2	4
Male/female percent	38/62	38/62	38/62
Familiarity percent	73	50	48
Group percent	27	33	29
Friends percent	56	29	37
Social interactions			
A/C index	13	26	26
F/C index	20	21	22
S/C index	1	3	4
Aggression/friendliness percent	35	54	53
Victimization percent	71	59	48
Befriender percent	60	44	40
Physical aggression percent	33	36	23
Settings			
Indoor settings percent	34	57	56
Familiar settings percent	74	39	41
Other			
Negative emotions percent	88	83	93
Percentage of dreams with at least one			
Aggression	27	47	42
Friendliness	23	40	54
Sex	3	10	10

than in the other two. Moreover, as we see when we turn to the continuity between his dream reports and waking life, some of the inconsistencies may reflect his transition from the familiar world of his community and small high school to the more impersonal world of a large university.

Figure 8.1 presents Person One's h-profiles for the 1990 and 1995 samples. The indicators of interest to us in these two profiles are the ones that show large and consistent deviations from the norms and those that changed the most from 1990 to 1995. Because Person One is known to us, making a blind analysis impossible, we do not go beyond the most obvious findings. The most unusual finding for Person One is his very low male/female percent of 38/62 (h = .60), something we rarely see in individual male series. He reports that his father died when he was very young, and he did not have a stepfather until age 10. The vast majority of his friends are women, and his only close family members are his mother and grandmother. He does not like men as much as women and does not form close friendships with them.

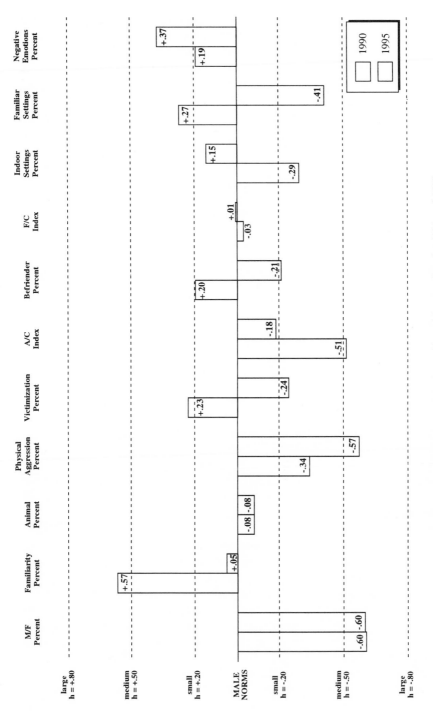

Figure 8.1. A comparison of the h-profiles of Person One for 1990 and 1995.

Person One is also unusually low on his physical aggression percent, and somewhat below the norm on his A/C index. These findings also typify Person One. He is an unaggressive person who spends most of his time with a few close friends, mostly women, and his aggressions in both his dreams and waking life involve hostile thoughts, critical comments, and rejections.

There are three differences between 1990 and 1995 that we think are comprehensible in terms of changes in Person One's waking life. His familiar characters, familiar settings, and friends percents were all high in 1990, when he was still living in his hometown and seeing his high school friends. However, all three figures were much lower in 1995, after four years at a large out-of-state university and then a move to still another large university in an urban setting. Just as there are now more unfamiliar people and settings in his life, so too, it seems, there are more of both in his dreams. Person One says that this inference is consistent with how he perceives the change in his circumstances over the five-year period. Whether that inference is correct or not, what makes Person One's dream series important for our purposes is the way in which the coding system picked up the two issues on which he is an atypical male—his strong preference for women friends and his low level of physical aggressions—with only 30 dream reports in each of the first two samples.

DREAM CONTENT IN PATIENT POPULATIONS

There have been many studies of dream content in various psychiatric populations over the past 40 years, but most of them are anecdotal in nature, use untested coding systems, or include only small numbers of subjects. The earlier studies are summarized by Kramer (1969, 1970) and Kramer and Roth (1979b), who conclude that there are only a few consistent findings, such as more family members in the dreams of depressives and more hostility, emotionality, and bizarreness in the dreams of schizophrenics. Some studies using the Hall/Van de Castle coding system since the Kramer and Roth (1979b) review was completed show more promise, but the results are inconsistent.

There are several likely reasons for why the findings on psychiatric patients have been so meager and inconsistent. There may be variation from hospital to hospital in how patients are diagnosed and classified. Patients within the same diagnostic categories may have been in different phases of their illnesses. The possible effects of medication or hospitalization on dream content are not controlled. It also may be that there are not large-scale group differences from what "normal" people dream about, as will be suggested when we consider the first psychiatric dream content study using the Hall/ Van de Castle system (Hall, 1966b).

We think at least part of the problem lies in the inadequacy of the measures utilized in previous studies, which is why we proposed a number of possible psychopathology indicators in Chapter 2. That is, there may be more differences than the older measures have been able to detect. We first summarize several suggestive findings from studies using the Hall/Van de Castle coding system, and then we suggest that the "h-profile" might be of use in future studies.

Rather than reporting on the relevant studies in a one-by-one fashion, or grouping the studies in terms of the type of patient studied, we organize the findings in terms of our psychopathology indicators, showing which psychiatric groups have been found to be atypical on a given indicator in one or more studies. Because some of the findings are contradicted in other studies, we are claiming only that the "positive" results are "suggestive."

Lack of Friends and Friendliness

There are several studies suggesting a smaller number of friends and friendly acts in the dream reports of some types of patients. In fact, a low F/C index with female characters was the major finding in Hall's (1966b) study of 211 dream reports collected from 50 male patients who were grouped into four diagnostic categories: 5 patients who were both schizophrenic and alcoholic, 20 patients who were schizophrenic, 15 patients who were alcoholics, and 10 patients with a variety of other diagnoses. The dream reports of the four groups were compared with each other and with the male norms.

The dream reports were coded for characters, social interactions, success and failure, misfortune and good fortune, and food and eating. The differences among the patient groups were few and unrevealing: dream reports from schizophrenics were shorter, and there were more food and eating elements (actually, drinking) and fewer sexual interactions in the alcoholics' dream narratives. Moreover, there were only a few differences between the patients as a group and the Hall/Van de Castle norms. For example, there was a lower male/female percent (58/42 versus 67/33, h = .19), which may be worth a look in future psychopathology studies of males. But the biggest and most interesting difference—in fact, the only other difference—concerned friendly interactions, especially with females. This is seen in the atypical aggression/friendliness percents displayed in Table 8.8. The same finding is revealed in the familiar 2 × 2 table of A/C and F/C scores with male and female characters (Table 8.9).

Low friendliness also was a striking finding in a study of female patients in Paris, France. Fifteen were schizophrenic, and 12 were other types of psychotics (Schnetzler & Carbonnel, 1976). Although these authors did not calculate an aggression/friendliness percent, we can use the figures in their Table 3 to determine that it is 62 in the schizophrenic group and 78 in the other psychotic group, as compared to 47 for their control group of 15 normal

Table 8.8.   Aggression/Friendliness Percent
with Male and Female Characters in Dream Reports
of Male Patients and Male College Students

	Patients	Norms	h
Aggression/friendliness percent with males	74	63	.24
Aggression/friendliness percent with females	66	37	.59

female subjects and 52 for the Hall/Van de Castle female norms (Schnetzler & Carbonnel, 1976:373).

A similar finding is reported in a study of female outpatients in London, England, who suffered from high anxiety states (Gentil & Lader, 1978). Twenty patients each mailed in five dream reports in stamped envelopes that the researchers provided. These dream narratives were compared with those collected from 25 female volunteers. According to the authors (1978:301), one of the "most significant" findings was the lack of friendly interactions, but the statistic used does not make it possible for us to make comparisons with our norms.

Findings in a comparison of dream reports from depressed and schizophrenic patients studied in the laboratory point to a low level of friendliness as well as a lack of friends in patient dreams (Kramer & Roth, 1973). Ten depressed patients, 5 male and 5 female, contributed 91 dream reports, and 13 schizophrenics, 11 male and 2 female, contributed 217. There were more strangers in the schizophrenics' dream reports (71%) and more family members in the depressed patients' reports, but it is striking that both groups had an extremely low friends percent, 18 for the schizophrenics and 22 for the depressives. We conjecture that a similarly low friends percent would be found in other studies reporting more relatives in depressives' dreams (e.g., Bollea et al., 1978).

Table 8.9.   A/C and F/C Indexes
for Male Patients (A/F Square)[a]

	Aggressions	Friendliness
Male characters	24 (28)	09 (17)
Female characters	19 (18)	10 (29)

[a]Norms in parentheses.
h = .24 for friendliness with male characters
h = .50 for friendliness with female characters

Aggression and Victimization

Several studies suggest that there is more aggression in the dream reports of various patient groups than in control groups or the Hall/Van de Castle norms. For example, Firth et al. (1986) found more of what they called "destructive violence" in the dream reports of violent patients. Often this finding is independent of any findings for low friendliness; that is, it is not part of an aggression/friendliness percent. Some of these studies report that patients are more often victims in their dream reports. In our terms, the patients have a very high victimization percent. In this brief review, we focus on the studies reporting high victimization percents.

The Paris study by Schnetzler and Carbonnel (1976), previously discussed in terms of low friendliness, found that psychotic patients are more likely to be victims in aggressive interactions. A study of acute depressive patients in a laboratory in Italy had similar findings (Bollea et al., 1978). The study of highly anxious women outpatients in London also found higher victimization in the patient group than in the control group (Gentil & Lader, 1978). A Canadian study reports higher victimization for male and female asthmatics than for neurotics or hypertension patients (Levitan & Winkler, 1985). This study did not use Hall/Van de Castle scales, so the several patient groups are not comparable with our norms. Stretching things a bit, perhaps we can include here Hauri's (1976) finding of more "masochism" in the dream reports of people who had come out of a reactive depression.

Patricia Carrington's (1972) excellent study of 30 female schizophrenics in a New York City hospital provides impressive evidence for a high degree of aggression and victimization in a patient population. Carrington's subjects were mostly first-admission patients in an acute phase of their illness. None had received electroshock within the previous 3 months. They ranged in age from 15 to 39, with a median age of 19. Compared to Carrington's control group, a comparable number of college women in the same age range, the schizophrenics' reports contained more aggression, especially physical aggression against the dreamers. In our terms, they were high on victimization percent and physical aggression percent.

Anger and victimization were important elements in dream reports from anorexic and bulimic women. Brink and Allan (1992) compared dream reports from 12 women with eating disorders to those of 11 normal women on a 91-item rating scale. The anorexic and bulimic dreamers had more instances of being attacked, being ineffective, hating themselves, and feeling anger.

We do not want to imply that all studies of patient groups show a higher rate of victimization. Riemann et al. (1990) did not find this to be the case in their study of depressive patients in Germany. Similarly, Barrett and Loeffler (1992) compared 20 college females classifiable as depressed by the Beck

Depression Inventory with 21 nondepressed college females and found differences suggesting that there is not much of anything in depressives' dreams: fewer dreams are reported, their length is shorter, there are fewer characters, and there is less anger. In fact, the generally mixed findings on depressives are one reason why we say that the positive studies we are reporting are merely "suggestive."

Negative Emotions

There is some suggestion in the literature of a higher negative emotions percent in patient populations. This was the case, for example, in the study by Bollea et al. (1978) of acute depressives in Italy. There is also some evidence of a decline in negative emotions in the dreams of depressed patients after 4 weeks of treatment with trimipramine (Riemann et al., 1990:97); however, these findings are *self-ratings* of dream emotions by the patients themselves, so they may reflect the general improvement in their condition, not changes in the dreams themselves.

Miscellaneous Findings

There are a few other suggestive findings in the literature relating to our hypothesized psychopathological indicators. The anxious patients in the Gentil and Lader (1978) study had more mentions of body parts, and the depressives in the Kramer and Roth (1973) study had a very low success percent. Carrington's (1972) study of 30 hospitalized female schizophrenics found more misfortunes, including misfortunes to the dreamer's body, than in the control group.

New Directions

The general findings on low friendliness, high victimization, and high negative emotions in several different patient groups make us hopeful that more differences could be found in studies using our psychopathology indicators relating to these issues: friends percent, F/C physical index aggression percent, and A/C index. As for our other indicators, they are basically untested in the literature except in the individual case studies earlier in this chapter. They thus provide us with the possibility of entirely new directions. Indexes like the physical aggression percent, the A/F square, the torso/anatomy percent, and the bodily misfortunes percent seem especially promising to us. To aid in the use of these indicators, we have put the male and female normative expectations for each of them into Table E.1 in Appendix E.

Given that none of these indicators is likely to be specific to any particular diagnostic category, a further step needs to be taken. There is potential in using the h-profile to see if there are *patterns* of deviations from the norms indicative of different types of psychopathology. For example, the patterning of the victimization percent and the physical aggression percent *might* differ in physically violent people and people who were physically abused as children. Both groups might have a high physical aggression percent, but abused people might have a higher victimization percent.

The indicators to be included on the h-profile in psychopathology studies could be determined in much the same way the MMPI was created, that is, by seeing which indicators actually differentiate "normals," neurotics, and various types of psychotics. In the short run, however, the h-profile is likely to be most useful in studying lengthy dream series from individuals, rather than groups of patients. This is because of the difficulties in securing a good, complete set of dream reports from any psychiatric population.

CONCLUSION

In all, the findings presented in this chapter are good evidence for our claim that the conceptions and concerns found in dream content appear to be the same ones operating in waking life. The waking mind and the dreaming mind seem to be basically one and the same, which is a strong argument for the idea that there is meaning in dreams.

We recognize, however, that much more research needs to be done before this conclusion can be stated with confidence. We need to demonstrate continuities in representative samples of subjects who have been shown through testing or observation to vary along behavioral dimensions corresponding to our findings on dream content. The degree of aggressiveness is the most obvious candidate here, but so is assertiveness, which can be measured with a dominance scale. We also need a wider range of case studies with long dream series where more in-depth personal information can be obtained from the subjects. In this regard it would be ideal to work with people who have written down their dreams as part of a Jungian analysis so that personal information could be obtained from their analysts as well. We also need to see if the h-profile can help us identify various types of psychopathologies, which would be all the more interesting if some patterns on the h-profiles corresponded with various psychopathology profiles on the MMPI.

Now that we have presented our findings, we can return to the issue of predictions not corroborated by the dreamer. How should we deal with Sam's denial of an interest in guns or Karl's claim that he is not an aggressive person? There are two main answers. First, we need to compile a catalog of failed predictions to see if any pattern emerges in them. Are there common issues where dreamers do not support our claims? Second, we need to develop more case studies where we can obtain corroborating testimony. For example, if a man's women friends or his Jungian analyst said he was hostile to women, thereby agreeing with the content finding, we would be less inclined to accept his denial of our inference.

The hypothetical example at the end of the previous paragraph leads to another point. We need to elaborate Hall's (1953b) claim that some people are more open to their conceptions than others. We also need to extend it to say that people may be open to *some* of their conceptions and blind to others. It is not enough, however, to put forth such a hypothesis. We must have psychological tests permitting us to predict in advance the kinds of conceptions the dreamer is likely to deny.

This chapter shows that the quantitative content analysis of dream series and dream sets can tell us something new and interesting about some aspects of people's motivation and personality. We do not claim we have said anything new about character traits or defenses in this chapter, but we do think we have shown that dreams are a good window into people's conceptions, concerns and interests. As Foulkes (1985:192) puts it from a cognitive point of view, "Because they are so little responsive to anything but what's on our mind, dreams may be one of the purest reflections we have of the structure and processes of our mind." In Hall's (1947, 1953a) terms, dreams bypass cultural and personal defenses to reveal underlying conceptions and concerns with an uncluttered clarity.

We now have reached the end of our quantitative road, at least for the time being. We hope we have shown readers how the quantitative study of dream content can be rigorous, systematic, and revealing, and that further studies using our methods and statistical conventions would be a valuable contribution to the literatures on both dreams and personality. We hope we have shown there is meaning in dreams.

Although we have reached the end of our quantitative road, we have not quite reached the end of the book. In the final chapter, we make use of our quantitative findings for two general purposes: as an anchor point for a slightly new way of thinking about dreams in general, and as a link to recent work on the content of daydreaming, reveries, thought intrusions, and similar types of relaxed waking cognition.

The Repetition Dimension
in Dreams and
Waking Cognition

INTRODUCTION

In this chapter, we put some of our findings into a larger context to suggest that there is an overlooked dimension, a repetition dimension, underlying much of our dreaming. We also connect the "unfinished business" driving the repetition dimension to similar findings on the content of our thoughts when our waking minds are drifting, wandering, or daydreaming.

The repetition dimension refers in the first instance to those aspects of dream content repeated over and over, but it also concerns the repetition of whole dreams. We have seen some of the more subtle manifestations of this dimension in earlier chapters, but here we connect the routine repetitions of dream content to the more dramatic evidence for a repetition dimension. In so doing, we draw on a wider range of dream research than quantitative content analysis: clinical, questionnaire, and thematic studies.

The repetition dimension manifests itself most obviously in traumatic dreams that reproduce overwhelmingly negative experiences again and again, to the great discomfort of the dreamers. It then moves to the recurrent dreams that puzzle or frighten many people at one time or another in their lives. It next turns to "typical" dreams, meaning dreams such as flying or appearing inappropriately dressed in public that many people report they have experienced at least once. From recurrent and typical dreams it is only a small jump to repetitive themes within long dream series, examples of which are given in the main body of the chapter. The continuum ends with the characters, interactions, activities, and objects that appear in ordinary dreams consistently over decades in long dream series, or appear more frequently in an individual's or group's dreams than might be expected on the basis of our norms for dream content.

The theoretical significance of the repetition dimension is its support for the idea that people dream about ongoing personal concerns and interests, whether pleasant or unpleasant, trivial or profound, past or future, which makes dream life similar to much of waking cognition (Klinger, 1971, 1990; Singer, 1988, 1993). In the following sections, we examine what is known about traumatic dreams, recurrent dreams, typical dreams, repeated themes, and frequent dream elements to see if a common thread emerges. Whether dreams are attempts at resolving emotional preoccupations, as many have suggested (e.g., Breger, 1967; Cartwright, 1977; Kramer, 1982), or "unintentional" revelations of what is on the dreamer's mind, as Foulkes (1985: Chap. 5, 1993a) claims, the repetition dimension suggests that dream content makes sense in terms of the dreamer's life and therefore has psychological meaning. Our argument derives primarily from Hall and Van de Castle's (1966:13–14) notion that the intensity of a preoccupation can be inferred from the frequency with which a particular dream character or dream activity appears. Generalizing this notion to include the frequency of certain types of dreams leads to a theory of dreams as expressing or reflecting emotional concerns and interests. This theory can encompass infantile wishes, societally repressed insights, worries about the future, present-day conflicts, and strong everyday interests.

At the very least, this chapter poses a new question for dream theorists. Just as no theory of cognition should be taken seriously if it cannot encompass dreaming, as the work of Antrobus (1978, 1986, 1994) and Foulkes (1985, 1993a) suggests, so too should no theory of dreams be taken seriously if it cannot deal with the repetition dimension we show to be prominent in dream content.

TRAUMATIC DREAMS

Traumatic dreams, now understood as a major symptom of posttraumatic stress disorder, are experienced by soldiers in war, people engulfed in natural catastrophes, individuals involved in terrible accidents, and women and children who have been raped or assaulted. They are notable because they tend to repeat the traumatic event in all its emotional detail and horror. People suffering from traumatic dreams often dread the thought of going to sleep.

Despite the dramatic and overwhelming nature of traumatic dreams, they have not been at the center of theoretical attention. They are often seen as atypical and peripheral. Freud's thinking may be the ideal example on this point. Although early in his work he hypothesized a role for infantile trauma in causing neuroses, traumatic dreams did not figure at all in *The Interpretation of Dreams* (1900). Instead, he came to his insights through analyzing free associations to complex and puzzling everyday dreams. Just how far traumatic dreams were from his attention can be seen in the fact that he began his theoretical argument about dreams as wish fulfillments by pointing to the most simple of dreams, namely, children's short dreams of things they longed for the day before.

In the years between 1900 and 1914, many critics suggested that certain types of dreams, such as anxiety and punishment dreams, did not fit Freud's theory. But Freud vigorously argued that there were indeed wishes underlying these seemingly non-wishful dreams. Only new material on "war neurosis" dreams that was brought to his attention during World War I led him to believe there was a type of dream that may not fit his theory. Indeed, this realization was one reason for the major changes he made in his instinct theory after the war, when he emphasized a compulsion to repeat (Freud, 1920).

Still, when it came to dream theory, Freud (1920:13) minimized war neurosis dreams by saying that "the function of dreaming, like so much else, is upset in this condition [traumatic neuroses] and diverted from its purposes." In his final formulation on dreams, he admitted that traumatic dreams did not fit his theory, but he nonetheless stuck with the old theory by saying "the exception does not overturn the rule" (Freud, 1933:29). Dreams were now defined as a disguised "attempt" at wish fulfillment, but more important, he explained traumatic dreams away by saying a more basic mechanism aimed at mastering overwhelming stimuli took control of psychic functioning in rare situations (Freud, 1920:32, 1933:29).

In a way, then, our argument begins where Freud left off the second time around, with traumatic dreams and the phenomenon of repetition. Contrary to Freud, we are saying that we should not start with the allegedly easiest of dreams, young children's short dreams, which in any case may be mere sleeptalking during arousals from NREM sleep according to Foulkes's (1982:44–47) finding of virtually no dreaming in preschool children. Instead, we should begin with the most difficult of dreams, traumatic dreams, and search for a theory encompassing them as well as wish fulfillment dreams.

The most systematic studies on traumatic dreams concern Vietnam veterans because they can be studied in large numbers due to their common experience; then, too, they also make themselves available to researchers through VA hospitals. This work makes it possible to go beyond a mere summation of a wide variety of individual instances in a search for generalizations. Research by Hartmann and his associates (1984) and by Kramer, Schoen, and Kinney (1987) discovered the following about traumatic dreams and those who suffer them. First, the combat soldiers who suffered later from traumatic dreams were younger, less educated, and more likely to be emotionally involved with a close buddy who was killed or injured as compared with nonsufferers with similar combat experiences. Those who did not have such dreams put up a wall between themselves and other people while in Vietnam; they decided very early not to become emotionally close to anyone (Hartmann, 1984:209).

Second, the dreams begin to change slightly over time as the person recovers, gradually incorporating other elements and becoming less like the exact experience. That is, the traumatic dreams slowly come to resemble ordinary dreams (Hartmann, 1984:219). Third, there seems to be a decline in traumatic dreams if they are discussed in groups with other veterans who suffer from them (Wilmer, 1982). Hartmann (1984:238–239) reports that early discussion also seems to decrease such dreams in those who suffer from other kinds of traumas as well.

Finally, those who have recovered often suffer a relapse to the old dream content when faced with new stressors. Kramer et al. (1987) provide good examples of this phenomenon for veterans dealing with marital disruption; war scenes from the past then return with all their pain and anxiety. Thus, "the Vietnam experience serves as a metaphor to express the [new] difficulties" (Kramer et al., 1987:79). At this point, we see how the study of traumatic dreams and their aftermath illuminates the general study of dreams, because dreams as an expression of our conceptions and emotional preoccupations is an important strand of dream theorizing (Antrobus, 1977; Baylor, 1981; Baylor & Deslauriers, 1985, 1986–1987; Hall, 1953a, 1953b).

We draw the following implications from the work on traumatic dreams. First, such dreams should not be put aside as exceptions of one sort or another. They are legitimate, "real" dreams, and the dreamers experience them as dreamlike. Second, these dreams deal, quite obviously, with emotional problems that have overwhelmed the person. They are about emotional events that people cannot handle or assimilate. The person's defenses are down or overwhelmed; something is able to slip by the psychological radar and wreak havoc with normal psychic functioning. Third, the dreams decrease in frequency and become altered in content to the degree that the experience is assimilated. Fourth, the way in which the experiences sometimes reappear when new problems arise suggests that the old traumas have become metaphors for new stressful situations.

Traumatic dreams, then, reflect a preoccupation with problems we have not resolved. This is a possible starting point for a theory to explain what we dream about. Before making too much of one type of dream, however, it is necessary to look at the closest relative of traumatic dreams, the recurrent dream, to see what conclusions can be drawn from studying it.

RECURRENT DREAMS

Recurrent dreams have not been studied with the depth and intensity of traumatic dreams. Most of the studies have been clinical–anecdotal in nature or based on brief surveys. However, the combined results from several studies provide the basis for generalizations and inferences about recurrent dreams (Cartwright & Romanek, 1978; Cermak, 1992; D'Andrade, 1985; LaRue, 1970; Robbins & Houshi, 1983).

Fifty to 80% of college students report on questionnaires that they have experienced a recurrent dream at one time or another in their lives (Cartwright & Romanek, 1978; Cermak, 1992; D'Andrade, 1985; Robbins & Houshi, 1983). There is great variation in the length of the period in which they occur, ranging from a few months to decades. There also is great variation in the frequency with which the dream appears within that time period—from once or twice a week to once or twice a year (D'Andrade, 1985).

Recurrent dreams most often begin in childhood. Adolescence is also a frequent time of onset, with only a few beginning in adulthood (D'Andrade, 1985; Robbins & Houshi, 1983). The affective tone of recurrent dreams is negative in at least 60% to 70% of the cases, making them reminiscent of traumatic dreams (Cartwright & Romanek, 1978). Two content analyses find that recurrent dreams are much more likely than ordinary dreams to contain only the dreamer (D'Andrade, 1985; LaRue, 1970). The most frequent content theme of recurrent dreams is being attacked or chased, accounting for 43% of recurrent dreams in one study:

> A content analysis of the recurrent dreams that students reported revealed that only one type of dream occurred with any frequency, an anxiety dream in which the dreamer was being threatened or pursued. The threatening agents were wild animals, monsters, burglars, or nature forces such as storms, fires, or floods. The dreamer was watching, hiding, or running away. (Robbins & Houshi, 1983:263)

Recurrent dreams often begin at times of stress, such as the death of a loved one, separation from parents, or the divorce of parents. However, the content usually does not reflect the stressful situation directly. The following recurrent dream, reported by a woman in college as beginning at age 14, when she left her mother's house to live with her father and stepmother, is typical in this regard, as well as in its lack of any characters except the dreamer:

> I am asleep in my bed at home. I know I'm in bed, in my room—but I have no tangible sensations in regard to my surroundings. It is pitch black and like a vacuum. There is a vague feeling of dizziness. A large, hairy (masculine) hand reaches out and pushes me into my closet. The door cannot be opened. The hand sets the closet on fire and I suffocate and die in the heat and smoke. (LaRue, 1970:7)

There are, however, occasional recurrent dreams that deal exactly with the emotional problem facing the dreamer, as with a virgin woman who was anguished about whether or not to sleep with her boyfriend. In the dream she is making love with her boyfriend: "The dream is very active and does not involve climax, merely tension, fear and a subsequent shame and day of headaches on awakening" (LaRue, 1970:4).

Clinical studies and surveys suggest that recurrent dreams sometimes disappear when the problem is resolved (Cartwright, 1979). Systematic evidence related to this observation has been provided by Brown and Donderi (1986), who gave a battery of well-being measures to recurrent dreamers, former recurrent dreamers, and nonrecurrent dreamers. The current recurrent dreamers scored significantly lower on well-being measures than former recurrent dreamers. The investigators also found that the everyday dreams of the current recurrent dreamers contained "larger proportions of aggressive, anxious, and dysphoric dream content, relative to the other two groups" (Brown & Donderi, 1986:619).

The conclusion we draw from this work on recurrent dreams is that most of them are very similar to traumatic dreams. More exactly, we hypothesize that most of them are watered-down editions of traumatic dreams. They have their origins in some stressful situation, usually in childhood or adolescence, they are repeated, and they are mostly unpleasant. They differ from the traumatic dreams of those diagnosed with posttraumatic stress disorder because they usually are not a re-experiencing of the stressful situation. Instead, they seem to be more metaphoric in content, with wild animals, untamed nature, monsters, or scary strangers chasing, attacking, or entrapping the dreamer.

Not all recurrent dreams can be tied to obvious stressors, as in the case of traumatic dreams, which presents a problem for linking the repetition dimension with emotional preoccupation. In some instances, the stressors may be forgotten, but findings from a study (Hartmann, 1984) of an unusual type of recurrent dream suggests a new angle: what is ordinary for some people may be stressful for others. The unusual recurrent dreams to which we refer are the nightmares of the very small number of people who suffer from lifelong nightmares. These dreams and those who dream them have been studied by Hartmann (1984) through psychiatric interviews and a battery of psychological tests with 50 subjects. The subjects were the most extreme from among many who responded to a newspaper ad asking for interviews with those who suffer from frequent nightmares.

Although lifelong nightmare sufferers do not have exactly the same nightmare each time, there tends to be a thematic pattern making the nightmares very similar to recurrent dreams. As Hartmann (1984:61) notes, "Some of the subjects described having had 'some form of this nightmare' or 'something like this' many times." Moreover, only a few themes make up most nightmares for most of the subjects. As was found with the college students who reported recurrent dreams in the aforementioned survey studies (e.g.,

D'Andrade, 1985; Robbins & Houshi, 1983), by far the most important theme is of being chased and attacked:

> Typically, a subject would recall childhood nightmares in which he or she was chased by a monster, something big, strange, and unknown. Later on, the chaser was more likely to be a large unidentified man, a group of frightening people, a gang, or a troop of Nazis. Often, the dreamer was not only chased, but attacked, or hurt in some way. Sometimes there was only a threat that something would happen and the dreamer awakened in fright. However, in many cases the dreamer was actually caught, beaten, stabbed, shot, or mutilated. (Hartmann, 1984:60)

In terms of their content, as well as in their repetition and emotional intensity, the nightmares of those who are lifelong sufferers are very similar to traumatic dreams. And yet, these people seldom recall any obvious traumas. Nor do they suffer from excessive anxiety, anger, or guilt according to personality tests and psychiatric appraisals. Instead, they are relatively normal people who work mainly as artists, teachers, and therapists; some are in graduate school. They are service-oriented people who responded to the ads because they wanted to help others by helping science.

What seemed to differentiate these people from various control groups utilized by Hartmann was their extreme sensitivity and openness from early childhood onward. They were likely to be upset by little things as children; they thought of themselves from the start as unusual, and they seemed to be exceptionally self-conscious and aware for youngsters. Hartmann concludes that these people remain especially "thin-skinned," whereas most of us are rather "thick-skinned." Hartmann makes the contrast in terms of thin and thick "boundaries" and provides many examples of how this distinction holds, whether it be in the rejection of rigid sex roles or the lack of strong psychological defenses (cf. Hartmann, 1992, for his further studies of boundaries).

These findings suggest that there is a small percentage of highly sensitive people for whom many everyday experiences are highly traumatic. Their congenital makeup and/or early life experiences have made daily life into a combat zone metaphorically comparable to what Vietnam was for average people who were not old enough or sophisticated enough to put on hard personal shells. If we conceive of the thin–thick dimension of the human personality interacting with a dimension of experience ranging from very nonthreatening to overwhelming, then we can suggest that many dreams might be reactions to traumatic experiences, even if the traumatic experience for some people is no more than interviewing with a potential employer or talking to a large group.

The findings on recurrent dreams thus seem to reinforce the idea that many dreams express our emotional preoccupations. However, a theory based on traumatic dreams and recurrent dreams is not broad enough—there are too many people who do not report having either of these types of dreams, and too many dreams are neither traumatic nor recurrent. It is therefore necessary to search for the repetition dimension in the everyday dreams of everyday dreamers.

TYPICAL DREAMS

Typical dreams, as noted at the outset of the chapter, are dreams that many people say they have experienced at least once. There have been several questionnaire studies asking people if they have ever had this or that typical dream, with a few percent saying "yes" to themes concerning "losing teeth" or "finding money" and a majority answering in the affirmative to "flying under their own power" or "falling helplessly through space" (e.g., Griffith, Miyago, & Tago, 1958; Ward, Beck, & Rascoe, 1961).

However widespread such dreams may be, it is certain that they occur infrequently. In that sense they are atypical. We had Susan Cermak search through 983 dream reports from 2-week journals from 126 students at the University of California, Santa Cruz, in 1992. She found that virtually none of 10 common dreams occurred more than a few times even though many of the students had reported on an earlier questionnaire that they recalled having had such a dream at least once. For example, 59% of the males and 53% of the females said they recalled a dream of flying, but there were only five flying dreams in the 2-week sample, 0.5% of the total. Barrett (1991:131) reports a similarly low figure for flying dreams from a study of 1,910 dream reports at the University of North Carolina, Chapel Hill; 17 subjects reported 22 flying dreams, 1.2% of the total dream report sample. Our figures for several other typical dreams were even lower. Only one person reported a falling dream in the 2-week period. One lost his teeth, two found money, two became lost, and two were taking an examination. Therefore, typical dreams are not very important in terms of the general dream life in the American population. They may, however, be useful in finding meaning in dreams precisely because there is a great deal of commonality in some very unrealistic dream content. This commonality across individuals earns these dreams a place on the repetition dimension.

In this section, we report on work on typical dreams by ourselves and others that we think answers some questions about dreams or has potential for further development. Some of this work deals with types of dreams not usually included on lists of typical dreams, namely, dreams of recently deceased loved ones and dreams of weddings. The dreams about recently deceased loved ones are of special interest because they seem to have a developmental sequence, and the dreams of weddings may be of theoretical significance because they are one of the few dreams of any kind that are experienced primarily by one gender. We also focus on two of the most frequent of typical dreams, inappropriate dress dreams and flying dreams.

Dreams of being inappropriately clad usually are accompanied by a feeling of embarrassment. Flying dreams, on the other hand, are the most typically pleasant of people's dreams.

We begin this section with Barrett's (1992) research on dreams about deceased people because it is more complete than our studies and provides a model for future work. We then turn to our tentative findings on dreams of weddings, inappropriate dress, and flying.

Dreams of Deceased Loved Ones

Dreams of deceased people are dreams in which the dreamer knows that she or he is interacting with a person who is dead. Dreams of a dead person concerning a time from before the person's death do not qualify. The dreamer has to be aware that the person has in effect come back from the dead.

Our most systematic knowledge concerning such dreams comes from a study by Barrett (1992). Although her general focus was on how any deceased person is depicted in dream reports, it turned out that most such dreams concerned deceased people who can be described as loved ones. Dreams about a deceased loved one are only a small percentage of all dream reports, but they often occur in the months or years after a loved one dies and have a similar enough content to be considered "typical" dreams. Moreover, some of the subjects report that these dreams occur more than once, making them "recurrent" dreams as well as "typical" ones. In addition, there are certain changes in the content of these dreams that make them of considerable theoretical interest.

Barrett's study of this type of dream is based on two sources. First, she went through 149 dream diaries kept by 58 male and 91 female students in courses at the University of North Carolina, Chapel Hill, for time periods ranging from 2 to 6 weeks. Second, she distributed a questionnaire to 96 students (39 male, 57 female), asking for any such dreams they recalled from the past. The study of the large sample from dream diaries yielded only 29 reports with any deceased characters in them, or about 2% of the total dream sample. These reports came from 18 students, or 12% of the sample. Moreover, 11 of these 29 reports were in the dream diaries of three women whose friend had committed suicide during the time their diaries were being kept. Thirty-nine percent of the people who filled out the survey questionnaire reported that they had had one or more such dreams. They turned in a total of 48 dream reports. In all, then, Barrett had a total of 77 reports to work with from the two different samples.

Barrett found she could classify the dream reports into four categories. Only seven of the reports seemed to fit into two or more categories. We will now discuss all four categories and their content characteristics, but the first three of them are of theoretical interest to us.

The first category contained dreams in which the dreamer was amazed or upset to see the deceased loved one alive. These "back-to-life" dreams made up 39% of the 77 dreams of the dead. They tended to occur within a few days or months of the loved one's death. They often contained a mixture of intense positive and negative emotions, involving the denial of death often found in early stages of grieving. All of the dream reports from the three women who were keeping a dream diary at the time of their friend's suicide were of this type. Here is an example of such a dream:

> I have a recurring dream that my grandmother calls me at my house while my mother, sister, and I are preparing dinner. I answer the phone and she says "Hi, it's me." I said, "Hi Grandma." She asks, "How are you?" Then I want my mother to talk to her and she says "No, I called you." When my mother comes to the phone, my grandmother hangs up. My mother replies, "Stop saying it's Grandma, she's not there." Another recurring dream I have is that my grandmother visits me in a hotel. I say, "Oh, you've come back to me," and she says "Yes, we are going to try it again and see if I live this time." Suddenly she collapses on the bathroom floor. I try to revive her, but I can't. I am panic-stricken and scream, "You can't die, I have to do this right this time."

The second category contained dreams in which the deceased person was giving the dreamer advice. The topics ranged from the trivial to the important and highly personal. These "advice" dreams, as Barrett called them, made up 23% of the sample. They tended to occur many months to years after the person had died. Their emotional tone was usually pleasant. Here is an example of such a dream report:

> My father died nine years ago but I often dream that he returns, especially at times of stress in my life. He looks older than he ever got to be in real life and very wise looking. I tell him problems I am having and sometimes he just listens and I feel better but usually he gives me advice, sometimes very clear, sometimes garbled. In the instances where it is clear, it is always good advice but things I already know I should do. But just seeing him and hearing it from him makes me feel better.

The third category consisted of "leave-taking" or "resolution" dreams. In these dream reports, the loved one explained the circumstances of his or her death, or assured the dreamer that everything had worked out for the best. These dreams made up about 29% of the sample. They occurred anywhere from several months to many years after the loved one died. In a dream series, these dreams almost always occurred after back-to-life dreams (category one) and usually after advice dreams (category two). The feeling tone of these dreams was extremely positive. They often brought great relief to the dreamer and helped to resolve guilt in waking life. Here are two moving examples of this type. The first one comes from the same woman who had the recurring dream quoted earlier in which her grandmother collapses and the dreamer can't revive her:

I had a lucid dream [i.e., she was aware she was dreaming during the dream] about my grandmother that was probably the best dream I have ever had. In this dream I was little, about 5 or 6 years old, and I was in the bathroom at my grandmother's house. She was giving me a bath in this big claw-footed tub. The old steam radiator was turned on, making it very cozy. I knew that I was dreaming and that I was getting to see my grandmother well again. After the bath, she lifted me out onto the spiral cotton rug and dried me with a blue towel. When that was done she said she had to leave now; this seemed to mean for heaven. I said, "Good-bye, Grandma. I love you." She said, "I love you too Mary." I woke up feeling wonderful. She had been delirious in the last few months of her life, so I'd never really gotten to say good-bye.

The second dreamer resolved her guilt about not having seen her grandmother shortly before the grandmother's death:

After my grandmother died, I felt terrible because I had visited her when she was in the hospital but I never went to see her in the hospice. I thought she would be coming home; she died suddenly just when we thought things were getting better. The first thing I thought of when I was told of her death was that I didn't get to say good-bye or tell her that I loved her. For two months after her death I was tormented by guilt and anger over not saying how I felt to her. However, one night I dreamed that I was awakened by a phone ringing in the hallway upstairs in my house. I got up out of bed and went to answer the phone. As I picked up the phone, the dark hallway I was standing in became fully illuminated. I said, "Hello," and my grandmother's voice said, "Hello, Sally, this is Grandma." I said, "Hi, how are you?" We spoke for about 10 minutes until we were ready to hang up (I can't recall what we spoke about). Finally, my grandmother said she had to go. I said, OK Gram, take care, I love you." She said "I love you too, good-bye." I said "good-bye." As I hung up the phone, the illuminated hallway became dark again. I walked back to bed and fell asleep. When I awoke (for real this time) the next morning, and ever since then, I have been at peace with my grandmother's death.

Barrett's fourth category contained dreams in which the nature of death was discussed with a deceased person. The deceased person may have been a distant relative or friend, or more generally someone who was not emotionally close to the dreamer. If a deceased loved one was involved, the dream was likely to have occurred many years after the person died. These dreams sometimes seemed philosophic in content, a contemplation of the mysteries of death or the possibilities of immortality. They seemed to express the dreamer's concerns about his or her own mortality. Some were pleasant; some were not. They made up about 18% of Barrett's sample.

One striking contingency of these "philosophic" death dreams is the frequent utilization of a telephone as the medium of interaction with the deceased person. Fifty-three percent of the dreams in this category involved telephone calls from the deceased person. By comparison, telephone calls appeared in 24% of the dreams in the other three categories, and in only 3% of a random sample of 300 dream reports in Barrett's University of North

Carolina dream collection. In short, Barrett's analysis suggests that the telephone may be a metaphoric way of expressing abstract communication in American culture. Here are two examples of these philosophic dreams, both with telephones in them:

> I had a lucid dream that the phone rang and it was my deceased mother. I knew it was a dream but I thought it was really her and that she could contact me in the dream state. I was frightened to talk to her but I didn't want to let that show and hurt her feelings, so I tried to act cheerful and make banal conversation. I said "Hi, how are you?" She said, "I'm pregnant." I thought she must have gone insane and think she's alive and young again, but to humor her I asked, "Are you going to have a boy or a girl?" She said, "I am going to be a girl." I felt more and more uncomfortable and said, "I've got to go now; I'll talk to you later," and hung up. As soon as I woke up, the dream sounded like a reincarnation statement but during the dream it just sounded crazy and threatening somehow.

> This dream was really strange. I was talking on the phone to a man who was describing a wonderful place where he was. The man was very familiar. I was told by another person (or perhaps it was a thought) that I was talking to Pa (my boyfriend's dad, who just died). I saw his face in a phone booth floating among the clouds. There were angels flying around too. Three angels. When I asked if this was Pa, he said, "No, Pa died, how could you talk to him?" But Pa's image and voice were the ones that told me that.

The changing nature of the themes in dreams about deceased loved ones is especially significant in terms of our claim that the repetition dimension reveals the way in which dreams express emotional preoccupation. Not only do dreams of deceased loved ones show that many different individuals "repeat" the same type of dream in reaction to the loss of a loved one, but the changes in the content of these dreams seem to reveal the underlying psychological processes following from the loss. We are a long way from saying the dreams themselves "resolve" grief, but the bereavement dreams reported by Barrett do seem to reflect where the dreamers are in the grieving process.

Wedding Dreams

In the process of reading through the dream series he collected at Case Western Reserve University, Hall (1953c:134–135) noticed that some students occasionally dream of getting married and that more of these students are women than men. Moreover, things often seemed to go wrong in the women's wedding dreams—wrong groom, wrong bridal gown, wrong church, or the groom doesn't show up. Note that we say "often." Some wedding dreams are positive for women. Twenty-five years later, Garfield (1988:134–142) reported similar observations on wedding dreams.

A type of dream frequent in one gender and relatively rare in the other might help us to understand meaning in dreams, especially if that dream has frequencies in some Hall/Van de Castle content categories significantly different from the norms. Using a questionnaire for collecting past dreams, we found a considerable gender difference in the frequency of memory for wedding dreams in two different samples of college students at the University of California, Santa Cruz. Those results are displayed in Table 9.1.

If we next ask what percentage of these dreams have "negative" elements in them, meaning misfortunes, aggressions, failures, and negative emotions, we find that negative dreams are more likely for the women than for the men, but the men's sample is too small to be conclusive. A closer look at the women's negative wedding dreams shows that the negative element is usually a misfortune, and these misfortunes are much more likely in dream reports where the groom turns out to be a stranger. (The fact that the groom is a stranger, a surprise in itself for such a momentous occasion, is not counted as a misfortune.) We also learned that some women have this type of dream several times. Our questionnaire also showed that the frequency of this dream is not related to whether the dreamer has a boyfriend or is about to be married.

If dreams express concerns and conceptions, what can we learn from wedding dreams? Can we find evidence that women in general are more preoccupied than men with weddings? Do men and women have different conceptions of weddings? We do not know the answers to these questions, but we think they are useful to ask. We also think that studies comparing women who have frequent, few, or no wedding dreams would be informative about meaning in dreams.

Inappropriate Dress Dreams

Dreams of being inappropriately dressed in public are of interest to us because they usually are accompanied by a feeling of extreme embarrassment. We therefore approach this dream by asking people to write down the dream in which they felt the greatest embarrassment during the dream itself. The reports we receive almost invariably concern the theme of inappropriate dress in public. By starting with the issue of embarrassment, this type of typical dream becomes of interest as a possible metaphoric expression of an emotion experienced by most people at one time or another.

We find that 40% to 50% of both males and females think they have had such a dream, usually in their mid-teens, and sometimes recurring. Most of

Table 9.1. Frequency
of Wedding Dreams

	Males	Females
1991 sample	6/30 (20%)	20/44 (45%)
1992 sample	1/37 (3%)	27/88 (31%)

these dreams involved inappropriate dress rather than a complete lack of clothing, and the most frequent setting was the person's school. The fact that there was no gender difference should not go unremarked, of course. Content analysts do not always find gender differences.

To our mild surprise, the content of these embarrassing dream reports is more varied than we expected. Even though most of the reports involve being nude or partially nude or being at school in pajamas, there are nonetheless some where the person only has the wrong clothes or shoes for the occasion, or only lacks shoes, and yet the same feeling of embarrassment and mortification is present for the dreamer. The hypothesis thus arises that these dreams express concern with social roles, conformity, and acceptance by peers. Nudity may be the most dramatic metaphoric statement of the issue, and males are a little more likely to be completely naked, but nudity does not seem to be the main concern. That is, "inappropriateness" may be the concern.

If we can appeal to the waking mind for a moment for guidance, we know that social embarrassment can be expressed with such metaphors as "caught naked" or "caught with your pants down." They are instances of the more general conceptual metaphor called "embarrassment is exposure," as developed in an interview study on embarrassment in American subjects by Holland and Kipnis (1994:320–321). The famous story of the Emperor's New Clothes also is relevant here because it concerns social roles and conformity. The little boy who couldn't see the alleged new suit of clothes was not yet properly socialized into the role conformity of being a dutiful subject to the king.

Rather than speculate on the basis of waking metaphors, we need to do further studies with this simple dream that can be collected in abundance. We need to find out more about feelings and events on the day of its occurrence, or about forthcoming events of concern to the dreamer. We need to make a concerted effort to understand the range of events (are they in relation to social roles?) that might be triggering this dream. We need to find dream series in which inappropriate dress dreams are frequent so that we can compare them with other dreams in the series. Most of all, we need to see if there is a correlation between the occurrence and frequency of these dreams and such individual differences as (1) frequency of feeling embarrassed in waking life; (2) shyness; (3) nervousness in new social roles; and (4) concern with peer acceptance. In short, this single typical dream may be ideal for a number of reasons in developing an understanding of the repetition dimension in dreams.

Flying Dreams

We conclude this section with one of the few dreams of any type, typical or individual, that is primarily positive in emotional content. We refer to dreams of flying, soaring, gliding, and floating above the earth without the aid of airplanes, balloons, gliders, or any other of the devices that are required for human beings to fly. On our questionnaire, we have included a question on flying dreams and their emotional tone (pleasurable, unpleasurable, or both) because they have the potential for being linked to waking metaphors based on the experience of flying.

Three-fourths of the men and 55% of the women in our first Santa Cruz sample and 59% of the men and 53% of the women in the second sample reported experiencing a dream where they were flying under their own power. Most of these dream experiences were judged to be highly positive, although some of the positive feelings sometimes turned into apprehension later in the dream.

In pleasurable flying dreams, people report that they merely flapped their arms and went straight up like a helicopter, or put their arms in front of them and took off like superman, or just suddenly found themselves floating along looking down at the ground. Such dream experiences may be based in the conceptual metaphor that "happy is up" (Lakoff, 1987; Lakoff & Johnson, 1980). This metaphor allows people to express their pleasure by saying they are "up," "high," "flying," "high as a kite," "walking on air," "floating on air," or "on top of the world." The fact that pleasurable flying dreams can contain an edge of concern, or turn apprehensive, does not contradict this metaphoric theory. People often express fear that positive feeling states will come to an end with comments about "crashing" or "coming down."

Conclusion on Typical Dreams

Typical dreams, if they are considered within the context of the repetition dimension, may be of greater theoretical interest than has been realized in the past. They may reveal the expression of emotional preoccupations, both negative and positive, common to everyone at one time or another (e.g., grief, embarrassment, elation). However, the study of such dreams as a window into the repetition dimension is clearly at a very early stage. The results are suggestive and encouraging, but much more work would have to be done before typical dreams could have the same standing on the repetition dimension as the other points along it.

REPETITIVE DREAM THEMES

Clinical researchers, especially Jungians, have given us some intimations of the degree to which certain themes may repeat themselves in dreams. However, Hall's systematic work with lengthy dream series revealed how pervasive and consistent repeated elements and themes are in dreams. Because much of that work has been presented in earlier chapters, we will direct most of our attention here to one new dream series and to new aspects of a series already discussed. The general point is that the repetitive themes and elements found in long dream series can be seen as denatured versions of recurrent dreams, and thus as another point on the repetition dimension.

A look at the themes in Dorothea's 50-year series (see Chapter 7), a topic not previously discussed in full, provides a good starting point. Ten themes appeared with considerable regularity in Dorothea's dreams. Six appeared with basically the same frequency throughout the entire 50 years. In roughly one out of every four dreams she was eating or thinking of food. The loss of an object, usually her purse, occurred in one out of every six dreams. Dorothea was in a small or disorderly room, or her room was being invaded by others, in every 10th dream. Another 10% of her dreams involved the dreamer and her mother. She was trying to go to the toilet in 1 out of every 12 dreams, usually being interrupted in the process, and she was late, concerned about being late, or missing a bus or train in 1 out of every 16 dreams. These six themes alone account for at least part of the content in almost 75% of her dreams, which is strong support for the idea of a repetition dimension. Unfortunately, because we do not know enough about Dorothea, it is not possible to explain how all these themes might relate to stresses in her life. The important point to be drawn from her series is the sheer repetition of themes over five decades: this repetition appears to have echoes, however emotionally faint, of traumatic dreams and recurrent dreams.

One of Hall's (1982) unpublished analyses not discussed in previous chapters provides an opportunity to show how at least some of the themes discovered in a long dream series are connected to the dreamer's main preoccupations. This analysis of 449 dreams covers "only" 16 years, but the themes are unusual. The subject of this analysis, called "T" by Hall, wrote Hall the following letter in the late 1970s:

> May I say how much I enjoyed your books about dreams. I have utilized them as I sought help through psychotherapy to moderate certain character defects.
> I have reached the age where I am aware of my own mortality. I have probably two thousand dreams written down through the nights over sixteen years. Some are typed. Some are in handwriting. If you're interested in such a group of dreams, I will type them out and send them to you. (Hall, 1982:2)

Hall replied that he would like to see a few of the typed dreams before he decided whether to do anything with the series. The letter and typed dreams that came back convinced Hall he was dealing with a literate and reasonable person. In addition, the dreams were interesting because they were so unrealistic, a feature of a dream series that we have shown to be more atypical than the common image of dreams might lead one to expect.

Hall then asked for half the dreams, including the first and last 100 and ones from all other years. The dreamer, who greatly overestimated the number of dreams in his collection, sent back 449 dreams. Later he sent the remaining 514 on his own initiative (Hall, 1982:3). The analysis to be presented here was completed before the second half of the dreams arrived. Our careful reading of the remaining dreams convinced us they are no different in their thematic content from those Hall analyzed.

As Hall later learned, T was indeed to all outward appearances a normal and satisfied person. In his early 50s at the time he first contacted Hall, he was a former law enforcement official who had earned a degree in creative writing after his retirement. He was happily married after marital stress when he was in his 30s and 40s, and his two grown children were doing well. He reported that psychotherapy had helped him with his tendencies toward anxiety, anger, and depression—he no longer became so angry with authority figures, he did not become depressed, and he was a recovering alcoholic who had not had a drink in 17 years. He had stopped the womanizing of his earlier years and controlled his compulsive gambling.

His dreams, however, did not change between 1963 and 1979. The same themes are present in the first 100 dream reports as in the last 100 (Hall, 1982:64–65), and they are very different from what is found in most dream series. The five main themes for our purposes here are (1) the overbearing but seductive mother; (2) the weak but lovable father; (3) the dangerous homosexual who makes advances and must be attacked; (4) males with female characteristics and females with male characteristics; and (5) metamorphoses of all kinds and descriptions, including men into women, women into men, humans into animals, young into old, and objects into animals and people.[1]

There are 31 dreams where his mother appears and 26 with his father present. The mother is variously "depicted as being insincere, self-pitying, overbearing, cold, quarrelsome, rude, and contemptuous," and in only one dream, where she consoles T, is she presented in a positive way (Hall, 1982:14). In one dream she turns into a werewolf, and in another characteristic dream T is trying to break free as she clings to him, demanding to be kissed. Conversely, T's love for his father is demonstrated in five dreams, and in four dreams the father is helpful and concerned in regard to T. There are three dreams where the father acts as a moral authority, but five in which he is weak, passive, or inadequate, sometimes in relation to T's mother. In one dream T sucks his father's penis, and in another dream T notices that his father has no penis.

Homosexuals are extremely rare in the dreams of heterosexuals, but T has 28 dreams in which they appear. Usually they approach him and make advances toward him; he is disgusted or frightened, and he tries to repulse them, sometimes quite violently with a knife or other weapon. There are also

---

[1]The one strongly positive relationship in his dream reports is with his wife. She is quite often portrayed as supportive of him, and he is protective of her. She may be the reason why both T and the marriage survived (Hall, 1982:21–25).

11 dreams in which T is surprised or confused by women with penises, men with breasts, or men without penises. In one such dream, "a beautiful woman appeared naked with a penis. My feelings are confusion, disbelief in what I saw." T makes advances toward her, but she rejects him; he keeps asking her if she has a penis. Then, "she shows it to me growing out of her left breast. She described how she made it by pushing a small stick or object into her breast. It is like the hard penis of an eight or ten-year-old boy" (Hall, 1982:34–35).

There are 73 metamorphoses in T's dreams, and they are far more varied and far less benign than those found in Ovid's *Metamorphoses*. Of the most relevance to this brief summary of the study are the 12 dreams where a man changes into a woman, or vice versa. In 2 of these 12, it is T himself who makes the change. Sometimes there is an age change as well as a gender change, as when an enemy soldier changes into a 15-year-old girl or a 10-year-old girl changes into T (Hall, 1982:39–40).

Taken as a whole, the unusual themes in this dream series suggested to Hall that T was plagued by three emotionally troubling questions: Am I male or female? Am I heterosexual or homosexual? Am I an adult or a child? (Hall, 1982:41). T's conception of his mother as overbearing in contrast to his father as passive may have been one cause of these questions. When Hall presented his inferences to T, he readily agreed with the characterizations of his mother and father. He also said he had struggled to become an adult. However, he said that he never doubted his maleness, nor did he have any concerns over whether he was homosexual. He did not recall any experiences of homosexual advances toward him. Thus, the recurring themes in this series must remain in part a mystery to us.

Much work of great potential remains to be done with themes in long dream series. For now, though, the findings on T, and on Dorothea and Jason in Chapter 7, provide the basis for a tentative conclusion: at least some themes in dreams may be residues of difficult relationships or painful experiences, thereby linking repetitive dream themes with traumatic dreams and recurrent dreams.

It is now time to consider briefly how the usual content of ordinary dreams from average dreamers might relate to the repetition dimension. That is, it is now time to add the findings presented in this book to the repetition dimension.

REPEATED DREAM ELEMENTS

Most clinical theorists, with the exception of Jung (1974) and French and Fromm (1964), tend to focus on one dream at a time, and they attempt to understand each dream in terms of material from outside of it—events of the previous day, biographical information, free associations, amplifications, or the acting out of the dream. These approaches do not lend themselves to finding that a person dreams consistently about certain themes or has higher frequencies for some dream elements than most people. Thus, most clinical theorists probably would not expect everyday dream life to be part of a repetition dimension. Too many dream reports do not seem to fit.

As this book demonstrates, however, quantitative content analysis of both series and sets of dreams shows there is a large amount of repetition in the everyday dreams of everyday people. There is repetition in the classes of characters and types of social interactions people dream about, and there are individual, age, gender, and cultural differences in relative frequencies, and hence, we can infer, in concerns and interests. For example, Kafka fits on the repetition dimension in one way, the child molester in another. Men are high in some categories, women in others. In terms of the hypothesis being considered in this chapter, quantitative consistencies and high frequencies are evidence for the repetition dimension. Quantitative findings on ordinary dreams have allowed us to link these dreams with what we know about more dramatic types of dreams from clinical, questionnaire, and qualitative studies.

In closing our argument, we emphasize that we have not said all dream content is repetitive and past-oriented. We recognize that new elements appear in dreams and that we can dream about concerns in the future. Young, unmarried women's dreams about fouled-up weddings, discussed earlier in the chapter, come to mind here, as do the anxious dreams about deformed babies and difficult labor experienced by some pregnant women (Maybruck, 1989; Stukane, 1985; Van de Castle, 1971:39–40). We have argued that the repetition dimension inplies that dreams reflect emotional concerns, but we do not preclude emotional concern with the new as well as the old, the happy as well as the sad, or the trivial as well as the profound. As we will now see, the wide range of concerns found in dream content are also found in studies of waking cognition. The repetition dimension in dreams may be one end of a longer continuum.

DREAMING AND WAKING COGNITION

There is now impressive evidence on the similarities between dreaming and waking cognition, suggesting that they lie along a continuum rather than being distinctive forms of thinking. The first evidence for this similarity is developmental. Foulkes's longitudinal and cross-sectional studies of dreaming in young children, reported in Chapter 5, show that the ability to produce a coherent and animated dream narrative parallels the development of waking cognitive capabilities. Most children under age 6 or 7 do not dream very well. They report a few static images on a minority of awakenings from REM sleep, and only gradually between ages 7 and 8 introduce action and their own selves into the process (Foulkes, 1982, 1993b).

Studies of brain-damaged patients' inability to produce visual imagery also point to this similarity. People who lose their ability to create visual imagery in waking thought also report an inability to dream, or else to produce visual imagery in their dreams (Kerr, 1993). The high quality of the many speech acts in dream reports argues for the same parallel. Sentences in dream reports are as complex and grammatically correct as in waking life, and they are appropriate to the situation in the dream. For example, bilingual subjects in laboratory studies with REM awakenings use the language appropriate for the person to whom they are talking or to the situation they are in during the dream (Meier, 1993). This implies that the brain is functioning at just as high a level in dreams as in waking.

With regard to parallels with waking cognition, several different studies report dreamlike mentation in samples of free-flowing thought. Foulkes and Scott (1973) found that 24% of sampled thoughts from 16 female college students were described as visual, dramatic, and dreamlike in a laboratory study where subjects reclined in a moderately lighted room while their wakefulness was monitored by EEG recordings. Foulkes and Fleisher (1975) then found a similar figure, 19%, in a replication study using 10 men and 10 women who were each signaled to report their thoughts 12 times in sessions of 45 to 60 minutes. In a comprehensive sampling of everyday thought in 29 undergraduates (13 men, 16 women) who were signaled randomly over a period of 7 days by means of a pager, Klinger and Cox (1987/1988:124) reported that 9% of the 1,425 thought samples were rated as involving "more than a trace" of dreamlike thought and another 16% as having "a trace" of such thought.

What about the seemingly "symbolic" nature of dreaming as opposed to waking thought? As this book has shown, much of our dream life seems to involve straightforward narratives about our lives, but to the degree it does not we can turn to literature suggesting that dream symbolism may be a form of metaphoric thinking during sleep (Hall 1953b; Lakoff, 1993; Langer, 1948). This parallel is strengthened by the fact that metaphoric and other forms of figurative thinking seem to be more extensive in waking thought than is generally recognized (e.g., Gibbs, 1994: Chap. 4). Lakoff (1987; with Johnson, 1980) has suggested a long list of "metaphors we live by," that is, ones we take for granted and often do not consciously register as metaphors. For example, we conceptualize the mind as a "container" and anger as "heated fluid in a container," so we can talk of people "blowing their stacks" or "flipping their lids." Moreover, there is evidence to show that some figurative speech has a basis in mental imagery. When people are asked about idioms such as "spilling the beans" or proverbs such as "a rolling stone gathers no moss," the great majority produce visual images containing considerable commonality (Gibbs, 1994: 163, 315–317; Gibbs & O'Brien, 1990).

The content as well as the process of spontaneous waking thought seems to have many similarities with dreaming. Summarizing a wide range of studies on children's play and imaginings between ages 4 and 12, Klinger (1971: Chap. 3) concludes that they most frequently reflect current concerns. Studies of the content of adults' daydreams with Singer and Antrobus's (1970) Imaginal Processes Inventory suggest current concerns as the primary content of this form of spontaneous waking thought (e.g., Klinger, 1990; Singer, 1988), and there is evidence of recurrent daydreams as well (Singer 1975:17ff). Further, the daydream diaries of people who filled out Klinger's Concern Dimensions Questionnaire reflect the same concerns expressed on the questionnaire. Fifty percent of the daydreams in one study, as we briefly reported in Chapter 8, contained one of the top five concerns on people's lists. Here we can add that 65% included at least one of the concerns mentioned on the questionnaire (Gold & Reilly, 1985/1986). These findings with questionnaires and diaries have been confirmed in random thought samples obtained by signaling people via pagers as they go about their everyday lives. As with dreams, the current concerns of waking life can reflect ongoing conflicts from childhood, continuing regrets about the past, newly arisen problems, or worries and rehearsals regarding the future, but we also savor more good memories in these waking samples than we do in dreams (Klinger, 1990: 18–19).

If we combine the findings on the similarities between dreaming and waking cognition on both process and content, it seems likely that we can extend the repetition dimension into waking thought. There are parallels to traumatic dreams in the waking "flashbacks" of posttraumatic stress disorder. There are recurrent and typical daydreams (Singer, 1966, 1975). There are individual styles and themes in people's daydreams (Klinger, 1990: Chap. 4), and of course there are individual differences in the frequency of different kinds of current concerns in everyday thought samples. These parallels lead to a conclusion very similar to the one drawn by Singer (1988) and Klinger (1990): emotionally arousing events in real life are the basis for concerns expressed in daydreams, random thought intrusions, and dreams. Our everyday consciousness, concludes Singer (1988:303), is full of "unfinished intentions as well as current concerns."

Having stressed the continuity of waking cognition and dreaming at an underlying level, including the possible presence of the repetition dimension in both states, we now need to remember the differences as well. Daydreams are generally more pleasant, more satisfactory in outcome, and more transparent in meaning to us, and we usually feel more in control of them as well (Klinger, 1990:16, 64; Singer, 1966). They may express the same concerns as dreams, but not as dramatically. Dreams are a very real experience for us. We seem to lose our self-reflectiveness in dreams, that is, our ability to comment on our thinking and realize it is "only" thinking. We become extremely "single-minded" in our dreams (Foulkes, 1985; Rechtschaffen, 1978). We are caught "in" them. They happen to us. They can leave us shocked, upset, or puzzled to a far greater degree than daydreams.

Not even drug-induced states or hallucinations have the same experiential qualities as dreams, despite the tendency of many theorists to think of them as linked to dreams because they feel beyond our control. Drug-induced states usually lack an ongoing narrative quality, that is, a story line, or even more, a sense of personal involvement in some continuing interaction with other people. As for hallucinations, they are overwhelmingly auditory in nature, consisting of voices that interrupt thinking, or persecutory figures who make criticisms and issue commands.

Dreams, then, are unique picture stories that we enter into at night. They are dramas that occupy our minds while we are asleep. Most preliterate peoples throughout the world believe that dreams are the real adventures of the soul as it wanders about outside the body during sleep, meeting up with other souls and various kinds of spirits. If we put aside our theories for a moment, this is not very different from the subjective sense we have when we awaken from a dream: dreams are real while they are happening. For us, though, they can serve as a direct route to our conceptions and concerns, as shown with considerable precision through the quantitative study of dream content.

Appendix A

Coding Rules for the Hall/Van de Castle System of Quantitative Dream Content Analysis

INTRODUCTION

This appendix presents the original Hall/Van de Castle coding system, complete with coding examples for each category, with only a few stylistic changes and updates (Hall & Van de Castle, 1966: Chaps. 4–12). It is included here because the book in which the coding system appeared has been out of print for many years. The examples help to maintain coding continuity with the past. No one should hesitate to return to the rules and examples when there is the slightest question about how to code an element. Few people, if any, have been able to use categories of the coding system without referring back to the coding rules. The system needs to be understood and mastered through hours of practice, but it need not be memorized.

THE CLASSIFICATION AND CODING OF CHARACTERS

Characters—people, animals, and mythical figures—are present in most dream reports, and the chief character in almost every dream is the dreamer. Because characters are usually so central to all else that appears or happens in a dream narrative, it is appropriate to start our discussion of the coding system with them.

Because the dreamer is such a constant factor in almost every dream, he or she is not listed as a character or coded among the classes of characters listed below. To include the dreamer would be redundant. It should be pointed out, however, that in subsequent sections the dreamer's emotions and interactions with other characters and with the environment are always categorized and coded. Consequently, the dreamer is given a coding symbol, which is D.

Definition of a Character

Characters, as already mentioned, consist of people, animals, or mythical figures. They are "coded" as characters, meaning they are "categorized" or "classified," when any one of the conditions set forth below can be satisfied. It should be kept in mind that the term "character" is used to refer both to an individual person or animal and to a group of such individuals. A couple or a crowd is therefore called a character. In the examples that are included to help make each coding rule more understandable, capital letters are used to indicate codable items, and italics are used for noncodable items. However, neither capitals nor italics will be used to designate the dreamer.

1. The character is described as being physically present in the dream.

Examples:

"I met a GIRLFRIEND for lunch."
"My FATHER drove me and my BROTHER to school."
"A GIRL was being chased by a GANG OF MEN."
"I saw a DEER and raised my gun to fire."
"A GIANT walked out of the woods."

2. The character is heard or seen by some form of communication, but he or she is not physically present in the dream.

Examples:

"I spoke with my WIFE on the telephone."
"LOWELL THOMAS was giving the news on the radio."
"I was watching DANNY KAYE on television."
"A telegram arrived from UNCLE FRANK."
"I saw a movie. LASSIE was in it."
"There was a picture of CHRIST on the wall."
"The painting had a LOT OF ANIMALS in it."

3. The character is mentioned in the dream report.

Examples:

"The POLICE were supposed to come."
"My FRIENDS were going to meet me at the station."

"My HUSBAND was in New York."
"VAN GOGH is my favorite painter."
"I was saving my money to buy a HORSE."
"I expected to see a GHOST in the old house."

4. A character is referred to in order to establish the ownership of an object or the relationship of the character to another character.

Examples:

"I went into my BROTHER'S room."
"My FAMILY'S car is a blue Ford."
"I was wearing my SISTER'S dress."
"I saw GRANT'S tomb."
"The BOYFRIEND of my best FRIEND came to visit me."
"MR. SMITH'S DOG began to bark."

5. A part of the character appears in the dream.

Examples:

"I just saw the legs of the BAND MEMBERS marching down the street."
"The head of DONALD DUCK was sticking out of the bag."
"I held my BOYFRIEND'S hand."

Do not code any of the following cases as characters.

1. A character is referred to in a generic sense.

Examples:

"*Everyone* has a right to happiness."
"I wonder if *people* believe in *ghosts* anymore."
"*Anyone* can do that."
"*No one* seemed to be reacting but me."
"*Dogs* are friendly *animals*."

2. A character is referred to in order to establish that it is not that character but another character.

Examples:

"I was with another BOY, not my *boyfriend*."
"It was my OLDER SISTER, not my *younger one*."
"They were OLD WOMEN, not *witches*."

3. A character is not mentioned in the dream report, but his or her presence is implied by the action that is described.

Examples:

"I heard guns being fired."
"My car was run into by another car."
"The airplane took off and suddenly burst into flames before crashing."

Classes of Characters

After the characters of a dream have been determined using the foregoing criteria, each codable character, except animal characters, is classified
under each of the four following headings:

1. Number
2. Gender
3. Identity
4. Age

The order of these headings is from the more general to the more specific,
and the coding system for characters used throughout this book always
appears in the following sequence: Number, Gender, Identity, and Age.

Number

Number refers to whether a single individual or a group of characters is
involved. There may be any number from two to a very large number in a
group, but no distinction is made in this coding system between groups of
different sizes.

1. An individual character is one who is described in the dream report as
being a separate and distinct entity. This ordinarily means that he or she is
described as doing something or being somebody or having certain characteristics that set him apart from others.

Examples:

"The CLERK showed me a pair of shoes."
"I asked my TEACHER if I could speak to my GIRLFRIEND."
"I was being chased by a WITCH riding a black HORSE."
"ONE DOG was a collie, and the OTHER DOG was a poodle."

2. A group consists of two or more individuals who are not individually
identified or distinguished.

Examples:

"I went home to visit my PARENTS."
"THREE BOYS whistled at me."
"A HERD OF BUFFALO was running across the field."
"A big CROWD gathered around the wreck."
"I was attending a meeting of the BOARD OF DIRECTORS."
"The SEVEN DWARFS marched across the stage."

The coding symbol for an individual character is 1; for a group, the
coding symbol is 2.

Animals are classified as individuals or groups, but they are not classified by Gender, Identity, or Age. (Coding symbol: 1ANI for a single animal;
2ANI for a group of animals.)

Gender

In addition to the two gender subclasses of male and female, there has to be a subclass for groups made up of both genders and a subclass for characters whose gender is not known by the dreamer or whose gender is not clearly identified in the dream report.

1. *Male* (Coding symbol: M). Classify as Male any character identified as being male, or for whom the masculine pronoun is used, or whose role is typically a male one.

Examples:

"The MAN spoke to me."
"HE was coming closer and closer and then I awoke."
"The POLICEMAN stopped me."
"The two FOOTBALL TEAMS lined up on the field."

2. *Female* (Coding symbol: F) . Classify as Female any character identified as being female, or for whom the feminine pronoun is used, or whose role is typically a female one.

Examples:

"This GIRL threw me a towel."
"My teacher gave me an angry look, and then SHE asked me to leave the room."

If a character changes gender in the course of a dream, classify the character as both Male and Female. See below under Metamorphoses for a description of such changes and how to treat them.

3. *Joint Gender Group* (Coding symbol: J). Classify a group as a Joint Gender Group when the group is described as being made up of both males and females or when the group is known by its nature to consist of both genders, or when the group is a large one so that it might be expected to include members of both genders.

Examples:

"There were both MEN AND WOMEN in the audience."
"My PARENTS asked me where I was going."
"There was a large CROWD in the street."

4. *Indefinite Gender* (Coding symbol: I). Classify as Indefinite Gender any character or small group whose gender is not identified in the dream report. Classify also as Indefinite Gender any character who is identified by occupational role alone, when that occupational role may be either a masculine or feminine one.

Examples:

"SOMEONE hurried by me."
"There were a FEW OTHER PEOPLE in the room."
"The TEACHER wrote something on the blackboard."

Identity

There are eight subclasses of identity. These subclasses are arranged below in a hierarchical order of decreasing familiarity to the dreamer. If a character can be assigned to more than one identity subclass, he or she should always be coded for the subclass indicating the greater familiarity; for example, "my family doctor" is coded as Known (subclass 3) rather than Occupational (subclass 5).

1. *Immediate family members of the dreamer.* Table A.1, containing relevant coding symbols, is inclusive.

2. *Relatives of the dreamer* (Coding symbol: R). These are characters other than immediate family members who are related to the dreamer by blood, marriage, or adoption. The list in Table A.2 is illustrative and not exhaustive.

3. *Known characters* (Coding symbol: K). If it seems clear that the dreamer is currently, or was formerly, personally acquainted with a character or the probability seems very high that the dreamer could, if requested to do so, identify by name a character in his or her dream, the character is coded as Known. If a large majority of a group consist of familiar characters, code the group as Known.

Examples:

"My ROOMMATE cut her hand."
"The BOY who lives next door came over."
"Our POSTMAN handed me a letter."
"My BOSS gave me a lot of work to do."
"My CLASSMATES were all wearing class rings."
"My FRIEND'S BOYFRIEND bought a new car."
"Some BUDDIES of my FRATERNITY BROTHER drove by the house."

4. *Prominent persons* (Coding symbol: P). Score as Prominent any character who is well known by her or his general reputation but who is not known personally by the dreamer. Fictional, dramatic, imaginary, and supernatural figures are also coded under this heading as they are usually familiar because of their reputation. (See additional coding rule 7 for the coding of fictional, dramatic, imaginary, and supernatural characters.)

Table A.1.   Immediate Family Members

Father (F)	Husband (H)	Child (C)
Mother (M)	Wife (W)	Infant or baby (I)
Parents (X)	Son (A)	Family member (Y)
Brother (B)	Daughter (D)	
Sister (T)		

Table A.2.   Relatives

Grandmother	Nephew	Stepmother
Grandfather	Niece	Foster father
Aunt	Cousin	Ex-husband
Uncle	Brother-in-law	Half-brother

Examples:

"I saw WINSTON CHURCHILL sitting at the end of the table."
"It was like I was seeing a cartoon strip with ORPHAN ANNIE in it."
"HAMLET walked out on the stage holding his sword in front of him."
"Then GOD appeared and said everything would be all right."

5. *Occupational identification* (Coding symbol: O). Any character whose occupation is designated but who is not otherwise identified by the dreamer as being more familiar is coded as Occupational. Occupation includes not only vocations and professions and other forms of gainful employment, but also avocations such as stamp collector, golfer, and hunter, as well as illegal or nonsanctioned pursuits such as gangster and prostitute. A student at any educational level who is not otherwise identified as being more familiar is coded O.

Examples:

"The WAITRESS asked me what I wanted to eat."
"The ARMY OFFICER pointed his gun at the SOLDIER."
"The JUDGE said I was guilty and sentenced me to death."
"The CHOIR sang a hymn."
"The man turned out to be a COUNTERFEITER."

6. *Ethnic, nationality, and regional identifications* (Coding symbol: E). These are characters whose race, nationality, or regional identification is designated but who are not otherwise identified as being more familiar by the dreamer.

Examples:

"I was being tortured by INDIANS."
"I dreamed I was living with a GERMAN FAMILY."
"This man who was a SOUTHERNER said he knew all about growing cotton."

7. *Strangers* (Coding symbol: S). A character is considered a stranger if the dreamer specifically indicates that the character is unknown or unfamiliar or his identity remains hidden because the character is faceless or wearing a mask. If, from the language used in the dream report, the probability seems very high that this is the first time that the dreamer has become acquainted with the character, the character is coded as a Stranger. A crowd,

unless otherwise being identified as more familiar, is coded as a group of Strangers.

Examples:

"There was a little BOY I had never seen before."
"I was being chased by some mean-looking MEN."
"I was lost in the CROWD."

8. *Uncertain identity* (Coding symbol: U). The dream report frequently does not contain sufficient information as to whether a character is known or a stranger to the dreamer. When degree of familiarity cannot be established, the character is coded as Uncertain. This coding is also used when the character is described as known in the dream but this character cannot be identified later by the dreamer when he or she is reporting the dream.

Examples:

"I was with a bunch of KIDS my age."
"SOMEONE asked me if I were going to the meeting."
"I showed this GIRL my engagement ring."
"I was mad because THEY wouldn't let me out of the cellar."
"Several BOYS asked me to dance."
"A MAN had called me while I was at the store."
"I wasn't sure that I knew HIM."
"I was with a GIRLFRIEND, but I didn't know who she was."
"This FELLOW … I knew him in the dream but I can't remember him now … took me for a ride in his car."

Age

There are four age groups. These are arranged below in order of decreasing chronological age.

1. *Adult* (Coding symbol: A). All characters are coded as Adults unless they meet the requirements for inclusion in one of the other three age groups.

2. *Teenager* (Coding symbol: T). Any character whose age is indicated as being from 13 through 17 or who from the context of the dream report appears to be an adolescent should be included in this age group. All high school students, whether of junior or senior level, are coded as Teenagers. All college students are coded as Adults. The use of such terms as "kid," "youth," "boy," or "girl" does not in itself identify a character as a teenager, since these terms are also used in referring to other age groups. The decision as to how to classify characters referred to by these terms has to depend on the context in which they are used. Friends and acquaintances of teenage dreamers are presumed to be teenagers unless otherwise stated.

3. *Child* (Coding symbol: C). Any character whose age is from 1 through

12 or who is referred to as a child is included in this age group. Any elementary school pupil is coded as a Child.

4. *Baby* (Coding symbol: B). A character who is less than 1 year old or who is referred to as an infant or baby is coded Baby, except when the word "baby" is used as a term of endearment or one of reproach for a character who is older than 1 year.

Coding the Characters

The procedure for coding characters is illustrated in this section. In actual practice, the characters in a dream report are classified and coded at the same time. The order of coding is Number, Gender, Identity, and Age. It will be recalled that italics are used below for all individuals except the dreamer who should not be coded as a character.

Examples:

"My FATHER (1MFA) and MOTHER (1FMA) were in the AUDIENCE (2JUA) when I sang one of COLE PORTER'S (1MPA) songs."

"My TEENAGE BROTHER (1MBT) got the measles, so I couldn't go out with my BOYFRIEND (1MKA)."

"My SISTER-IN-LAW (1FRA) invited me to come over and see the INFANT TWINS (2IRB) she had just adopted from *Children's* Hospital."

"Three of my CLASSMATES (2IKA) and several of my FRATERNITY BROTHERS (2MKA) were standing around at the party with a lot of older PEOPLE (2JUA)."

"I dreamed I had a date with SOPHIA LOREN (1FPA), and she told me how difficult the life of a *movie star* is."

"A parade of SOLDIERS (2MOA) marched by and ONE OF THEM (1MOA) was riding a HORSE (1ANI) and ANOTHER (1MOA) was leading a pair of HORSES (2ANI)."

"A group of my FRIENDS (2IUA) ... well, anyway I think they were my friends, but I can't be sure now ... came over to the house and said my BROTHER'S (1MBA) car had been stolen by an ORIENTAL MAN (1MEA) and that I should call the POLICE (2JOA)."

"When I finally walked past the last GUARD (1IOA) and into the PRESIDENT'S (1MPA) office, there were all these FAMOUS PEOPLE (2JPA) and they were looking at a picture of the *Washington* monument. Some MAN (1MSA) I didn't know began to slash at the picture with a knife until the White House GUARDS (2IOA) came running and took him off to jail. *No one* seemed to notice that I was there. The next thing I remember I was home with my MOTHER (1FMA) and STEPFATHER (1MRA) and they were asking me whether I wanted to be a *doctor* or *lawyer*. There was SOMEONE (1IUA) else in the room, too, and I heard some DOG (1ANI) barking outside, and that's all I can remember of that dream."

"I was in a room with TWO PEOPLE (2ISA) who were *strangers* to me and a

CHILD (1IUC) and a BABY (1IUB). The RUSSIANS (2IEA) began to break down the door, and I hid in a secret room that my GRANDFATHER (1MRA) had built for just such an emergency. The room was full of SPIDERS (2ANI) that were covered with little green ANTS (2ANI). Three BOYS (2MUA) discovered my hiding place, and *they* were going to tell on me. ONE OF THE BOYS (1MKA) turned out to be my BROTHER'S (1MBA) *friend*, and then I remember I had seen *him* around the house. *He* asked me if my *brother* had got out of the *Army* yet, and I said he might go to OTS and become an *officer*."

Metamorphoses

Sometimes, a character changes his or her sex, identity, or age in the course of the dream. It is also possible for a human being to change into an animal or vice versa. When this occurs, the character is coded in its original form and for its metamorphosis as well. The numeral 7 is the coding symbol used for the original form, and the numeral 8 is used for his changed form. These numerals precede the character's coding symbol and appear in the same number column used to indicate whether an individual (1) or group (2) character is involved. If a character dies or a dead character comes to life, this is not coded as a metamorphosis.

Examples:

"My GIRLFRIEND (7FKA) suddenly changed into my BOYFRIEND (8MKA)."
"When I turned around the DOCTOR (7MOA) had turned into my FATHER (8MFA)."
"The MAN (7MUA) grew smaller and smaller until he was a CHILD (8MUC)."
"A BEAR (7ANI) was chasing me, and then it was no longer a bear but a strange MAN (8MEA)."

Additional Coding Rules

1. A character who makes several appearances in the same dream should be coded only once in each dream.
2. If several characters are simply enumerated and the dreamer does not further describe the appearance or activities of any of these individual characters at any point in the dream, the enumerated characters are coded as a single group.

Examples:

"My *mother, father, brother,* and *sister* (2JYA) came to my graduation."
"I was being chased by a *lion,* a *tiger,* and two *snakes* (2ANI)."
"First, *one* man, then *another,* and *another* (2MUA) climbed the ladder and entered my room."

3. If some, but not all, of the members of a group are distinguished with regard to appearance or activities as individuals, code as an individual

character each of them who is so distinguished and code the remainder as a group.

Examples:

"My whole FAMILY (2JYA), all 10 of us, were sitting around talking in the living room. My FATHER (1MFA) got up to fix the fire and then started to talk to my oldest BROTHER (1MBA), who began to laugh."

"A GROUP OF FIREMEN (2MOA) marched by. ONE (1MOA) was very tall, and ONE OF THEM (1MOA) waved at me."

4. If one or more small groups are differentiated out of a large group because of their appearance or activities, code both the small groups and the large group.

Example:

"There was a big CROWD (2JUA) at the party. THREE SOLDIERS (2MOA) were fooling around and began a fight with THREE SAILORS (2MOA)."

5. If the dreamer says that a character might be either one person or another person, code for the first mentioned character unless the dreamer later resolves his or her uncertainty.

Example:

"I wasn't sure whether it was my MOTHER (1FMA) or my *wife*."

6. The numeral 3 is the coding symbol used to indicate individual dead characters; numeral 4 is the symbol for a group of dead characters. These numerals appear in place of the numerals 1 or 2, which would have been employed if the characters were not dead. The numerals 3 or 4 are not used if a character dies during the dream.

Examples:

"I cried as I saw my FATHER'S (3MFA) body in the coffin."

"There were the corpses of SEVERAL YOUNG WOMEN (4FSA) whom I didn't know."

"These STRANGERS (2ISA) were laughing when suddenly they dropped dead with a horrible look on their faces."

7. The numeral 5 is the coding symbol used to indicate a single imaginary character or one that is a fictional or dramatic portrayal; the numeral 6 is used to indicate group characters of this type. These numerals precede the character's coding symbol and appear in the same number column ordinarily used to indicate individual or group status. These numerals, therefore, appear in place of the numerals 1 or 2, which would have been employed if the characters were not imaginary.

Examples:

"I was so surprised because in my dream I was going to a dance with SUPER-MAN (5MPA)."

"She was playing the part of QUEEN VICTORIA (5FPA)."
"I dreamed I gave birth to TWINS (6IIB), but I'm not even pregnant.
    8. Very infrequently, a character cannot be identified as either human or animal, or is referred to as a creature. In either case, code it as a Creature (Scoring symbol: CZZ).

Examples:

"SOMETHING (1CZZ) was chasing me. I couldn't tell what it was."
"Then these ROBOTLIKE CREATURES (2CZZ) climbed on my bed and I was terrified."

Summary of Coding Symbols

To obtain an overall view of the various coding symbols employed for characters, Table A.3 should prove useful.

THE CLASSIFICATION AND SCORING OF SOCIAL INTERACTIONS

In treating the social interactions present in dreams, we code three classes: aggressive, friendly, and sexual interactions. Coding procedures are identical for these three classes, and the same notational system is also followed for some of the classes in the Activities classification that will be discussed in the next section. This section will deal only with social interactions.

Table A.3. Summary of Scoring Symbols for Characters

Number	Gender	Identity		Age
1: Individual	M: Male	F: Father	I: Infant	A: Adult
2: Group	F: Female	M: Mother	Y: Family member	T: Teenager
3: Individual dead	J: Joint	X: Parents	R: Relative	C: Child
4: Group dead	I: Indefinite	B: Brother	K: Known	B: Baby
5: Individual imaginary		T: Sister	P: Prominent	
6: Group imaginary		H: Husband	O: Occupational	
7: Original form		W: Wife	E: Ethnic	
8: Changed form		A: Son	S: Stranger	
		D: Daughter	U: Uncertain	
		C: Child		
		Miscellaneous		
		ANI: Animal		
		CZZ: Creature		

Aggressive Interactions

The first class of social interaction to be described is that of aggression. We code eight subclasses of aggression, which are numbered from 1 to 8. Those numbered from 1 to 4 involve various forms of nonphysical aggression. Verbal remarks constitute the most frequent form of nonphysical aggression, although on occasion, expressive behavior may be used for the same purpose. Feelings of aggression that the character experiences but that do not reach any overt level of expression are also included within this grouping. The subclasses numbered from 5 to 8 involve various forms of physical aggression. Included are those acts where a character kills, hits, chases, or robs another character.

In all the subclasses that follow, except for A1, the situations involve a *deliberate, intentional* act on the part of one character to harm or annoy some other character. The classification of Misfortunes, which will be discussed in a later section, is used to handle those situations where injury, mishap, or adversity occurs to a character through chance or environmental circumstances over which it is impossible to exert personal control.

Subclasses of Aggressions

A8: An aggressive act that results in the death of a character.

Examples:

"This dark stranger sprang at the blonde woman and HACKED HER TO PIECES with a big knife."
"I SQUASHED the bug with my foot."

A7: An aggressive act that involves an attempt to harm a character physically. The attempt may be carried out through personal assault or through use of a weapon. Threatening a character with a weapon is also included in this subclass.

Examples:

"I SLAPPED him in the face."
"These two boys were THROWING STONES at each other."
"He POINTED A GUN at me and told me to hurry up."

A6: An aggressive act that involves a character being chased, captured, confined, or physically coerced into performing some act.

Examples:

"I kept trying to run faster, but the gorilla was CATCHING UP with me."
"The little baby had been KIDNAPPED by someone."

"The police PUT the suspect IN JAIL."
"HE HELD MY WRIST AND HE PULLED ME ALONG the street with him."

A5: An aggressive act that involves the theft or destruction of possessions belonging to a character.

Examples:

"My room was all messed up, and the TV WAS MISSING."
"He SET FIRE to the farmer's barn."
"She THREW her father's spectacles INTO THE LAKE."

A4: An aggressive act in which a serious accusation or verbal threat of harm is made against a character.

Examples:

"This old lady kept SHOUTING THAT I WAS THE MAN THE POLICE WERE LOOKING FOR."
"Jim told his boss that if he didn't stop, he was GOING TO PUNCH HIM ON THE NOSE."

A3: This subclass covers all situations where there is an attempt by one character to reject, exploit, control, or verbally coerce another character. Such activity may be expressed through dismissals, demands, refusals, disobedience, or any other type of negativistic or deceitful behavior.

Examples:

"My boyfriend from back home sent me a letter saying that HE WASN'T GOING TO WRITE ME ANYMORE."
"She TURNED HER BACK on her husband and WALKED OUT OF THE ROOM."
"This fat lady INSISTED that the crying child finish all his supper."
"My roommate's parents WOULDN'T ALLOW her to go to New York."
"I found out that my brother HAD LIED ABOUT ME to my teacher."

A2: Aggression displayed through verbal or expressive activity. Included are such activities as one character yelling or swearing at another or when a character criticizes or scowls at another.

Examples:

"I could hear the couple next door ARGUING."
"My father SAID I WAS A LOUSY DRIVER."

A1: Covert feeling of hostility or anger without any overt expression of aggression.

Examples:

"I KEPT GETTING MADDER AND MADDER at him BUT NEVER SAID ANYTHING."
"I FELT LIKE SPANKING my son BUT I DIDN'T."

Terminology Employed for Aggressive Interactions

For an aggressive act to occur, one character usually initiates the activity and another character has this aggressive activity directed against him or her. The character who initiates the aggression is called the *aggressor*, and the person who is the recipient of the aggression is called the *victim*. If the victim responds with any type of counteraggression, it is called a *reciprocated aggression*. In those cases where no aggressor or victim can be clearly identified because the characters are engaging in the same aggressive activity at the same time, the interaction is called a *mutual aggression*.

As the preceding section mentions, the dreamer is not listed as a character because he or she is present in virtually every dream. The dreamer is coded (coding symbol: D) for interactions, however, because he or she is a participant in many of them. Aggressions in which the dreamer is not a participant are called *witnessed aggressions*. When a character aggresses against himself or herself, this is called a *self-directed aggression*.

Procedure for Coding Aggressive Interactions

In the examples given below, the coding symbol for the aggressor is written first. The type of aggression displayed by the aggressor is then indicated by placing the number of the appropriate subclass after the coding symbol for the aggressor. This is followed by a "sideward V" (>) pointing toward the coding symbol for the character who is the victim. Reciprocated aggressions are designated by placing the letter R after the aggressive subclass number rather than a sideward V. Mutual aggressions are indicated by an "equals" (=) sign. If more than one character is involved, either as aggressor or as victim, the coding symbols for the characters are joined by plus (+) signs. Self-directed aggressions are denoted by placing an asterisk (*) after the number of the aggressive subclass.

Examples:

"I HIT my brother with all my might on the head."

D 7 > 1MBA

"My girlfriend SAID I WAS A TIGHTWAD."

1FKA 2 > D

"This fellow and I started to TRADE PUNCHES."

D 7 = 1MUA

"This tough-looking guy started to TIE UP the policeman."

1MSA 6 > 1MOA

"The two boys ... I should judge they were about 15 ... were CALLING EACH OTHER BAD NAMES."

1MST 2 = 1MST

"As I entered my bedroom, my mother who had been sweeping the floor and my sister who had been cleaning the woodwork suddenly took all my clothes out of the closet and began THROWING ALL MY CLOTHES OUT the window."

1FMA + 1FTA 5 > D

"This sinister-looking man LUNGED AT ME with a club in his hand so I KICKED HIM in the groin."

1MSA 7 > D

D 7R 1MSA

"I CALLED HER A SIMPLETON, and she GRABBED MY BLOUSE AND TORE IT."

D 2 > 1FUA

1FUA 5R D

"She told her husband she WAS GOING TO GET A DIVORCE. Then he grabbed a gun from the drawer and KILLED HER."

1FUA 3 > 1MUA

1MUA 8R 1FUA

"I SAID that I WAS A LOUSY DANCER."

D 2*

"The old man started to SLASH HIS OWN WRISTS."

1MUA 7* 1MUA

Coding Rules

1. It is considered an aggressive act even though the aggressor may be a sanctioned agent of punishment or professionally employed for such a purpose.

Examples:

"My 9-year-old cousin Tommy was BEING SPANKED BY HIS MOTHER."

1FRA 7 > 1MRC

"The POLICEMAN CAPTURED THE ITALIAN MOB LEADER."

1MOA 6 > 1MOA

2. Criticism of a character's possessions is treated as criticism of the character himself or herself.

Examples:

"My sorority sister said that MY NEW FORMAL LOOKED VERY UNATTRACTIVE."

1FKA 2 > D

"My 16-year-old brother Jack said MY CAR SHOULD BE IN A JUNK YARD."

1MBT 2 > D

3. If the aggressor or the victim is unknown, use a Q to indicate this lack of identification.

Examples:

"The miners REFUSED to go to work."

2MOA 3 > Q

"The company FIRED me."

Q 3 > D

4. If there is a continued sequence of aggressive acts between the same aggressor and victim and these acts are identical as to the subclass of aggression involved, only one aggression is coded.

Example:

"This big sailor PUSHED the little sailor, then *began hitting* him, and after he *had knocked him down*, he began to *kick* him."

1MOA 7 > 1MOA

5. If more than one aggressive act takes place between the same aggressor and victim, code each aggression where a different subclass of aggressions occurs and indicate this linkage by placing a { mark in front of the linked aggressive interactions.

Example:

"This wild-looking fellow came out of the alley and approached my boyfriend, Sam, and me. He CALLED SAM YELLOW, then he said he WAS GOING TO CALL HIS GANG TO TAKE CARE OF SAM. We didn't say or do anything, and then he TOOK A KNIFE AND STARTED TOWARD Sam."

$$\left\{ \begin{array}{l} \text{1MSA 2 > 1MKA} \\ \text{1MSA 4 > 1MKA} \\ \text{1MSA 7 > 1MKA} \end{array} \right.$$

6. When aggressive acts are separated in time through intervening events, code each aggression even if the same subclass of aggression is involved between the same aggressor and victim.

Example:

"I RIPPED UP some of my husband's love letters from an old girlfriend that were up in the attic, but then thought about it and quit. I went downstairs and started to sew. After a while I turned on the TV but I kept thinking about the other letters, so I went back up to the attic and RIPPED UP all the rest of them."

$$D\ 5 > 1MHA$$
$$D\ 5 > 1MHA$$

7. Reciprocated aggressions are coded according to the same rules that are applied to initiated aggressions.

Friendly Interactions

The second type of social interaction that we code is friendliness. Seven subclasses of friendliness are distinguished below. These subclasses cannot be grouped as easily as the aggressive ones into physical versus nonphysical or verbal forms of expression. Again, we urge that the numbers associated with the subclasses not be treated as if they represented some measure of intensity or strength of response. The various subclasses discussed below all involve a *deliberate, purposeful* attempt on the part of one character to express friendliness toward another. This may eventuate in some pleasant outcome for the person receiving the friendliness. The classification of Good Fortunes, to be discussed in a later section, is used to handle those situations where some pleasant outcome (e.g., finding money) occurs as the result of environmental circumstances rather than as a result of personal interaction with another character.

Subclasses of Friendliness

F7: Friendliness expressed through a desire for a long-term close relationship with a character. Included in this subclass are getting married, becoming engaged, and falling in love.

Examples:

"I dreamed my boyfriend and I WERE GETTING MARRIED in this unusual-looking church."
"I was so happy because my boyfriend had just GIVEN ME A BEAUTIFUL ENGAGEMENT RING."

F6: Friendliness expressed through socially acceptable forms of physical contact. Included in this subclass are such acts as shaking hands, cuddling a baby, and dancing. Kissing and embracing are also included when they are clearly nonsexual in intent. Sexual activity is not included here but is treated later in this section as a separate interaction.

Examples:

"My son began TO PET the new puppy."
"I was so glad to see Mom that I GAVE HER A BIG KISS."
"My brother gave me A PAT ON THE SHOULDER."

F5: Friendliness expressed by taking the initiative in requesting a character to share in a pleasant social activity. Included are situations where one character requests another to accompany him or her to some event, asks for a date, or visits someone. In the latter case, friendliness is coded because visiting implies that someone is taking the initiative or an active role in furthering a relationship with another character. Simply associating with a character or jointly participating in an activity is not coded as a friendly act.

Examples:

"My roommate ASKED ME TO SPEND THE WEEKEND at her home."
"I phoned Judy to ASK FOR A DATE."
"The boy *I had a date with* and *I went bowling*."

F4: Friendliness expressed through extending assistance to a character or offering to do so. Included in this subclass are helping, protecting, and rescuing acts.

Examples:

"When we received the news, our family BEGAN TO PRAY FOR HIS RECOVERY."
"I found out where the poor child lived and TOOK HER HOME."

F3: Friendliness expressed by offering a gift or loaning a possession to a character.

Examples:

"John GAVE ME A LOVELY BLANKET for our anniversary."
"I let my brother BORROW MY CAR for the trip."

F2: This subclass covers a wide variety of expressions of friendliness that may be conveyed through either verbal or gestural means. Included are such activities as welcoming, greeting, waving hello or goodbye, introducing one person to another person, smiling at someone, phoning or writing someone for a friendly purpose, and sympathizing with or praising someone.

Examples:

"He TOOTED THE CAR HORN IN RECOGNITION as he passed me on the street."
"I CALLED my father TO TELL HIM THE GOOD NEWS."
"I COMPLIMENTED Jean on her new dress."

F1: Friendliness is felt toward a character but it is not expressed overtly.

Examples:

"I FELT SO GOOD INSIDE just to be with Tom."
"I FELT VERY SORRY when I heard what happened to Mrs. Smith."
"I THOUGHT that the new girl LOOKED VERY ATTRACTIVE."

Terminology Employed for Friendly Interactions

The initiator of a friendly act is called the *befriender*, and the recipient of a friendly act is called the *befriended*. If the befriended responds with any type of friendliness, it is called *reciprocated friendliness*. In those cases where no befriender or befriended can be clearly identified because the characters are engaging in the same friendly exchange at the same time, the interaction is called *mutual friendliness*. If the dreamer does not participate in the friendly interaction, it is called *witnessed friendliness*. When a character may express friendliness to himself or herself it is called *self-directed friendliness*.

Procedure for Coding Friendly Interactions

The procedures are exactly the same as those for coding aggressive interactions. The coding symbol for the befriender is written first, followed by the number of the appropriate subclass. Next the "sideward V" (>) appears and points toward the coding symbol for the befriended character. Reciprocated friendliness is denoted by placing the letter R after the friendly subclass number rather than a sideward V. Mutual friendliness is indicated by an "equals" (=) sign. If more than one character is involved, either as befriender or befriended, the coding symbols for the characters are joined by a plus (+) sign. Self-directed friendliness is indicated by placing an asterisk (*) after the number of the friendly subclass.

Examples:

"I noticed this little kitten meowing high in the tree. I CLIMBED UP AND BROUGHT IT DOWN."

D 4 > 1ANI

"Mother had sent some kind of CONGRATULATORY CARD to the Browns on the birth of their new son."

1FMA 2 > 2JKA

"Jim and I rushed toward each other, then STARTED TO SHAKE HANDS AND SLAP EACH OTHER ON THE BACK."

D 6 = 1MKA

"The principal came from the burning school building CARRYING a little girl. Just before he put her down, SHE GAVE HIM A BIG HUG."

1MOA 4 > 1FUC

1FUC 6R 1MOA

"My cousin ASKED ME TO GO TO THE FAIR with him, and I SAID I WOULD BE GLAD TO GO."

1MRA 5 > D

D 5R 1MRA

"I SMILED AT MYSELF IN A PLEASED WAY in the mirror."

D 2* D

Coding Rules

1. It is considered to be a friendly act even though the befriender may be acting in a societal or professional role.

Examples:

"I dreamed our house caught on fire and a FIREMAN HELPED ME CLIMB DOWN A LADDER from the second floor."

1MOA 4 > D

"The DOCTOR SET my baby's broken leg."

1IOA 4 > 1IIB

2. If a character treats another character's possessions in a friendly manner, it is coded as a friendly treatment of the character himself.

Example:

"My girlfriend ADMIRED MY NEW CAR."

1FKA 2 > D

3. If the befriender or the befriended is not specified in the dream report, use Q to indicate this lack of identification.

Examples:

"The WELCOME WAGON left some gifts for me."

Q 3 > D

"I gave the CHURCH a hundred dollars."

D 3 > Q

4. If there is a continued sequence of friendly acts between the same befriender and befriended characters and these acts involve the same subclass of friendliness, only one friendly act is coded.

Example:

"After class, she SMILED, said 'Hello,' and then began to tell the professor how much she enjoyed his lecture."

1FUA 2 > 1MOA

5. If more than one friendly act takes place between the same befriender and befriended characters, code each different subclass of friendly acts separately and indicate their linkage by placing a { mark in front of the linked interactions.

Example:

"The truck driver gave me a BIG SMILE, and then he HELPED me change the tire."

$$\begin{cases} 1 \text{ MOA } 2 > D \\ 1 \text{ MOA } 4 > D \end{cases}$$

6. When friendly acts are separated in time through intervening events, code each friendly act even if the same subclass of friendliness is involved between the same befriender and befriended characters.

Example:

"I WAVED HELLO to Sally as I walked into Grants. I bought some records, watched part of a TV show, and ate lunch at the snack bar there. As I walked out the door I saw Sally again and WAVED HELLO a second time."

D 2 > 1FKA

D 2 > 1FKA

7. Reciprocated friendliness is coded according to the same rules that are applied for initiated friendliness.

Sexual Interactions

The remaining class of social interactions is sexual. Five subclasses of sexual interaction are described below. The most frequent form of sexual expression involves some type of physical contact, although we have one subclass to handle sexual fantasies.

Subclasses of Sexual Interactions

S5: A character has or attempts to have sexual intercourse with another character.

Example:

"My girl was willing and I was just getting ready to INSERT MY PENIS when I woke up."

S4: This subclass involves the various types of nonintercourse activities often preceding intercourse. Included are handling another character's sex organs and related fondling and petting activities. Masturbation is also included in this category.

Example:

"I dreamed I looked in the window across the street and I saw this man I didn't recognize FONDLING THE NEIGHBOR LADY'S BREASTS."

S3: This subclass covers necking and "nonplatonic" kissing. Kissing as a form of greeting (e.g., between family members) is coded under friendliness.

Example:

"And then my boyfriend KISSED me long and hard."

S2: A character makes sexual overtures to or "propositions" another character.

Example:

"This good-looking woman who was a stranger to me SUGGESTED WE GO TO HER APARTMENT AND MAKE LOVE."

S1: A character has sexual thoughts or fantasies about another character.

Example:

"I IMAGINED what it would be like to SLEEP WITH Elizabeth Taylor."

Terminology Employed for Sexual Interactions

The character who takes the initiative in starting a sexual interaction is called the *initiator*; the character who is the object of the sexual interaction is called the *recipient*. If the recipient responds with any type of sexual activity, it is called *reciprocated sexuality*. When no initiator or recipient can be clearly identified, the interaction is called a *mutual* one. If the dreamer does not participate in the sexual interaction, it is called a *witnessed sexuality*. When a character indulges in solitary sexual activity, it is called *self-directed sexuality*.

Procedure for Coding Sexual Interactions

The procedure is exactly the same as that for coding the other social interactions. The coding symbol of the initiator is written first, followed by the subclass number and a   pointing toward the coding symbol for the recipient. Reciprocated sexuality is designated by placing the letter R after the sexual subclass number rather than a sideward V. Mutual sexual interactions are indicated by an equals (=) sign. If more than one character is involved, either as initiator or as recipient, the coding symbols for the characters are joined by a plus sign (+). Self-directed sexuality is denoted by placing an asterisk (*) after the number of the sexual subclass.

Coding Rules

1. It is considered a sexual act even though the initiator is acting in a professional role.

Example:

"A red-headed PROSTITUTE walked up and ASKED ME if it were worth five dollars for a little fun up in her room."

1 FOA 2 > D

2. If there is a continued sequence of sexual activities between the same initiator and recipient and these activities involve the same subclass, only one sexual activity is coded.

Example:

"I dreamed that J. R. and I were married and it was our wedding night. WE WERE MAKING LOVE and trying out different positions. First J. R. *lay on top of me*, then we had relations *lying on our side*, and then finally I got *on top of* him."

D 5 = 1MKA

3. If more than one sexual activity takes place between the same initiator and recipient, code each different subclass involved and indicate their linkage by placing a { mark in front of the linked interactions.

Example:

"I was in a hotel room with some gorgeous-looking blond wearing a flimsy nightgown. I walked over to the bed where she was and started to KISS HER. I got into bed and began to RUN MY HANDS OVER HER BODY. Just as I started to ENTER HER, I woke up and had to change my pajamas."

$$\left\{ \begin{array}{l} D\ 3 > 1FSA \\ D\ 4 > 1FSA \\ D\ 5 > 1FSA \end{array} \right.$$

4. When sexual activities are separated in time through intervening events, code each sexual activity even if the same subclass of sex is involved between the same initiator and recipient.

Example:

"My boyfriend and I WERE NECKING on my living room couch. My parents came home and we all watched TV for a while and had some coffee later. After they went upstairs to bed, we BEGAN TO NECK AGAIN."

D 3 = 1MKA

D 3 = 1MKA

5. Reciprocated sexual acts are coded according to the same rules applied to initiated sexual acts.

THE CLASSIFICATION AND CODING OF ACTIVITIES

In this section, a system of classifying what characters *do* in dreams is presented. It includes activities that may be done by a character acting alone or in conjunction with other characters as well as interactions between characters. We have already taken up some social interactions in the preceding sections. These social interactions and the interactions described in this section are not mutually exclusive. For example, a hostile act of one character hitting another, which would be coded A7 on the aggression scale, is also coded as a physical activity on the activities scale. In the same way, a friendly remark made by one character to another, which would be coded F2 on the friendliness scale, is also coded as a verbal activity on the activities scale of this section.

Eight classes of activities are included in our coding system. They are described below.

Classes of Activities

Physical

(Coding symbol: P). Any voluntary movement of the whole body or of part of the body while the character remains more or less in one place is coded as a physical activity. Physical activity in a limited spatial area is emphasized, because physical activity such as walking or running that results in the character moving into a different location is coded in the subsequent class of movement. For a physical activity to be coded, the nature of the physical activity should be clearly recognizable from the dream report. Reference to a character shopping, for example, is too vague to be coded because the description does not explain the precise activities of the character. It is possible that it might have referred primarily to visual activities, as in window shopping; or to verbal activities, as in telephone shopping or haggling with a merchant; or to movement activities, in walking from store to store; or to physical activities, in handling various objects. A rough criterion that may be employed for judging whether a physical activity should be coded is as follows: can the coder, with the information provided in the dream report, pantomime the activity successfully enough so that an observer could correctly identify the activity? If the answer is yes, a physical activity is coded. A few examples of codable physical activities are dressing, combing one's hair, brushing one's teeth, sitting down, getting up, bending, writing, picking up an object, and chopping wood.

Movement

(Coding symbol: M). When a character changes his or her physical location by self-propelled movements of his or her body, a code is given for movement. Change in location through various means of transportation is coded in the subsequent class. Walking and running are the most frequent forms of movement activity, but a number of other possibilities such as crawling, sliding, swimming, and climbing are also reported. Terms such as "entering" or "leaving" are also codable if they refer to a character voluntarily carrying out these activities under his or her own muscular power. Entering a house would be scorable as movement if it seems clear that the character walked into the house, but entering a hospital on a stretcher would not be scorable in this class. Involuntary movements such as falling, slipping, or being thrown through space are not coded as movement.

Location Change

(Coding symbol: L). Whenever a character moves in a spatial dimension and arrives at a different location through any means other than self-propelled muscular activity, a location change code is given. The change in location may occur because the character uses some means of transportation such as a car, plane, or boat, or the character may fall through space, be carried, or be dragged by someone else. Any verbs that suggest a change in location, even though they are somewhat vague as to how the change was effected, are grounds for coding a location change. A few examples of such verbs are "went," "came," "arrived," "departed," "journeyed," and "traveled." If a character suddenly finds himself or herself in a new location because there has been an abrupt shift in setting, a location change code should not be entered. For a location change code to be given, there must be an indication that the new surroundings have appeared after some intervening travel by the character, even though the means of travel have not been specified. Movement activities such as walking and running, which were described in the immediately preceding class, are not included in the location change class.

Verbal

(Coding symbol: V). Any type of vocalization, whether it be a breakfast conversational grunt, a thundering speech, a whispered affectionate term, an abusive curse, a recited poem, or a dramatic soliloquy, is coded as verbal activity. Singing is also coded as verbal activity.

Expressive Communication

(Coding symbol: E). Included in this class are those nonverbal activities associated with emotional states that are sometimes not under voluntary control. Numerically, it is a very infrequently used class. Laughing and crying are the most common forms of expressive communication, although smiling, scowling, baring one's teeth, drooling, and gasping all belong to this class.

Visual

(Coding symbol: S). All types of seeing activities are included here. Among the large number of words denoting visual activities are those such as "see," "notice," "read," "watch," "peek," "glance," "view," "inspect," and "distinguish."

Auditory

(Coding symbol: A). Whenever a character is described as being engaged in any type of hearing or listening behavior, a code for auditory activity is given.

Thinking

(Coding symbol: C). The remaining class consists of the most *covert* form of activity—thinking activity. To be coded as a thinking activity, the description should indicate that deliberate continued mental effort was involved. This thinking should possess a goal-directed or problem-solving quality. Some verbs reflecting this quality of thinking are "concentrate," "puzzle over," "contemplate," "ponder," "brood," "ruminate," "preoccupy," "engross," "study," "weigh," "speculate," "deliberate," and "think about." Attempts to decide, figure out, understand, grasp, and plan are also reflective of the kind of sustained ideation that is included in this class. Brief, transient mental activities are not coded. For example, such reports as "I think it was blue," "I remember the room was familiar," "I forgot my coat," and "I couldn't recognize him" do not convey any sense of prolonged or intentional thinking activity. Wishes, feelings, and sensations represented in such reports as "I wished I were home," "I felt sorry for him," or "I was thrilled by the view" are not included in the thinking class.

Procedure for Coding Activities

Most activities are coded as follows: If the dreamer alone engages in these activities, it will be coded as D X, where X is one of the activity codes (P, M, L, V, E, A, C, or S). If other characters, or the dreamer and other characters, engage in an activity together, the coding symbols for those characters are followed by the coding symbol for the activity class (e.g., 1MFA L). Joint activity by more than one character is indicated by a plus sign.

For two of the activity classes—physical and verbal activities—there can be interactions between two characters. In this case, the coding procedure is identical to that followed for social interactions. If a physical or verbal interaction occurs between two or more characters, the coding symbol for the character beginning the interaction is written first, followed by the letter P or

V, depending on the class involved, then a sideward V (>), and finally the coding symbol for the character toward whom the activity is directed. A character who is the recipient of a physical activity may return a physical activity to the initiator, or the recipient of a verbal activity may replay with a verbal activity to the initiator. These are called reciprocated physical or verbal activities and are coded by placing the letter R after P or V, in place of a > mark. When the physical or verbal interactions do not have a clearly defined initiator and recipient, they are called mutual interactions and are coded by placing an equal sign (=) after the P or V.

Of course, there are quite a large number of physical activities and some occasional verbal activities where only a single character is involved, or where two or more characters are engaged in a parallel physical or verbal activity at the same time. In such cases, the procedure is the same as for all other activities: list the name of the character(s), followed by P or V.

In Hall/Van de Castle's original coding scheme, activities were treated slightly differently. When the dreamer was the only character involved, the "D" was omitted. When there was no interactive P or V activity, the characters were written to the right of the activity code, separated by a comma. We have changed this convention slightly so that the data are easier to enter into a computer for further analysis; in our new system, the person(s) involved in the activity are always on the *left*.

Examples:

"I PUNCHED this guy in the stomach, and then he CONNECTED WITH AN UPPERCUT to my jaw."

D P > 1MUA

1MUA PR D

"The doctor and I HAD A LONG TALK TOGETHER about my mother's condition."

D V = 1IOA

"I SLICED A PIECE OF BREAD from the loaf on the table."

D P

"When Roger and I finally REACHED THE TOP OF THE MOUNTAIN we rested, and then HE PILED A GROUP OF ROCKS on top of each other to make a marker."

D + 1MKA M

1MKA P

"We LOOKED AT EACH OTHER for a while, and then we both SMILED."

D + 1IUA S

D + 1IUA E

Coding Rules

To be coded, an activity must be described as a current or completed activity. Do not code contemplated or anticipated activities. The latter are indicated by such terms as "would," "could," "should," and "might." An activity is indicated by the use of a verb. Because a dream report often contains a large number of verbs, the following rules are intended to serve as a guide with regard to the number of activities that should be coded.

1. A continuous sequence of similar actions performed by the same character is coded as one activity.

Examples:

"I was TALKING to my young son. I *asked* him what he did in second grade that day. When he didn't answer, I *asked* him again. Finally I *asked* in a very loud voice and he REPLIED, 'Nothing much.'"

D V > 1MAC

1MAC VR D

"The pitcher THREW the ball and the umpire YELLED, 'Ball one.' The pitcher *threw* again and the umpire called it a strike. The pitcher *threw* three more times and the count was three and two. Then the pitcher *threw* once more and the umpire *yelled*, 'Strike three.'"

1MOA P

1MOA V

2. A sequence of activities performed by the same character and belonging to the same class is coded as separate activities if different activities are involved.

Example:

"I WALKED into the bathroom, TURNED ON the light, TOOK A SHOWER, SHAVED, BRUSHED my teeth, and then COMBED my hair."

D M

D P

D P

D P

D P

D P

3. If activities belonging to the same class are separately engaged in by different characters, they are coded as separate activities.

Example:

"I was WALKING down one side of the street, and Mary was WALKING down the other side of the street."

D M

1FKA M

4. If activities belonging to the same class are jointly engaged in by different characters, they are coded as a single activity.

Example:

"Mary and I were WALKING down the street TOGETHER."

D + 1FKA M

5. If the same character engages in interactional activities with different characters, separate activities are coded.

Examples:

"I was TALKING to my mother, and then my father CAME HOME and I began TALKING to him."

D V > 1FMA

1MFA L

D V > 1MFA

"I SHOOK HANDS WITH my uncle John, then WITH my uncle Henry, and then WITH my cousin Jim."

D P = 1MRA

D P = 1MRA

D P = 1MRA

6. If intervening events occur, separate activities are coded even though they involve identical activities, identical characters, or identical interactional patterns.

Example:

"My sister and I WENT FOR A WALK in the woods. As we *turned* down one trail, we SAW two squirrels. One squirrel was RUNNING along a branch, and the other WAS CRACKING a nut. I HEARD a bluejay and CALLED to my sister to listen. We both LAUGHED at the sound. We then CONTINUED OUR WALK."

D + 1FTA M

D + 1FTA S

1ANI M

1ANI P

D A

D V > 1FTA

D + 1FTA E

D + 1FTA M

THE CLASSIFICATION AND CODING OF STRIVING: SUCCESS AND FAILURE

In dealing with the interactions and activities engaged in by characters, coding attention has been paid, so far, only to whether reciprocal acts follow some initial act. Left out has been an important consideration—does a character succeed or fail in carrying these activities through to some desired outcome? To take account of possible results, we have developed a classification for striving. Included within this classification are the two classes of Success and Failure.

In our efforts to fashion a workable striving scale, our greatest difficulty was encountered in deciding how much latitude should be allowed for the criteria governing success and failure. We eventually settled on a rather stringent and rigorous standard. First, it must be reasonably clear from the dream report that a character has formulated some definite task to accomplish or goal to achieve and sets out in a deliberate attempt to realize this ambition. If he or she is then successful in pursuing the objective to a satisfactory conclusion, a success is coded; if he or she is unsuccessful, a failure is coded. Coding examples are provided below.

Success

For a success to be coded, the character must be described as expending some energy and perseverance in pursuit of his or her goal. The objective need not be of epic significance; a successful handling of some difficulty encountered in a character's daily life is sufficient to qualify. What is important is that the character is confronted by some problem, decides to deal with it, and then works at its solution before eventually managing to succeed. Any type of magical solution would be coded as a good fortune, which will be discussed in the next section.

Examples:

"I discovered I had a flat tire, so I got my tools and began to change it. It turned out to be a rather difficult job, but I KEPT AT IT AND FINALLY MANAGED TO FIX IT."

"A man was chasing me with a gun. By running down some narrow dark alleys and climbing some high fences, I FINALLY WAS ABLE TO GET AWAY."

"The exam was a tough one but I was determined to get a good grade. I wrote as fast as I could and put down all the examples I had memorized. I FELT SURE THAT I HAD DONE WELL ON IT."

"I had asked this beautiful blond for a date earlier, but she said no. I sent her flowers, a box of candy, and a singing telegram. When I called again SHE SAID THAT SHE WOULD GO OUT WITH ME NEXT SATURDAY."

Failure

The same prerequisites described for success—willingness to deal with an existing problem and continuing efforts to master it—must also be met before failure can be coded. The difference is only in the matter of outcome. When a character is not able to achieve his or her desired goal because of personal limitations and inadequacies, a failure is coded. If a character is thwarted in the achievement efforts because of some adverse environmental intervention such as a storm or sudden illness, a misfortune is coded.

Examples:

"I wanted to board this boat and kept trying to climb the ladder, but every time I got near the top I SLIPPED BACK INTO THE OCEAN AGAIN."

"When I saw all the parts to the TV lying on the table top, I decided to repair the set. I kept trying to put the parts together but I NEVER WAS ABLE TO ASSEMBLE THEM CORRECTLY."

"My father COULDN'T FIND HIS GLASSES although he looked high and low for them all over the house."

"My sister kept trying to sell a raffle ticket to my uncle. She asked, pleaded, and begged him, but no matter what she tried, she still WASN'T ABLE TO SELL HIM ONE."

Coding Procedure for Success and Failure

The coding symbol for the type of achievement is listed first, followed by a comma. The coding symbol for success is SU; for failure it is FL. After the comma, the coding symbols for the relevant characters are recorded. Multiple characters are joined by a plus sign.

Examples:

"I wanted to hit a home run. After two consecutive strikes, I decided that it would be the next one that I would belt out of the park. I swung real hard and heard the ump yell, 'STRIKE THREE, YOU'RE OUT.'"

FL, D

"Betty, my roommate, and I came up with the idea to redecorate our room. We painted, wallpapered, and moved everything around. When IT WAS FINALLY COMPLETED, we were very pleased with the results, and everyone who saw it complimented us on how well done it was."

SU, D + 1FKA

"My brother, teenage sister, and cousin announced that they were going to climb a nearby mountain. They all came back later and said that it had been hard going but THEY HAD FINALLY MADE IT TO THE TOP."

SU, 1MBA + 1FTT + 1IRA

Coding for Consequences of Success and Failure

Sometimes after achieving a success or failure, something else will occur that will change the outcome for a character. Fate, or some other character, may step in to alter what a character has just achieved. The character himself or herself may make more effort, which again may result in a reversal of the previous outcome. To handle such situations, three subclasses of consequences that may modify the original outcome are coded for each of the striving outcomes. These consequences are represented by placing the coding symbols for them in parentheses after the coding that appears for the achievement outcome unit. Because these consequences are classifications that appear in other sections, these codes also appear separately and independently of their consequence status. The rationale for coding such consequences is that of preserving the sequence of dream events in order to answer certain interactional questions that might be raised. Such questions might take the form of "How often does a character succeed only to have his or her efforts nullified by the environment?" or "In what percentage of failures does some other character intervene and attempt to help the failing character?" The three consequences of success are illustrated below.

1. A character achieves success but it is nullified by a misfortune. The coding symbol for misfortunes is M. This class of events is discussed in the following section on environmental misfortunes and good fortunes.

Example:

"I had worked very hard to make the cheerleading squad. After finally receiving word that I had made it, I BROKE MY LEG AND COULDN'T BE A CHEER-LEADER."

SU, D (M)

MF, D

2. A character achieves success but subsequently overextends himself or herself and failure occurs.

Example:

"I was making a great deal of money by skillful maneuvering on the stock market. Then I began to speculate and LOST ALL MY MONEY."

SU, D (FL)

FL, D

3. Another character intervenes in an aggressive fashion and intentionally nullifies the success.

Example:

"My brother and I had been struggling to build this fancy model house out of wooden match sticks. After we finally glued the last one in place, my 11-year-old brother came along and INTENTIONALLY DROPPED A BRICK ON IT WHICH DEMOLISHED IT."

$$SU, D + 1MBA (A)$$
$$1MBC \ A5 > D + 1MBA$$

The three consequences of failure are:

1. A failure is reversed by a good fortune. The coding symbol for good fortune is GF. This class of events is discussed in the following section.

Example:

"I was really sweating over a chemistry problem and couldn't come up with the answer when, as if by magic, THE ANSWER APPEARED WRITTEN DOWN ON THE PAPER. I could hardly believe what I saw."

$$FL, D (GF)$$
$$GF, D$$

2. A failure is overcome when the character through unusual effort or new approach manages to succeed.

Example:

"My father kept trying to get a job but was always getting turned down. In desperation, he ran a newspaper ad and MANAGED TO GET ONE AT LAST."

$$FL, 1MFA (SU)$$
$$SU, 1MFA$$

3. A failure is overcome through the friendly intervention of another character.

Example:

"My teenage brother had his car apart and couldn't get it together. I GAVE HIM A DIAGRAM OF THE ENGINE, and then he was able to complete the job."

$$FL, 1MBT (F)$$
$$D \ F4 > 1MBT$$

THE CLASSIFICATION AND CODING OF MISFORTUNES AND GOOD FORTUNES

It sometimes happens that bad or good outcomes occur to a character independent of anything he or she may have done. Fate, in a sense, has stepped in and produced certain results over which no character has any control. We have labeled these impersonal "fatalistic" events as misfortunes, where bad things happen to a character, and good fortunes, where good things happen to a character.

Misfortune

We shall first deal with misfortune (Scoring symbol: M). A misfortune is any mishap, adversity, harm, danger, or threat that happens to characters as a result of circumstances over which they have no control; it happens to them through no fault of their own. A misfortune differs from the consequence of an aggressive act, since in an aggression there is an intent by one character to harm another character. There is no such intent in a misfortune. A misfortune also differs from a failure, as was pointed out in the last section. In a misfortune, a person is not trying to do anything; rather, something "bad" happens "out of the blue." The six subclasses of misfortune are listed below.

M6: A character is dead or dies as a result of accident or illness or some unknown cause. Death because of murder is categorically excluded because it is coded as an aggression.

Examples:

"I went up to the coffins and opened them. Lying in one box was my mother, in the other my sister, and in the third my brother. They all appeared TO BE DEAD."
"I was attending my FATHER'S FUNERAL."

M5: A character is injured or ill. This class includes pain, operations, any bodily or mental defects, insanity, amnesia, blindness, and so on. Elective plastic surgery is not counted as an "operation" because it is elective surgery.

Examples:

"Her baby boy had a serious congenital HEART DEFECT."
"My mother LOST HER MEMORY."
"A TOOTH BROKE OFF in my mouth."
"He had a CLUBFOOT."
"My boyfriend had a STOMACHACHE."

M4: A character is involved in an accident without suffering physical or mental injury; a character loses a possession or has one destroyed or damaged; a character has a defective possession.

Examples:

"As I was driving down the mountain, my car CRASHED BECAUSE OF THE ICY ROAD."
"The DIAMOND CAME OUT of my engagement ring."
"The LIGHTNING DAMAGED our house."
"My boyfriend's car had a FLAT TIRE."

M3: A character is threatened by something in the environment. A threat of falling is classified under the next heading.

Examples:

"The wall began to crack and bulge out, and I thought it was GOING TO FALL ON ME."

"The waves were very high, and I was afraid the boat we were in WAS GOING TO CAPSIZE."

M2: A character is falling or is in danger of falling.

Examples:

"I dreamed that I WAS FALLING AND FALLING and never hit bottom."

"As I stood on the edge of the cliff, the rocks began to move and I WAS AFRAID I MIGHT FALL."

M1: A character encounters an environmental barrier or obstacle; a character is unable to move; a character is lost; a character is late or is in danger of being late. This class of misfortunes includes situations that produce frustration for the character who confronts them. In some cases, the frustrating agent is clearly environmental in origin as when a road is washed out; in other cases, where the character is lost or late, it is possible that the character has made a contribution to the difficulty he or she encounters. However, since the character has not consciously or intentionally produced the difficulty and views the problem as external to himself or herself, it seems more appropriate to treat it as a misfortune that bears upon the character, rather than as a failure in achievement or as an intropunitive aggression. Once the obstacle that warrants the M1 coding has been encountered, it is possible for success or failure to be coded if the character makes an effort to overcome the barrier and the outcome is described in the dream report.

Examples:

"When we reached the river, we discovered that the BRIDGE HAD COLLAPSED so we couldn't get to the picnic grounds."

"As the truck bore down on me, I tried to run but found that MY LEGS WOULDN'T MOVE."

"I started toward home, but the streets became more and more unfamiliar until I finally realized that I WAS LOST."

"As I entered the office, I saw that I WAS LATE FOR WORK."

Good Fortune

Good fortune is the opposite of misfortune. A misfortune is coded when "something bad" happens to a character; a good fortune is coded when "something good" happens to a character. The "something good" is not the result of an *intentional* beneficial act by another character. That would be coded as friendliness. Neither is the "something good" the result of any purposeful striving by the character. That would be coded as success. A good fortune is coded when there is an acquisition of goods or something beneficial happens to a character that is completely adventitious or the result of a circumstance over which no one has control. A good fortune is also coded if the dreamer is in a bountiful environment. It might be said that a good fortune is coded whenever a character becomes "lucky." Good fortunes are rather rare in dreams. As the result of their paucity, we have not attempted to subclassify them. We code for only one class of good fortune; the coding symbol is GF.

Examples:

"I dreamed I FOUND A LOT OF MONEY."

"My girlfriend WON ONE OF THE DOOR PRIZES."

"I was out hunting when a LARGE HERD OF DEER JUST SEEMED TO APPEAR from out of nowhere."

"I dreamed I WAS LIVING IN A MANSION, HAD CLOSETS FULL OF NEW CLOTHES, AND WAS DRIVING A NEW ROLLS-ROYCE."

Coding Procedures

The coding procedure is the same as that followed in the last section. A comma is placed after the coding symbol for the environmental press, and then the coding symbols for the characters are shown. Multiple characters are joined by a plus sign.

Examples:

"I LOST MY WATCH over the side of the boat."

M4, D

"My buddy and I FOUND A BRAND-NEW BOAT that had drifted up on the beach."

GF, D + 1MKA

"My teenage brother and my new baby sister both CAME DOWN WITH THE MUMPS."

M5, 1MBT + 1FTB

Consequences

In the last section, it was indicated that consequences can occur that would modify the initial striving outcomes. In a similar fashion, the coding system for misfortune and good fortune includes provisions for consequences that alter the initial fate bestowed on a character. Three subclasses of consequences have been developed. These consequences are either a form of social interaction, a success or failure, or the opposite type of fatalistic event. They are also coded independent of their coding as a consequence. Their coding as a consequence is indicated by enclosing the relevant coding symbol in parentheses following the coding unit. The purpose of coding as a consequence is to preserve the sequence of events in order to answer certain questions that might be raised. Such questions might ask, "How often does a character struggle to overcome a misfortune and succeed?" or "In what percentage of good fortunes does fate intervene and turn an initial blessing into some misfortune?" The three consequences of misfortune are illustrated below.

1. The misfortune is transformed into a good fortune.

Example:

"My mother was very sick, but ALL OF A SUDDEN SHE APPEARED WELL AND HEALTHY."

M5, 1FMA (GF)

GF, 1FMA

2. The character suffering the misfortune tries to cope with the misfortune and succeeds.

Example:

"The door was locked and wouldn't open. After trying several times, I finally used a bent hairpin and MANAGED TO GET IT OPEN."

M1, D (SU)

SU, D

3. Another character intervenes in a friendly fashion and dispels the misfortune.

Example:

"I was hopelessly lost in the woods and wandering around in circles. Suddenly, a man I had never seen before appeared and SHOWED ME THE WAY OUT OF THE WOODS."

M1, D (F)

1MSA 4 > D

The three consequences of good fortune are as follows:
1. The good fortune is transformed into a misfortune.

Example:

"I found a lot of money, but on my way home IT DISAPPEARED."

GF, D (M)

M4, D

2. The character to whom the good fortune occurs tries to press his or her luck and fails.

Example:

"I dreamed I had found a lot of money. I invested it in order to make more money, but THEN I LOST IT ALL."

GF, D (FL)

FL, D

3. Another character intervenes in an aggressive fashion and intentionally destroys the good fortune.

Example:

"My teenage sister found this real cute puppy, but my father said SHE COULDN'T KEEP IT."

GF, 1FTT (A)

1MFA3 > 1FTT

Coding Rules

1. Score each misfortune that happens to the same character when the misfortunes belong to different subclasses.

Example:

"My brother's car WAS WRECKED, and HE GOT CUTS ON HIS FACE and *broke his arm* in the accident."

M4, 1MBA

M5, 1MBA

2. Score each misfortune or good fortune, even those that belong to the same subclass, if they happen to the same character at different times in the dream.

Examples:

"I was hungry and began to scratch my nose. All of a sudden A STEAK SUPPER APPEARED in front of me. I ate this and after a while I scratched my nose again. Suddenly, I WAS DRESSED IN THE FINEST OF CLOTHES. I began to wonder if my nose were magic."

GF, D

GF, D

"I was skiing when I ran into a tree and CUT MY LIP. I went back to the lodge and put a Band-Aid on it. Then I started out again. This time I SPRAINED MY ANKLE when one of my skis came off."

M5, D

M5, D

THE CLASSIFICATION AND CODING OF EMOTIONS

The classification of emotions was one of our most difficult tasks. The problem of reducing the hundreds of words in the English language that represent affective states to a fairly small number of classes that seemed to be fairly comprehensive, yet discrete in coverage, was a formidable one. Another stumbling block involved the question of extensity of coding; that is, should we try to classify the types of situations that caused the emotion as well as consequences following the emotion? After experimenting with a large number of coding schemes, we eventually arrived at the answer to this question and several others by limiting our emotional states to five in number and simply indicating which characters experienced these emotions.

When coders go over dream reports, they are generally surprised at how few emotions are actually reported, unless the dreamer is specifically and strongly urged to state what emotions are being experienced during the dream. Situations that would undoubtedly be terrifying or depressing for the average individual may be reported in some detail, but a description of their emotional impact on the dreamer is often lacking.

The five classes of emotion are presented below.

Anger

(Coding symbol: AN). This class of emotions is generally easy to identify. Representative of some of the terms coded under anger are "annoyed," "irritated," "mad," "provoked," "furious," "enraged," "belligerent," "incensed," and "indignant." As with the following emotional classes, all degrees of intensity are included within each class, and no coding distinction is made between weak expressions of anger such as being peeved or strong expressions such as being infuriated.

Apprehension

(Coding symbol: AP). The emotions included in this class can be considered related to fear, anxiety, guilt, and embarrassment. Although differences are recognizable among them, all these conditions lead to conscious concern on the part of the person experiencing them. The person feels apprehensive about the possibility of physical injury or punishment, or the possibility of social ridicule or rejection. Thus the common denominator underlying these emotions is that the person is uncomfortable because the threat of some potential danger exists . The following terms, which are not meant to be all inclusive, refer to various degrees of apprehension: "terrified," "horrified," "frightened," "scared," "worried," "nervous," "concerned," "panicky," "alarmed," "uneasy," "upset," "remorseful," "sorry," "apologetic," "regretful," and "ashamed."

Happiness

(Coding symbol: HA). All the words that describe a general state of pleasant feeling tone are included in this class. Some of the terms that would be coded as happiness are "contented," "pleased," "relieved," "amused," "cheerful," "glad," "relaxed," "gratified," "gay," "wonderful," "elated," "joyful," and "exhilarated."

Sadness

(Coding symbol: SD). All the words that describe an unhappy emotional state are coded in the sadness class. References to physical pain or physical distress are not included in any of the emotional classes. Some examples of terms that would be coded as sadness are "disappointed," "distressed," "hurt," "depressed," "lonely," "lost," "miserable," "hopeless," "crushed," and "heartbroken."

Confusion

(Coding symbol: CO). Although it may be debatable as to whether confusion is a condition possessing the same degree of autonomic involvement as the preceding emotions, we have chosen to place it in the classification of emotions. It is true that confusion resides more in the head as a state of cognitive ambiguity than it does in the viscera as a gut-type reaction. However, the feeling state accompanying uncertainty may begin to shade toward a type of free-floating anxiety, toward frustration, or toward depression. Because confusion is therefore "emotionlike," and also because it is reported fairly frequently in dreams, mention of it seems to belong most appropriately in the classification of emotions. Confusion is generally produced either through confrontation with some unexpected event or through inability to choose between available alternatives. Some words that may indicate confusion are "surprised," "astonished," "amazed," "awestruck," "mystified," "puzzled," "perplexed," "strange," "bewildered," "doubtful," "conflicted," "undecided," and "uncertain."

Coding Procedures

Because emotions are often not described, the coder may be tempted to infer emotions on the basis of the physical surroundings or activities mentioned in the dream report. This temptation should be resisted. If a dreamer says that he or she was in a torture chamber or being chased, the coder should not assume that apprehension was being experienced unless the dreamer says that such an emotion was being experienced. We make only one exception to this. If the dreamer describes definite autonomic activity accompanying an event, and it is clear from the combination of context and the autonomic description that the dreamer was experiencing an emotion that could be clearly classified as one of the five scorable emotions, we will code an emotion. For example, if the dreamer said, "Tears began running down my face when I received word of my mother's death," we would code an SD for that description. We would code AP if the dreamer said, "As the monster approached, I began to sweat and tremble and tried to cry out but no sound would come." The above situations appear infrequently, however, and restraint is urged as the general rule in attributing any emotion to a character unless the dream report provides ample material to do so.

The coder should not attempt to assign an emotion automatically on the basis of its listing in the preceding groups. In some cases, the same word may take on quite different meanings in different contexts. For example, the statement "I was shocked" might possibly indicate any one of the five emotional classes, depending on how the dreamer goes on to describe his or her reaction. The coding procedure followed in the last two sections is also employed for emotions. A comma is placed after the coding symbol for the emotion, and then the coding symbols for the characters are presented. As usual, multiple characters are joined by plus signs.

Examples:

"I became FURIOUS when I saw my boyfriend holding a girl's hand."

AN, D

"Suddenly, I realized that I was walking down the street with no clothes on. I became terribly EMBARRASSED."

AP, D

"My buddy and I were OVERJOYED when we finally found the treasure."

HA, D + 1MKA

"My sister was very DISAPPOINTED when she didn't get the job."

SD, 1FTA

"My aunt and uncle were SURPRISED to see a half-dog and half-cat creature walk across the floor."

CO, 1FRA + 1MRA

Additional Coding Rules

1. If the terms used to describe a reaction to a particular event all belong to the same class, that class of emotions is coded only once for that event.

Example:

"I was so PLEASED and *happy* to hear the news."

HA, D

2. The same class of emotion may be coded more than once if it appears as a reaction to different events.

Example:

"I was MAD at my wife for not fixing coffee. Then I got MAD at the bus driver because he wouldn't give me change for a ten-dollar bill. When I arrived at work, I became MAD at my boss because he asked me to do someone else's work besides my own."

AN, D

AN, D

AN, D

3. If more than one class of emotion is described as a reaction to the same event, each class is coded separately.

Example:

"I was SAD when I saw the damage to the roof but was GLAD that the rest of the house had not been damaged."

SD, D

HA, D

THE CLASSIFICATION AND CODING OF PHYSICAL SURROUNDINGS

Settings and Objects

The characters in a dream report do not act without a context. The dream report almost always contains physical surroundings that are divided into two very general categories in the Hall/Van de Castle system: settings and objects. Generally, settings and objects have not been quite as interesting as some of the categories that already have been presented, but they sometimes have their uses.

Settings

Almost all dream reports include some form of recognizable setting, and dreamers frequently begin their report by saying something about the setting. In the same way that there are often several acts and scenes to a play, so, too, is it common for the setting to change during the course of a dream narrative, sometimes quite abruptly.

Establishing the categories for settings was the most difficult aspect of the entire coding system. The initial efforts to classify settings included a rather extensive number of possible settings. It was impossible, however, to obtain adequate intercoder reliability when such a large number were involved, so we eventually collapsed all settings into two broad groupings— indoor and outdoor settings.

Indoor settings consist of those in which the dreamer is within a building. The building may be a house, hotel, church, factory, barracks, or some other structure. Any room such as a living room, cellar, or attic is therefore an indoor setting, as are offices, elevators, hallways, stairs, or other regions within buildings. Also considered indoor settings are those areas attached to or part of the exterior of a building. Examples of the latter that would be coded as indoor settings are instances where the dreamer is located on a porch, roof, fire escape, or ledge of a building. Open-air buildings such as amphitheaters or stadiums are also coded as indoor settings. The coding symbol for indoor settings is I.

Outdoor settings are those where the dreamer is described as being out-of-doors or outside a building. Settings occurring in nature, such as when the dreamer is at the beach, in the woods, or on a mountain, are included, as well as urban settings, such as streets, sidewalks, yards, parking lots, and cemeteries. The setting is considered an outside one if the dreamer is in a car, train, boat, or airplane, unless the car is in a garage or the airplane is in a hangar. Being in a tunnel or cave is coded as an outdoor setting. The coding symbol for outdoor settings is O.

The decision as to whether a setting should be coded I or O is generally not a difficult one, and a high level of coding agreement can be readily achieved for the distinction between them.

In a few cases, it appears that a setting is definitely present, but it cannot be determined whether it should be coded I or O because the dreamer has not supplied sufficient information. For instance, she might say, "We went to the country club," and it is not clear whether the dreamer is referring to some sort of building or whether she means the golf course, tennis area, or swimming pool. We handle these infrequent cases by coding such settings as ambiguous and indicate this by the coding symbol A.

An even more infrequent situation is the one in which no setting is described. Short dreams or those that seem to be only some fragment of a longer dream are the ones most likely not to contain any setting. These dreams are coded with the symbol NS, which stands for no setting. The presence of any object or description of any surroundings, no matter how vague, is sufficient to warrant some type of setting code, other than NS.

Once the locale of the dream has been determined, the next phase of coding settings involves determining the degree of familiarity that the dreamer reports for the setting. Five levels of familiarity are distinguished in our coding system.

Familiar settings (Coding symbol: F) are those in which it appears quite clear that the dreamer recognizes the setting as being a personally familiar one, such as his own or a friend's home, place of employment, or place of worship. If the setting is a well-known or famous one that the dreamer can identify, such as the Empire State Building, Mt. Everest, or Arlington Cemetery, it is coded as being a familiar setting, even though the dreamer may never have been there. Thus, if the dreamer is able specifically to identify a setting or indicates that he or she has prior acquaintance with it, an F code is given.

Distorted settings (Coding symbol: D) are familiar settings that the dreamer indicates involve an element of peculiarity or incongruity because they differ in some respect from the way the dreamer knows the setting to be in waking life. Coding is fairly liberal for this category so that a setting containing any distortion, even of a minor nature, is coded D. The distortion, however, must involve the physical surroundings rather than the appearance of any character. *The D code takes precedence over any other setting code.*

Geographical settings (Coding symbol: G) are those in which the dreamer identifies the settings according to their geographical location, such as Europe, Illinois, or San Francisco. If the dreamer also indicates that the setting is a personally familiar one, the F coding is given precedence over the G coding.

Unfamiliar settings (Coding symbol: U) are those that are not known to the dreamer. Sometimes the dreamer will be very explicit and state that the setting is a place he or she has never seen or visited before, or sometimes the adjective "strange" will be used to indicate that the setting is not recognized as a familiar one. In other instances, the vague description of the setting will often reveal the lack of familiarity. Statements showing this vague quality are "I was in some house," "I was driving down the street of a large city," "We went to what looked like a hotel," "The furniture suggested this was a kitchen where we were talking." If the coder can answer yes to the question "Does the description of the setting strongly suggest that the dreamer has not actually been in this setting in his waking life?" the setting is coded U. It should be kept in mind that the coding will not always be U if the dreamer has never been in the setting in waking life, for if the setting is a famous one it is coded F, if it is referred to as some specific geographical location it is coded G, and if there is something incongruous about the arrangement of the setting it is coded D.

Questionable settings (Coding symbol: Q) are coded when it cannot be determined whether the setting is a familiar or unfamiliar one. The description provided in the dream report is often insufficient to establish the familiarity or unfamiliarity of a setting with any degree of assurance, so Q is a frequently employed code.

Coding settings is generally fairly easy. Deciding whether a setting should be coded U or Q and determining the total number of settings are the coding problems that pose the greatest difficulty. To illustrate the various combinations of codes that may occur, a list of examples is provided below.

Examples:

IF: "I was in MY ROOM getting dressed."

ID: "It looked like my HISTORY CLASSROOM EXCEPT THE DESKS WERE OF KINDERGARTEN SIZE."

IG: "I looked out the hotel window and saw NEW YORK CITY below."

IU: "We were in what seemed to be A CELLAR."

IQ: "I was IN A STORE buying a pair of shoes."

OF: "I was yelling from OUR NEIGHBOR'S DRIVEWAY."

OD: "I was in OUR BACKYARD BUT THE BIG OAK TREE WAS MISSING."

OG: "We were swimming AT SOME HAWAIIAN BEACH."

OU: "The path THROUGH THESE UNFAMILIAR LOOKING WOODS was a very crooked one."

OQ: "THE FOOTBALL FIELD we were playing on was muddy."

AF: "THE VIEW OF THE EIFFEL TOWER was magnificent."

AD: "I WAS BACK AT COLLEGE BUT IT LOOKED MORE LIKE MY HIGH SCHOOL."

AG: "I WAS BACK SOMEWHERE IN VERMONT again."

AU: "I COULDN'T TELL MUCH ABOUT MY SURROUNDINGS BUT I KNEW I HAD NEVER BEEN THERE BEFORE."

AQ: "I was sitting ON TOP OF A FLAG POLE."

NS: "ALL I COULD SEE WAS THIS OLD LADY WHO KEPT SCOWLING AT ME. THAT WAS THE WHOLE DREAM."

Determining the Number of Settings

The rules for determining the number of settings are given below along with coding examples. Items to be coded will appear in capital letters, and items that may seem relevant, but that should not be coded, are italicized.

1. For a setting to be coded, the dreamer must appear as an observer in the setting. Do not code settings in which other characters are located unless the dreamer appears as an observer in the same place.

Examples:

"I was walking through what I thought were THE STREETS OF NEW ORLEANS (OG)."

"He said that he and my other fraternity brothers had gone for a drive through *the streets of New Orleans.*"

2. All changes in location within a single building are coded as a single indoor setting. Changes in location from one building to a different building are coded as separate indoor settings.

Examples:

"I stopped IN THE TODDLE HOUSE (IF) for a cup of coffee and then went to A BEAUTY PARLOR (IQ) to get my hair done."

"We hunted for it IN THE ATTIC (IQ) then went downstairs and continued the search in the *rooms on the second floor* and finally wound up looking *in the cellar* but without any success."

3. If any type of codable intervening setting occurs, the same indoor location may be coded more than once.

Examples:

"We quickly packed a lunch AT DOROTHY'S HOUSE (IF), then drove for a while IN THE COUNTRY (OQ) and returned to DOROTHY'S HOUSE (IF) and listened to records."

"I left the LIVING ROOM OF THIS OLD GLOOMY HOUSE (IU), walked THROUGH THE STRANGE GARDEN OUTSIDE (OU), and then for some reason returned again to THE HOUSE (IU) and walked through the back door."

4. Outdoor settings are coded separately if they involve clearly differentiated and separate regions. If the dreamer is describing different areas of a larger region, a single overall outdoor setting is coded.

Examples:

"We attended the burial at THE CATHOLIC CEMETERY (OF) then drove off to SOME NEARBY SMALL TOWN (OQ) to talk."

"As I was walking THROUGH SOME FOREST (OU) I came across a *group of pine trees*, then I walked through a *grove of aspen* and farther on through a small *stand of junipers*."

5. If any type of codable intervening setting occurs, the same outdoor location may be coded more than once.

Example:

"We were surfing at SOME BEACH THAT I COULDN'T RECOGNIZE (OU) when the scene shifted to some STRANGE ROOM THAT HAD PAINTINGS ALL OVER THE WALLS (IU), and then I was back surfing at the SAME BEACH (OU) again."

6. For an additional setting to be coded, some action should take place within the new setting or the dreamer must describe himself or herself as actually being located in the new setting.

Examples:

"AFTER WALKING IN THE RAIN (OQ) for what seemed a long time, I ARRIVED AT MY FRIEND'S HOME AND WENT INSIDE TO GET DRY (IF)."

"AFTER WALKING IN THE RAIN (OQ) for what seemed a long time, *I arrived at my friend's home*."

Objects

The settings of the dream provide the general background against which the various dream activities are viewed. To provide a more detailed picture of the physical surroundings that the dreamer creates, attention must also be paid to the various objects that appear in dream reports.

An object is a thing. It has tangibility, palpability, and dimensionality. It also has definite physical boundaries or limits. Intangibles such as air, wind, fog, and sky are excluded by such considerations as are songs or sounds, which have temporal boundaries but not physical ones. Locations such as cities, streets, rooms, and lakes have physical boundaries and consequently are classified as objects. In some cases, a thing such as a building that is always coded as an object may also be coded as a setting if the dreamer indicates she or he was engaged in some activity within the building. Persons and animals are not coded as objects because they are handled separately under the classification of characters, but parts of persons and animals are treated as objects.

Because any object we encounter in waking life can be represented in dreams, and some items may also show up in dreams that we would be startled to see with our eyes open, the problem of formulating a system for the classification of objects is a difficult one. The number of possible groupings could be very large if one chose to categorize by reference to size, shape, color, weight, age, composition, ownership, location, function, and other qualities that could readily be suggested. After several arrangements had been tried, we finally settled on a system that includes 12 broad classes, three of which are further subdivided, plus a miscellaneous class. All objects that appear in dreams are therefore classifiable under one of these headings. These classes are presented below.

Architecture

Architecture refers to buildings or structures and their component parts. Seven different subclasses of architecture are coded. The first letter of the coding symbol for architecture is A, which is followed by a second letter to indicate the class. The first four classes deal with entire buildings or units within buildings, while the next two deal with small component parts of buildings. Any architectural object not included in these six classes is coded in the subclass of miscellaneous architecture.

Residential (Coding symbol: AR). This subclass is composed of all buildings and units of buildings (rooms) that are used for residential purposes. It includes house, mansion, castle, palace, cabin, shack, hut, tent, and other types of private dwelling place. It also includes apartment house, dormitory, hotel, motel, inn, and other types of multiple dwelling places in which people reside temporarily or permanently. In addition to obvious residential rooms such as bedrooms and living rooms, AR includes hallways and stairways as well as levels within a residential building such as the second floor, downstairs, and basement.

Vocational (Coding symbol: AV). This subclass includes buildings and rooms in buildings devoted mainly to business transactions, manufacturing, employment, or education. What such buildings share in common is that they are primarily concerned with work or vocational activities. Included is any type of store, factory, and office. Classroom buildings and classrooms are also coded as vocational because of their implied work emphasis; other educational buildings such as school dormitories, cafeterias, and chapels are classified under other headings. Banks are included in the money class. Home workshops and study rooms are not included here. They are coded AR.

Entertainment (Coding symbol: AE). This subclass covers buildings and rooms that are used for recreation, entertainment, sports, or other pleasurable activities. Included are restaurant, cafeteria, diner, bar, nightclub, casino, dance hall, theater, museum, art gallery, bowling alley, stadium, gymnasium, and indoor swimming pool. Recreation or hobby rooms in a home are not included in this subclass; they are coded AR.

Institutional (Coding symbol: AI). This subclass is composed of buildings or units within them that society maintains for collective action in dealing with social or governmental problems. Such buildings are therefore generally supported by taxes or subscription. Included are hospital, infirmary, jail, penitentiary, court house, government building, military building, and church, as well as the units within them such as surgery room, cell, court room, tax collector's office, and choir loft.

Details (Coding symbol: AD). This subclass consists of all parts of a room or smaller units of a building not usually regarded as separate rooms. Included are door, window, wall, ceiling, fireplace, aisle, steps, and floor. In the last example, floor refers to the walked-on surface of a room, not to a level within a building. It does not matter what type of building is involved; a house door, restaurant door, or church door are all coded as AD. In addition to internal components, architectural details include those structures viewed from outside a building such as roof, chimney, spire, belfry, ledge, balcony, railing, fire escape, shutters, arch, and column.

Building Materials (Coding symbol: AB). Included in this subclass are those objects used to construct buildings such as boards, lumber, bricks, concrete blocks, and cement.

Miscellaneous (Coding symbol: AM). Any building or part of a building that cannot be classified within the preceding architectural groupings would be included here. Some examples are tower, dam, and fountain.

Household

(Coding symbol: HH). Contained within this class are all objects frequently encountered in a household setting. Included are furniture such as table, chair, and bed; appliances such as stove, refrigerator, and vacuum cleaner; furnishings such as rug, drapes, and lamp; and supplies such as sheet, light bulb, and soap. Silverware, dinner ware, and cooking utensils are coded HH. Examples of other objects coded HH are broom, clock, scissors, needle, safety pin, thermometer, medicines, cosmetics, bottle, mirror, faucet, rope, garbage can, and hose. Office furniture and furnishings are also considered HH.

Food

(Coding symbol: FO). Both food and drink are coded in this class. Included are all forms of food or drink whether on the shelf of a store, in a refrigerator, in a container, on a plate, or on the table. It does not include food that is growing. Growing food is coded in the nature class. It does include general terms such as groceries, drinks, and things to eat, but not a reference to a meal or to eating without any specification as to what the meal consisted of or what was eaten. Grocery store and meat market are coded as AV, restaurant and cafeteria as AE, dining room as AR, and dining room table as HH.

Implements

Three subclasses of implements are coded. The first letter of the coding symbol for implements is I. A second letter is attached to indicate the subclass.

Tools (Coding symbol: IT). This subclass includes tools, machinery, and machinery parts. Objects that are used in vocational activities are generally included here, although some, such as typewriter, are coded in the communication class. Examples of the IT subclass are hammer, nail, saw, screwdriver, wrench, pliers, shovel, rake, lawn mower, lathe, X-ray machine, jack, lever, and the starting button of a machine. Household appliances are coded in the household class, and parts of conveyances are coded in the travel class.

Weapons (Coding symbol: IW). This subclass consists of such weapons as gun, club, sword, grenade, missiles, or bomb. Tanks and bombers are coded here rather than in the travel class.

Recreation (Coding symbol: IR). This subclass incorporates sporting goods such as baseball bat, tennis racquet, balls, ice skates, and fishing pole; objects used in playing games such as cards, checkers, and dice; and toys such as dolls, miniature trucks, and blocks. This subclass also includes musical instruments.

Travel

(Coding symbol: TR). Encompassed within this class are all forms of conveyance such as car, truck, bus, streetcar, subway, train, boat, airplane, bicycle, elevator, and escalator. Parts of a conveyance such as wheel, brakes, motor, windshield, and propeller are also included. In addition, objects associated with travel such as bus depot, train station, airport, license plate, passenger ticket, and luggage are coded TR.

Streets

(Coding symbol: ST). Covered within this class are all types of roadways by which a person can go from one place to another. Included are street, highway, road, path, trail, alley, sidewalk, driveway, intersection, bridge, and train tracks.

Regions

(Coding symbol: RG). This class primarily takes in all land areas that are limited by some form of boundaries. It includes city, village, block, square, parking lot, yard, park, playing field, lot, cemetery, farm, college campus, and military camp. Also considered as regions are water areas whose boundaries have been established by human beings, such as outdoor swimming pools and reservoirs.

Nature

(Coding symbol: NA). This class consists of all outdoor objects that exist in nature. Included are all forms of plant life such as tree, flower, and grass; terrain such as mountain, plateau, cliff, cave, valley, field, meadow, swamp, and forest; natural bodies of water such as ocean, lake, pond, river, and waterfall; weather elements such as rain, snow, hail, and ice; heavenly bodies such as sun, moon, star, and planet; earth and its mineral products such as ground, soil, dirt, clay, mud, sand, pebbles, rocks, iron ore, gold ore, crude diamonds, rubies, or other gems. Growing fruits or vegetables are NA, but fruits or vegetables prepared for eating are FO. Similarly, water or ice as it appears in nature is NA, but a glass of water intended for drinking is coded FO.

Body Parts

Both human and animal parts are included under this heading. Five subclasses of body parts are coded. The first letter of the coding symbol is B, which is followed by a second letter to indicate the subclass.

Head (Coding symbol: BH). This subclass is composed of all visible body parts in the head region. It includes head, neck, throat, face, hair, horns, eyes, beak, nose, mouth, lips, tongue, real and false teeth, jaw, ears, and beard.

Extremities (Coding symbol: BE). All extremities of the body such as leg, arm, tail, and fin as well as parts of extremities such as finger, hand, elbow, toe, foot, knee, and claw are included in this subclass.

Torso (Coding symbol: BT). All visible parts of the torso such as shoulders, chest, abdomen, hips, side, and back are included in this subclass. Terms such as body, build, and physique are coded BT.

Anatomy (Coding symbol: BA). This subclass contains internal body parts, both bony and visceral, and includes such parts as skull, ribs, leg bone, tonsils, heart, lungs, and intestines. Terms such as "insides" or "guts" are coded BA. Also included are body secretions such as blood, perspiration, saliva, and pus. Note should be made of the following grouping before coding BA.

Sex (Coding symbol: BS). This subclass embraces all body parts and organs related to reproduction and excretion such as penis, testicles, vagina, clitoris, uterus, pelvis, pubic hair, breasts, nipples, buttocks, and anus. Also included are secretions or products from these organs such as semen, menstrual blood, urine, and feces. Embryo and fetus are coded BS.

Clothing

(Coding symbol: CL). Covered within this class are clothing and parts of clothing. Included are outer garments, underwear, headgear, and footwear, as well as such items as pocket, collar, and button. Accessories that are carried or worn by a person (such as handbag, cane, wristwatch, and eyeglasses) and jewelry (such as ring, necklace, and ornamental pin) are coded CL.

Communication

(Coding symbol: CM). This class is composed of all forms of visual, auditory, and written communications and the means for transmitting them. Included are TV set, movie, photograph, drawing, painting, picture, sculpture, telephone, radio, tape recorder, phonograph, book, magazine, newspaper, letter, telegram, postcard, advertisement, map, and test. Objects used to produce communications such as camera, film, microphone, typewriter, pen, pencil, and paper are also coded CM.

Money

(Coding symbol: MO). This class incorporates money and objects closely associated with money. Included is any type of money in the form of currency and coins; objects that can easily be exchanged for money such as checks, gambling chips, and subway tokens; negotiable objects such as stocks and bonds; records referring to monetary values such as check stubs, bills, receipts, and price tags; and containers for money such as piggy banks, wallets, and change purses. Unless a purse is mentioned as a coin or change purse, it is coded CL because a purse is considered a stylistic accessory that is a receptacle for a wide variety of objects beside money. Bank buildings are coded MO.

Miscellaneous

(Coding symbol: MS). An object that cannot be included in any of the preceding classes is coded MS.

Coding Rules

Some objects raise problems as to whether they should be coded in one class or another. Their placement must be decided on the basis of context, usage of the object, and the manner in which it is described. For example, a knife can be used as an aggressive implement (IW) or as cutlery (HH). A key may open a home (HH), or it may start a car (TR). To use rags for household cleaning (HH) is quite different from wearing them for clothing (CL). Thus, objects such as knives, keys, and rags cannot be mechanically assigned to the household class in every instance.

1. Each object is to be assigned to only one class. A knife, for example, cannot be both a household object (HH) and a weapon (IW).

Examples:

"My mother said to put the KNIVES (HH) and FORKS (HH) on the TABLE (HH)."
"He kept coming after me with a KNIFE (IW) in his HAND (BE)."

2. Any object that is mentioned in the dream is coded. An object need not be physically present to be coded.

Examples:

"I was planning to buy a CAR (TR)."
"We were reading about how they made CHEESE (FO)."

3. If the same object is mentioned several times in a dream, it is coded only once. If two or more similar but different objects of the same type are mentioned, each is coded.

Examples:

"I looked at the NECKLACE (CL) and passed it along to Jim; then he handed the *necklace* to Walt."
"There was a red BOOK (CM), a blue BOOK (CM), and a yellow BOOK (CM) lying on the FLOOR (AD)."

4. If an object is a part or subunit of a larger unit, each of the subunits as well as the larger unit is coded.

Examples:

"His NOSE (BH) was very large for his FACE (BH)."
"The LIVING ROOM (AR) of this HOUSE (AR) was all decorated in blue."
"The DOOR (AD) to the LIVING ROOM (AR) was made of oak."

5. An object is not coded if it is referred to in a generic sense, or if the dreamer mentions an object in order to exclude it.

Examples:

"I told her that I was eager to finish *school*."
"I got cold *feet* and couldn't go through with it."
"He said it was not a *flower* but a TREE (NA)."

THE CLASSIFICATION AND CODING OF DESCRIPTIVE ELEMENTS

In addition to reporting that people and objects appeared in a dream and that certain events took place, dreamers may also describe some attributes and qualities of objects, people, actions, and emotional states. They say it was "a red car," "a large house," "an old man," "a crowded church," "a cold day," "a crooked stick," "an intense fear," or "an ugly dog." In dream reports, a person may be characterized as "running rapidly," "working very hard," or "dancing beautifully." Dreamers may also note the passage of time—"We seemed to be riding for about an hour"—or refer to a particular time—"It was midnight." They may also describe things, people, and happenings not in terms of what they were but in terms of what they were *not*—"It was not my mother." We call all of these *descriptive elements*.

In coding descriptive elements, three different scales are involved—the modifier scale, the temporal scale, and the negative scale. Each of these is discussed below and illustrated by coding examples.

The categories and scales in the following section have not been routinely used in most studies. They are to be used by highly committed investigators, or to test very specific hypotheses, or when there seems to be a striking occurrence of an element that fits into one of these descriptive categories. By and large, the frequencies for these categories are low.

Modifiers

A modifier is any adjective, adverb, or phrase that is used for descriptive elaboration. Because any object can be classified with regard to an extremely large number of attributes, the number of modifier classes could be a large one. We have limited the number of classes to nine. These nine represent those on which satisfactory reliability could be obtained and for which psychological significance probably exists. Each of the nine classes can be considered to represent bipolar qualities, and each class of modifiers is therefore coded with a plus or minus sign to indicate which pole of the modifier is represented.

Color

(Coding symbol: C). Any mention of color or a color name is coded unless the term is used to describe an emotional state. Chromatic colors are coded C+, and achromatic colors (black, white, and gray) are coded C−. The same color can be coded more than once if it refers to separate things. In the following examples, the reader is reminded that italics represent nonscorable elements.

Examples:
"She was wearing a BLACK (C−) and YELLOW (C+) striped dress and was carrying a BLACK (C−) purse."
"The rainbow contained a great many COLORS (C+)."
"The WHITE-haired (C−) gentleman rose when I entered the room."
"Her cheeks turned RED (C+) with embarrassment."
"It was a *dark night*."
"I felt sad and *blue*."
"I called him a *yellow* coward."
"She *blushed* as the cheap *silver* utensils were put on the table."
"The dark-haired stranger was with a *blond* woman."

Size

(Coding symbol: S). This class contains all references to the largeness or smallness of things. Descriptive terms indicating a large size such as "big," "huge," "thick," "tall," "high," "broad," and "deep" are coded S+. The antonyms of these terms such as "small," "tiny," "thin," "short," "low," "narrow," and "shallow" are coded S−. The concept of size is ordinarily thought of as being appropriate only for objects that have height, width, and length—that is, for three-dimensional objects. As is evident from the above list of terms, we code a reference to any one of these three physical dimensions as a size term. References to the temporal dimension as when an interval of time is described as short or long are not coded as size modifiers. It should be remembered that although many nouns such as "midget" or "giant" could be classified as indicating size differences, only the modifying terms are included in the modifier scale.

Examples:

"I climbed a HIGH (S+) wall and ran down a NARROW (S−) street between TALL (S+) buildings."

"This boy, who was SHORT (S−), had on a shirt that was too SMALL (S−) for him and a LONG (S+) tie with TINY (S−) polka dots."

"A FAT (S+) lady with a MINIATURE (S−) poodle was walking down a WIDE (S+) street."

"I waited a *long* time for the train to arrive."

"We had a *narrow* escape."

"The baby was sitting on a ledge of the *skyscraper*."

Age

(Coding symbol: A). References to a person being old or to an object being old are coded A+. References to a person being young or to an object being new are coded A−. Synonymous terms for old, young, and new are also scorable, as are comparative age terms such as "older" and "younger." Only these bipolar distinctions in age are included in this class, and mention of a character's specific age is therefore not coded.

Examples:

"The YOUNG (A−) man was driving a NEW (A−) car."

"I walked up to this ANCIENT (A+) mansion and an ELDERLY (A+) man greeted me."

"My OLD (A+) boyfriend laughed at my YOUNGER (A−) brother."

"All of the rooms in this MODERN (A−) hotel had furniture of the LATEST (A−) style."

"I cuddled and sang to this *baby*."

"My grandfather *is 80 years old*."

Density

(Coding symbol: D). Modifiers included in this class must refer to a bounded area or to some type of container. References to such areas or containers as being full, bulging, or crowded are coded D+. If such areas or containers are described as empty they are coded as D−.

Examples:

"The church was CROWDED (D+) with people."

"I felt STUFFED (D+) after the large meal."

"The elevator was JAM-PACKED (D+) with passengers."

"His wallet was BULGING (D+) with dollar bills."

"The suitcase was EMPTY (D−)."

"The tree trunk was HOLLOW (D−)."

"I was unable to move in the *crowd*."

"*No one* was at home."
"I was all *alone* in the big house."

Thermal

(Coding symbol: T). References to contrasting temperatures are included in this class. Things that are described as warm or hot are coded T+; things that are described as cool or cold are coded T−. Other descriptive terms that refer to measurable qualities of temperature are also scorable. Objects that are inferentially known to be hot or cold or descriptions of verbal interactions as heated, etc., are not coded.

Examples:
"I suddenly felt WARM (T+)."
"The water seemed FRIGID (T−) when I stepped into it."
"The wind was CHILLY (T−)."
"The cowboy was cooking something over a *fire*."
"The *ice* on the lake was covered with *snowy* slush."
"He spoke *coldly* to me when I said that he wasn't such *hot* stuff."

Velocity

(Coding symbol: V). This class contains references to the speed with which objects or people move. Fast movement is coded V+, and slow movement is coded V−. Speed of mental activity is codable if described in such terms as "quickly" or "slowly," but the word "suddenly" is not coded.

Examples:
"I walked FAST (V+) down the street."
"I drove the car SLOWLY (V−) through the RAPIDLY (V+) flowing stream."
"I QUICKLY (V+) calculated the answer and wrote it down."
   "*All of a sudden*, I realized that this man who had *stopped* the truck was some sort of spy."
"She *ran* to meet her father who was *limping* toward her."
"The train was *suddenly* going about 70 *miles an hour* down the tracks."

Linearity

(Coding symbol: L). References to whether an object possesses linear or nonlinear qualities are included in this class. Objects that are described as straight or flat are coded L+, and objects that are described as curved, crooked, or in synonymous terms are coded L−. Knowledge that an object is straight or curved is not sufficient grounds for coding; the dreamer himself or herself must indicate that attention was paid to these qualities of linearity.

Examples:

"Ahead, the road across the FLAT (L+) prairie rose and TWISTED (L−) around the mountain."

"The girl with the STRAIGHT (L+) hair asked the CURLY-haired (L−) girl for a match."

"The floor was WARPED (L−) and the walks were very BUMPY (L−)."

"She drew a *line* with the *ruler*."

"He wanted a *straight* answer as to whether the deal was *on the level* or *crooked*."

Intensity

(Coding symbol: I). Contained within this class are modifiers that are used to describe force or expenditure of energy. Modifiers indicating a strong intensity are coded I+; modifiers indicating a weak intensity are coded I−. Intensity modifiers may refer to either physical or mental energy or to emotions and sensations. Simple mention of an emotion generally associated with a strong affect is not sufficient for coding; the dreamer must use some intensity modifier such as "very," or "greatly," in order to be considered scorable.

Examples:

"There was a LOUD (I+) clap of thunder followed by a BRIGHT (I+) flash of lightning and a STRONG (I+), VERY (I+) cold wind."

"I worked VERY HARD (I+) on solving the physics problem."

"I felt TERRIBLY (I+) happy for the winner and SLIGHTLY (I−) sad for the loser."

"It was a QUIET (I−), DIMLY-lit (I−) room, and as my boyfriend held me GENTLY (I−) in his STRONG (I+) arms, I became A LITTLE BIT (I−) aroused."

"The husband became *furious* because his wife kept *screaming*."

Evaluation

(Coding symbol: E). This class covers evaluative remarks that are made about people or objects. Because so many terms could be considered to represent a judgment, opinion, or evaluation of some sort, we found it difficult to obtain any appreciable degree of coding reliability until we finally limited our coding to only two areas. These two areas are those of aesthetic and moral evaluation. Descriptions indicating that something is considered aesthetically pleasing or morally correct are coded E+; descriptions indicating the aesthetically unpleasant or morally incorrect are coded E−. Reference to any type of stimulus considered to be pleasant or unpleasant to the senses is included in the aesthetic class. Included in the moral class are references to personal conduct as being right, correct, appropriate, or approved, as well as references indicating the opposite kind of evaluation.

Examples:

"The sunset was BEAUTIFUL (E+)."

"This HANDSOME (E+) boy asked me to dance while the band played a LOVELY (E+) tune."

"A DIRTY-LOOKING (E−) man came out of a SHABBY (E−) hut."

"I thought that was a TERRIBLE (E−) thing for him to say to his mother because she had always been GOOD (E+) to him.

"She made a *wrong* turn and caused a *bad* accident."

"None of my answers was *right* on the quiz, and I felt *terrible*."

Temporal Scale

Within the dream report, references may occur to various time intervals or to particular points in time. Such temporal references are indicated by the coding symbol T. No distinction is made between long and short units of time; thus, unlike the bipolar modifier scales, + and − differentiations are not included as part of the coding symbols. The thermal class is also indicated by the coding symbol T, but the + or − sign is always included in the thermal coding. Examples of the two subclasses of temporal references that are coded are included below as well as examples of situations that are not coded.

1. References to a specific unit of time such as a minute, hour, day, week, or year and references to a nonspecific interval of elapsed time.

Examples:

"My girlfriend spent the DAY with me."

"He worked on the NIGHT SHIFT."

"My roommate went home for the WEEKEND."

"My mother had had the ring for MANY YEARS."

"A FEW MINUTES later I got up and went outside."

"He kept me waiting for a LONG TIME."

"We talked for A WHILE and then he asked me to dance."

2. Reference to a particular time for the purpose of dating an event.

Examples:

"It was EARLY IN THE MORNING when we started out."

"I said I would meet him about 10 O'CLOCK."

"AT THAT MOMENT, I saw a snake cross the road."

"I thought to myself that the examination is TODAY."

"We were planning to go on a picnic TOMORROW."

"It was the FOURTH OF JULY."

Do not code the age of a person.

Examples:

"She was *10 years old.*"
"My father is *middle-aged.*"

Do not code the use of the word "time" when it refers to an occasion.

Examples:

"I had a good *time.*"
"I had a hard *time* starting the car."

Do not code a sequence of events.

Examples:

"*After* the parade, we went to get something to eat."
"*Then* the *next* thing that happened, we were in a car."
"*After* struggling hard, I *finally* got free."

Do not code salutations in which there is a reference to the time of day.

Examples:

"He said *good night* and left."
"I yelled *good morning* to the mailman."

Negative Scale

The remaining scale that appears in the classification of descriptive elements is the negative scale. Some dreamers use direct, straightforward language in describing what happened in their dreams, whereas other dreamers take a much more devious approach and describe what was not happening or what something did not resemble. Because these differences in descriptive approach can be discerned in reading dream reports, we decided that a negative scale should be constructed that would reflect these stylistic differences. This is the only scale in which comments by the dreamer on his or her dream such as "It was not a long dream" are coded. Scoring examples for the two types of negative words are given below. The coding symbol for negative words is N.

1. Use of any of the common negative words such as "no," "not," "none," "never," "neither," and "nor."

Examples:

"There was NO one at the door when I opened it."
"It was NOT a gun but a bottle that the man had in his hand."
"When I asked him for some candy, he said he had NONE."
"My brother NEVER wears a tie."

"It was NEITHER my mother NOR my father, but some strange couple that was living in our house."
"I recognized the person in my dream but I can NOT remember who it was now."
"There were NO other people in the dream."

2. Use of negative words that are created by adding certain prefixes to adjectives or adverbs. When these prefixes are added and used in such a way that the word *not* could be substituted for the prefix without changing the meaning, the word is counted as a negative. These prefixes are "un," "im," "in," "il," "ir," and "non."

Examples:

"I was UNSURE of my ability and thought I would be INCAPABLE of doing it."
"His behavior was INEXCUSABLE, and he broke an IRREPLACEABLE vase."
"We were UNAWARE that what we had done was IMPROPER, but the policeman said it was ILLEGAL."
"The mechanic said it was a NONESSENTIAL part that was missing."
"It seemed *imminent* that he would be *imprisoned*."
"I thought I was *infatuated* with this boy until I saw him *inebriated*."
"After the bomb exploded, the sky was *illuminated* and I knew the *irradiation* had begun."

TWO QUASI-THEORETICAL SCALES: FOOD AND EATING AND ELEMENTS FROM THE PAST

There is a great obsession with food and eating in industrial urban societies. There is also a belief that the elderly and the psychologically disturbed tend to live more in the past than other people. To see if either or both of these issues are reflected in dreams, two quasi-theoretical scales were developed as part of the Hall/Van de Castle system. One is called food and eating; the other is called elements from the past. As is shown in the main text, both have proved to be useful in studies of specific individuals.

Food and Eating

This scale consists of the consummatory activities of eating and drinking and of preparatory activities that precede and lead up to these consummatory activities. The five subclasses listed below are arranged in order of increasing distance from the consummatory responses that constitute the first subclass. The coding symbol for food and eating is OI (for oral incorporation).

OI1: A character is reported as actually eating, drinking, nursing, swallowing, and so on, or these activities are referred to although they do not actually occur during the dream.

Examples:

"My boyfriend and I ATE hamburgers after the movies."
"I was reminded of the fish we ATE on our last camping trip."
"They say he DRINKS a quart of liquor a day."
"I SWALLOWED the nasty stuff in spite of its bitterness."

OI2: A character is actually in an eating place such as a restaurant, bar, dining room, picnic ground, or cafeteria, or an eating place is referred to in the dream report. *Do not code* if it is explicitly stated that the character is in the eating place for a reason other than that of eating or drinking.

Examples:

"I went into the DINING ROOM to set the table."
"He said he had been at THE PUMP ROOM in Chicago."
"There was a small band playing in the TAVERN."
"We were in the *dining room* playing cards."
"I went into the *bar* to use the telephone."

OI3: A character is preparing food, cooking it, or seeing or using utensils associated with food, or these activities or objects are mentioned in the dream report.

Examples:

"My mother was MIXING SOME CAKE BATTER."
"There was a set of COPPER FRYING PANS hanging on the wall."
"My girlfriend got an ELECTRIC TOASTER for her birthday."
"My sister said I had better attend COOKING SCHOOL if I want to catch a husband."

OI4: A character secures food by buying it, picking it, or some other means, or a character is in a food store, or these are mentioned in the dream report. *Do not code* if it is explicitly stated that the character is in the food store for a reason other than that of buying food.

Examples:

"My mother sent me to BUY BREAD AND BUTTER."
"I told her I was going to PICK STRAWBERRIES."
"I saw the old man STEAL AN APPLE from the stand."
"I dreamed that a new SUPERMARKET was being built across the street from our house."
"I went into the *grocery store* to get change for a dollar."

OI5: Food is seen or mentioned in the dream report but not in connection with any of the foregoing activities; that is, it is not being eaten, served, prepared, or bought. If food is seen or mentioned in connection with one of the foregoing subclasses 1–4, do not give food an additional coding.

Examples:

"There were GRAPES hanging from a vine."
"She asked me if I liked APPLES, and I said yes."
"A still life painting of VEGETABLES hung on the wall."
"She was carrying a huge HAMBURGER in her hand."
"I BOUGHT two *candy bars*."

Additional Coding Rules

1. Code one point for each different subclass that is contained in the dream report.

Examples:

"We BOUGHT *marshmallows*, TOASTED them over the campfire, and ATE THEM." Three points
"We PICKED *blackberries* and MADE WINE." Two points

2. Code one point for each repetition of the same subclass in a dream report when the subclass repetitions take place in different locations or involve different characters.

Examples:

"My mother BOUGHT *bread* while I was PICKING OUT the *meat*." Two points
"First we went to a BAR for a *martini*, and then we went to the CAFETERIA for *roast beef*." Two points
"The neighbor's TOMATOES were larger than our TOMATOES." Two points

3. Code one point for each repetition of the same subclass when the subclass repetitions are separated by intervening events in the dream report.

Example:

"I ATE A QUICK BREAKFAST and dashed off to school because I was late. After class, I studied for a while and then had A SECOND BREAKFAST." Two points

4. *Do not code* mention of a food or food utensil if it is used as some standard of comparison.

Examples:

"It was a rock the size of a *grapefruit*."
"The dress had the same color as a *plum*."
"His eyes got as big as *saucers*."

The Elements from the Past Scale

Seven subclasses of events in dream reports are coded as elements from the past. The coding symbol for elements from the past is RE (for "regression").

RE1: The dreamer dreams of being in a setting or locale in which he has not been for over a year.

Example:

"I was teaching in a school that I taught in WHEN I WAS A YOUNG WOMAN."

RE2: The dreamer dreams of being younger by at least a year.

Example:

"In this dream, I SAW MYSELF AS A CHILD with long pigtails."

RE3: The dreamer dreams of someone he or she has not seen or heard from within a year.

Example:

"I was at a party when in walked Nancy Jones. I HAVE NOT SEEN HER OR THOUGHT ABOUT HER FOR YEARS."

RE4: The dreamer dreams of doing something he or she has not done for at least a year.

Example:

"My brother and I were climbing a mountain. I HAVE NOT BEEN ABLE TO DO ANY CLIMBING FOR THE LAST FIVE YEARS, although I used to do a lot when I was younger."

RE5: The dreamer dreams of someone who has been dead for at least a year.

Example:

"I SAW MY FATHER come into the room and kiss my mother. I knew he was my father, ALTHOUGH HE'S BEEN DEAD FOR OVER 50 YEARS, because he had a black beard that he used to let me pull when I was a child."

RE6: The dreamer dreams of another person as being younger, by at least a year, than he or she currently is.

Example:

"My sister appeared to be about 18 YEARS OLD in the dream although she is actually over 40."

RE7: The dreamer dreams of an object that he or she has not had for at least a year.

Example:

"I was wearing a dress THAT I GAVE AWAY YEARS AGO."

Do not code the following as being regressive:

1. The dreamer or another character is talking in the dream about something that happened in the past.

Example:

"My cousin recalled the time when *we were children* and we had got lost in the woods."

2. The dreamer or another character is reminded in the dream of something that happened in the past.

Example:

"We were all on this large boat that was pitching and tossing. I felt seasick. It reminded me of *the time I had been seasick on our first voyage to Japan.*"

3. Something in the dream is like something in the past but it is recognized as being different.

Example:

"*He looked like an old beau of mine* except he was much taller."

4. After the dreamer has awakened and recalls a dream, he or she associates something in the dream with something in the past.

Example:

"The car we were riding in—well, now that I think about it—*it was like one we had when I was in college.*"

The Unrealistic Elements Scale

I. Unusual activities
  A. Unusual activities of the dreamer.
     Example: "I was taking a shower in the pantry."
  B. Unusual activities of another character.
     Example: "The horse said he wouldn't carry the load."
  C. Unusual activities of plants and inanimate objects.
     Example: "The boat was sailing over dry land."

II. Unusual occurrences
  A. Unusual occurrences to the dreamer.
     Example: "The sword went through my heart without hurting me."
  B. Unusual occurrences to another character.
     Example: "My brother's home was flooded with urine."
  C. Unusual occurrences to plants and inanimate objects.
     Example: "The Vaseline burned a hole in the leather seat."

III. Distorted objects or arrangement of objects
  A. Distorted perception; sudden appearance or disappearance.
     Example: "He just evaporated while I was looking at him."
  B. Distortion (not due to faulty perception) of the usual shape, size, and place of the dreamer, others, or objects.
     Example: "The mountains were made of watermelons."

IV. Metamorphoses
  A. Dreamer changes into another person or vice versa.
     Example: "Actually I became my wife in the dream."
  B. A character changes into another character.
     Example: "The reporters changed into armed guards."
  C. A character changes into an animal or vice versa.
     Example: "The horse changed into my father."
  D. An inanimate object changes into an animate one.
     Example: "The football changed into a sheep."
  E. A dead person or animal becomes alive.
     Example: "The dead bird suddenly flew away."
  F. An object changes into another object.
     Example: "The whole countryside changed into a tank."

Appendix B

The Coding of a Sample Dream Series

To illustrate how the Hall/Van de Castle classification system is used in actual practice, we have appended this series of 10 dreams and an explanation of the coding rationale for each dream. These 10 dreams were obtained from a 21-year-old unmarried male college student who was working as a Fuller Brush salesman part-time. This particular dream series was selected because it contained an unusually large number of coding problems, and it was hoped that by discussing the rationale followed in resolving some of these problems, the potential user would gain a clearer understanding of our classification system. Readers are urged to code each dream before they read how Hall and Van de Castle coded them.

Three caveats before you begin. First, the discussion will seem even more overwhelming than an actual coding of dream reports because it includes codings for activities, objects, and descriptive elements. These are three of the longest and most detailed categories, but they are among the three that are least used except in normative studies or in individual cases where certain activities, objects, or descriptive elements stand out. Thus, the primary focus in reading this appendix probably should be on characters, social interactions, successes and failures, misfortunes and good fortunes, and emotions.

Second, we remind you that in actually coding a series or set of dreams, it is best to code the dreams for one category at a time, such as characters or friendliness. It is much more difficult to code one dream for each category and then go on to the second dream for all categories, and so on. There is just too much to keep in mind. If you code one category at a time for all the dreams, you can review the coding rules before you start and have the pages of this book open to the examples for that category so that you can refer to them quickly if you run into coding questions. Moreover, as we said in the main text, coding all dreams for a given category allows you to develop a mind-set that will assure that you are being consistent in your own coding.

Third, although this appendix suggests that codes be put on a specially designed 5 × 8 card illustrated in the context of each dream, many people may find it more convenient, in this age of easy photocopying, to make multiple copies of the dream reports and have each coder underline the elements that are coded and put the appropriate symbol in the margins. This also makes it easy for someone to check the coding.

You are finally ready to take the plunge. This is not the most dramatic dream series you will ever read. The basis for selection, as we said in the first paragraph above, is that this series contained a very large number of difficult coding decisions. Most series are easier to code, and more fun.

DREAM 1

"I was in a classroom teaching young women several things about cosmetics, hair care, and so on. I remember getting into a big discussion on the virtues of natural hair brushes versus nylon ones and the correct way to brush hair. The class was about 30 women about age 18 in a classroom much like we had in high school (fixed desks, and old building). The women all paid attention and discussed things well."

The coding of characters raises somewhat of a problem in this dream. It is clear that it is a group character and that the group consists of all females. Because no indication was given that the dreamer might be familiar with any of these young women, the group was coded as consisting of strangers. There is some question about age, but since the statement about age 18 was made, this information was used to code the group as an adult one. It will be recalled that age 13 through 17 is the age range covered in the teenage subclass. Because 18-year-olds are considered adults, this was the coding assigned here. It is possible that some of the women in this group may have been younger than 18, but our convention has been to code a group in accordance with the characteristics possessed by the majority of the members.

The only social interaction that occurred was a friendly one. This was coded as an F4 because it was considered that the dreamer was performing a helpful act by instructing the women about personal grooming. Even though such instruction is part of his employment role as a Fuller Brush man, Rule 1 under coding Friendliness states that "It is considered to be a friendly act even though the befriender may be acting in a societal or professional role."

In contrast to most dreams, this dream contains a paucity of activity. The only activity involved is a mutual verbal discussion that takes place between the dreamer and the young women on the virtues of various types of hair brushes.

Series: Dream #: 1   Lines: Words:

Char.	Aggression	Friendliness	Sexuality	Settings	Modifiers
2FSA		D 4> 2FSA		IQ	I+
					A+
				Objects	
				AV	
				HH	
				HH	
				HH	
				BH	
	Activities			HH	
	D V= 2FSA			AV	
					Temporal
					Negative
Success	Failure	Misfortune	Good Fortune	Emotions	Food
					Past

Figure B.1. Coding card for Dream 1.

It is clear that the setting was an indoor one in a classroom; a Q code was given for familiarity because there is some doubt as to whether the dreamer has ever been in this setting before. On the other hand, there is the possibility that he may use this classroom more or less regularly, and it may even be that the dreamer perceived it as the same classroom that he attended in high school. Because a Q code is intended specifically to reflect these situations where it cannot be ascertained from the report how familiar a setting is, it was the code given here.

In the Objects column, the two AV codes for Dream I are given for the classroom and old (high school) building. The four HH codes are for cosmetics, natural bristle hair brushes, nylon brushes, and desks. The BH code is for mentioning hair. The dreamer's high school was not coded because it is contained within the coding for building.

The final codable classification is that of modifiers. The I+ code was assigned for the "big" discussion. "Big" in this sentence does not refer to size but to a quality of intensity. The A+ code was given for describing the building as old. Although the comment that the women discussed things well might seem to be an evaluative statement, it was not coded as such because it could not be considered as belonging in either the aesthetic or moral realm of evaluation. The same rationale explains why teaching the women the correct way to brush hair was not coded. There are no scorable elements for any of the remaining scales.

DREAM 2

"I remember driving up a hill on a paved road. It was a steep hill, probably in Maine. The road made a right-hand turn, but I kept right on going in the same direction I was going. I was going up a trail that was very steep. I kept right on going till I reached the top of this hill. There was no road up there, just a trail and a lot of rocks. I felt rather foolish driving all the way up, and I came back down. Then the setting changed. It was flat-seeming, like Florida is. Then I stopped to see one of my customers, but this was no customer that I recognized. As I saw she was just a customer, I never even got out of the car. She just came to the car window, and I rolled it down to talk to her. She was a woman about 45 and had brown hair. I don't remember the conversation. It was pleasant though. It only lasted a few minutes. I drove on and that's about all I can remember."

Series:		Dream #: 2		Lines:	Words:		
Char.	**Aggression**	**Friendliness**		**Sexuality**		**Settings**	**Modifiers**
1 FOA						OQ	I +
						OQ	C+
						Objects	
						NA	
						ST	
						RG	
						ST	
						NA	
		Activities				RG	
	D P					RG	
	D L					TR	
	D S					TR	**Temporal**
	1 FOA M					BH	1
	D P						
	D V= 1 FOA						**Negative**
	D P						4
	D L						
Success	**Failure**	**Misfortune**	**Good Fortune**	**Emotions**			**Food**
		M1, D					
							Past

Figure B.2. Coding card for Dream 2.

The only character appearing in this dream is the 45-year-old woman. She was coded as O because she was known in a customer role to the dreamer. The subclass of Occupational Identification is not intended to include only long-term occupational pursuits such as doctor, teacher, or policeman; it also serves to cover temporary vocational or avocational roles such as athlete, student, cheerleader, or customer. The psychological rationale underlying the use of the O subclass is that characters so identified have some degree of familiarity in that the dreamer can expect them to behave in a manner consistent with their role characteristics.

No social interactions were coded, although it might be considered that a borderline case of friendliness existed when the woman came to the dreamer's car and he rolled down the car window to converse with her. Had this involved some effort on her part, such as coming downstairs from an upstairs apartment and going out of her way to approach the dreamer, her actions would have been coded as F5 for a friendly visit. Because the dreamer is not very specific about this, it is possible that she was already standing there and made no unusual efforts to initiate a friendly interaction. We do know that the dreamer rolled down his car window to talk to her, which would seem to indicate some minimal friendliness on his part. In the preceding sentence, however he says that he never even got out of the car when he saw that she was "just a customer," so it seems quite doubtful that he was expressing any scorable degree of friendliness toward her.

The activities will be discussed in the same sequence that they were coded within the dream. Both a P and an L were given for the dreamer driving up a hill. The L code is clear because the dreamer is changing his physical location; the P is included for the physical activity of driving the car under these circumstances. The dreamer's descent down the mountain was considered a part of this same driving activity and therefore was not coded. The S code was given for seeing the customer, and the customer was given an M for coming to the car window, since she would have done this through some sort of walking activity. The P was given for the dreamer rolling down the window, and then a mutual V was coded for the dreamer and the customer having a conversation. The final P and L codes were given for the dreamer driving on after the conversation.

In turning our attention to misfortunes, a problem presents itself as to whether an M1 code should be given for the lack of a road on top of the hill. After we considered the sentence about the dreamer feeling rather foolish when he had to drive down after his long trip up, we thought that he perceived he had encountered an obstacle or barrier that prevented him from continuing his drive. Because minor environmental barriers are coded M1, this code was utilized, although this situation would be considered a borderline one.

No emotions were coded, although it might be debated that the dreamer experienced some degree of pleasure or contentment because the conversation was described as pleasant. Because we warned against making inferences about emotional states, we followed our own advice here and refrained from inferring an emotion when the dreamer did not specifically state that this was his reaction. He did say he felt foolish as his reaction to driving up the hill, but this reaction is not classifiable as one of our five coded emotions.

Two settings were coded in this dream: one for the steep hill that the dreamer was attempting to drive up, and the other for the flat area where the dreamer was in his car talking to a customer. The first hill setting is obviously an outdoor one, and the second one appears to be some sort of outdoor street setting, since the dreamer mentions driving away after the conversation. Both settings were coded as Q, because in each, the dreamer indicates some vague familiarity with the settings by being able to classify them approximately geographically; on the other hand, he never provides sufficient information to indicate his exact locale. The Q coding seems best to handle this questionable level of familiarity.

In the Objects class for Dream 2, the two NA codes are for hill and rocks, and the two ST codes are given for road and trail. Two TR codes were assigned: one for the car and one for the car window. The BH code was entered for the woman's hair. An interesting coding problem is raised by the dreamer's reference to Maine and Florida because in both cases he is careful to insert a comment indicating that these are not necessarily those regions. If he had stated that he was in Maine and in Florida, two separate RG codes would definitely be indicated. They do, however, seem to qualify as mentioned objects even though they do not exist with any substantive reality in the dream, and therefore they were coded. Rule 2 under coding Objects states, "Any object that is mentioned in the dream is coded. An object does not need to be physically present to be coded." Hill is coded only once even though it is mentioned in three instances, because it is clear that the dreamer is referring to the same hill. If he described a different hill, one off in the distance, for example, another NA code for the additional hill would have been awarded. Even though the top of the hill might be considered a subunit of the larger unit (i.e., hill), it was felt that it was not a sufficiently demarcated part of the larger unit to warrant being coded in this case.

Several coding problems are also raised with regard to modifiers. Some might consider a paved road to be a straight road with regard to its surface quality, but because a paved road can also be a winding road, a code for linearity would be inappropriate. Similarly, mention of a steep hill might be considered as a size referent, since we code tall or high objects as S+. However, since it seems more appropriate to consider steep as referring to angularity rather than exclusively to height, it was not coded. An I+ was included because the trail was referred to as being very steep. The reference to a "lot of" rocks was not coded as D+ because this subclass requires that a type of bounded area or container must be involved with the implication of fullness or some pressure being exerted against the sides. A lot of rocks in a box would therefore qualify for coding, but a lot of rocks lying on the top of a hill would not. The dreamer's comments about feeling "rather" foolish were not coded as I+ because it's not clear from the word "rather" that he felt strongly or intensely foolish. Foolish was not coded as an evaluative reference because it did not seem to refer to either an aesthetic or a moral judgment. No V− code was awarded for the dreamer when he "stopped," because a V− code is given only for a reference to moving slowly, not to stopping. The C+ code was assigned for the brown hair. The final coding problem occurs in connection with the mention of "pleasant" conversation. Although the aesthetic criteria involved in coding E+ are broad enough to allow any sensation that is pleasant to the senses, the enjoyment here seems to be more a matter of intellectual enjoyment rather than visual, auditory, or other sensual enjoyment.

One temporal code was awarded for mention of the conversation "lasting a few minutes." The four items coded on the negative scale were as follows: "no" road up there, "no" customer that I recognized, I "never" even got out of the car, and I "don't" remember the conversation.

DREAM 3

"In the beginning of this dream I was in the back of a large open truck with a bunch of other boys. It seems that we were going back to school. I cannot remember what we were talking about. We stopped at the edge of a small town, and everyone was getting out to go swimming. I threw down the helmet to my skin-diving wet suit and said "five dollars." Immediately a boy took it and gave me the five dollars (which was for renting it). The place where we swam was much like a place we used to go to in Colorado when I was in summer camp. It was a gorge full of deep pools and a lot of fast-moving water. The boy I rented the helmet to was in the place I wanted to go, but it was so small only I could fit. Finally he moved out and I got in. I had my mask on, so I was doing some diving. I remember thinking I could really earn a lot if I rented out my whole suit. The dream becomes hazy now, but I do remember something about a red and white '57 Ford going up the road. It had a New York plate on it."

The two characters involved in the dream are a bunch of boys and the boy who rented his helmet. Because there is a good possibility that the boys may have been familiar to the dreamer, although they were not so identified, a U coding is relevant. Both characters were coded as adults because this is our convention when no other information is given. Describing them as boys is not a sufficient basis to classify them as teenagers or as children.

Series: Dream #: 3   Lines: Words:

Char.	Aggression		Friendliness		Sexuality	Settings	Modifiers
2MUA						OU	S+
1MUA						OQ	S−
							S+
							V+
							S−
							I+
						Objects	C+
						TR	C−
						RG	
						CL	
						MO	
						RG	
			Activities			RG	
	D +		1MUA	P		NA	
	2MUA	L	1MUA	P>	D	NA	
	D +		1MUA	M		I R	*Temporal*
	2MUA	V	D	M		CL	
	D +		D	M		TR	
	2MUA	M	D	C		ST	*Negative*
	D	P				TR	1
	D	V					
Success		Failure	Misfortune		Good Fortune	Emotions		Food
								Past

Figure B.3. Coding card for Dream 3.

No social interactions were coded. A question might be raised as to whether there was a friendly act on the part of the dreamer in renting out his helmet, but this was not coded. The dreamer says that he threw the helmet down and then announced the price. His actions were impersonal in nature and intended more to benefit himself rather than some individual that he had selected to be the recipient of his friendliness.

The activities will be described in the same sequence in which they appeared within the dream. The L code for the dreamer and the bunch of boys was given for riding in the back of the truck. Although the dreamer does not say specifically that the truck was moving, it becomes evident that it was when he does refer to it stopping. The V code was included for the talking in which the dreamer and the boys engaged, since the wording of the report strongly suggests that some talking was going on while they were in the truck. Getting out of the truck was coded as an M for the dreamer and the boys. The dreamer then engages in a P when he throws down his helmet and a V when he mentions the five dollars. The boy who took the helmet was given a P code for this action. He receives another P code when he gives the dreamer the five dollars. This is coded as a physical interaction because both characters become a part of the physical activity. The boy next receives an M code for moving out of the place where the dreamer wanted to be, and the dreamer receives an M code for getting into this place. An M code is also credited to the dreamer for his diving activities. The dreamer receives a C for thinking about how he could earn a lot of money. The latter is a rather marginal case as C codes are generally reserved for more sustained cognitive activity than that described in this report. It seems, however, that the dreamer was calculating how much he could get for the whole suit at the rate of five dollars for just the helmet, and this would require some degree of concentration.

No strivings, misfortunes, or good fortunes were coded for this dream. Although the dreamer does acquire five dollars in the dream, this is accomplished through his own efforts and therefore cannot be coded as a good fortune. On the other hand, these efforts cannot be treated as a Success because the dreamer does not have to expend any effort pursuing some stated goal.

The coding problems posed by settings revolve first about the issue of how many settings are present. It is clear that one outdoor setting is present where the various swimming activities take place, but it is less clear whether a separate setting code should be given for the initial part of the dream involving the open truck. Because the truck did seem to represent a different locale and the dreamer was apparently there long enough to become engaged in some unremembered conversation with the other boys, it was decided that two outdoor settings should be coded. The truck setting was coded as U because the dreamer does not give any indication that the area they were passing through was familiar. The swimming setting was coded as Q because apparently it was very similar and yet also dissimilar to a familiar place, so that its degree of familiarity to the dreamer remains questionable.

Because so many objects are mentioned in Dream 3, they will be discussed in the same sequential order that they appeared in the dream. The TR code was given for truck, but no separate code was given for mention of the back of the truck, since this was not considered to represent a clearly demarcated part of the vehicle. No code was given for the school reference, since the word "school" here was used in a generic sense and not to denote a specific building. The RG was given for town, but the edge of town is not a scorable region item, since it does not represent a distinguishable part of a larger unit. The wet suit helmet was coded CL, although a strong argument might be offered in favor of considering this as a recreational item, which would then be coded as IR. IR is used more for sporting goods items such as an aqualung, football, or tennis racquet. The MO code was given for the reference to five dollars. Both Colorado and summer camp were coded as RG and are examples of mentioned objects rather than objects that tangibly appear within the dream. Two NA codes were given for the gorge and the pools, but no NA code was given for the mention of water. We do code water as an NA object if it is mentioned in isolation, but do not code it if a body of water is also mentioned (e.g., a reference to the water in the ocean). This convention is followed because the ocean consists of water and does not exist independent of it, and to code mention of both the ocean and the water leads to double coding of the same item. We do, however, code separate and relatively independent parts of a larger unit, as for example, in this dream when the helmet and the whole wet suit are separately coded. The word "place" was not coded because it is too vague and does not seem to refer to any clearly bounded area that would qualify for an RG code. The diving mask was coded as IR because it seemed to be closer to the sporting goods category than to the clothing one. A clothing code was given for the mention of the whole wet suit, however. The two TR codes were given for the '57 Ford and for the New York plate, and the ST code was for the road.

In coding for modifiers, an S+ code was given for the large truck and an S− for the small town. There may be a question regarding whether density should be coded for mention of the bunch of boys in the truck. As indicated earlier, a D+ code is generally reserved for situations where there is an implication of pressure or fullness. If the dreamer had said that the boys were bunched up in the truck, a D+ code would have been appropriate. This same rationale for not coding density also applies for the description of the gorge as full of pools. An S+ code was indicated for the pools being deep, since a description of any one of the three dimensions is sufficient for a size code. The fast-moving water was coded V+, and the place that was so small was given an S− for being small and I+ for the intensifying term "so." The colors on the '57 Ford were handled by assigning a C+ code for the red and a C− code for the white color. The modifier "really" was not coded as I+ because it seems to carry the meaning of realistically rather than any intensity connotation. One negative code was credited for "I *cannot* remember what we were talking about."

DREAM 4

"The time is winter and a group of students and myself are on a field trip. The instructor is telling us about the formation of sand dunes and snow drifts as we walk through the snow. We all have a drawing board and are making a drawing of the areas he tells us about. The lecture then seems to get more artistic than scientific as the beauty of the drifts, trees, and few buildings is pointed out. I remember I was making my drawing with a Bic pen just like the one I am using on this report. I tried to show the way the snow looked as it formed little clouds at the lips of the snow banks as it blew. The ones we were seeing were in beautiful pastels of red, green, and blue. The instructor also pointed out the beauty of the noise of the wind. I made a slight whistle that sounded much like it, and someone else did the same. Just before I awakened, the instructor told us about a canoe that was awarded to the student at Yale who could make the best academic recovery and hold it for a month."

The first character is the group of students coded as J because there is no reason to believe that the group would not be composed of both male and female students. Being identified as students is sufficient to warrant a coding of O, as pointed out in Dream 2. The instructor is coded as a male because in the third sentence, the dreamer uses the masculine pronoun to identify this instructor. Being an instructor clearly qualifies for an O identification code. Had the dreamer indicated he knew the instructor, the coding would have been K, since K takes precedence over O. The remaining character is the someone who whistled after the dreamer whistled. Because no indication of this person's sex was given, an I code is necessary. Although no information is provided as to this character's identity, it seems reasonable to assume that it must have been a student, since they are the only persons, except for the instructor, mentioned in the report. It also seems unlikely that anyone else would have been close enough to hear the dreamer's slight whistle unless this person were also a student. If this had been a field trip to a city, it is much more probable that other people would have been nearby, and in that situa-

Series:		Dream #: 4		Lines:	Words:		
Char.	*Aggression*	*Friendliness*		*Sexuality*		*Settings*	*Modifiers*
2JOA		1MOA 4> D +				OU	E+
1MOA		2IOA					S-
1IOA							E+
							C+
							C+
							C+
						Objects	E+
						NA	I-
						NA	
						CM	
						CM	
						RG	
		Activities				NA	
	1MOA V> D +	D +				AM	
	2JOA	2JOA S				CM	
	D +	D P				CM	*Temporal*
	1IOA+	1IOA P				TR	2
	2JOA M	1MOA V> D +					
	D +	2JOA					*Negative*
	2JOA P						
Success	*Failure*	*Misfortune*	*Good Fortune*	*Emotions*			*Food*
							Past

Figure B.4. Coding card for Dream 4.

tion, a U code would have been given. The student at Yale was not coded as a character because this is an example of a generic reference (that is, no actual student was referred to).

A friendly interaction was coded for the instructor telling the students about the formation of sand dunes. His explanation is considered as a helpful act and therefore coded F4, even though the instructor is only carrying out his teaching role. This point was explained in the discussion of Dream 1.

The first activity is a verbal one, when the instructor tells the dreamer and the students about the sand dunes. An M code is given for the dreamer, students, and instructor, who are all walking through the snow. The dreamer and the students engage in a physical activity when they make drawings of the areas that are pointed out. No code is given for pointing out because it is not clear whether this is done through physical or verbal means. No additional P code was used for the dreamer explaining in the report how he proceeded to make his drawing, since this was the same drawing activity for which the earlier P code was assigned. An S code was given to the dreamer and the students for seeing the little clouds of snow. The whistling engaged in first by the dreamer and later by someone else was coded as two separate physical activities, since it was not done jointly but separately by each character. Another V code was given for the instructor telling the dreamer and the students about the canoe. This was coded as a different verbal activity even though it seems as if there were a continuing dialogue between the instructor and the students, because in this instance it refers to an entirely different topic unrelated to the preceding nature talk and because there were some intervening activities.

Although a success theme was mentioned in the latter part of the dream, no SU coding was introduced because no specific character experienced it. The Yale student was treated as a generic nonscorable character and therefore cannot be associated with any other elements in the dream. Success, in our classification system, can be dealt with only when it is achieved by some scorable character.

Only a single setting is involved in this dream, and this is clearly an outdoor one. This setting was coded as being unfamiliar to the dreamer because although he devoted a great deal of description to it, he never indicated that any part of it was familiar to him. The more lengthy the description of a setting becomes without any indication of familiarity being provided, the greater is the likelihood that a setting is unfamiliar to the dreamer.

Objects will be taken up in the same order that they appeared in Dream 4. Two NA codes were given for the sand dunes and snow drifts. The next reference to snow was not coded separately as it was thought that snow and snow drifts were not different objects, just as the water and pools of the previous dream did not receive two separate NA codes. The two CM codes were given for the drawing board and the drawing. An RG code was given for the areas the instructor tells them about. This represents borderline acceptability, as a more specific designation of some region should generally be provided to receive such a code. The next NA code was given for the trees, but the drifts were not coded because they were coded earlier. The buildings are given an AM code because no information is provided as to what types of buildings they might be. The two CM codes are for the Bic pen and for the report. No code was allowed for snow or snow banks, since snowdrifts had previously been coded. Clouds were not coded because they were clouds of snow, rather than celestial clouds, which would have received an NA code. Similarly, lips were not coded because they obviously do not refer to a body part. Neither noise nor whistle are codable items because it was pointed out in the chapter on coding objects that sounds and things with temporal boundaries are not included in the object class. The final item that was coded was the canoe as a TR object. Yale is not scorable as an object because it does not have a specific enough referent such as a campus or building.

The first modifier is an E+ for the reference to the beauty of the surroundings. S− was given for the little clouds and another E+ for the mention of the beautiful pastels. Red, blue, and green are each given separate C+ codes, since they refer to different colors. Another E+ code was entered for the reference to the beauty of the noise of the wind. I− was used for the mention of the slight whistle that the dreamer made.

Two temporal codes were given: one for indicating the time is winter, and the second for the mention of one month in the last sentence. No negative codes were present, which is unusual in a dream report of this length.

DREAM 5

"The first part of this dream I can remember was about grade school children voting on some issue. They were using red ballots so that collection would be easier. It seems that the ballots were left by the doors of their houses. While this was going on, I was talking with a street sweeper. He was quite well informed and had run for several offices. The last one he ran for had something to do with assisting the town manager. He said he had really done a job at cleaning out the corruptions in the offices then. (This man was a gas station attendant and school bus driver in my home town.)"

The grade school children were coded as J because there is no reason to believe that they do not consist of both male and female children. These children were coded as possessing uncertain identity, because although they were identified as grade school children, they were not identified as pupils. Had they been identified as pupils, the coding would have been O. Since all children of grade school age are coded as C, this presents no coding problem.

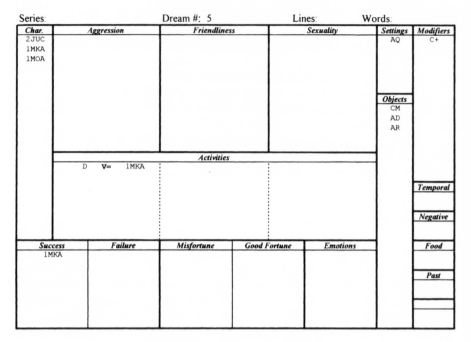

Series: Dream #: 5   Lines: Words:

Figure B.5. Coding card for Dream 5.

The next two characters are both single male adult characters, and it is evident from the dreamer's remarks in parentheses that one of them was personally known to him. It is not clear, however, whether it was the street sweeper or the town manager. It seems somewhat more probable that he is referring to the street sweeper, since the dreamer does describe some interaction with him but not with the town manager. The street sweeper was therefore given a K coding and the town manager an O coding.

The only scorable activity in this report is the mutual verbal interaction between the dreamer and the street sweeper. Although voting and ballots being used were mentioned, it is not clear if the children were actually voting during the dream or just planning to do so. The reference to "this going on" was ambiguous as to whether it refers to the voting or the ballots being left. With regard to the ballots that were being left, no information is provided as to what characters were engaged in this activity, so it is therefore uncodable. The reference to cleaning out the corruptions is also too vague to be coded, since it is unclear what activities were involved.

A code for success was given for "really having done a job of cleaning out the corruptions." Exactly who cleaned them out, the street sweeper or the town manager, is uncertain but it seems as if it were the street sweeper. The only scorable modifier was a C+ for the red ballots. No intensity codes were given for "quite" and "really" because these words represent an indeterminate amount of intensity.

The setting for this dream is very ambiguous, and although it seems as if the dreamer were probably out of doors on some street, this would be making too much of an inference. The fuzziness of the locale description for this setting is best handled by coding it as AQ.

Just three objects were coded in Dream 5: the ballots (CM), the doors (AD), and the houses (AR). The mention of offices was not coded because it does not refer to rooms in a building but to political positions.

DREAM 6

"I was in a coed boarding school or college by the edge of the sea. Many of the classes were outside. I remember one in which about 50 of us were all on one big rock next to the water. I cannot remember the subject of the class, however. We had some classes inside also. In one, I remember I had an assignment to deliver a short talk on the value of the education I was getting at the school and how it differed from other schools. I did a very poor job preparing, but I was sure I would not be called. As it turned out the professor (female) stopped just one person before me. For this class we were in a large room somewhat like a cafeteria. In the corner I was sitting in there were some strange foods that had just been brought in for dinner. I remember one was mastodon meat. After that class we had one outside on the rocks. I left early and did not clean up the things I was working with, but someone else did it for me. After this I remember being tired and wanting to lie down on one of the ceremonial couches but I didn't. Two young women were lying on these, however."

The first character is the group of 50 students from the coed school. Because they are students, the O identification is used. The next character is the female professor who is also coded as O. The person with whom the teacher stopped was treated as a character because it was a specific person called on by the professor rather than a generic character. The sex of the student was not specified, and an I code is therefore indicated. Another individual of indefinite sex appears when the dreamer mentions that someone else cleaned up the things that the dreamer was working with. This character was coded as U because there is a possibility that a janitor or custodial person, rather than another student, cleaned up the dreamer's things. The final character consists of the two young women lying on the couches. Because there is a possibility that this may have been a setting apart from the college, no great confidence could be placed in assuming that these

Series:		Dream #: 6		Lines:	Words:	
Char.	**Aggression**	**Friendliness**	**Sexuality**		**Settings**	**Modifiers**
2JOA		1IOA 4> D			OU	S+
1FOA					IU	I+
1IOA					OU	E-
1IUA						S+
2FUA						
					Objects	
					AV	
					NA	
					NA	
					AE	
					FO	
		Activities			FO	
	D M				NA	
	1IOA P				HH	
						Temporal
						Negative
						4
Success	**Failure**	**Misfortune**	**Good Fortune**	**Emotions**		**Food**
	D (GF)		D			2
						Past

Figure B.6. Coding card for Dream 6.

young women were students, and they were therefore also coded as possessing uncertain identity.

One social interaction occurred in this dream. An F4 was coded for the person who performed a helping act in cleaning up the dreamer's things. There are only two scorable activities, and these develop from this same situation. The first involves an M code for the dreamer when he left class and the other a P for the person who cleaned up. An M code was given rather than an L for the dreamer leaving because it seems implausible that he could have arrived outside on the rocks in any way except through a physical movement on his part.

A failure was attributed to the dreamer because he acknowledged that he did a very poor job in preparing for his classroom assignment. The dreamer, however, did not have to face up to the failure because he was "lucky" not to be called on. A consequence of good fortune was therefore included as part of the overall coding for this situation. Because this latter coding represents an additional type of code, a primary GF code must also be listed in the good fortune column. Any consequence code must also appear as a primary coding in some other column.

The first setting was an outdoor one where the class was held on a big rock next to the water. The next setting is an indoor one that took place in the cafeterialike room. Following that, the next setting occurs outdoors on the rocks. There is a possibility that another setting may have been involved when the dreamer mentions that he wanted to lie on one of the ceremonial couches. These were probably not located outside on the rocks, but since it is not clear that a definite change in locale was involved, no further settings were coded. All three of these settings were coded as being unfamiliar, since the school was not named nor was the region identified, and the dreamer himself seems somewhat confused by the appearance of the cafeterialike room.

In the Object column for Dream 6, the AV code was given for the college. Two NA codes were entered: one for the sea and one for the big rock. Water was not coded as NA because it was already included in the coding for sea. School was not coded because this refers to the previously coded college, and the other schools referred to were not coded because the term is used in a generic sense. The question as to how to code the large room in which the class took place poses a problem. It appears to be a classroom, but it also appears to be a cafeteria where one can have dinner. Because more emphasis was given to the cafeteria aspects in terms of mentioning the foods, dinner, and mastodon meat, it was coded as AE. Two FO codes were given, one for the strange foods and the other for the mastodon meat. Another NA code was given for the rocks where the class took place, and the HH coding represented the ceremonial couches.

For modifiers, an S+ was given for the "big" rock, but an S− was not given for the short talk, since short refers to temporal duration and not to physical length. An E− code was given for the poor job of preparing, and an I+ was also included because it was described as a "very" poor job. This lack of preparation is socially inappropriate, thereby qualifying for a "moral" type of evaluation. An S+ was included for the description of the cafeterialike classroom as being large.

No temporal reference was coded because the dreamer did not refer to any specific unit of time, nor did he attempt to date any event. His mention of leaving class early would therefore not qualify for a temporal code. Four negative codes were given for the following: the dreamer "cannot" remember the subject, he was sure he would "not" be called, he did "not" clean up the things, and he "didn't" lie down on one of the couches. Food and Eating was coded twice: once for the eating setting (i.e., the cafeteria type room) and the other for the dinner preparations. The references to the strange foods and the mastodon meat were not coded because food is scorable only when it appears in isolation, not when it appears with any other scorable Food and Eating items.

DREAM 7

"I cannot remember the beginning of this dream, but in the first part I can recall I was back in the country in Michigan talking with two girls. One was unattractive and the other was fairly nice-looking. I began to get friendly with this one, but not too enthusiastically. She took my display of affection to mean more than I had intended and started trying to get me aroused by pushing her breasts into me. At this point the thought came to my mind that her mother had taught her to do this to enable her to get a boy to marry her. However, I wasn't too concerned with this as I was rather enjoying her. Then we stopped because another girl, a very cute one, came on the scene. I liked her at once and knew that she was a girl I could love. I went over and talked with her for a while and soon was kissing her as the other two girls and the mother looked on sadly. She was great and I remember I wished I could have dreamed more about her or remembered more about her when I woke up."

Four female characters are involved in this dream. They are an unattractive girl and a fairly nice-looking one with whom the dreamer was initially talking, the mother of one of these girls, and the cute girl who later arrived on

Series:			Dream #: 7			Lines:		Words:	
Char.	**Aggression**			**Friendliness**			**Sexuality**		**Settings**	**Modifiers**
1FSA	D	3>	1FSA	D	5>	1FSA	1FSA	4>	D	AG	E–
1FSA				D	2>	1FSA	D	3>	1FSA		E+
1FSA				D	1>	1FSA					I –
1FSA											I –
											E+
											E+
										Objects	I+
										RG	
										BS	
				Activities							
	D	V=	1FSA+								
			1FSA								
	1FSA	P>	D							**Temporal**	
	D	C								1	
	1FSA	L									
	D	M							**Negative**	
	D	V=	1FSA							4	
	D	P>	1FSA								
Success	**Failure**		**Misfortune**		**Good Fortune**		**Emotions**		**Food**	
							AP, D			
							HA, D			
							SD, 1FSA+		**Past**	
							1FSA+			
							1FSA			

Figure B.7. Coding card for Dream 7.

the scene. Because these girls were never referred to by name and there is nothing in the dream report to indicate that the dreamer had ever met them before, all four characters were coded as strangers.

A large number of social interactions take place, and it is exceedingly difficult to disentangle them and assign them to their appropriate classes. An A3 code was given to the dreamer because he appeared to be rejecting the one girl whom he was initially with, since he left her when the cute girl appeared on the scene. This was also apparently perceived as a rejection by the other characters, because the dreamer describes them as looking on sadly. The dreamer says that he began to get friendly with the nice-looking girl. His words were taken at face value, and therefore an F5 was assigned for taking the initiative in visiting or dating another character. From later remarks that the dreamer makes, it is quite probable that he was actually making sexual overtures to this girl, since he elicited a sexual response from her, but this was thought to be too great an inferential jump and the dreamer's own words about getting friendly were therefore accepted. The dreamer was also credited with verbal friendliness (F2) for talking to the cute girl, but once again it is probable that he was making some sort of overtures to this girl because soon afterward he was kissing her. However, since a sexual response may unexpectedly follow an initial friendly response, it was decided to preserve his talking with this girl as a separate friendly act. The dreamer was also credited with a covert feeling of friendliness (F1) toward this same girl when he says that she was great and he wished he could have dreamed about her more. Under the sexual interactions, an S4 code was given to the first girl for taking the initiative in trying to arouse the dreamer through pushing her breasts into him. The dreamer is also credited with an S3 code for kissing the second girl.

The first activity that occurs is a mutual verbal activity between the dreamer and the two girls. No code was given for the dreamer becoming friendly, since it was not specified how this was accomplished. The girl received a P for pushing her breasts into the dreamer. The C code was for the thinking that the dreamer engaged in concerning the mother and the intentions that the girl had toward him. The cute girl who came on the scene received an L code, since it was not specified how she arrived. An M was coded for the dreamer going over to her, since this seems to have been effected by his walking over. The dreamer then engages in a mutual verbal interaction with this girl, followed by a P for the dreamer kissing her. The final activity is a seeing one that is engaged in by the two girls and the mother.

In contrast to most of the other reports, some emotions are mentioned in this dream. The AP was coded for the dreamer mentioning he "wasn't too concerned." Because intensity is not a prerequisite for an emotion to be coded, not being too concerned is coded as readily as being very concerned. The HA was coded for the dreamer "rather enjoying" the girl. The two girls' and the mother's emotions as they looked on the kissing scene constituted the SD code, since they were so described by the dreamer.

Only one overall setting is involved in this dream. It is coded as ambiguous because it is unclear whether the activities are taking place outdoors or indoors. When the dreamer says that he was back in the country, this would suggest an outdoor setting was involved, but it is also possible that some sort of shack or cabin may have been the setting for the dream. The setting is coded as a geographical one because it is identified as taking place in Michigan and the dreamer does not indicate any greater degree of familiarity with the locale.

Only two objects were coded in Dream 7. The first was an RG code for mention of Michigan and the other a BS code for breasts. The reference to "in the country" is too indefinite to warrant coding as a region.

Several aesthetic modifiers are contained in this report. The first one, an E−, was for the description of one of the girls as unattractive; the other girl who was fairly nice-looking was represented by an E+. An I− code was given for the mention of "not too enthusiastically," since what is conveyed by this expression was that the dreamer was only slightly or minimally enthusiastic. The same rationale holds for the description of not being too concerned, so this was also coded I−. The mention in the same sentence of "rather enjoying" is ambiguous as to whether he was slightly or greatly enjoying this experience and so was not coded as an intensity modifier. The two E+'s were coded for labeling the girl as cute and being great. Because the girl was described as very cute, an I+ code is also indicated.

The temporal reference occurs in connection with talking to the cute girl "for a while." The first of the four negative codes appears in the first sentence when the dreamer mentions that he "cannot" remember the beginning of the dream. It will be recalled that the negative scale is the only scale wherein general comments about the dream are also coded. The next N code was for the "unattractive" girl. The remaining two N codes are for "not" too enthusiastically and "wasn't" too concerned.

DREAM 8

"I was in an apartment building and I hinted something to my boss that I might quit Fuller Brush. He said nothing but went down to the patio and started talking with two other Fuller men, one of them the branch manager, and the other a German. When I came in the German began talking about quitting, and the others tried to get him not to. They showed him how much money he was making, etcetera and how foolish it would be to quit. Then they turned to me to ask if I didn't agree with all this. I said I did, and then he asked me why I wanted to quit. The little act they had been putting on was just to show me how foolish I would be if I did quit. I said I wouldn't quit until I was not making any money or my school work was hurt. They said okay. But then the manager began talking about my sales record. He said he wanted to see more than the $65 I turned in last week. I really turned in over $100 but my boss needed some of it to fill his quota. At this point I walked away, but I heard my boss saying that I had worked for him and earned another $50. This seemed to satisfy the men."

The three characters appearing in this dream are all individual male characters. The boss and the branch manager were both coded as being known, because the dreamer did work for the Fuller Brush Company and it was thought that he could name both of these individuals if he were so requested. The German could have been identified on the basis of his accent and may have been known to the dreamer personally. Because the German was also identified as a Fuller Brush man, he was coded as O because this takes precedence over an ethnic coding.

Coding of social interactions in this dream presents some problems. The dreamer's hint that he might quit Fuller Brush sounds as if it might be an aggressive action involving rejection by the dreamer. Yet whom is he reject-

Series:			Dream #: 8			Lines:		Words:	
Char.	**Aggression**			**Friendliness**			**Sexuality**	**Settings**	**Modifiers**
1MKA	D	3>	1MKA	1MKA	4>	D		IQ	
1MKA	1MKA	3>	D						
1MOA									
								Objects	
								AV	
								AR	
								MO	
								MO	
		Activities						MO	
	D	V>	1MKA	1MKA+			1MKA+	MO	
	1MKA	L		1MKA+			1MKA+		
	1MKA	V=	1MKA+	1MKA	V>	D	1MOA VR		
			1MOA	D	VR	1MKA+	1MKA V		**Temporal**
	D	M				1MKA+	D M		1
	1MOA	V				1MOA	D A		
	1MKA+			1MKA	VR	D	1MKA V> 1MKA+		**Negative**
	1MKA+			D	VR	1MKA	1MOA		5
	1MOA	P							
Success	**Failure**			**Misfortune**		**Good Fortune**	**Emotions**		**Food**
									Past

Figure B.8. Coding card for Dream 8.

ing? Is it an actual character such as the boss or branch manager, or should it be coded with a question mark for the impersonalized brush company? We decided that his boss would be the probable victim, so the victim was coded as 1MKA. In actuality, this coding does not distinguish between the boss and the branch manager, which is preferable in this particular situation. A more specific aggression is involved when the branch manager begins to discuss the dreamer's sales record and says that he wishes to see more money turned in. This apparent aggression was coded as an A3 with the dreamer as the victim of the manager's remarks. Things become a bit tangled again as one tries to unravel the boss's actions in filling his quota. With some hesitation, a helping friendly act was coded for the boss because of his speaking in defense of the dreamer and satisfying the others that the dreamer had been doing a satisfactory job. Of course, it could be said that the boss had also behaved aggressively in using some of the dreamer's money initially, but it is not clear whether this may have been company policy. What is clear, however, is that without being requested to do so, the boss did spontaneously exonerate the dreamer, regardless of the preceding events.

The first activity was a verbal one from the dreamer to his boss when he hinted about quitting. The next activity was the boss going down to the patio. This was coded as an L rather than M because it was not specified that the boss walked down. It is possible that he might have taken an elevator. A mutual verbal activity was coded for the boss talking with the branch manager and the German. The dreamer received an M code for coming into the patio, since this would have involved walking. No code was given for the dreamer coming down to the patio as there was for the boss, since the dreamer's trip was not mentioned in the report. A code of V was listed for the German when he began talking, but the others trying to get him to remain and showing him about the money he was making did not receive a code because it was not clear what methods they used to accomplish this. The three characters received a P code for turning to the dreamer, and all three are credited with a verbal activity directed toward the dreamer for asking him why he wanted to quit. In actuality, probably only one person asked him, but since the report states that "they" turned to ask, all three are represented in the coding. A series of reciprocal verbal replies follows. First the dreamer is credited with a VR when he replies to them that he did agree, then another is entered for someone, probably the boss, asking why the dreamer wanted to quit. The dreamer then receives a VR for replying that he won't quit, and the final VR appears when they, presumably all three, reply by saying okay. The preceding coding is intended to reflect that there was one continuing verbal activity going on, and the various questions and replies that made up the bulk of this conversation were coded as reciprocal activities. Then a V was coded for the manager who began talking about the sales record. This introduced a new topic of conversation and was coded separately from the preceding conversation. No S code was given for the boss mentioning that he wanted to see more than $65, because this does not refer to any current or completed activity but to a colloquial way of speaking. The same explanation holds for why the dreamer "turning in" money was not coded. The dreamer walking away received an M code, and an A code was recorded for hearing his boss. The last V appears for the boss explaining to the other two men about the other $50.

Only one setting was coded, an indoor one for being in the apartment building. Although mention is made of going down to the patio, it is not clear that this was located outside, and it was therefore treated as if it were a part of the building itself. With regard to familiarity, it might appear that the apartment building was not too familiar, since it is described only by the word "an," but the patio is described by the definite article "the," suggesting that the dreamer may have had some experience with this building. A Q code therefore seemed best to handle this ambiguity. In the latter part of the report, the dreamer describes walking away, but it was never stated how far away he walked or to where, so no additional setting was coded.

The first two objects in Dream 8 are AR and are coded for the apartment building and the patio. Four MO codes were assigned: the first for the mention of how much money the German was making, and the remaining three for the specific sums of money mentioned, (i.e., $65, $100, and $50).

A temporal code was entered for the reference to last week. The negative codes were given for the boss saying "nothing," the others trying to get the German "not" to quit, asking the dreamer if he "didn't" agree with this, the dreamer saying he "wouldn't" quit, and the dreamer "not" making any money.

DREAM 9

"The first part of the dream I can remember started in a monstrous hunting lodge that, for some reason, had live deer walking around. This did not seem to excite me or the others who were there (all male and only one I knew in real life—a man I used to hunt with). The deer were mostly doe, but there were a few buck. Only spike horns however. Later, I went outside and saw two hunters and told them about the deer. Then a doe came out and one of the hunters shot it, but only I could see this, since it went behind a tree right after he shot. I heard him say 'I missed' and then the next thing I knew, he had hit me in the ankle, but only with a couple pieces of buckshot. I went to a hunting store to get a first aid kit but ran into a Spanish-speaking saleslady that couldn't understand me. Finally, I got the kit and fixed myself up."

The first character mentioned in this report is the live deer. Although later on the dreamer distinguishes between them on the basis of sex, only one group of deer is listed because coding distinctions are not made within the

Series: _____   Dream #: 9   Lines: _____   Words: _____

Char.	Aggression			Friendliness			Sexuality	Settings	Modifiers
2ANI	D	3>	2ANI	D	4>	2MOA		IU	S+
1MKA	1MOA	7>	1ANI					OU	
2MSA								IU	
2MOA									
1ANI									
1MOA									
1FOA								**Objects**	
								AE	
								BH	
								NA	
								BE	
								IW	
				Activities				AV	
	2ANI	M		D	A			HH	
	D	M		1MOA	V				
	D	S		D	L				*Temporal*
	D	V>	2MOA	D	P				
	1ANI	M							
	1MOA	P>	1ANI						*Negative*
	D	S							2
	1ANI	M							

Success	Failure	Misfortune	Good Fortune	Emotions	Food
D	1MOA	M5, D			
		M1, D (SU)			*Past*

Figure B.9. Coding card for Dream 9.

animal subclass with regard to age, sex, or familiarity. The man the dreamer knew in real life was given a K code. The other males that the dreamer did not know were coded as strangers. They would have been coded as O if they were identified as hunters. The two hunters were coded as O. An individual code was given for the one doe that came out and an individual code for the one hunter who attempted to shoot it. Individual characters differentiated from a larger group are coded separately. The Spanish-speaking saleslady was coded as O rather than E, because occupational identification takes precedence over ethnic identification.

As in the last dream, social interactions pose some coding problems. The difficulties are encountered in handling the dreamer's activities when he tells the hunters about the deer. We decided that to inform hunters where they might be able to obtain their sought-after goal of deer would be a friendly thing to do, and we coded it as an F4. In doing so, however, the dreamer must play the role of accomplice or intermediary in causing the expected death of the deer. The dreamer was therefore also credited with an aggressive act (A3) against the group of deer. The hunter who shot at the one doe clearly displayed aggressive behavior toward this animal. Even though the hunter in this case missed hitting the deer, his aggression qualifies as A7 because he engaged in a threatening act with a weapon.

Under activities the M code was given for the group of deer walking, and an M code was also given for the dreamer when he went outside. The S code is for seeing the two hunters, and the V is for the dreamer telling the hunters about the deer. The doe who came out of the lodge was given an M, and a P was credited to the hunter who shot at it. The dreamer receives another S code for seeing this. Another M was given to the deer for going behind the tree, because this seems to represent an activity different from coming out of the lodge, since it did not occur until after the hunter had shot. An A was credited to the dreamer for hearing the hunter and a V to the hunter when he said he missed. It was not explained how the dreamer arrived at the hunting store, so this was coded with an L. It is not clear exactly what was involved in the dreamer fixing himself up with the first aid kit, but it would seem to necessitate some physical activity and was therefore coded as a P.

In the striving classification, a success code was given to the dreamer for finally obtaining the first aid kit and fixing himself up. This was the task that he set for himself in going to the hunting store, and after overcoming the obstacle of the saleslady who couldn't understand him, the dreamer did manage to achieve his goal. An FL code was recorded for the hunter who failed to hit the deer he was attempting to shoot and who acknowledged his failure by saying he missed. An M5 was coded for the dreamer because of the injury he accidentally received. It is true that he was shot by one of the hunters, but this was not an intentional act on the part of the hunter and therefore qualifies as a misfortune. An M1 was also coded for the dreamer encountering the obstacle of the Spanish-speaking saleslady who couldn't understand him. Again the misfortune occurs indirectly as the result of another individual, but the saleslady was not being intentionally unhelpful to the dreamer, so a misfortune rather than an aggression should be coded. Because the dreamer was able somehow to secure the kit, an additional successful consequence is recorded as part of the M1 coding. There is a question as to whether a good fortune was present in terms of the bountiful environment provided by the lodge full of deer, but since neither the dreamer nor the others in the lodge had any apparent intentions of hunting, this would not constitute any special good luck for them. Had the two hunters come upon the deer themselves, a GF could have been coded for them. Because their awareness of the group of deer was made possible through the dreamer's information, they do not encounter any impersonal good luck but rather a friendly act on the part of another person.

The initial setting was an indoor one located within the hunting lodge. The dreamer then went outside and talked to the hunters, so the dream locale shifted to an outdoor one. Eventually the dreamer enters a hunting store, so a final indoor setting is indicated. All three settings were coded U because no indication was given that the dreamer had ever seen any of these settings in real life.

In Dream 9, the AE was coded for the hunting lodge and the BH for the mention of the spike horns on the buck. An NA code appears for the tree and a BE for the dreamer's ankle. The pieces of buckshot were placed in the weapon subclass and the hunting store was coded AV. The difference between a hunting lodge being coded AE and a hunting store being coded AV is that the former is used for recreational purposes, while the latter is a place where business transactions occur. The first aid kit was coded HH, since medicines are considered household items.

The only modifier present in this dream is the S+ for the description of the hunting lodge as monstrous. Two negative codes were present: this did "not" seem to excite me, and the saleslady "couldn't" understand the dreamer. For two reasons, no code for emotion was given to the dreamer's statement that this didn't seem to excite him. First, the verb "excite" is too nondifferentiating in describing the type of emotion involved for it to be classified as one of the five scorable emotions. Second, the dreamer has effectively negated the presence of any emotion through the wording of his report. Note that this wording is different from saying something such as "I did not seem to be very excited," which would indicate that the dreamer was at least slightly excited.

DREAM 10

"I was in a bar drinking beer with my roommate. The bar was in Fort Carson, but did not resemble any one we had been in. It most closely resembled a little lunch counter. In fact, the more I think of it, it was exactly the same. My roommate and I were fairly high on the beer we had been drinking. A male friend we had brought with us was asleep on the floor between us. We were talking and joking about various things. The subject of age came up, and my roommate was telling me how lucky I was because I never had to worry about I.D. cards now that I am 21. The bartender heard this conversation and thought it was I who was underage. He asked for my I.D. so I gave it to him, sure that he would find it okay. He didn't, however, and thought the card was a fake, so he booted me out. My roommate was laughing so hard it was all he could do to keep his seat. I, too, was laughing but was a little mad at the bartender, so I started beating on the door. The bartender finally came and this time looked at all my identification. Then he let me back in. I went over to my roommate, hit him on the back and bought him a beer."

Three individual male characters were described in this dream. The first was the dreamer's roommate, the second was a friend they had brought with

Series: Dream #: 10   Lines: Words:

Char.	Aggression			Friendliness			Sexuality	Settings	Modifiers
1MKA	1MOA	7>	D	D	6>	1MKA		IU	S-
1MKA	D	2R	1MOA	D	3>	1MKA		OU	I+
1MOA								IU	I-
									A-
									E-
								Objects	
								AE	
								RG	
								AE	
								FO	
								AD	
			Activities					CM	
	D	+		1MOA	P>	D		HH	
	1MKA	P		1MKA	E			AD	
	D	V=	1MKA	D	E				**Temporal**
	1MKA	V>	D	D	P				
	1MOA	A		1MOA	M				**Negative**
	1MOA	V>	D	1MOA	S				3
	D	P>	1MOA	D	M				
	1MOA	C		D	P>	1MKA			

Success	Failure	Misfortune	Good Fortune	Emotions	Food
D				AN, D	3
					Past

Figure B.10. Coding card for Dream 10.

them, and the third was the bartender. The roommate and friend were coded as K because they would be familiar to the dreamer, and the bartender was coded as O.

The bartender was being aggressive when he forced the dreamer to leave the bar. There is some question as to how this was accomplished. Because the dreamer used the words "booted me out," the bartender's act was coded A7. The dreamer reciprocated with a mild form of aggressive activity when he began beating on the door. The language of the report structures this as the consequence of the dreamer being a little mad at the bartender. If the dreamer had only felt a little mad without doing anything about it, it would have been an A1, but since the dreamer did attempt to express his aggression in some more overt fashion, it was coded as an A2. This subclass can be used for such indirect expressive behavior as slamming a door to show one's anger. The dreamer initiated two friendly acts toward his roommate: one when he hit him on the back and the other when he bought him a beer. The back slapping is a form of expressing friendliness through physical means and is therefore an F6, while the purchasing of the beer is similar to offering a gift and was coded as F3.

Under activities, a code of P was used for the dreamer and his roommate drinking beer. A mutual V appears for the dreamer and his roommate talking and joking. The roommate then initiates a V to the dreamer, and an A code is given to the bartender for hearing this remark. The bartender then receives a V for asking the dreamer about his I.D. card, and the dreamer interacts in a physical activity with the bartender when he hands him his card. The C is credited to the bartender for the thinking activity that he engages in when he first thinks that the dreamer is underage and then later when he decides that the dreamer's card is a fake. Following this the bartender performs a physical act when he puts the dreamer out. The roommate laughing was coded as E, and an E was also included for the dreamer laughing. The next P is coded for the dreamer beating on the door. The bartender's arrival at the door is coded as M, since he would have to walk to reach there. An S code is given to the bartender for looking at the identification, and the dreamer receives an M for going over to the roommate, after which a P is coded for the dreamer slapping the roommate on the back.

A successful striving was coded in this dream for the dreamer being able eventually to get back into the barroom. He had made this his goal, and after engaging in beating on the door, he was able to prove his age and be readmitted as he intended. The emotion of anger was coded for the dreamer because he stated that he was a little mad at the bartender.

Three settings were involved. The first consisted of an indoor setting when the dreamer and his roommate were in the bar or lunch counter. The second occurred when the dreamer was booted out and he was standing outside beating on the door. This was coded as an outdoor setting. Finally, the dreamer was able to re-enter the bar, and some of his activities after returning inside are described. The dreamer specifically said that the bar did not resemble any that he had visited in real life, so both indoor settings were coded as unfamiliar. It appears probable that the area immediately adjacent to the bar or lunch counter, that is, the area around the front door where he stood, was also unfamiliar to the dreamer, so the outdoor setting was also coded U.

In Dream 10, the code of AE appeared for the bar and RG for Fort Carson, which is a city. Another AE was coded for mention of the lunch counter. FO was recorded for the beer, and the floor was coded as AD. The I.D. card was coded as CM. The HH was coded for referring to seat, although it is a little vague as to whether seat means bar stool, or whether it means that the roommate had difficulty keeping his balance. A second AD was included for the door and a BT for the roommate's back. Another FO code was given for the beer that the dreamer bought, since this represented a different beer.

Reference to the lunch counter being little received an S− code, but no code was given for mention of being fairly high on beer. In some ways this sounds as if a reference to intensity is being made, but both the terms of "fairly" and "high" are too vague to be coded in this case. An I+ was coded for the roommate laughing so hard, and an I− was coded for being a little mad at the bartender. The reference to being underage was coded as an A−. It will be recalled that mention of a specific age is not scorable as an age modifier, but the term "underage" here has the meaning of being too young. An E− code was given for the bartender initially judging that the card was a fake.

Three negative codes appear for this dream. The first was for the bar, which did "not" resemble any they visited; the second was for "never" having to worry about I.D. cards; and the third was for when the bartender "didn't" find the card okay. Three food and eating codes were given for this dream: one for the overall setting of being in a bar or lunch counter, another for the activity of drinking beer, and the third for the activity of buying the roommate a beer. Mention of the word "beer" itself was not coded in this case, because food or drink are not coded separately if they appear as part of the coding for any of the food and eating subclasses. A clean copy of the coding card (Figure B.11) is provided on the next page for those who want to make copies.

Series: Dream #:   Lines: Words:

Char.	Aggression	Friendliness	Sexuality	Settings	Modifiers
				Objects	
		Activities			
					Temporal
					Negative
Success	Failure	Misfortune	Good Fortune	Emotions	Food
					Past

Figure B.11. Blank coding card.

Appendix C

Instructions for Reporting Dreams in Written Form

The following instructions, with minor variations, have been used in the quantitative studies of dream content carried out by Hall, Van de Castle, their students, and their colleagues:

> Please describe the dream exactly and as fully as you remember it. Your report should contain, whenever possible, a description of the setting of the dream, whether it was familiar to you or not; a description of the people, their sex, age, and relationship to you; and a description of any animals that appeared in the dream. If possible, describe your feelings during the dream and whether it was pleasant or unpleasant. Be sure to tell exactly what happened during the dream to you and the other characters. Continue your report on the other side and on additional sheets if necessary.

INSTRUCTIONS FOR OBTAINING "MOST RECENT DREAMS"

For our study of Most Recent Dreams, we prefaced the above instructions as follows:

Your Most Recent Dream

Age: _____

Gender: _____

Date: _____

We would like you to write down the last dream you remember having, whether it was last night, last week, or last month. But first please tell us the date this dream occurred: _____. Then tell us what time of day you think you recalled it: _____ .

Please describe the dream exactly and as fully as you can remember it. Your report should contain, whenever possible, a description of the setting of the dream, whether it was familiar to you or not; a description of the people, their sex, age, and relationship to you; and a description of any animals that appeared in the dream. If possible, describe your feelings during the dream and whether it was pleasant or unpleasant. Be sure to tell exactly what happened during the dream to you and the other characters. Continue your report on the other side and on additional sheets if necessary.

_____

_____

_____

_____

_____

_____

_____

_____

_____

_____

_____

_____

_____

Turn over if more space is needed.   Thank You

Appendix D

Statistical Appendix

In this appendix, we discuss the rationale for the statistical approach we use. We also explain how to use two tables that make it possible to derive our two statistics with relative ease.

To bring context and perspective to what follows, we paraphrase a reflection on several decades of work by the perceptive statistical psychologist Jacob Cohen, on whose insights and formulations we have relied very heavily. Looking back on 40 years of statistical work, Cohen (1990) makes the following observations that we think worthy of careful consideration by anyone contemplating quantitative studies of dream content.

First, "less is more," meaning it is far better to work with fewer variables on highly targeted issues than to put many variables into a large matrix with the hope that sophisticated statistics will bring forth new findings (they can, but the new findings are often hard to interpret unless you have a good theory to begin with). Second, the sample sizes in most psychological studies are much too small to conclude anything with confidence; for example, it takes samples of over 160 observations to have a 60% chance of detecting a real difference of about 15 percentage points at the .01 level of confidence.

Third, "simple is better," especially clear and simple graphic representations of results. Fourth, the significance levels of concern to most psychological investigators (which really should be called "stability" or "reliability of findings" levels) are far less important than "effect sizes," that is, the *magnitude* of the differences between samples. In fact, rather than reporting significance levels, it would be better—and more sobering—if we stated "confidence intervals," meaning the range of values within which new findings are likely to fall if we repeat the study many times. Confidence intervals can tell us if there is likely to be great variability in "highly significant" findings, which is especially important when the study is based on a small sample. Cohen (1994) demonstrates these points in a second reflective paper devoted primarily to the irrelevance of significance levels. Fifth, no matter how large the sample size or how sophisticated the statistical analysis, there is no substitute for the systematic replication of findings.

In the spirit of Cohen's reflections, we have decided to use just one closely related pair of statistics from among several that are possible. This narrowing of statistical focus allows us to be consistent throughout and to minimize any confusion that might arise for those who are unfamiliar with statistics. The statistical approach we have chosen, as noted in the introduction to Chapter 4, uses simple percentages and the differences between those percentages. Technically, we are dealing with "proportions," but percentages are just a special case of a proportion in which the denominator is 100.

An approach based in percentages is useful for us for two relatively unique reasons. First, our content categories, as stated in Chapter 1, are nominal ones, and nominal categories lend themselves very readily to percentage data (e.g., Reynolds, 1984:36–37). Second, percentages are a good approach to analyzing our data because the test for statistical significance between two independent proportions is equivalent to better-known statistics with two-sample comparisons, and we are usually comparing only two samples. For example, as will be shown later in this discussion, percentages in a two-sample comparison are the equivalent of the better-known and more widely used 2×2 table. With a 2×2 table, as also will be shown, several different statistical tests provide equivalent results.

Using percentages, we can determine both the statistical "significance" or "stability" of differences between two samples and the relative magnitudes (psychological significance) of differences. Our test for statistical significance is called the "significance of differences between two independent proportions"; the result it yields is usually called a "z" score (e.g., Ferguson, 1981:186). The statistic for effect size with proportions has been named "h" by its creator (Cohen, 1977:180). The effect size statistic h is determined first in Table D.2 and then used to find the significance level in Table D.3. Thus, there is no need to use the usual formula for determining the z score, although a very simple formula is provided for determining a z score on the basis of h. We also provide a simple method to determine confidence intervals for our sample h values.

Given that an approach based in percentages is possible, the next question becomes whether this type of analysis is as good as the other statistics we could have chosen. The simple answer is that this approach is equivalent to the other statistics we could have used. This may come as a surprise to some readers; therefore, we take a few paragraphs to compare proportion-based statistics with the alternatives.

First, it is important to realize that a proportion is merely a type of mean where all the values in the distribution of scores are either zero or one. As Cohen (1977:179) explains:

A proportion is a special case of an arithmetic mean, one in which the measurement scale has only two possible scores, zero for the absence of a characteristic and one for its presence. Thus, one can describe a population as having a proportion of males of .62, or, with equal validity (if not equal stylistic grace), as having a mean "male-ness" of .62, the same value necessarily coming about when one scores each male 1, each nonmale 0, and finds the mean.

Cohen (1977:179) then notes that "the same kind of inferential issues" are involved with proportions as with means in general (cf. Ferguson, 1981:185 for the same point). Given the fact that the same logic underlies both mean-difference and proportional-difference testing, there is no particular advantage for our purposes to determining the mean number of characters or aggressions or emotions per dream, as some researchers do. Indeed, there are major problems with such an approach, as explained in the introduction to Chapter 4, unless there is a correction for dream length (cf. Hall, 1969a, 1969b, for discussions of this issue).

Second, percentage differences between two samples can be viewed in correlational terms (Cohen, 1977:179). Moreover, as Rosenthal and Rubin (1982) have shown, the percentage difference between two samples is exactly equal to the Pearson r between the two samples. For example, a difference of 13 percentage points between two samples can be understood as an r of .13 between two dichotomous variables. Thus, there is nothing to be gained by working with correlational statistics instead of percentages with our kind of data.

Third, percentage differences between two samples are also exactly equivalent to a chi-square analysis of a 2×2 table. For example, we could put our findings on gender differences in the percentage of familiar characters, as presented in Chapter 4, in the format shown in Table D.1.

In effect, this 2×2 table displays both the "familiarity" and the "unfamiliarity" percents. Although chi-square is a very versatile and useful statistic because it can be used to analyze tables with any number of rows and columns, it yields exactly the same results with a 2×2 table as our test for the significance of differences between proportions; specifically, $z = \sqrt{\chi^2}$. (See Ferguson, 1981:211–213, for an excellent discussion of the relationship between proportional differences and chi-square.) Moreover, the effect size statistic derived from chi-square, called phi, is exactly equivalent to the

Table D.1. Gender Differences
in Familiarity Percent

	Male dreamers	Female dreamers
Familiar characters	501 (45%)	796 (58%)
Unfamiliar characters	607 (55%)	567 (42%)

difference between the percentages in the top row of a 2×2 table. That is, r = phi in a 2×2 table. Lambda, a widely used measure of association in tabled data, also is equal to r and phi in a 2×2 table when percentages are used. Thus, there is no advantage for us in using chi-square and phi (or lambda) instead of z and h.

Even though a percentage-based approach is equivalent to the alternatives with our nominal categories and two-sample designs, and percentages also are useful in multidimensional tables (Reynolds, 1984:36), why should a percentage-based approach be favored over the others? The main reason is to be found in the two crucial analytical problems we discussed at the outset of Chapter 4, namely, correcting for (1) differences in dream length and (2) variations in raw frequencies of elements. Once we adopt a solution to those problems using percentages and indexes, we are in a situation where a test of significance using differences between two independent proportions (percentages and indexes in our terminology) makes the most sense.

Each new investigator makes her or his decision on what statistics to use on the basis of a variety of considerations. However, given the fact that the statistics we have chosen are equivalent to the alternatives with our kind of data, we hope others will adopt our statistical conventions when using the Hall/Van de Castle coding system so that all future studies with it will be easily comparable.

DETERMINING AND UNDERSTANDING EFFECT SIZE: h

As we noted earlier in this appendix, it is very easy to determine effect sizes using percentages. Basically, the difference between the two percentages is the "effect size." As so often happens when things seem too good to be true, however, there is unfortunately a slight complication. The same percentage difference means slightly different things at the extremes of the 0–100% distribution than it does in the middle. For example, the 10 percentage points between, say, 15% and 5%, or between 95% and 85%, both of which are at the extreme ends of the range, do not mean the same thing as the same percentage difference in the middle of the range, say between 50% and 40%. We don't need to understand why this is so, although it has to do with the fact that "the standard deviation of the sampling distributions depend upon their population parameters, which are unknown." (See Cohen, 1977:180, and Section 4.2 for the explanation.) Nor do we have to understand the mathematics used to correct the problem. We simply use Table D.2 to convert our two percentages into the needed corrections and then subtract one from the other to derive h, our effect size.

To show how to use Table D.2, let us return to the gender difference in familiarity percent (45% for males, 58% for females). We simply find 58% in

Table D.2. Determining "h" from the Differences between Two Percentages

To determine the "effect size" of the difference between two percentages, change each percentage (P) into an X using the table below, then subtract the smaller X from the larger one. The remainder is the effect size h.

Example: P_1 is .16 and P_2 is .55. First, go down the first P column until you reach .16, and then write down the .823 in the X column to the right. Second, go to the third P column, find .55, and then write down the 1.671 in the X column to the right. Third, subtract .823 from 1.671. The result is h = .848, which we round off to .85.

P	X	P	X	P	X	P	X
0	.000	25	1.047	50	1.571	75	2.094
1	.200	26	1.070	51	1.591	76	2.118
2	.284	27	1.093	52	1.611	77	2.141
3	.348	28	1.115	53	1.631	78	2.165
4	.403	29	1.137	54	1.651	79	2.190
5	.451	30	1.159	55	1.671	80	2.214
6	.495	31	1.181	56	1.691	81	2.240
7	.536	32	1.203	57	1.711	82	2.265
8	.574	33	1.224	58	1.731	83	2.292
9	.609	34	1.245	59	1.752	84	2.319
10	.644	35	1.266	60	1.772	85	2.346
11	.676	36	1.287	61	1.793	86	2.375
12	.707	37	1.308	62	1.813	87	2.404
13	.738	38	1.328	63	1.834	88	2.434
14	.767	39	1.349	64	1.855	89	2.465
15	.795	40	1.369	65	1.875	90	2.498
16	.823	41	1.390	66	1.897	91	2.532
17	.850	42	1.410	67	1.918	92	2.568
18	.876	43	1.430	68	1.939	93	2.606
19	.902	44	1.451	69	1.961	94	2.647
20	.927	45	1.471	70	1.982	95	2.691
21	.952	46	1.491	71	2.004	96	2.739
22	.976	47	1.511	72	2.026	97	2.793
23	1.000	48	1.531	73	2.049	98	2.858
24	1.024	49	1.551	74	2.071	99	2.941

Note: This table is taken from Cohen (1977:183), who abridged it from Table 9.9 in D. B. Owen, *Handbook of Statistical Tables* (Reading, MA: Addison-Wesley, 1962). It is reproduced with the permission of both publishers.

For those who might want to calculate h directly with a software program, the formula is:

$X = \cos^{-1}(2(1 - P) - 1)$, or

$h = \cos^{-1}(2(1 - P_1) - 1) - \cos^{-1}(2(1 - P_2) - 1)$

P is a proportion between 0 and 1, not a percentage.

The $\cos^{-1}$ operation should return a value in radians, *not* degrees.

the third "P" column from the lefthand side of the table and convert it to 1.731, the number to its right in the X column. We then locate 45% in the second "P" column and convert it to 1.471. Next we subtract 1.471 from 1.731, which gives us an h of .26.

To situate this particular h of .26 in the context of more familiar numbers, and thus give it more meaning, we return to the Pearson r and the arithmetic difference between two percentages. Roughly speaking, h is about twice as large as a Pearson r or the arithmetic difference between two percentages, at least for all but the extremes of the 0–100% range. Therefore, when readers see a difference of 5 to 20 percentage points between two samples on some content category, they can make a mental note that the effect size is a small one (h = .10 to .40). If there is a difference ranging from 20 to 35 percentage points, this is a medium effect size (h = .41 to .70). If they see a difference of 35 percentage points or greater, they can note that the effect size is a large one (h = .71 or greater).[1]

Relatively few effect sizes in our studies can be described as "large," and in fact large effect sizes are relatively rare in most psychological research. Our largest effect sizes appear in Chapter 8 when individuals are compared with the norms. In the area of gender differences, most of our findings are in the small to medium range. Thus, most of the gender differences presented in Chapter 4 can be characterized as statistically significant, that is, as very likely to be real differences, but not as large differences in the sense of magnitude. Men and women are far more similar than different in their dream content when it comes to our content categories. Nonetheless, as we also say in Chapter 4, the differences are important enough that we have to use different norms for seeing how an individual dream series of a male or female is typical or atypical.

As shown in Chapter 4, we also use the h statistic to create what we call the "h-profile," the kind of clear "graphic representation" Cohen (1990) stresses. The h-profile is simply the graphic display, for any combination of our major percentages and indexes, of the h difference between our norms and any new series or set of dream reports. By comparing h-profiles, we may

---

[1]In years past, psychologists were not impressed with correlational findings between .10 and .30, which are similar to small and medium effect sizes, because they supposedly are not accounting for much of the variance, as determined by squaring the correlation. Thus, a correlation of .30 was said to be accounting for "only" 9% of the variance. More recently, it has been shown that such an interpretation is erroneous (e.g., Hunter & Schmidt, 1990:199–201; Rosenthal & Rubin, 1982). To put the point most dramatically, a correlation of .32 is "the correlational equivalent of increasing a success rate from 34% to 66% by means of an experimental treatment procedure" (Rosenthal & Rubin, 1982:166). Thus, Rosenthal and Rubin argue psychologists have been selling their findings short over the years. We agree with their argument, and think that the same reasoning applies to the percentage differences we find in quantitative studies of dream content.

be able to see if there are systematic patterns in the dream reports of specific types of individuals or groups.

DETERMINING SIGNIFICANCE LEVELS

Now that we have discussed h and its relationship to other measures, and shown how to derive it from Table D.2, the next task for this statistical appendix is to show how h can be used in conjunction with sample size to determine statistical significance from Table D.3. As noted earlier in this appendix, Table D.3 is a substitute for using the formula for determining the significance of differences between two independent proportions.

To illustrate the use of Table D.3, let us assume that we are comparing two samples each having 140 observations in them and an h difference of .32. Because the N in both samples is the same, we simply look down the column marked N or N' until we come to 140. We look to our right and see that an h

Table D.3. Determining Statistical Significance from h using N or N'

N or N'	.05	.01	N or N'	.05	.01	N or N'	.05	.01
15	.72	.95	36	.47	.61	88	.30	.39
16	.70	.92	37	.46	.60	92	.29	.38
17	.68	.89	38	.45	.60	96	.29	.38
18	.66	.86	39	.45	.59	100	.28	.37
19	.64	.84	40	.44	.58	120	.26	.34
20	.62	.82	42	.43	.57	140	.24	.31
21	.61	.80	44	.42	.55	160	.22	.29
22	.60	.78	46	.41	.54	180	.21	.28
23	.58	.76	48	.41	.53	200	.20	.26
24	.57	.75	50	.40	.52	250	.18	.24
25	.56	.73	52	.39	.51	300	.17	.22
26	.55	.72	54	.38	.50	350	.15	.20
27	.54	.71	56	.37	.49	400	.14	.19
28	.53	.69	58	.37	.48	450	.14	.18
29	.52	.68	60	.36	.48	500	.13	.17
30	.51	.67	64	.35	.46	600	.12	.15
31	.50	.66	68	.34	.45	700	.11	.14
32	.49	.65	72	.33	.43	800	.10	.13
33	.48	.64	76	.32	.42	900	.10	.13
34	.48	.63	80	.31	.41	1000	.09	.12
35	.47	.62	84	.31	.40	1200	.08	.11

Note: The decimal numbers in this table are h values. Round-off error leads to the same h value for slightly different sample sizes in a few cases.
This table is adapted from Cohen (1977, Tables 6.3.4 and 6.3.5, pp. 192–195). It is used with the permission of the publisher and the author.

of .23 or above is significant at the .05 level of confidence and an h of .31 is significant at the .01 level. Because the h in this hypothetical example is .32, the difference between the two samples is statistically significant at the .01 level of confidence, meaning there is less than one chance in a hundred that the difference we have found is not a real difference.

Because it is widely known that a z of 1.96 is significant at the .05 level of confidence and a z of 2.58 is significant at the .01 level, some researchers might want to display the significance finding in terms of a z score. There is an easy formula for finding z from h:

$$z = h\sqrt{\frac{N}{2}}.$$

In the above example, the N for both samples was the same. In many cases, however, the samples will be of different sizes. Then N' must be determined with the following straightforward formula, where n_1 is one sample and n_2 is the other:

$$N' = \frac{2n_1n_2}{n_1 + n_2}.$$

Once N' is determined, it also can be used in the formula to convert h to z:

$$z = h\sqrt{\frac{N'}{2}}.$$

As can be seen by a casual inspection of Table D.3, it does not take a very large h for statistical significance when sample sizes are in the hundreds. Because, as noted, our sample sizes are usually large, the question of statistical significance is not a primary one for us. Perhaps this table makes it even more clear why we are concerned with effect sizes rather than statistical significance.

DETERMINING CONFIDENCE INTERVALS

A confidence interval (CI) is the range of values within which new findings would fall with a certain degree of probability if we were to draw many new samples. For example, a 95% CI provides figures between which h is likely to fall 95% of the time with repeated samples. In effect, CIs are the inverse of levels of significance, which state the probability that new samples will fall outside the CI. A 95% CI is the complement of the .05 level of significance; a 99% CI is the complement of the .01 level. The advantage of the

CI is that its width makes clear how much variability there is likely to be in h from sample to sample. The narrower the CI, the more impressive the finding.

Once h is determined, it is very easy to establish CIs because they are a function of the size of the samples. To demonstrate this point, let us return to the gender differences in familiarity percent displayed in Table D.1, where h was found to be .26. We will run through the steps necessary to establish a confidence interval in order to show how simple each step is. To begin, we determine the "standard error" of h in the following steps:

1. Add the number of characters in male dream reports (1,108) to the number of characters in female dream reports (1,363). This equals 2,471.
2. Then multiply the number of characters in male dream reports (1,108) by the number of characters in female dream reports (1,363). This equals 1,510,204.
3. Then divide the sum obtained in step 1 (2,471) by the product found in step 2 (1,510,204). This equals .00164.
4. Then find the square root of .00164. This equals .041, which is the standard error of h for the familiarity percent.

   What we have just done can be expressed in a formula that should be easy to face now that we have shown the simple steps it entails:

$$SE_h = \sqrt{\frac{N_1 + N_2}{N_1 N_2}}.$$

5. Once we have the standard error of h, we multiply it by 1.96 if we want the 95% confidence interval, or by 2.58 if we want the 99% confidence interval. For the purposes of this book, we will use the 95% CI, so we multiply the standard error of h (.041) times 1.96, which equals .08.
6. Now we add the number obtained in Step 5 (.08) to our h of .26, which gives us the upper level of the 95% CI, .34.
7. Then we subtract the number obtained in Step 5 (.08) from our h of .26 to establish the lower level of the 95% CI, which equals .18.

Ergo, we can be 95% certain that the h value for the familiarity percent falls between .18 and .34.

This is a fairly wide CI even though the N in our example is quite large. It is no wonder Cohen (1994:1002) suspects that confidence intervals are seldom reported because they are usually "embarrassingly large." A 95% CI of .18 to .36 does not sound as impressive as a finding of .26 that is "significant" at the .0000 level of confidence. We hope, however that the reporting of 95% CIs for several findings in Chapter 4 will lead future dream content researchers to use CIs in their work, and thereby deter them from making too much out of findings that in actuality differ only slightly from ours.

Now we are ready for the formula that condenses this whole process into one phrase. It can be entered into a computer for easy calculation:

$$95\% \text{ CI} = \sqrt{\frac{N_1 + N_2}{N_1 N_2}} \times 1.96 \pm h.$$

CONCLUSION

The method of statistical analysis adopted for this book reflects the spirit of Cohen's (1990, 1994) accumulated wisdom. Our statistics are simple and easily displayed, and they emphasize magnitude of effects and likely range of variability rather than the statistical "significance" of differences. They were chosen with the specific problems of our kind of data in mind. We recognize that other statistics could have been employed, but we have demonstrated that they yield the same results with our kind of data as our approach based on percentages.

Appendix E

Normative Tables

The purpose of Appendix E is to bring together the detailed normative tables containing the original Hall/Van de Castle findings in one place so that they can be easily located by those wishing to use them for research purposes. The appendix begins with a table summarizing the percentages and indexes we use in analyzing the findings from our major content categories. The indicators with an asterisk by them in Table E.1 are the ones we singled out in Chapter 2 as possible indicators of psychopatholgy in dream reports. Any combination of the indicators in Table E.1 could be included on an h-profile for a given person or group, depending on the purposes of the study.

Table E.1. Normative Expectations on All Major Indicators for Main Content Categories in the Hall/Van de Castle System

	Men	Women
Characters		
Animal percent	6	4
Male/female percent	67/33	48/52
Familiarity percent	45	58
Friends percent*	31	37
Social interactions		
A/C index*	34	24
F/C index*	21	22
Aggression/friendliness percent*	59	51
Befriender percent	50	47
Victimization percent*	60	67
Physical aggression percent*	50	34
Settings		
Indoor setting percent	48	61
Familiar setting percent	62	79
Other content categories		
Dreamer-involved success percent*	51	42
Bodily misfortunes percent*	29	35
Torso/anatomy percent*	31	20
Negative emotions percent*	80	80
Percentage of dream reports with at least one:		
Aggression	47	44
Friendliness	38	42
Sexuality	12	4
Misfortune*	36	33
Success	15	8
Failure	15	10
Food or eating	16	17

*A/F Square**

	Men		Women	
	Aggressions (A/C index)	Friendliness (F/C index)	Aggressions (A/C index)	Friendliness (F/C index)
With male characters	28	17	22	24
With female characters	17	29	14	15

Note: Indicators with asterisks are possible psychopathology indicators.

Table E.2.   Frequencies and Percentages
of Types of Dream Characters

	Men		Women	
	f	%	f	%
Total characters	1,180		1,423	
Average number per dream	2.4		2.8	
Total animals	71	6	60	4
Total creatures	1	0	0	0
Single animals	43	4	41	3
Plural animals	28	2	19	1
Total human characters	1,108	94	1,363	96
Total single human characters	761	69	980	72
Total plural human characters	347	31	383	28
Total male	587	53	507	37
Total female	286	26	547	40
Total joint sex	145	13	181	13
Total indefinite	90	8	127	9
Total familiar	501	45	796	58
Total unfamiliar	607	55	567	42
Familiar males	280	25	308	23
Unfamiliar males	307	28	199	15
Familiar females	178	16	392	29
Unfamiliar females	108	10	155	11
Familiar indefinite	14	1	33	2
Unfamiliar indefinite	76	7	94	7
Familiar joint sex	29	3	62	5
Unfamiliar joint sex	116	10	119	9
Total adults	1,078	97	1,271	93
Total teenagers	7	1	20	1
Total children	20	2	57	4
Total babies	3	0.3	15	1

Note: The percentages in lines 3–7 were obtained by dividing frequencies by the total number of characters (line 1); the percentages in lines 8–27 were computed by dividing the various frequencies by the total number of human characters (line 7). In this table, and all other tables, familiar characters are those who are coded in one of the following four identity subclasses: Family, Relatives, Known and Prominent. Unfamiliar characters are those who are coded in the following identity subclasses: Occupational, Ethnic, Stranger, and Uncertain. The few imaginary and dead characters, as well as those few involved in metamorphoses, are classified as familiar or unfamiliar according to their identity class.

Table E.3. Frequencies and Percentages
of Character Subclasses for Total Human Characters

	Men		Women	
	f	%	f	%
I. Family	105	9	201	15
II. Relatives	25	2	62	5
III. Known	347	31	502	37
IV. Prominent	18	2	14	1
V. Occupational	189	17	116	9
VI. Ethnic	22	2	29	2
VII. Strangers	257	23	233	17
VIII. Uncertain	132	12	181	13
IX. Dead, imaginary, and metamorphoses	14	1	27	2
Dead	1		6	
Imaginary	3		7	
Metamorphoses	10		14	
Friends percent = $\dfrac{\text{III}}{\text{All human characters}}$	31		37	

Note: Table E.3 presents the frequencies and percentages for the different types of human characters in the overall human characters category. We have not included the many different subtypes within each category. These subtype findings, which we rarely use, can be found in Table 14-6 in Hall and Van de Castle (1966:165–168).

Table E.4. Frequencies and Percentages of
Aggressions by Subclasses of Aggression

Subclass	Male		Female	
	f	%	f	%
8: Murder	24	6	7	2
7: Attack	89	22	49	15
6: Chasing-confining	62	15	43	13
5: Destruction	26	6	15	4
4: Serious threat	19	5	15	4
3: Rejection	71	18	122	36
2: Verbal	70	17	50	15
1: Covert	41	10	36	11
Total aggressions	402	100	337	100
Total 5–8 (physical)	201	50	114	34
Total 1–4 (nonphysical)	201	50	223	66

Note: The percentages in the table were computed by dividing each frequency within a column by the total number of aggressions in that column. The frequency of "physical" aggressions was obtained by summing the frequencies for subclasses 5 through 8 and that for "nonphysical" aggressions by adding up subclasses 1 through 4.

Table E.5. Nature of Aggressive Interactions in Male and Female Dream Reports

	Men		Women	
	f	%	f	%
Dreams in which aggression occurs	235	47	222	44
Total aggressions	402		337	
Dreamer-involved aggression	321	80	272	81
Witnessed aggression	81	20	65	19
Dreamer as aggressor	100	31	76	28
Dreamer as victim	153	48	155	57
Dreamer as reciprocal	43	13	27	10
Dreamer mutual	15	5	10	4
Dreamer self-aggression	12	4	10	1
Victimization percent		60		67

Note: The victimization percent uses only those interactions where the dreamer is an aggressor or victim, not witnessed, reciprocal, mutual, or self-aggressions.

Table E.6. Frequencies and Percentages of Friendly Interactions by Subclasses of Friendliness

	Men		Women	
Subclass	f	%	f	%
7: Marriage	11	4	23	7
6: Physical	23	9	25	8
5: Inviting, dating	19	8	47	15
4: Helping, protecting	106	42	99	32
3: Gift, loan	27	11	32	10
2: Verbal	50	20	59	19
1: Covert	14	6	23	7
Total	250	100	308	100

Note: The percentages were computed by dividing each frequency in a column by the total number of friendly acts in that column.

Table E.7. Nature of Friendly Interactions
in Dreams in which Friendliness Occurs

	Men		Women	
	f	%	f	%
Dreams in which friendliness occurs	191	38	211	42
Total friendliness	250		308	
Dreamer-involved friendliness	225	90	258	84
Witnessed friendliness	25	10	50	16
Dreamer as befriender	102	45	106	41
Dreamer as befriended	101	45	119	46
Dreamer reciprocal	6	3	3	1
Dreamer mutual	15	7	10	4
Self-friendliness	None		None	
Befriender percent		50		47

Table E.8. Aggressions/Friendliness
Percent (Aggressions Divided by
Aggressions Plus Friendliness)

	Men %	Women %
Total	62	52
Dreamer involved	59	51
Witnessed	76	57
D with males	63	48
D with females	37	49
D with familiar characters	45	45
D with unfamiliar characters	63	54
D with familiar males	51	40
D with unfamiliar males	72	63
D with familiar females	36	52
D with unfamiliar females	40	43
D with animals	82	77

Table E.9. Frequencies and Percentages
of Sexual Interactions

	Male		Female	
	f	%	f	%
Number of dreams in which any sex occurs	58	12	18	4
Total sexual interactions	73	—	19	—
Dreamer-involved sexual interaction	68	93	13	68
Witnessed sex	5	7	6	32
D with opposite sex familiar	22	32	10	77
D with opposite sex unfamiliar	37	54	3	23
D reciprocates	5	7	0	0
D to self	4	6	0	0
S/C index		6		1
Classes of sexual interactions				
5: Sexual intercourse	20	27	5	26
4: Petting	13	18	5	26
3: Kissing	8	11	4	21
2: Sexual overtures	22	30	3	16
1: Sexual fantasies	10	14	2	11

Note: The percentages in lines 3 and 4 and those under "Classes of sexual inter-actions" were obtained by dividing the frequencies by total sexual interactions (line 2). The proportions in lines 5–8 were computed by dividing the frequencies by the number of sexual interactions in which the dreamer was involved. The S/C index is similar to the A/C and F/C index: it is the total number of sexual elements divided by the total number of characters. It is of most use in comparing sexual interactions with different types of characters.

Table E.10.   Frequencies and Percentages of Activities

	Male		Female	
	f	%	f	%
I. Total of all activities	2,362		2,470	
P: Physical	627	27	482	20
M: Movement	586	25	621	25
L: Location change	194	8	182	7
S: Visual	280	12	307	12
A: Auditory	38	2	36	1
V: Verbal (talking)	511	22	646	26
E: Expressive	51	2	83	3
C: Cognitive	75	3	113	5
Physical activities percent		60		52
Dreamer-involved physical activities percent[a]		61		56

[a]The male norms for all dreamer-involved activities were the only ones Adam Schneider was unable to replicate within one percentage point when he recalculated all the male norms from the original coding cards for the 500 male dream reports. We used his new finding for the dreamer-involved physical activities percent for males, and we made an estimate of the percentage for females by assuming that the same errors occurred in calculating the female norms as Schneider found with the male norms. Because of the errors, we have not included the norms for all dreamer-involved activities because we cannot locate the original coding cards for the women's 500 dream reports. It did not seem sensible to include new norms for men and old, possibly inaccurate, norms for women. Fortunately, the physical activities percent is the finding we have found most useful within the context of dreamer-involved activities, and we are confident that we have provided a solid normative figure for it, especially in the case of males. As for the women's figure, we do not think it could be off by more than one or two percentage points.

Table E.11. Frequencies and Percentages
of Successes and Failures

	Men		Women	
	f	%	f	%
Number of dreams with success	75	15	38	8
Number of dreams with failures	77	15	49	10
Number of successes	81	—	38	—
Number of failures	80	—	54	—
Dreamer-involved successes	72	89	33	87
Dreamer-involved failures	69	86	45	83
Dreamer-involved success percent		51		42
Consequences of success				
Misfortune	1	1	0	0
Failure	None		None	
Aggression	None		None	
Consequences of failure				
Good fortune	1	1	1	2
Success	5	6	1	2
Friendliness	1	1	3	6

Table E.12. Frequencies and Percentages of Misfortunes,
Subclasses of Misfortunes, and Consequences

	Men		Women	
	f	%	f	%
Dreams with misfortunes	181	36	167	33
Number of misfortunes	205	—	206	—
Misfortunes to dreamer	146	71	139	67
Misfortunes to other characters	59	29	67	33
By subclass				
6: Death	17	8	21	10
5: Injured or ill	43	21	51	25
4: Accident, destruction, or loss of possession	51	25	39	19
3: Threat from environment	27	13	26	13
2: Falling	10	5	7	3
1: Obstacle	57	28	62	30
Consequences				
Good fortune	14	7	6	3
Success	7	3	5	2
Friendliness	2	1	3	1

Table E.13. Frequencies and Percentages of Good Fortunes

	Men		Women	
	f	%	f	%
Number of dreams with good fortune	30	6	28	6
Number of good fortune	30	—	29	—
GF to D	27	90	23	79
GF to other characters	3	10	6	21

Table E.14. Frequencies and Percentages of Emotions

	Men		Women	
	f	%	f	%
I. Total number of emotions expressed	282		420	
Total happy	55	20	82	20
Total sad	26	9	54	13
Total anger	44	16	53	13
Total confusion	61	22	75	18
Total apprehension	96	34	156	37
II. Dreamer's own emotions	241		351	
Happy	51	21	63	18
Sad	21	19	46	13
Anger	29	12	33	9
Confusion	55	23	69	20
Apprehension	85	35	140	40

Table E.15. Frequencies and Percentages of Settings

	Men		Women	
	f	%	f	%
Total number of settings	644		654	
Average number per dream	1.29		1.31	
Total indoor	284	44	362	55
Total outdoor	302	47	229	35
Total ambiguous	46	7	56	9
Total familiar	197	31	241	37
Total unfamiliar	123	19	65	10
Total distorted	14	2	38	6
Total geographical	51	8	23	4
Questionable familiarity	247	38	280	43
No setting	12	2	7	1

Note: The percentage for each type of setting was determined by dividing by the total number of settings. Ambiguous settings are ignored in determining indoor/outdoor percent and distorted, geographical, and questionable settings are ignored in determining familiar/unfamiliar percent.

Table E.16. Frequencies and Percentages
of Objects

	Men		Women	
	f	%	f	%
Total number of objects	2,422		2,659	
Average number per dream	4.8		5.3	
Architecture	655	27	843	32
AR: Residential	272	11	389	15
AV: Vocational	117	5	138	5
AE: Entertainment	75	3	69	3
AI: Institutional	28	1	39	1
AD: Detail	152	6	186	7
AB: Building materials	6	0.2	3	0.1
AM: Miscellaneous	5	0.2	19	1
HH: Household articles	197	8	278	10
FO: Food or drink	44	2	55	2
Implements	160	7	52	2
IT: Tools	35	1	7	0.3
IW: Weapons	73	3	20	1
IR: Recreational	52	2	25	1
TR: Travel	271	11	223	8
ST: Streets	163	7	118	4
RG: Regions	135	6	126	5
NA: Nature	221	9	199	7
Body Parts	246	10	314	12
BH: Head	80	3	161	6
BE: Extremities	90	4	91	3
BT: Torso	34	1	31	1
BA: Anatomy	20	1	28	1
BS: Sex	22	1	3	0.1
CL: Clothes	139	6	271	10
CM: Communication	95	4	112	4
MO: Money	36	1	19	1
MS: Miscellaneous	60	2	49	2

Table E.17. Frequencies and Percentages
of Modifiers

	Men		Women	
	f	%	f	%
Total number of modifiers	1,110		1,458	
Average number per dream	2.22		2.92	
C+: Chromatic	75	6.8	166	11.4
C−: Achromatic	43	3.9	67	4.6
S+: Large	199	17.9	194	13.3
S−: Small	106	9.5	114	7.8
I+: Intense	326	29.4	439	30.1
I−: Weak	56	5.0	55	3.8
D+: Filled	18	1.6	22	1.5
D−: Empty	9	0.8	3	0.2
L+: Straight	4	0.4	7	0.5
L−: Crooked	13	1.2	19	1.3
T+: Hot	5	0.5	12	0.8
T−: Cold	8	0.7	11	0.8
V+: Fast	40	3.6	30	2.1
V−: Slow	8	0.7	10	0.7
A+: Old	46	4.1	61	4.2
A−: Young	57	5.1	61	4.2
E+: Pretty, good	58	5.2	103	7.1
E−: Ugly, bad	39	3.5	84	5.8

Table E.18.
Frequencies and
Percentages of
Negatives per Dream

	Men		Women	
	f	%	f	%
0	141	28	93	19
1	145	29	134	27
2	111	22	117	23
3	62	12	68	14
4	20	4	43	9
5	12	2	22	4
6+	9	2	23	5

Table E.19.
Frequencies and
Percentages of
Temporal References
per Dream

	Men		Women	
	f	%	f	%
0	328	66	299	60
1	119	24	128	26
2	38	8	52	10
3+	15	3	21	4

Table E.20. Frequencies and
Percentages of Food and Eating
References per Dream

Oral incorporation	Men		Women	
	f	%	f	%
0	420	84	415	83
1	50	10	54	11
2	21	4	22	4
3	9	2	9	2

References

Antrobus, J. (1977). The dream as metaphor: An information processing and learning model. *Journal of Mental Imagery, 2*, 327–338.

Antrobus, J. (1978). Dreaming for cognition. In A. Arkin, J. Antrobus, & S. Ellman (Eds.), *The mind in sleep: Psychology and psychophysiology* (pp. 569–581). Hillsdale, NJ: Lawrence Erlbaum.

Antrobus, J. (1983). REM and NREM sleep reports: Comparisons of word frequencies by cognitive classes. *Psychophysiology, 20*, 562–568.

Antrobus, J. (1986). "Dreaming: Cortical activation and perceptual thresholds. *Journal of Mind and Behavior, 7*, 193–211.

Antrobus, J. (1990). The neurocognition of sleep mentation: Rapid eye movements, visual imagery, and dreaming. In R. Bootzin, J. Kihlstrom, & D. Schacter, (Eds.), *Sleep and cognition*, (pp. 1–24). Washington, DC: American Psychological Association.

Antrobus, J. (1993). "Dreaming: Could we do without it?" In Alan Moffitt, Milton Kramer, & Robert Hoffman, (Eds.), *The functions of dreaming*. Albany: State University of New York Press.

Archer, D., & Gartner, R. (1984). Violence and crime in cross-cultural perspective. New Haven: Yale University Press.

Armitage, R. (1992). Gender differences and the effect of stress on dream recall: A 30-day diary report. *Dreaming, 2*, 137–142.

Aserinsky, E., & Kleitman, N. (1953). Regularly occurring periods of eye motility and concomitant phenomena during sleep. *Science, 118*, 273–274.

Baekland, F., & Lasky, R. (1968). The morning recall of rapid eye movement period reports given earlier in the night. *Journal of Nervous and Mental Diseases, 147*, 570–579.

Barrett, D. (1991). Flying dreams and lucidity: An empirical test of their relationship. *Dreaming, 1*, 129–134.

Barrett, D. (1992). Through a glass darkly: Images of the dead in dreams. *Omega, 24*, 97–108.

Barrett, D., & Loeffler, M. (1992). Comparison of dream content of depressed vs. nondepressed dreamers. *Psychological Reports, 70*, 403–407.

Baylor, G. (1981). Dreams as problem solving. In W. Koella, (Ed.), *Sleep 1980* (pp. 354–356). Basel, Switzerland: Karger.

Baylor, G., & Deslauries, D. (1985). Understanding dreams: Methods, maps and metaphors. *Dreamworks, 5*, 46–57.

Baylor, G. & Deslauries, D. (1986–1987). Dreams as problem solving: A method of study—Part I. Background and theory. *Imagination, Cognition, and Personality 6*, 105–118.

Beck, A. T., & Hurvich, M. S. (1959). Psychological correlates of depression: I. Frequency of "masochistic" dream content in a private practice sampling. *Psychosomatic Medicine, 21,* 50–55.

Beck, A. T., & Ward, C. H. (1961). Dreams of depressed patients: Characteristic themes in manifest content. *Archives of General Psychiatry, 5,* 462–467.

Bell, A., & Hall, C. S. (1971). *The personality of a child molester: An analysis of dreams.* Chicago: Aldine.

Ben-Horin, P. (1967). *The manifestation of some basic personality dimensions in wakefulness, fantasy, and dreams.* Doctoral Dissertation, University of Chicago.

Berger, R. J. (1963). Experimental modification of dream content by meaningful verbal stimuli. *British Journal of Psychiatry, 109,* 722–740.

Berrien, F. (1933). A statistical study of dreams in relation to emotional stability. *Journal of Abnormal and Social Psychology, 28,* 194–197.

Binswanger, L. (1957). *Sigmund Freud: Reminiscences of a friendship.* New York: Grune and Stratton.

Blagrove, M. (1992). Dreams as a reflection of our waking concerns and abilities: A critique of the problem-solving paradigm in dream research. *Dreaming, 2,* 205–220.

Bokert, E. (1967). *The effects of thirst and a related auditory stimulus on dream reports.* Doctoral Dissertation, New York University.

Bolgar, H. (1954). Consistency of affect and symbolic expression: A comparison between dreams and Rorschach responses. *American Journal of Orthopsychiatry, 24,* 538–545.

Bollea, E., Carbonetti, P., Donini, G., Marrucci, M., Piccione, M., & Vella, G. (1978). Dream activities of depressives. *Archivo di Psicologia, Neurologia e Psichiatria, 39,* 473–501.

Bonato, R., Moffitt, A., Hoffman, R., Cuddy, M., & Wilmer, F. (1991). Bizarreness in dreams and nightmares. *Dreaming, 1,* 53–61.

Bose, V. S. (1983). *Dream content transformations: An empirical study of Freud's secondary revision hypothesis.* Unpublished manuscript, Department of Psychology, Andhra University, India.

Bose, V. S., and V. Pramila. (1993). Do Indian and American college students dream differently? Unpublished manuscript, Department of Psychology, Andhra University, India.

Breger, L. (1967). Function of dreams. *Journal of Abnormal Psychology Monograph, 72*(5), 1–28.

Brenneis, C. (1967). *Differences in male and female ego styles in manifest dream content.* Doctoral Dissertation, University of Michigan.

Brenneis, C. (1970). Male and female ego modalities in manifest dream content. *Journal of Abnormal Psychology, 76,* 434–442.

Brenneis, C. (1975). Developmental aspects of aging in women: A comparative study of dreams. *Archives of General Psychiatry, 32,* 429–434.

Brenneis, C. (1976). Dream patterns in Anglo and Chicano young adults. *Psychiatry 39,* 280–291.

Brenneis, C., & Roll, S. (1975). Ego modalities in the manifest dreams of male and female Chicanos. *Psychiatry, 38,* 172–185.

Brink, S., & Allan, J. (1992). Dreams of anorexic and bulimic women: A research study. *Journal of Analytical Psychology, 37,* 275–297.

Brown, R., & Donderi, D. (1986). Dream content and self-reported well-being among recurrent dreamers, past-recurrent dreamers, and nonrecurrent dreamers. *Journal of Personality and Social Psychology, 50,* 612–623.

Buckley, J. (1970). *The dreams of young adults: A sociological analysis of 1,133 dreams of black and white students.* Doctoral Dissertation, Wayne State University.

Carrington, P. (1972). Dreams and schizophrenia. *Archives of General Psychiatry, 26,* 343–350.

Carswell, C., & Webb, W. (1985). Real and artificial dream episodes: Comparisons of report structure. *Journal of Abnormal Psychology, 94,* 653–655.

Cartwright, D. (1953). Analysis of qualitative material. In L. Festenger & D. Katz, (Eds.), *Research methods in the behavioral sciences* (pp. 421–470). New York: Holt, Rinehart, and Winston.

Cartwright, R. (1977). *Night life.* Englewood Cliffs, NJ: Prentice-Hall.

Cartwright, R. (1979). The nature and function of repetitive dreams: A speculation. *Psychiatry, 42*, 131–137.

Cartwright, R. (1986). Affect and dream work from an information processing point of view. *Journal of Mind and Behavior, 7*, 411–428.

Cartwright. (1990). A network model of dreams. In R. Bootzin, J. Kihlstrom, & D. Schacter, (Eds.), *Sleep and cognition* (pp. 179–189). Washington, DC: American Psychological Association.

Cartwright, R. (1992). Masochism in dreaming and its relation to depression. *Dreaming, 2*, 79–84.

Cartwright, R., & Lamberg, L. (1992). *Crisis dreaming*. New York: Harper Collins.

Cartwright, R., & Romanek, I. (1978). Repetitive dreams of normal subjects. *Sleep Research 7*, 174.

Cavallero, C., Cicogna, P., Natale, V., & Occhionero, M. (1992). Slow wave sleep dreaming. *Sleep, 15*, 562–566.

Cavallero, C. & Foulkes, D. (Eds.) (1993). *Dreaming as cognition*. New York: Harvester Wheatsheaf.

Cavallero, C., & Natale, V. (1988–1989). Was I dreaming or did it really happen? A comparison between real and artificial dream reports. *Imagination Cognition and Personality, 8*, 19–24.

Cermak, S. (1992, June 23–27). *Personal dream histories and recurrent dreams*. Paper presented to the annual meeting of the Association for the Study of Dreams, Santa Cruz, CA.

Chodorow, N. (1978). *The reproduction of mothering*. Berkeley: University of California Press.

Chow, E. (1984). The acculturation experience of Asian-American women. In A. Sargent, (Ed.), *Beyond sex roles* (pp. 238–251). St. Paul: West.

Cicogna, P. (1994). Dreaming during sleep onset and awakening. *Perceptual and Motor Skills, 78*, 1041–1042.

Cicogna, P., Cavallero, C., & Bosinelli, M. (1986). Differential access to memory traces in the production of mental experience. *International Journal of Psychophysiology, 4*, 209–216.

Clark, J., Trinder, J., Kramer, M., Roth, T., & Day, N. (1972). An approach to the content analysis of dream scales. In M. Chase, W. Stern, & P. Walter, (Eds.), *Sleep research* (Vol. 1, p. 118). Los Angeles: Brain Research Institute, UCLA.

Cohen, D. B. (1970). Current research on the frequency of dream recall. *Psychological Bulletin, 73*, 433–440.

Cohen, D. B. (1971). Dream recall and short term memory. *Perceptual and Motor Skills, 33*, 867–871.

Cohen, D. B. (1973). A comparison of genetic and social contributions to dream recall frequency. *Journal of Abnormal Psychology, 82*, 368–371.

Cohen, D. B. (1974). Presleep mood and dream recall. *Journal of Abnormal Psychology, 83*, 45–51.

Cohen, D. B. (1979). *Sleep and dreaming*. New York: Pergamon Press.

Cohen, D. B., & Wolfe, G. (1973). Dream recall and repression: Evidence for an alternative hypothesis. *Journal of Consulting and Clinical Psychology, 41*, 349–355.

Cohen, J. (1977). *Statistical power for the behavioral sciences*. New York: Academic Press.

Cohen, J. (1990). Things I have learned (so far). *American Psychologist, 45*, 1304–1312.

Cohen, J. (1994). The earth is round (p < .05). *American Psychologist, 49*, 997–1003.

Cook, W. R. (1956). *Nomothetic personality patterns in dreams*. Doctoral Dissertation, Case Western Reserve University.

Cory, T. L., Ormiston, D. W., Simmel, E., & Dainoff, M. (1975). Predicting the frequency of dream recall. *Journal of Abnormal Psychology, 84*, 261–266.

D'Andrade, J. (1985). *On recurrent dreams*. Unpublished term research paper for a course on dreams taught by G. William Domhoff, University of California, Santa Cruz.

D'Andrade, R. G. (1961). Anthropological studies in dreams. In F. K. Hsu, (Ed.), *Psychological anthropology* (pp. 296–332). Homewood, IL: Dorsey Press.

Darbes, A. (1952). A comparison of made-up dreams and real dreams. Master's thesis, Case Western Reserve University.

Dement, W. (1955). Dream recall and eye movements during sleep in schizophrenics and normals. *Journal of Nervous and Mental Diseases, 122*, 263–269.

Dement, W., & Kleitman, N. (1957). Cyclic variations in EEG during sleep and their relation to eye movement, body motility and dreaming. *Electroencephalograph Clinical Neurophysiology, 9,* 673–690.

Dentan, R. (1983). *A dream of Senoi.* Special Studies Series, Council on International Studies, State University of New York. Amherst: State University of New York at Buffalo.

Dentan, R. (1986). Ethnographic considerations in the cross-cultural study of dreaming. In J. Gackenbach, (Ed.), *Sleep and dreams* (pp. 317–358). New York: Garland.

Dentan, R. (1988). Lucidity, sex, and horror in Senoi dreamwork. In J. Gackenbach & S. LaBerge, (Eds.), *Conscious mind, sleeping brain* (pp. 37–63). New York: Plenum Press.

Domhoff, G. W. (1962). *A quantitative study of dreams content using an objective indicator of dreaming.* Doctoral Dissertation, University of Miami.

Domhoff, G. W. (1969). Home dreams and laboratory dreams. In M. Kramer, (Ed.), *Dream psychology and the new biology of dreaming* (pp. 199–217). Springfield, IL: Charles C. Thomas.

Domhoff, G. W., & Gerson, A. (1967). Replication and critique of three studies of personality correlates of dream recall. *Journal of Consulting Psychology, 31,* 431.

Domhoff, G. W., & Kamiya, J. (1964a). Problems in dream content study with objective indicators: I. A comparison of home and laboratory dream reports. *Archives of General Psychiatry, 11,* 519–524.

Domhoff, G. W., & Kamiya, J. (1964b). Problems in dream content study with objective indicators: III. Changes in dream content throughout the night. *Archives of General Psychiatry, 11,* 529–532.

Dorus, E., Dorus, W., & Rechtschaffen, A. (1971). The incidence of novelty in dreams. *Archives of General Psychiatry, 25,* 364–368.

Dudley, L., & Fungaroli, J. (1987). The dreams of students in a women's college: Are they different? *ASD Newsletter, 4*(6), 6–7.

Dudley, L., & Swank, M. (1990). A comparison of the dreams of college women in 1950 and 1990. *ASD Newsletter, 7*(5), 3.

Eagle, C. (1964). An investigation of individual consistencies in the manifestation of primary process. Doctoral Dissertation, New York University.

Eggan, D. (1949). The significance of dreams for anthropological research. *American Anthropologist, 51,* 177–198.

Eggan, D. (1952). The manifest contents of dreams: A challenge to social science. *American Anthropologist, 54,* 469–486.

Eggan, D. (1961). Dream analysis. In Bert Kaplan, (Ed.), *Studying personality cross-culturally* (pp. 551–577). Evanston, IL: Row, Peterson.

Eggan, D. (1966). Hopi dreams in cultural perspectives. In G. E. Von Grunebaum & R. Cailles, (Eds.), *The dream and human societies* (pp. 237–265). Berkeley: University of California Press.

Ellman, S., & Antrobus, J. (Eds.). (1991). *The mind in sleep.* New York: Wiley.

Farley, F., Schmuller, J., & Fischbach, T. (1971). Dream recall and individual differences. *Perceptual and Motor Skills, 33,* 379–384.

Ferguson, G. (1981). *Statistical analysis in psychology and education.* (5th ed.). New York: McGraw-Hill.

Firth, S., Blouin, J., Natarjan, C., & Blouin, A. (1986). A comparison of the manifest content in dreams of suicidal, depressed, and violent patients. *Canadian Journal of Psychiatry, 31,* 48–53.

Fiss, H. (1979). Current dream research: A psychobiological perspective. In B. Wolman, (Ed.), *Handbook of dreams* (pp. 20–75). New York: Van Nostrand Reinhold.

Fiss, H. (1983). Toward a clinically relevant experimental psychology of dreaming. *Hillside Journal of Clinical Psychiatry, 5,* 147–159.

Fiss, H. (1986). An empirical foundation for a self psychology of dreaming. *Journal of Mind and Behavior, 7,* 161–192.

Fiss. (1991). Experimental strategies for the study of the function of dreaming. In S. Ellman & J. Antrobus, (Eds.), *The mind in sleep* (pp. 308–326). New York: Wiley.

Fitch, T., & Armitage, R. (1989). Variations in cognitive style among high and low frequency dream recallers. *Personality and Individual Differences, 10,* 869–875.

Fletcher, M. (1970). A study of the relationship between aggression in the verbally reported content of dreams and some conceptually related measures of personality. Doctoral Dissertation, University of Tennessee.

Fong, S. (1973). Assimilation and changing sex roles of Chinese Americans. *Journal of Social Issues, 29,* 115–127.

Foulkes, D. (1962). Dream reports from different states of sleep. *Journal of Abnormal and Social Psychology, 65,* 14–25.

Foulkes, D. (1979). Home and laboratory dreams: Four empirical studies and a conceptual reevaluation. *Sleep, 2,* 233–251.

Foulkes, D. (1982). *Children's dreams.* New York: Wiley.

Foulkes, D. (1985). *Dreaming: A cognitive-psychological analysis* Hillsdale, NJ: Lawrence Erlbaum.

Foulkes, D. (1993a). Data constraints on theorizing about dream function. In A. Moffitt, M. Kramer, & R. Hoffman, (Eds.), *The functions of dreaming.* Albany: State University of New York Press.

Foulkes, D. (1993b). Children's dreaming. In D. Foulkes & C. Cavallero (Eds.), *Dreaming as cognition.* New York: Harvester Wheatsheaf.

Foulkes, D. (1994). Point of view in spontaneous waking thought. *Perceptual vs. Motor Skills, 78,* 681–682.

Foulkes, D., & Fleisher, S. (1975). Mental activity in relaxed wakefulness. *Journal of Abnormal Psychology, 84,* 66–75.

Foulkes, D., Hollifield, M., Sullivan, B., Bradley, L., & Terry, R. (1990). REM dreaming and cognitive skills at ages 5–8: A cross-sectional study. *International Journal of Behavioral Development, 13,* 447–465.

Foulkes, D., Larson, J., Swanson, E., & Rardin, M. (1969). Two studies of childhood dreaming. *American Journal of Orthopsychiatry, 39,* 627–643.

Foulkes, D., Pivik, T., Steadman, H., Spears, P., & Symonds, J. (1967). Dreams of the male child: An EEG study. *Journal of Abnormal Psychology, 72,* 457–467.

Foulkes, D., & Rechtschaffen, A. (1964). Presleep determinants of dream content: Effects of two films. *Perceptual and Motor Skills, 19,* 983–1005.

Foulkes, D., & Schmidt, M. (1983). Temporal sequence and unit comparison composition in dream reports from different stages of sleep. *Sleep, 6,* 265–280.

Foulkes, D. & Scott, E. (1973). An above-zero waking baseline for the incidence of momentary hallucinatory mentation. In M. Chase, W. Stern & P. Walter, (Eds.), *Sleep research* (Vol. 2). Los Angeles: Brain Research Institute.

Frayn, D. (1991). The incidence and significance of perceptual qualities with anorexia nervosa. *Canadian Journal of Psychiatry, 36,* 517–520.

French, T., & Fromm, E. (1964). *Dream interpretation.* New York: Basic Books.

Freud, S. (1900). *The interpretation of dreams.* The Standard Edition of the Complete Psychological Works of Sigmund Freud (Vols. IV and V). London: Hogarth Press.

Freud, S. (1901). *On dreams.* The Standard Edition of the Complete Psychological Works of Sigmund Freud (Vol. V). London: Hogarth Press.

Freud, S. (1920). *Beyond the pleasure principle.* The Standard Edition of the Complete Psychological Works of Sigmund Freud, (Vol. XVIII). London: Hogarth Press.

Freud, S. (1933). *New introductory lectures on psychoanalysis.* The Standard Edition of the Complete Psychological Works of Sigmund Freud (Vol. XXII). London: Hogarth Press.

Garfield, P. (1988). *Women's bodies, women's dreams.* New York: Ballantine Books.

Gentil, M., & Lader, M. (1978). Dream content and daytime attitudes in anxious and calm women. *Psychological Medicine, 8,* 297–304.

Giambra, L. (1977). Daydreaming about the past: The time setting of spontaneous thought intrusions. *Gerontologist, 17,* 35–38.

Gibbs, R. (1995). *The poetics of mind*. New York: Cambridge University Press.

Gibbs, R., & O'Brien, J. (1990). Idioms and mental imagery: The metaphorical motivation for idiomatic meaning. *Cognition, 36,* 35–68.

Gold, S. & Reilly, J. (1985/1986). Daydreaming, current concerns and personality. *Imagination, Cognition, and Personality, 5,* 117–125.

Goodenough, D. (1991). Dream recall: History and current status of the field. In S. Ellman & J. Antrobus, (Eds.), *The mind in sleep* (pp. 143–171). New York: Wiley.

Goodenough, D. R., Lewis, H. B., Shapiro, A., Jaret, L., & Sleser, F. (1965). Dream reporting following abrupt and gradual awakenings from different types of sleep. *Journal of Personality and Social Psychology, 2,* 170–179.

Gordon, H. L. (1953). A comparative study of dreams and responses to the thematic apperception test: A need-press analysis. *Journal of Personality, 22,* 234–253.

Gregor, T. (1977). *Mehinaku: The drama of daily life in a Brazilian Indian village*. Chicago: University of Chicago Press.

Gregor, T. (1981a). A content analysis of Mehinaku dreams. *Ethos, 9,* 353–390.

Gregor, T. (1981b). Far, far away, my shadow wandered ...: Dream symbolism and dream theories of the Mehinaku Indians of Brazil. *American Ethnologist, 8,* 709–722.

Gregor, T. (1986). *Anxious pleasures: The sexual lives of an Amazonian people*. Chicago: University of Chicago Press.

Grey, A., & Kalsched, D. (1971). Oedipus east and west: An exploration via manifest dream content. *Journal of Cross-Cultural Psychology, 2,* 337–352.

Griffith, R., Miyago, O., & Tago, A. (1958). The universality of typical dreams: Japanese vs. Americans. *American Anthropologist, 60,* 1173–1179.

Hall, C. S. (1947). Diagnosing personality by the analysis of dreams. *Journal of Abnormal and Social Psychology, 42,* 68–79.

Hall, C. S. (1951). What people dream about. *Scientific American, 184,* 60–63.

Hall, C. S. (1953a). A cognitive theory of dream symbols. *Journal of General Psychology, 48,* 169–186.

Hall, C. S.. (1953b). A cognitive theory of dreams. *Journal of General Psychology, 49,* 273–282.

Hall, C. S. (1953c). *The meaning of dreams*. New York: Harper.

Hall, C. S. (1956). Current trends in research on dreams. In D. Bower & L. Abt, (Eds.), *Progress in clinical psychology* (Vol. 2). New York: Grune and Stratton.

Hall, C. S. (1964). *Ethnic similarities in manifest dream content*. Unpublished paper, Institute of Dream Research, Miami, FL.

Hall, C. S. (1966a). Studies of dreams collected in the laboratory and at home. *Institute of Dream Research Monograph Series* (No. 1).

Hall, C. S. (1966b). A comparison of the dreams of four groups of hospitalized mental patients with each other and with a normal population. *Journal of Nervous and Mental Diseases, 143,* 135–139.

Hall, C. S. (1969a). Content analysis of dreams: Categories, units, and norms. In G. Gerbner (Ed.), *The analysis of communication content*. New York: Wiley.

Hall, C. S. (1969b). Normative dream content studies. In M. Kramer, (Ed.), *Dream psychology and the new biology of dreaming* (pp. 175–184). Springfield, IL: Charles C. Thomas.

Hall, C. S. (1982). *T's dreams: A case study*. Unpublished monograph.

Hall, C. S. (1984). A ubiquitous sex difference in dreams, revisited. *Journal of Personality and Social Psychology, 46,* 1109–1117.

Hall, C. S., & Domhoff, G. W. (1963a). A ubiquitous sex difference in dreams. *Journal of Abnormal and Social Psychology, 66,* 278–280.

Hall, C. S., & Domhoff, G. W. (1963b). Aggression in dreams. *International Journal of Social Psychiatry, 9,* 259–267.

Hall, C. S., & Domhoff, G. W. (1964). Friendliness in dreams. *Journal of Social Psychology, 62,* 309–314.

Hall, C., Domhoff, G. W., Blick, K., & Weesner, K. (1982). The dreams of college men and women in 1950 and 1980: A comparison of dream contents and sex differences. *Sleep, 5,* 188–194.

Hall, C. S., & Lind, R. (1970). *Dreams, life and literature: A study of Franz Kafka.* Chapel Hill: University of North Carolina Press.

Hall, C. S., & Nordby, V. (1972). *The individual and his dreams.* New York: New American Library.

Hall, C. S., & Van de Castle, R. (1965). An empirical investigation of the castration complex in dreams. *Journal of Personality, 33,* 20–29.

Hall, C. S., & Van de Castle, R. (1966). *The content analysis of dreams.* New York: Appleton-Century-Crofts.

Hartmann, E. (1967). *The biology of dreaming.* Springfield, IL: Charles C. Thomas.

Hartmann, E. (1984). *The nightmare.* New York: Basic Books.

Hartmann, E. (1992). *Boundaries of the mind.* New York: Basic Books.

Hartmann, E., Elkin, R., & Garg, M. (1991). Personality and dreaming: The dreams of people with very thick or very thin boundaries. *Dreaming, 1,* 311–324.

Hauri, P. (1975). Categorization of sleep mental activity for psychophysiological studies. In G. Lairy & P. Salzarulo, (Eds.), *The experimental study of sleep: Methodological problems* (pp. 271–281). New York: Elsevier Scientific Publishing Co.

Hauri, P. (1976). Dreams in patients remitted from reactive depression. *Journal of Abnormal Psychology, 85,* 1–10.

Hiscock, M., & Cohen, D. (1973). Visual imagery and dream recall. *Journal of Research in Personality, 72,* 179–188.

Hobson, J. (1988). *The dreaming brain.* New York: Basic Books.

Hobson, J., & McCarley, R. (1977). The brain as a dream state generator: An activation-synthesis hypothesis of the dream process. *American Journal of Psychiatry, 134,* 1335–1348.

Hoelscher, T., Klinger, E., & Barta, S. (1981). Incorporation of concern—and noncern—related verbal stimuli into dream content, *Journal of Abnormal Psychology, 90,* 88–91.

Holland, D. & Kipnis, A. (1994). Metaphors for embarrassment and stories of exposure: The not-so-egocentric self in American culture. *Ethos, 22,* 316–342.

Howard, M. (1978). *Manifest dream content of adolescents.* Doctoral Dissertation, Iowa State University.

Howe, J. B., & Blick, K. (1983). Emotional content of dreams recalled by elderly women. *Perceptual and Motor Skills, 56,* 31–34.

Hsu, F. (1971). *The challenge of the American dream: The Chinese in the United States.* Belmont, CA: Wadsworth.

Hunt, H. (1986). Some relations between the cognitive psychology of dreams and dream phenomenology. *Journal of Mind and Behavior, 7,* 213–228.

Hunt, H. (1989). *The multiplicity of dreams.* New Haven: Yale University Press.

Hunter, J., & Schmidt, F. (1990). *Methods of meta-analysis.* Newbury Park, CA: Sage.

Jerasitis, G. (1992, June 23–27). *Sexual interactions and emotionality in dreams.* Paper presented to the Annual Meeting of the Association for the Study of Dreams, Santa Cruz, CA.

Jones, E. (1953, 1955, 1957). *The life and work of Sigmund Freud.* (Vols. 1–3). New York: Basic Books.

Jung, C. (1963). *Memories, dreams, reflections.* New York: Pantheon Books.

Jung, C. (1974). *Dreams.* Princeton: Princeton University Press.

Kane, C., Mellen, R., Patton, P., & Samano, I. (1993). Differences in the manifest dream content of Mexican-American and Anglo-American women: A research note. *Hispanic Journal of Behavioral Sciences, 5,* 134–139.

Kerr, N. (1993). Mental imagery, dreams, and perception. In D. Foulkes & C. Cavallero, (Eds.), *Dreaming as cognition.* New York: Harvester Wheatsheaf.

Kilner, L. (1988). Manifest content in dreams of Gusii and U.S. females: Social and sexual interactions, achievement and good fortune. *Psychiatric Journal of the University of Ottawa, 13,* 79–84.

Klinger, E. (1971). *Structure and functions of fantasy.* New York: Wiley-Interscience.

Klinger, E. (1990). *Daydreaming.* Los Angeles: Jeremy Tarcher, Inc.

Klinger, E. & Cox, W. (1987/1988). Dimensions of thought flow in everyday life. *Imagination, Cognition, and Personality, 7,* 105–128.

Kracke, W. (1987). Everyone who dreams has a bit of Shaman: Cultural and personal meanings of dreams—Evidence from the Amazon. *Psychiatric Journal of the University of Ottawa, 12,* 65–72.

Kracke, W. (1979). Dreaming in Kagwahiv: Dream beliefs and their psychic uses in an Amazonian culture. *Psychoanalytic Study of Society, 8,* 119–171.

Kramer, M. (1969). Manifest dream content in psychopathologic states. In M. Kramer, (Ed.), *Dream psychology and the new biology of dreaming* (pp. 377–396). Springfield, IL: Charles C. Thomas.

Kramer, M. (1970). Manifest dream content in normal and psychopathologic states. *Archives of General Psychiatry, 22,* 149–159.

Kramer, M. (1982). The psychology of the dream: Art or science? *Psychiatric Journal of the University of Ottawa, 7,* 87–100.

Kramer, M., Baldridge, B. J., Whitman, R. M., Ornstein, P. H., & Smith, P. C. (1969). An exploration of the manifest dream in schizophrenic and depressed patients. *Diseases of the Nervous System, 30* (Suppl.), 126–130.

Kramer, M., Kinney, L., & Scharf, M. (1983). Sex differences in dreams. *The Psychiatric Journal of the University of Ottawa, 8,* 1–4.

Kramer, M., & Roth, T. (1973). Comparison of dream content in laboratory dream reports of schizophrenic and depressive patient groups. *Comprehensive Psychiatry, 14,* 325–329.

Kramer, M., & Roth, T. (1979a). The stability and variability of dreaming. *Sleep, 1,* 319–325.

Kramer, M., & Roth, T. (1979b). Dreams in psychopathology. In B. Wolman, (Ed.), *Handbook of dreams* (pp. 361–367). New York: Van Nostrand Reinhold Co.

Kramer, M., Schoen, L., & Kinney, L. (1987). Nightmares in Vietnam veterans. *Journal of the American Academy of Psychoanalysis, 15,* 67–81.

Kramer, M., Whitman, R. M., Baldridge, B., & Lansky, L. (1965). Depression: Dreams and defenses. *American Journal of Psychiatry, 122,* 411–417.

Kramer, M., Whitman, R. M., Baldridge, B., & Lansky, L. (1966). Dreaming in the depressed. *Canadian Psychiatric Association Journal, 11* (Special Suppl.), 178–192.

Kramer, M., Winget, C., & Whitman, R. (1971). A city dreams: A survey approach to normative dream content. *American Journal of Psychiatry, 127,* 1350–1356.

Kremsdorf, R., Palladino, L., & Polenz, U. (1978). Effects of the sex of both interviewer and subject on reported manifest dream content. *Journal of Consulting and Clinical Psychology, 46,* 1166–1167.

Kuiken, D. (1986). Dreams and self-knowledge. In J. Gackenbach, (Ed.), *Sleep and dreams: A sourcebook* (pp. 225–250). New York: Garland.

Lakoff, G. (1987). *Women, fire, and dangerous things.* Chicago: University of Chicago Press.

Lakoff, G. (1993). How metaphor structures dreams. *Dreaming, 3,* 77–98.

Lakoff, G., & Johnson, M. (1980). *Metaphors we live by.* Chicago: University of Chicago Press.

Langer, S. (1948). *Philosophy in a new key.* New York: Penguin Books.

LaRue, R. (1970). *Recurrent dreams.* Unpublished term research paper for a course on dreams taught by G. William Domhoff, University of California, Santa Cruz.

Leman, J. (1967). *Aggression in Mexican-American and Anglo-American delinquent and non-delinquent males as revealed in dreams and thematic apperception test responses.* Doctoral Dissertation, University of Arizona.

Levine, J. (1991). The role of culture in the representation of conflict in dreams: A comparison of Bedouin, Irish, and Israeli children. *Journal of Cross-Cultural Psychology, 22,* 472–490.

LeVine S. (1982). The dreams of young Gusii women: A content analysis. *Ethnology, 21,* 63–77.

Levitan, H., & Winkler, P. (1985). Aggressive motifs in the dreams of psychosomatic and psycho-neurotic patients. *Interfaces, 12,* 11–19.

Lortie-Lussier, M. (1995). Continuity and change: The dreams of women throughout adulthood. Paper presented to the meeting of the Association of the Study of Dreams, New York.

Lortie-Lussier, M., Schwab, C., & De Koninck, J. (1985). Working mothers versus homemakers: Do dreams reflect the changing roles of women? *Sex Roles, 12,* 1009–1021.

Lortie-Lussier, M., Simond, S., Rinfret, N., & De Koninck, J. (1992). Beyond sex differences: Family and occupational roles' impact on women's and men's dreams. *Sex Roles, 26,* 79–96.

Martinetti, R. (1983). Dream recall, imaginal processes, and short-term memory: A pilot study. *Perceptual and Motor Skills, 57,* 718.

Maybruck, P. (1989). *Pregnancy and dreams.* Los Angeles: Jeremy P. Torcher.

McCarley, R. (1989). The biology of dreaming sleep. In M. Kryger, T. Roth, & W. Dement, (Eds.), *Principles and practice of sleep medicine* (pp. 173–183). Philadelphia: W. B. Saunders.

McNicholas, P. & Avila-White, D. (1995). *A quantitative analysis of 7th grade most recent dreams.* Unpublished term research paper for a course on dreams taught by G. William Domhoff, University of California, Santa Cruz.

Meer, S. J. (1955). Authoritarian attitudes and dreams. *Journal of Abnormal Social Pyschology, 51,* 74–78.

Meier, B. (1993). Speech and thinking in dreams. D. Foulkes & C. Cavallero, (Eds.), *Dreaming as cognition.* New York: Harvester Wheatsheaf.

Meier, B., & Strauch, I. (1990). *The phenomenology of REM-dreams: Dream settings, dream characters, dream topics, and dream realism.* Paper presented to the annual meeting of the Association for the Study of Dreams, Chicago.

Meier, C., Ruef, H., Zeigler, A., & Hall, C. (1968). Forgetting of dreams in the laboratory. *Perceptual and Motor Skills, 26,* 551–557.

Meng, H., & Freud, E. (1963). *Psychoanalysis and faith: The letters of Sigmund Freud and Oscar Pfister.* New York: Basic Books.

Moffitt. A. (1990). *Presidential address.* Paper presented to the annual meeting of the Association for the Study of Dreams, Chicago.

Moss, C. (1970). *Dreams, images, and fantasy: A semantic differential casebook.* Urbana: University of Illinois Press.

Munroe, R. L., & Munroe, R. H. (1977). Sex of dream characters in East Africa. *Journal of Social Psychology, 103,* 149–150.

Munroe, R. L., & Munroe, R. H. (1992). Friendliness: Sex differences in East African dreams. *Journal of Social Psychology, 132,* 401–402.

Munroe, R. L., Munroe, R. H., Brasher, T., Severn, S., Schweickart, R., & Moore, T. (1985). Sex differences in East African dreams. *Journal of Social Psychology, 125,* 405–406.

Munroe, R. L., Munroe, R. H., Turner, J., Zaron, E., Potter, P., & Woulbroun, T. (1989). Sex differences in East African dreams of aggression. *Journal of Social Psychology, 129,* 727–728.

Nathan, S. (1981). Cross-cultural perspectives on penis envy. *Psychiatry, 44,* 39–44.

O'Nell, C., & O'Nell, N. (1977). A cross-cultural comparison of aggression in dreams: Zapotecs and Americans. *International Journal of Social Psychiatry, 23,* 35–41.

Osgood, C. (1959). The representation model and relevant research methods. In I. de Sola Pool, (Ed.), *Trends in content analysis.* Urbana: University of Illinois Press.

Osterberg, M. N. (1951). *A comparison of aggression dreams and TAT stories.* Master's thesis, Case Western Reserve University.

Paolino, A. (1964). Dreams: Sex differences in aggressive content. *Journal of Projective Techniques and Personality Assessment, 28,* 219–226.

Pitcher, E., & Prelinger, E. (1963). *Children tell stories: An analysis of fantasy.* New York: International Universities Press.

Polster, E. (1951). An investigation of ego functioning in dreams. Doctoral Dissertation. Case Western Reserve University.

Pope, K. (1978). How gender, solitude and posture influence the stream of consciousness. In K. Pope & J. Singer, (Eds.), *The stream of consciousness.* New York: Plenum.

Prasad, B. (1982). Content analysis of dreams of Indian and American college students—A cultural comparison. *Journal of Indian Psychology, 4*(1), 54–64.

Rechtschaffen, A., & Kales, A. (Eds.). (1968). *A manual of standardized terminology, techniques and scoring system for sleep stages of human subjects.* Washington, DC: U.S. Public Health Service.

Redfering, D., & Keller, J. (1974). Comparison between dream reporters and low reporters as measured by the MMPI. *Social Behavior and Personality, 2,* 201–203.

Reichers, M., Kramer, M., & Trinder, J. (1970). A replication of the Hall-Van de Castle character scale norms. *Psychophysiology, 7,* 238.

Reis, W. (1951). *A comparison of the interpretation of dream series with and without free association.* Doctoral Dissertation, Case Western Reserve University. Abridged version in M. F. DeMartino, (Ed.). (1959). *Dreams and personality dynamics* (pp. 211–225). Springfield, IL: Charles C. Thomas.

Reynolds, H. (1984). *Analysis of nominal data.* Newbury Park, CA: Sage.

Riemann, D., Low, H., Schredl, M., Wiegand, M., Dippel, B., & Berger, M. (1990). Investigations of morning and laboratory dream recall and content in depressive patients during baseline conditions and under antidepressive treatment with trimipramine. *Psychiatric Journal of the University of Ottawa, 15,* 93–99.

Rinfret, N., Lortie-Lussier, M., & de Koninck, J. (1991). The dreams of professional mothers and female students: An exploration of social roles and age impact. *Dreaming, 1,* 179–191.

Robbins, M. C., & Kilbride, P. L. (1971). Sex differences in dreams in Uganda. *Journal of Cross-Cultural Psychology, 2,* 406–408.

Robbins, P., & Houshi, F. (1983). Some observations on recurrent dreams. *Bulletin of the Menninger Clinic, 47,* 262–265.

Robbins, P., & Tanck, R. (1971). MMPI scales and dream recall: A failure to confirm. *Perceptual and Motor Skills, 33,* 473–474.

Roll, S., & Brenneis, C. B. (1975). Chicano and Anglo dreams of death: A replication. *Journal of Cross-Cultural Psychology, 6,* 377–383.

Roll, S., Hinton, R., & Glazer, M. (1974). Dreams of death: Mexican-Americans versus Anglo-Americans. *Interamerican Journal of Psychology, 8*(1–2), 111–115.

Rosenthal, R., & Rubin, D. (1982). A simple, general purpose display of magnitude of experimental effect. *Journal of Educational Psychology, 74,* 166–169.

Rubenstein, K. (1990). How men and women dream differently. In Stanley Krippner, (Ed.), *Dreamtime and dreamwork* (pp. 135–142). Los Angeles: Jeremy P. Tarcher.

Rubenstein, K. & Krippner, S. (1991). Gender differences and geographical differences in content from dreams elicited by a television announcement. *International Journal of Psychosomatics, 38,* 40–44.

Rychlak, J. (1960). Recalled dream themes and personality. *Journal of Abnormal Social Psychology, 60,* 140–143.

Rychlack, J., & Brams, J. (1963). Personality dimensions in recalled dream content. *Journal of Projective Techniques, 27,* 226–234.

Sampson, H. (1969). Home dreams versus laboratory dreams. In M. Kramer, (Ed.), *Dream psychology and the new biology of dreaming* (pp. 218–223). Springfield, IL: Charles C. Thomas.

Schneider, D. (1969). The dream life of the Yir Yoront. In D. Schneider & L. Sharp, (Eds.), *The dream life of primitive people: The dreams of the Yir Yoront of Australia* (pp. 12–56). Ann Arbor: University Microfilms International.

Schnetzler, J., & Carbonel, B. (1976). Etude thematique des recits de reves de sujets normaux, schizophrenes et autres psychotiques. *Annales Medico-Psychologiques, 3,* 367–380.

Sharp, L. (1934). The social organization of the Yir-Yoront tribe, Cape York Peninsula. *Oceania, 4,* 404–431.

Sharp, L. (1939). Tribes and totemism in north-east Australia. *Oceania, 9,* 254–275, 439–461.

Sharp, L. (1952). Steel axes for stone-age Australians. In E. H. Spicer, (Ed.), *Human problems in technological change*. New York: Russell Sage Foundation.

Sharp, L. (1969). The Yir Yoront of Australia. In D. Schneider & L. Sharp, (Eds.), *The dream life of primitive people: The dreams of the Yir Yoront of Australia* (pp. 1–11). Ann Arbor: University Microfilms International.

Sheppard, E. (1963). Systematic dream studies: Clinical judgement and objective measurements of ego strength. *Comprehensive Psychiatry, 4*, 263–270.

Sheppard, E. (1964). *Dream rating scales*. Mimeographed. Summarized in C. Winget & M. Kramer, 1979. *Dimensions of dreams*. Gainesville: University of Florida Press.

Sheppard, E. (1969). Dream content analysis. In M. Kramer, (Ed.), *Dream psychology and the new biology of dreaming* (pp. 225–254). Springfield, IL: Charles C. Thomas.

Singer, J. (1966). *Daydreaming*. New York: Random House.

Singer, J. (1968). The importance of daydreaming. *Psychology Today, 1*, 18–26.

Singer, J. (1975). *The inner world of daydreaming*. New York: Harper and Row.

Singer, J. (1978). Experimental studies of daydreaming and the stream of thought. In K. Pope & J. Singer (Eds.), *The stream of consciousness*. New York: Plenum.

Singer, J. (1988). Sampling ongoing consciousness and emotional experience. In Mardi Horowitz (Ed.), *Psychodynamics and cognition*. Chicago: University of Chicago Press.

Singer, J. (1993). Experimental studies of ongoing conscious experience. In Ciba Foundation Symposium, *Experimental and theoretical studies of consciousness*. New York: Wiley and Sons.

Singer, J. & Antrobus, J. (1970). *Imaginal processes inventory*. Princeton: Educational Testing Service.

Smith, M., & Hall, C. S. (1964). An investigation of regression in a long dream series. *Journal of Gerontology, 19*, 66–71.

Snyder, F. (1970). The phenomenology of dreaming. In L. Madow & L. Snow, (Eds.), *The psychodynamic implications of the physiological studies on dreams* (pp. 124–151). Springfield, IL: Charles C. Thomas.

Stairs, P., & Blick, K. (1979). A survey of emotional content of dreams recalled by college students. *Psychological Reports, 45*, 839–842.

Starker, S. (1978). Dreams and waking fantasy. In K. Pope & J. Singer, (Eds.), *The stream of consciousness*. New York: Plenum.

Stern, D., Saayman, G., & Touyz, S. (1983). The effect of an experimentally induced demand on nocturnal dream content. *Journal of Mental Imagery, 7*, 15–31.

Stickel, E. (1956). *Dream frequency and personality variables*. Doctoral Dissertation, Case Western Reserve University.

Strauch, I. (1969). *Psychological aspects of dream recall*. Paper presented at a symposium on sleep and dreaming, 19th International Congress of Psychology, London.

Strauch, I. (1995). *Self-representation in REM dreams and waking fantasies at ages 9–11 and 11–13: A longitudinal study*. Paper presented to the meetings of the Association for the Study of Dreams, New York.

Strauch, I., & Meier, B. (1992). *Den träumen auf der spur*. Bern, Switzerland: Verlag Hans Huber.

Strauch, I., & Meier, B. (1996). *In search of dreams: Results of experimental dream research*. Albany: State University of New York Press.

Stukane, E. (1985). *The dream worlds of pregnancy*. New York: Quill Press.

Tedlock, B. (1981). Quiché Maya dream interpretation. *Ethos, 9*, 313–330.

Tedlock, B. (1987). *Dreaming: Anthropological and psychological interpretations*. Cambridge: Cambridge University Press.

Tedlock, B. (1991). The new anthropology of dreaming. *Dreaming, 1*, 161–178.

Tonay, V. (1990–91). California women and their dreams: A historical and sub-cultural comparison of dream content. *Imagination, Cognition, and Personality, 10*, 83–97.

Tonay, V. (1993). Personality correlates of dream recall: Who remembers? *Dreaming, 3,* 1–8.

Trinder, J., & Kramer, M. (1971). Dream recall. *American Journal of Psychiatry, 128,* 296–301.

Trinder, J., Kramer, M., Riechers, M., Fishbein, H., & Roth, T. ((1970). The effect of dream length on dream content. *Psychophysiology, 7,* 333.

Urbina, S. P. (1981). Methodological issues in the quantitative analysis of dream content. *Journal of Personality Assessment, 45,* 71–78.

Urbina, S. P., & Grey, A. (1975). Cultural and sex differences in the sex distribution of dream characters. *Journal of Cross-Cultural Psychology, 6,* 358–364.

Van de Castle, R. (1968). Differences in dream content among psychiatric inpatients with different MMPI profiles. *Psychophysiology, 4,* 374.

Van de Castle, R. (1969). Problems in applying methodology of content analysis. In M. Kramer, (Ed.), *Dream psychology and the new biology of dreaming* (pp. 185–197). Springfield, IL: Charles C. Thomas.

Van de Castle, R. (1971). *The psychology of dreaming.* New York: General Learning Press.

Van de Castle, R. (1983). Animal figures in fantasy and dreams. In A. Katcher & A. Beck, (Eds.), *New perspectives on our lives with companion animals.* Philadelphia: University of Pennsylvania Press.

Van de Castle, R., & Holloway, J. (1970). Dreams of depressed patients, nondepressed patients, and normals. *Psychophysiology, 7,* 326.

Vogel, G. (1978). An alternative view of the neurobiology of dreaming. *American Journal of Psychiatry, 135,* 1531–1535.

Ward, C. H., Beck, A. T., & Rascoe, E. (1961). Typical dreams: Incidence among psychiatric patients. *Archives of General Psychiatry, 5,* 606–615.

Waterman, D., De Jong, M., & Magdelijns, R. (1988). Gender, sex role orientation and dream content. *Sleep '86* (pp. 385–387). New York: Gustav Fischer Verlag.

Wehr, G. (1985). *Jung: A biography.* Boston: Shambhala.

Weisz, R., & Foulkes, D. (1970). Home and laboratory dreams collected under uniform sampling conditions. *Psychophysiology, 6,* 588–596.

Whitman, R., Kramer, M., & Baldridge, B. (1963). Which dream does the patient tell? *Archives of General Psychiatry, 8,* 277–282.

Whitman, R., Pierce, C., Maas, J., & Baldridge, B. (1961). Drugs and dreams. II. Imipramine and prochlorperazine. *Comprehensive Psychiatry, 2,* 219–226.

Wilmer, H. (1982). Vietnam and madness: Dreams of schizophrenic veterans. *Journal of the American Academy of Psychoanalysis, 10,* 47–65.

Winget, C., & Kramer, M. (1979). *Dimensions of dreams.* Gainesville: University of Florida Press.

Winget, C., Kramer, M., & Whitman, R. M. (1972). Dreams and demography. *Canadian Psychiatry Association Journal, 17,* 203–208.

Witkin, H. (1969). Influencing dream content. In M. Kramer, (Ed.), *Dream psychology and the new biology of dreaming* (pp. 285–343). Springfield, IL: Charles C. Thomas.

Witkin, H., & Lewis, H. (1967). Presleep experience and dreams. In H. Witkin & H. Lewis, (Eds.), *Experimental studies of dreaming* (pp. 148–201). New York: Random House.

Yamanaka, T., Morita, Y., & Matsumoto, J. (1982). Analysis of the dream contents in Japanese college students by REM-awakening technique. *Folia Psychiatrica et Neurologica Japonica, 36,* 33–52.

Zepelin, H. (1980–1981). Age differences in dreams: I. Men's dreams and thematic apperceptive fantasy. *International Journal of Aging and Human Development, 12,* 171–186.

Zepelin, H. (1981). Age differences in dreams: II. Distortion and other variables. *International Journal of Aging and Human Development, 13,* 37–41.

Zimmerman, W. (1970). Sleep mentation and auditory awakening thresholds. *Psychophysiology, 6,* 540–549.

Index

Aborigines, 108
Absolute constancy, 132, 134–135, 136–137, 138, 140
A/C index
  in African-American dream studies, 74, 75, 76
  in childhood dream studies, 90, 94
  in college student dream studies, 53, 59–60, 74, 75, 76
  consistency and, 136, 138, 139
  continuity and, 160, 164, 181–182, 184, 185, 186
  in multi-society cross-cultural study, 119
  psychopathology and, 26
  sample size of dream reports and, 65
  in teenager dream studies, 87
  in Zapotec study, 122
Activities
  classification and coding of, 18, 237–242
  in college student dream studies, 61, 79
  consistency of, 151
  continuity of, 165, 173
  frequencies and percentages of, 328
  in India study, 111
  in Japan study, 112
  in sample dream series, 280, 283, 286–287, 292, 297, 300–301, 303, 306
  in young versus older adult dream studies, 85
Adults
  as characters, 220
  older, 83–86
  young. *See* Young adults

Advice dreams, 200
African-Americans, 73–76
A/F square, 60, 141, 172
Age
  of characters, 14, 220–221, 224
  coding of, 268
  differences in, 83–97; *see also* specific age groups
Aggression/friendliness percent, 326
  in college student dream studies, 59
  continuity of, 172, 177, 185, 186, 187
  in Netherlands study, 100
  psychopathology and, 26
  in teenager dream studies, 87
Aggressive interactions
  in African-American dream studies, 73–74
  in childhood dream studies, 90, 92, 93, 94, 95
  coding of, 16–17, 225–230
  in college student dream studies, 57–58, 59–60, 70, 71–72, 73–74, 79
  consistency of, 136, 137–140, 144, 146, 147
  continuity of, 154, 160–161, 164, 165, 167–168, 172, 177, 178, 179–180, 187–188
  in dramatic dream reports, 23
  dream recall and, 46
  frequencies and percentages of by sub-class, 324
  friendliness compared with, 59–60
  in Gusii women study, 125
  in India study, 109
  intercoder reliability and, 29
  in Japan study, 114, 115